The Civil Society Reader

Civil Society: Historical and Contemporary Perspectives

Series Editors:

VIRGINIA HODGKINSON
Public Policy Institute, Georgetown University

KENT E. PORTNEY
Department of Political Science, Tufts University

JOHN C. SCHNEIDER
Department of History, Tufts University

BRIAN O'CONNELL
Civil Society: The Underpinnings of American Democracy

PHILIP H. ROUND
By Nature and by Custom Cursed: Transatlantic Civil Discourse and New England Cultural Production, 1620–1660

BOB EDWARDS, MICHAEL W. FOLEY, AND MARIO DIANI, EDS.
Beyond Toqueville: Civil Society and the Social Capital Debate in Comparative Perspective

KEN THOMSON
From Neighborhood to Nation: The Democratic Foundations of Civil Society

HENRY MILNER
Civic Literacy: How Informed Citizens Make Democracy Work

VIRGINIA A. HODGKINSON AND MICHAEL W. FOLEY, EDS.
The Civil Society Reader

The Civil Society Reader

Edited by
Virginia A. Hodgkinson
and Michael W. Foley

Tufts University
Published by University Press of New England
Hanover and London

Tufts University

Published by University Press of New England,

37 Lafayette St., Lebanon, NH 03766

© 2003 by Trustees of Tufts University

Printed in the United States of America

5 4 3 2 1

Library of Congress Cataloging-in-Publication Data

The civil society reader / edited by Virginia A. Hodgkinson and Michael
W. Foley.
    p.   cm. — (Civil society)
Includes bibliographical references and index.
  ISBN 1-58465-278-0 (pbk. : alk. paper)
  1. Civil society—History. 2. Political science—History.
I. Hodgkinson, Virginia Ann. II. Foley, Michael W. III. Series.
  JC337 .C58 2002
  300—dc21   2002014986

The publisher gratefully acknowledges the following:

Chapter one, *The Politics,* is excerpted from Barnes, Jonathan; *THE COMPLETE WORKS OF ARIS-TOTLE.* Copyright © 1984 by Princeton University Press. Reprinted by permission of Princeton University Press.

Chapters two and three, "Ideas for a Universal History with a Cosmopolitan Purpose" and "Perpetual Peace," are from Immanuel Kant, *Political Writings,* ed. Hans S. Reiss, trans. H. B. Nisbet. Copyright © Cambridge University Press 1970, 1991. Reprinted with the permission of Cambridge University Press.

Chapter four, *An Essay on the History of the Civil Society,* is excerpted from Adam Ferguson, *An Essay on the History of Civil Society,* ed. Fania Oz-Satzberger. Copyright © 1995. Reprinted with the permission of Cambridge University Press.

Chapter seven, *Philosophy of Right,* is excerpted from G. W. F. Hegel, *Philosophy of Right,* translated with notes by T. M. Knox (1942). Reprinted by permission of Oxford University Press.

Chapter eight, "On the Jewish Question," from THE MARX-ENGELS READER, SECOND EDITION by Robert C. Tucker. Copyright © 1978, 1972 by W. W. Norton & Company, Inc. Used by permission of W. W. Norton & Company, Inc.

Chapter nine, *Democracy in America,* is from DEMOCRACY IN AMERICA by Alexis DeTocqueville, translated by Henry Reeve, copyright 1945 and renewed 1973 by Alfred A. Knopf, a division of Random House, Inc. Used by permission of Alfred A. Knopf, a division of Random House, Inc.

Chapter ten, *The Public and Its Problems,* is excerpted from *The Collected Works of John Dewey, Later Works: Volume 2 "The Public and Its Problems"* © 1984 by the Board of Trustees, Southern Illinois University, reprinted by permission.

(continues on page 363)

Contents

Michael W. Foley and Virginia A. Hodgkinson
Introduction

The notion of civil society is more than just the vague but often powerful slogan of the last several years. The term has a distinguished pedigree in Western efforts to grapple with fundamental problems in the shape and direction of modern societies. Yet thinkers over the last two hundred years have held competing visions of what civil society is and what it means for our lives in common. This collection of readings attempts to convey the richness of the civil society tradition and debate. The following pages propose a framework for understanding the contending positions in the civil society debate.

In the broadest terms, the civil society debate is about the conditions of citizenship and the character of the good society—about what shapes citizens and contributes to civic virtue and civic engagement, about what role the ordinary occupations and preoccupations of citizens play in the public sphere and in building the good society, about the function and place of the associations that make up modern societies in the polities that attempt to govern them. In that sense, the debate can be traced back as far as Plato and Aristotle, with the latter arguing against his mentor that the good society was one in which human nature reached its perfection through the practice of the arts of civic responsibility. The political order, the *polis,* was the "association of associations" in Aristotle's eyes, and only by sharing in ruling and being ruled could human beings achieve genuinely human virtue. Aristotle was as concerned with the nature of the best sort of political system, and its relations to the elements of society that made it up, as with civic virtue. Indeed, in his conception the two went hand in hand.

The authors assembled in this volume thus reflect varying sides of a debate that stretches back through all of Western history. We start with some passages from Aristotle's *Politics* in recognition of his role even in contemporary discussions. Nevertheless, if the larger questions reflected here are perennial, the civil society debate poses them in the specific context of modernity, with its seemingly sharp distinction between the modern, bureaucratic state and a complex society built on the division of labor and increasing acknowledgment of difference among its citizens. The volume's real engagement with the idea of civil society thus starts with two thinkers of the Enlightenment, Immanuel Kant and Adam Ferguson, because the modern notion of civil society was born in the late eighteenth century, at the dawn of the modern condition.

Two broad strands of thinking about the conditions of citizenship emerge from the peculiar problems of modernity. On the one hand, we find thinkers who concern themselves with the moral compass of citizenship in the modern context: What are the virtues and dispositions necessary to sustain the modern polity, they ask, and where do they come from? While many thinkers have acknowledged that the political system shapes the person, modernity raises in special ways the question how and to what ends society itself shapes the political lives of citizens. Do the division of labor and the competing interests that characterize modern life undermine care for the whole, as Adam Ferguson and countless thinkers since have worried? Or are the very associations in which citizens express their differences "schools of democracy," as de Tocqueville and his many followers have argued? How can citizens of diverse interests and experiences come together in the common project of citizenship? What incentives and what sorts of virtues are available to enable modern citizens to pursue and protect their private interests and at the same time maintain a healthy regard for the common good?

A second strand concerns itself with the conditions of participation in a modern polity or, more profoundly, the arenas available for meaningful and active citizenship. Has the proliferation of interests and experiences that accompany modern society eroded the public sphere (as John Dewey feared, echoing a long tradition) and thus undermined all attempts at forging a common purpose and even a common language of politics? Or are these competing interests the very stuff of modern politics, providing citizens of diverse outlooks and cares vehicles for a level of participation and contestation they could not sustain by themselves (as David Truman insisted)? Can we rebuild a public sphere by building alternative and autonomous spaces for citizen action (as Sarah Evans and Harry Boyte have suggested)? Or is such a project dangerous to democracy, as the critics of multiculturalism argue, and better designed for the overthrow of oppressive orders along lines enunciated by Antonio Gramsci and, later, Vaclav Havel?

These questions run through this collection of readings, but some thinkers take a broader and more systematic view than others. Kant and Ferguson, Hegel and Marx were concerned with understanding the shape of the modern polity as a whole, even as they differed in how they characterized it and where they looked for solutions. Similarly, in the twentieth century, Antonio Gramsci, Jean Cohen and Andrew Arato, Edward Shils and Michael Walzer attempt to characterize the situation in which we find ourselves in global terms, working out the kinds of citizen action appropriate to that situation as part of a broader vision of how we might achieve the good society. But differing readings of the modern condition and differing conceptions of the good society emerge from each of the selections in this volume; and the reader should be attentive to such differences and to how they shape each writer's argument.

The following pages offer a brief history of the idea of civil society in its various incarnations, with special emphasis on the contributions of the thinkers represented. A great many more writers than we have been able to present here have contributed to the ongoing debates around the themes just set forth, particularly in the last twenty years. We hope these excerpts will interest readers to read and inquire further.

Origins

Although some authors have attempted to identify discussions of civil society in all the major writers of the Western philosophical tradition, we confine ourselves here to its distinctly modern usages, in part because contemporary uses of the term virtually all stem from the fundamental rethinking of modern society that emerged in the eighteenth century, and particularly from the extended essay by Adam Ferguson, *On the History of Civil Society.*[1]

In the vague usage of Ferguson's day, the term "civil society," derived from the Latin *societatis civilis,* referred to an ordered and peaceful society, one governed by law.[2] Ferguson's problematic lay precisely in the contrast between modern versions of such a society, characterized by a growing division of labor and "refined manners," with the decidedly more unitary and warlike, but to his mind more vigorous, societies that were the basis for the classical republican ideal. What would be the effect on republican virtue and citizenship, Ferguson asked, of the diversity of interests and peaceful inclinations of modern societies? Would such societies fall prey to more warlike ones, or, equally troubling, to the emerging national state, with its bureaucratic apparatus and standing army? What sources of unity and resistance might citizens have at their disposal, given the inherent divisions of civil society and the "softening" effects of a way of life that gave ordinary citizens little practice in the arts of war? Ferguson gave no final answer to these questions, but by sketching the problem of the increasing division of labor in modern industrializing societies and its impact on citizenship and the social order, he raised critical questions which subsequent scholars were anxious to confront.[3]

The ancient roots of contemporary discussions, we noted already, can be found in Aristotle's interpretation of the ancient Greek *polis* as the "association of associations," founded on bonds of friendship and religious loyalty to the homeland and oriented, by nature if not always in practice, toward the cultivation of virtue.

---

1. One example of the alternative approach is John Ehrenberg's *Civil Society: The Critical History of an Idea* (New York: New York University Press, 1999).

2. The selection from Kant's writings included here is an ample illustration of this usage, but Locke uses the term in this way as well, conflating "civil society," "political society," and "the Commonwealth" in ways that later discussions find utterly confusing. See, for example, Locke's *Second Treatise of Government,* Book II, §87, in John Locke, *Two Treatises of Government,* rev. ed. (New York: New American Library, 1965) p. 367.

3. Adam Seligson claims to have found Ferguson's answer in a Scottish theory of "moral sentiments" that sees the new source of unity in modern society in the sense of honor and shame that accompanies human beings' concern for their "good reputation." There is scant trace of such a stance in Ferguson's text, however; and Seligson's interpretation seems to be based on a wholesale transfer of Adam Smith's argument from the *Theory of Moral Sentiments* to the work of his predecessor. Smith's theory does not, moreover, address the specific problems that Ferguson poses. Consequently, it seems illegitimate to see it as part of a "Scottish" theory of civil society, as Seligson and others, following him, including Ehrenberg, have done. See Adam Seligson, *The Idea of Civil Society* (New York: The Free Press, 1992).

The major strands of Aristotelian thought on politics part and rejoin in new mixes over the course of the centuries. In the following pages, we trace three major strands of the Aristotelian tradition that have re-emerged in contemporary debate about civil society and the quality of our democracies: civic republicanism; the natural law tradition and its mutation into liberal theories of the harmony of competing interests under the rule of law; and the modern civil society tradition *per se*. By and large, the selections in this volume represent only the last of these traditions, but understanding the contemporary debate around "civil society" requires a familiarity with all three.

Civic Republicanism and Civic Virtue

The most obvious descendent of the Aristotelian tradition is the body of thought sometimes called "civic republicanism" crystallized by Machiavelli and other defenders of the independent Italian Renaissance city state, and reformulated in England in the wake of the English Civil War.[4] Central to this approach was the notion that the survival of the republic, and of the freedoms which it represented, depended upon the civic virtue of its citizens, a notion echoed in much contemporary discussion, as in Ferguson's classic restatement of the problem.[5] Both for Machiavelli and for his later English and American followers, the key to the survival of the republic was an armed, land-owning citizenry—a theme which recurs, remarkably, in the contemporary militia movement in the United States, with its subterranean connections to the English Machiavellians of the seventeenth century.

In early modern civic republicanism, an armed citizenry was essential, not only to defend the republic in times of war, but to defend it against usurpers from within. Machiavelli was scornful of states that employed mercenaries, whom he thought could not be relied upon to fight; but more profoundly, he feared that mercenaries could be turned against the republic itself, just as the English republicans several centuries later opposed a standing army as an instrument of tyranny. Neither Machiavelli nor his English counterparts favored a democratic republic. Theirs was a "mixed republic" on the Aristotelian model, combining features of monarchy, aristocracy, and rule by the many. But for just that reason, it was important that the many be equipped to defend their liberties.

At the same time, the Machiavellian republic owed its existence to a certain degree of equality among citizens. No republic could be built upon a society of landed lords, with their serfs and armed retainers. The republic required wide-

---

4. This discussion relies on the indispensable work of J. G. A. Pocock, *The Machiavellian Moment: Florentine Political Thought and the Atlantic Republican Tradition* (Princeton, N.J.: Princeton University Press, 1975).

5. Notice that Ferguson, unlike contemporary theorists, does not confuse the "civil" in civil society with the "civic" in civic virtue. On the contrary, Ferguson's concern is precisely that "civilization" has eroded the basis of civic virtue that ruder societies possessed in the tradition of the citizen warrior.

spread ownership of land, giving the populace both a stake in the polity and sufficient independent income to make them immune to the blandishments of demagogues, as Aristotle had suggested. But it was military training, above all, which
instilled civic virtue in a citizenry, according to the Machiavellians, because such
training combined courage and cunning in the service of the *patria.*

Civil society in the contemporary sense of the assemblage of associations that
stand between state and citizen had little or no place in the thinking of these civic
republicans. In a telling passage of the *Discourses,* Machiavelli sided with the
Roman Senate in its decision to execute Spurius Maelius, one of its number who,
in a time of famine, had taken it upon himself to open his granaries for the poor.
The Senate decided rightly, Machiavelli argues, because only the institutions of
the republic should have the right to decide upon action in the public good. By
putting himself forward as savior of the poor, Spurius threatened the ascendancy
of the Senate itself.[6] For Machiavelli, as for the radical republicans of the French
Revolution and even for their friend Thomas Jefferson, the public good was best
entrusted to public institutions, not to private ones, no matter how well inten-
tioned.[7] While Jefferson was convinced that civic virtue would grow in the measure that America's yeoman farmers became educated (in public institutions), the
Jacobins went further, legislating everything from dress to speech and abolishing
intermediary institutions of all sorts so as to ensure the citizenry's loyalty to the
republic alone. A new, civic religion would provide the basis for civic loyalty, as
the ancient rites of the hearth and the *polis* had grounded Aristotle's polity. Virtue
might be central to the life of the polity, but it would have to be a virtue crafted to
civic needs by the institutions of the republic.

The Natural Law Tradition and Liberalism

The liberal tradition, by contrast, has famously left aside the question of civic virtue to construct a polity which might function freely and fairly without having to
depend upon the dubious prospects of abolishing egoism and replacing it with virtue. Liberalism has largely abandoned the concerns of the Aristotelian synthesis,
but it has its roots, nevertheless, in an intellectual tradition that can be traced back
to the Greek *polis.* From the Middle Ages, it inherited a pessimistic view of
human nature, a preoccupation with the rule of law, and a diminished notion of
what governance might accomplish. In many respects, this heritage is more Stoic
and Augustinian than Aristotelian; but all three come together in the work of
Thomas Aquinas.

6. Niccolo Machiavelli, *The Discourses of Niccolo Machiavelli,* trans. by Leslie J. Walker, S.J.
(London: Routledge, 1991), Book III, 28.

7. This interpretation of Jefferson has been contested by some Jefferson scholars. It is developed
in the context of the rise of secondary associations in the United States by Peter Dobkin Hall, "Inventing the Nonprofit Sector," in *Inventing the Nonprofit Sector and Other Essays on Philanthropy, Voluntarism, and Nonprofit Organizations* (Baltimore: Johns Hopkins University Press, 1992), pp. 13–84.

Aquinas and other scholastics refashioned Aristotle's notion of the *polis* as a *"societatis civilis"* founded on the dictates of reason and oriented, above all, toward ensuring peace, and thus, Aquinas argued, an arena in which virtue might develop and flourish.[8] Where Aristotle argues that humankind is by nature a "political animal," Aquinas describes the species as essentially "social," thus in need of common governance and of a social sphere in which to fulfill itself. This is more than a change of terms. For Aristotle, human nature could reach its highest natural expression in the exercise of political virtue, even if he left open the possibility of some higher fulfillment in the contemplative life. For Thomas Aquinas there could be no question of complete fulfillment through political action; only communion with God could provide that, and for Aquinas, in contrast to Aristotle, this possibility was open to all. Following Augustine, Aquinas considers the primary goal of political life to be ensuring the peace that people needed to pursue their primary goal. Unlike Augustine, and closer to Aristotle, Aquinas thought that human beings could attain virtue through engagement in worldly affairs. And if peace was the limited good for which political rule was ordained, government nevertheless had to be based upon the laws of God, which were manifest, for believers and nonbelievers alike, as the laws of nature. *Societatis civilis* was achieved when good governance under the rule of law could achieve that peace essential to the pursuit of virtue and, ultimately, eternal salvation.

The scholastic tradition of which Thomas Aquinas was a key exponent was carried over into Protestant theology and provided the basis for growing efforts in the wake of the religious strife of the sixteenth century to reimagine politics—both domestic and international—as something more than the clash of conflicting interests and wills. A series of thinkers in the seventeenth and eighteenth centuries sought the foundations of the *societatis civilis*—better translated as the "well-governed society," or even the "civil state," than as "civil society"—first in natural law, then in a social contract that would sacrifice natural liberty for a state in which civil liberties might be guaranteed. Hobbes, Locke, Rousseau, Montesquieu, and Hume all offered variations on the argument that a well-governed society must be founded, not on the presumptions of kings, but on a fundamental societal agreement as the constitutive basis for any legitimate rule of law.

At the same time, various thinkers attempted to uncover some mechanism to guard the new order against the divisions to which the manifest differences in the interests of citizens might lead it. They found a solution in the notion that competing interests would balance against one another in a sort of competitive equilibrium, accepting the rule of law as the limit to their competition. In Kant's "Perpetual Peace," no less than in Madison's *The Federalist, No. 10* (see chapters three and six), the liberal conception emerges that a plurality of interests might ultimately serve a polity better than social harmony could, just as relatively unfettered economic competition, according to Adam Smith, would contribute to greater

---

8. This translation of the Aristotelian notion of the *polis* actually goes back to Cicero.

wealth than could be achieved through any attempt to regulate commerce or create monopolies subservient to the state. Here lie the roots of subsequent liberal engagement with the modern problematic of civil society. Kant's "competing interests" and Madison's "factions" will become the "interest groups" of pluralist theory in American political science at the beginning of the twentieth century.

Tom Paine's enthusiastic paean to civil society without the state stands in contrast to the general pessimism about human nature often encountered in this tradition, but shares its optimism about outcomes. Paine's notion that individuals come together willingly for common purposes in the frontier conditions of the American colonies represents a concrete application of Locke's social contract theory, and reflects as well older English republican notions about the civic virtue of an independent yeoman class. Though Paine has received little attention in subsequent discussions of civil society,[9] his work represents a powerful strand of American political thought, undergirding its more anarchist and localist manifestations; and it anticipates de Tocqueville's better-known contribution.

The Emergence of the Modern Civil Society Tradition

The optimistic predictions of the liberal tradition were not shared by the thinkers who first used the term "civil society" in its modern sense. The Scottish thinker Adam Ferguson celebrated the wealth and refinement that a new division of labor brought the industrializing West, England in particular; but he also worried—very much in the tradition of the civic republicans—that specialization, wealth, and refinement would together undermine the civic virtue necessary to sustain the greatness of the nation. "Civil" society was thus "civilized" society—refined thanks to the peace that good government had provided, but potentially corrupted by its very refinement. Civil society thus underlined a problem according to Ferguson, more than a solution to the problem of the good polity.

Simultaneously, civil society for the first time came to signify not the whole of an ordered *polis,* but society apart from the state, its foundation but also potentially in tension with it. Ferguson's thought reflected, in this respect, the changed circumstances of the emerging modern polity. The centralizing states of the seventeenth and eighteenth centuries, with their bureaucracies and standing armies, had recast the problem of governance as a relation, not of ruler and ruled, but of state and society, where states took on lives of their own, and governance—no matter how "democratic"—could no longer readily be seen, in the Aristotelian fashion, as "sharing in ruling and being ruled."[10]

G. F. W. Hegel, impressed with Ferguson's work, also called into question the

---

9. But see John Keane, *Tom Paine: A Political Life* (Boston: Little, Brown, 1995).

10. Pocock's discussion of seventeenth-century English debate on the standing army is particularly instructive in this regard. See *The Machiavellian Moment,* chap. XII.

optimistic solution of the liberal theorists, insisting that the conflict of interests inherent in civil society could never resolve itself by itself. Only the state could provide the unity which society needed to govern itself. In Hegel's mind the newly autonomous state expressed the "universal," as opposed to the particularistic divisions of civil society, which was first and foremost an expression of a "system of needs." Civil society, nevertheless, encompassed the "ethical" ideal in its concrete preoccupation with everyday relationships. Civil society is thus characterized by arbitrary inequalities, class divisions, and bewilderingly diverse efforts to meet the growing variety of human needs. But it is also the realm in which human beings shape themselves through ethical norms to master their environment and find ways to work together. Its very existence, however, depends upon the state, which recognizes one of the fundamental sources of division embodied already in "civil law"—the right to property—and which administers a whole system of justice designed to guarantee contracts and adjudicate disputes among the competing elements of society. But the state is more than the guarantor of individual rights and "particularities." It is the unity of all these diverse needs, interests, and claims to rights; it is the rule of law and thus is "absolutely rational" (see our excerpt from Hegel's *Philosophy of Right,* no. 257).[11]

Karl Marx rejected both terms of the Hegelian synthesis, while retaining Ferguson's insights and the basic structure of Hegel's portrait of modern societies. Civil society as the realm of inequality, plurality, and competing interests meant little more than "man's exploitation of man" in Marx's eyes; and the supposed universalism of the liberal state, with its "rights of man" and rule of law, was an abstract mask for the oppressive relations at the heart of liberal society, embodied especially in the workplace.[12] In his utopian moments Marx envisioned a social order founded on specialization but governed directly by its members, whose free and equal participation in the productive process would give them a direct stake in the good of the whole. Marx thus harkens back to the notion of a *societatis civilis* self-governed by individuals whose common property gives them the insight to perceive their common good and the motivation to pursue it together.

Alexis de Tocqueville was more optimistic than Hegel or Marx in his appraisal of the diverse associational life of the new United States, and he gave the civil society tradition a significant twist in arguing that America's diverse associations

11. In Hegel's philosophy—sometimes labeled "philosophical idealism"—concrete reality is an expression of "the Idea," whose development is "dialectical" or evolutionary rather than strictly logical. Much of the difficulty of Hegel's text stems from his constant recourse to this language and its conception of historical process. Civil society thus expresses "contradictory" sides of the Idea, both human need (embodied, above all, in economic relations) and human solidarity (embodied in law and the ethical life). Only the state, in Hegel's schema, can resolve the "contradiction" in a synthesis that subsumes conflicting needs and ethical imperatives in a system of universal law expressing the common good.

12. Thus, Marx's convoluted polemic against religion in "On the Jewish Question," excerpted here, has its root in the argument that religion, and the division among the religious traditions in particular, is merely a reflection of the deeper economic and class divisions of modern society.

produced the "habits of the heart" and civic skills necessary for political life in a democratic republic. But he was still cautious, particularly when it came to political associations, which might occasionally threaten to tear apart the polity in pursuit of this or that passionate interest. The polity might be an "association of associations," as Aristotle put it, but the constituent associations often had lives of their own, which might easily threaten the state as well as sustain it.

Association as Problem

Though the term "civil society" had already disappeared from de Tocqueville's discussion, diverse thinkers in the late nineteenth and early twentieth centuries continued to worry over the new associational complexity of industrial society. Indeed, the problem signaled by Ferguson became only more acute. While Madison—and even Locke—recognized the competition of various interests for political influence (Madison mentions landed, commercial, financial, and manufacturing interests as the most basic), neither of them, in Alessandro Pizzorno's words, "could have imagined such interests formally organized and durable over time or the presence of the interests not linked with private property. Moreover, they never dreamed of stable organizations, permanent agents on the political scene, which would be inspired by an ideology distinct from the dominant one of the political system. Only religious groups were thought to have such characteristics."[13]

The proliferating "factionalization" of society and politics struck many of the thinkers of the later nineteenth and early twentieth century as problematic, and it generated a variety of studies of the new professional leadership of parties, interest groups and bureaucracies. As Pizzorno notes, "Mosca's view of the political class as an autonomous subject; Kautsky, Lenin, and Gramsci's elaborations on professional revolutionaries and intellectuals; Michel's description of party and union functionaries; and Weber's analysis of professional vs. charismatic politicians were all tentative theories meant to explain why there is no one-to-one correspondence between civil society and the state, between class and party, and between the represented and the representatives."[14]

But the problem lay not just in apparently autonomous and professionalized leaders, but in the proliferation of interests, organized in opposition to one another

13. Alessandro Pizzorno, "Interests and Parties in Pluralism," in *Organizing Interests in Western Europe: Pluralism, Corporatism, and the Transformation of Politics,* edited by Suzanne Berger (London: Cambridge University Press, 1981), p. 248. Pizzorno here echoes the words of John Dewey, writing more than fifty years earlier, who recalled eighteenth-century English and American sentiment against factions and noted: "Extensive and consolidated factions under the name of parties are now not only a matter of course, but popular imagination can conceive of no other way by which officials may be selected and governmental affairs carried on." For Dewey these "intermediary groups" at the heart of the new politics signaled the "eclipse of the public." See the excerpt from Dewey's *The Public and Its Problems* reprinted in chapter ten.

14. *Ibid.,* p. 249.

and in competition for the attention of the state. Over the course of the next century, a variety of solutions to the problem of the relation of state and civil society were offered, some authoritarian, if still implicitly republican, others renewing the liberal solutions of Kant and Madison, others still calling for a renewal of the civic community and civic virtue of an idealized republican tradition. In Leninist versions, society was to be organized in groups of all sorts under the direction of a cadre party. In notions of the corporate or "organic" state, functional organizations encompassing employers and workers would be chartered by the state, given monopoly control over representation, and serve simultaneously as organs of representation and transmission belts for state policy. In practice, in Hitler's Germany, Mussolini's Italy, and Franco's Spain, such notions were supplanted by overtly exclusionary policies. The Nazi model was closer in practice to Leninism than to corporatism, while Mussolini and Franco suppressed groups they could not control and deactivated those they could.[15]

In the United States, John Dewey posed the problem more globally as one of the decline and loss of "the public"—of a shared experience of political life capable of informing public deliberation on the problems of the day. Like Ferguson, Dewey traced the difficulty of enforcing a sense of common concern and destiny to the growing specialization of industrial society. But Dewey added that the sort of knowledge necessary to formulate "public judgments" was increasingly technical in character and, therefore, increasingly out of the reach of even well-educated citizens. Characteristically, Dewey thought that a renewal of the public could be achieved through a new social science and a new education attuned to the realities of the modern division of labor. Dewey's preoccupation with the character of public life and public deliberation anticipated, and in many ways laid the groundwork for, subsequent debate on the conditions for a genuinely civic form of deliberation. Contributors to that debate today range from the German political philosopher Jürgen Habermas to contemporary proponents of "deliberative democracy."[16]

Groups in Politics

The period following World War II, however, brought a re-evaluation of the role of autonomous groups in democratic polities. On the one hand, the mass society theorists revived the concerns of turn-of-the-century thinkers such as Durkheim, Tönnies, and Sorel about modernity's effects on traditional sources of social control. In attempting to explain the rise of Nazism in Germany, they argued that a

15. For a review of the relevant theories and an influential re-conceptualization of "corporatism," see Philippe C. Schmitter, "Still the Century of Corporatism?" *The Review of Politics* 36, 1 (January, 1974): 85–131.

16. See, for example, James S. Fishkin, *The Voice of the People: Public Opinion and Democracy* (New Haven: Yale University Press, 1995) and, in a more skeptical vein, Jon Elster, ed., *Deliberative Democracy* (New York: Cambridge University Press, 1998).

lack of social moorings characteristic of rapid modernization had contributed to people's susceptibility to extremist messages and the appeal of a charismatic leader.[17] (As Sheri Berman has pointed out, in doing so they ignored the rich associational life of Weimar Germany and the ways in which the Nazis built their organizations upon it.)[18] On the other hand, the American pluralists, starting with David Truman, revived the liberal notion of a competitive equilibrium among competing interests, arguing that the American polity worked well precisely because a broad variety of interests were represented. Truman saw the proliferation of interests rooted in the division of labor, like many of his predecessors, but noted that interests became organized precisely where government could be appealed to in pursuit of solutions.[19]

Gabriel Almond and Sidney Verba's five-nation study of "the civic culture," meanwhile, was part of a general revival of the Toquevillian tradition. They presented empirical evidence that membership in associations was correlated with support for democracy, trust in others and in government, and greater willingness to participate in civic life. Nonpolitical attitudes and affiliations, in their view, lay behind distinctively political behavior; and voluntary associations were particularly important because they involved citizens "in the broader social world" while making them "less dependent upon and less controlled by [their] political system."[20] Finally, drawing on early survey research, some pluralists added that representation at the level of interest groups perhaps served American politics so well because the elites who led such groups tended to have more democratic attitudes than the general populace.[21] Though this view has not survived entirely the scrutiny of subsequent researchers, the pluralist revaluation of groups continues to be the dominant thread in contemporary American thinking on the subject.[22]

Nevertheless, there were critics. Reflecting Cold War preoccupations with "political stability" and the dilemmas of U.S. policy making for a turbulent world,

17. See, among many others, Hannah Arendt, *The Origins of Totalitarianism* (New York: Harcourt Brace, 1973) and William Kornhauser, *The Politics of Mass Society* (London: Routledge Kegan Paul, 1960).

18. Sheri Berman, "Civil Society and the Collapse of the Weimar Republic," *World Politics* 49 (1997).

19. In this respect, Truman anticipates the findings of Jack Walker that American nonprofits generally have spread during the post–WWII period partly in response to growing government programs of all sorts. See Jack L. Walker, Jr., *Mobilizing Interest Groups in America: Patrons, Professions, and Social Movements* (Ann Arbor: University of Michigan Press, 1991).

20. See the excerpt published here, p. 173.

21. See the excerpts from the work of David Truman, this volume. A pluralist whose long career reflects growing questions within the pluralist tradition is Robert Dahl. See especially his *Dilemmas of Pluralist Democracy: Autonomy vs. Control* (New Haven: Yale University Press, 1982).

22. Still the most trenchant critique is that of E. E. Schatschneider, *The Semi-Sovereign People: A Realist's View of Democracy* (New York: Holt, Reinhart and Winston, 1960). For a recent review of the challenges and failings of the empirical analysis of group power in American politics, see Frank Baumgartner and Beth L. Leech, *Basic Interests : The Importance of Groups in Politics and in Political Science* (Princeton, N.J.: Princeton University Press, 1998).

Samuel Huntington raised renewed fears about the politicized "social forces" unleashed by modernization in the developing world. Huntington insisted that political institutions must come to dominate "raw social forces," so that "the power of
each group is exercised through political institutions which temper, moderate, and
redirect that power so as to render the dominance of one social force compatible
with the community of many."[23] That one "social force" might dominate did not
much trouble Huntington, who, though no friend of communism, viewed the
Communist Party of the Soviet Union as a prime example of a political institution
capable of properly governing a developing society. For Huntington, "a government with a low level of institutionalization is not just a weak government; it is
also a bad government."[24]

Closer to home, theorists in the public choice tradition began to concern themselves with what they saw as the "rent-seeking" activity of groups. In an influential series of articles and books, James Buchanan and Gordon Tulloch argued that
interest groups sought primarily to gain particular advantage (in the economists'
language, "rents") from their special relationships with legislators and bureaucrats.[25] Mancur Olson's *The Rise and Decline of Nations* claimed to show that as
the organizational density of countries increased, their economies slowed and
their political institutions became more and more sclerotic.[26] Even liberal econo-
mist Lester Thurow, writing in the late 1970s, worried about the growing "ungovernability" of the United States and other Western democracies as more and
more interests claimed a voice in policy making.[27]

Such concerns recalled some of the worries of turn-of-the-century theorists,
writing of the new power of organized groups in industrial societies and their relative immunity to public accountability. Politically, the two currents of thought reflect similar situations: in the late nineteenth century, organized labor, farmers',
and women's groups emerged to challenge the hegemony of business and finance
in public affairs;[28] in the 1970s and 1980s environmentalists, women (again!), and
a large-scale peace movement were on the minds of analysts—not to mention the
breakthrough by African Americans and, increasingly, by Hispanics and Asian
Americans as a result of the civil rights movement. The continuing concerns in the
current debate about the "incivility" of American politics may well reflect little
more than this sense that too many new contenders from hitherto quiescent groups

23. Samuel P. Huntington, *Political Order in Changing Societies* (New Haven: Yale University
Press, 1968), p. 9.

24. Huntington, p. 28.

25. James M. Buchanan, R. D. Tollison, and Gordon Tullock, eds., *Toward a Theory of the Rent-
Seeking Society* (College Station: Texas A&M University Press, 1981).

26. Mancur Olson, *The Rise and Decline of Nations: Economic Growth, Stagflation, and Social
Rigidities* (New Haven: Yale University Press, 1982).

27. Lester C. Thurow, *The Zero-Sum Society: Distribution and the Possibilities for Economic
Change* (New York: Basic Books, 1980).

28. Elizabeth S. Clemens, *The People's Lobby: Organizational Innovation and the Rise of Interest
Group Politics in the United States, 1890–1925* (Chicago: University of Chicago Press, 1997).

have gained a voice at the expense of older, ostensibly "quieter" interests.[29] At the same time, these worries reflect a growing concern in the pluralist tradition with the perennial problem of civil society: how to reconcile the competing, particularistic interests of modern societies with the ideals of the "civic republic."[30]

The dominant note in Western thinking about groups today, however, is positive; and the renewal of the language of civil society is key evidence that the older problem of groups has been set aside or submerged in subtle turns to the contemporary debate. The origins of this renewal, nevertheless, are paradoxical. Not only did the term "civil society" originate in efforts to understand the suddenly problematic character of the relations among competing interests in the emerging states of Western Europe; but its modern revival was tied initially to notions of conflict between the state and dissident elements within society. Current efforts to find in civil society sources of social harmony and political comity stem paradoxically from a discourse that sets society against the state in a struggle for control of the state.

Gramsci and the Renewal of Civil Society Language

The Italian Marxist Antonio Gramsci may be single-handedly responsible for the revival of the term "civil society" in the post–World War II period. Gramsci, who wrote and died in one of Mussolini's prisons, expanded Marxist understanding of civil society as part of an effort to understand the ability of the modern state to maintain control over society with only limited application of force. His writing was dedicated to plotting a course of action for social transformation with this reality in mind. For Gramsci, as for Marxists more generally, the state is an expression of the power of a dominant class, though holders of state power may have their own interests, at times at variance with those of economic elites. But state power is not just domination, not simply a matter of brute force. It is also, in the stable state, a matter of "hegemony," or the ideological and cultural acceptance of class rule by members of dominated classes. Civil society, in Gramsci's view, is the arena in which the struggle for hegemony unfolds. Thus it provides an opening for counter-hegemonic (read: revolutionary) projects to gain strength.[31]

Gramsci's work—largely fragmentary notes, often difficult and sometimes contradictory—was published only after his death, in the first two decades after World War II.[32] Despite the difficulties of interpretation, Gramsci's thought had

29. Thanks to Bob Edwards for this observation.

30. See Robert Dahl, *Dilemmas of Pluralist Democracy: Autonomy vs. Control* (New Haven: Yale University Press, 1982). For a careful recent attempt to struggle with the meaning of associational life for democracy, see Mark E. Warren, *Democracy and Association* (Princeton, N. J.: Princeton University Press, 2001).

31. Norberto Bobbio, "Gramsci and the Concept of Civil Society," in John Keane, ed., *Civil Society and the State: New European Perspectives* (London: Verso, 1988), pp. 73–100, provides a more subtle (and controversial) reading of Gramsci's intent and his relation to orthodox Marxism.

32. The excerpts published here contain most of Gramsci's best-known reflections on civil society and the state.

considerable impact on the Left in the West and the Third World, but also in the countries of the communist world. Thanks to Gramsci, "cultural struggle" became a part of the repertoire of oppositionist movements around the world. Left opposition movements in Western Europe and elsewhere were thus freed to abandon the exclusive focus on organized labor maintained by the various communist parties and to direct their energies instead to a wide array of popular causes, from feminism to environmentalism.

Gramsci's influence can also be seen in the decision by dissidents such as Adam Michnik in Poland and Vaclav Havel in Czechoslovakia to develop the struggle against the "post-totalitarian" dictatorships of Eastern Europe through refusal to cooperate with projects of the state and by efforts to build up and align with independent organizations and movements in society. Michnik opened the eyes of the secular Polish opposition to the importance of the Catholic Church as a source of independent life in Polish society, while Havel developed an analysis of the ways in which even subtle forms of "living within the truth" could become the basis for social change under the oppressive weight of the "post-totalitarian" state.[33]

These ideas were important not only in Eastern Europe and among a new left in Western Europe, but in Latin America, where military dictatorships ruled much of the region during the 1970s. There, Gramsci's notion that forces of the opposition could work within civil society in what would eventually become a "war of position" for control of the state appealed to leftists who despaired of a frontal attack on the military dictatorships of the region and sought (and won) broad alliances in the struggle against authoritarianism. Nevertheless, the result in case after case was not "social transformation" but a return to forms of liberal democracy that, in the difficult economic circumstances of the 1980s and 90s, were largely incapable of realizing the aspirations for a better way of life that had driven much of the struggle on the left. In these circumstances, "civil society" quickly became the slogan of a new generation of professionally staffed nongovernmental organizations committed to public advocacy around narrow questions of policy.[34]

33. See the excerpts from the seminal essay by Michnik in this volume, and Vaclav Havel's "The Power of the Powerless," in *Open Letters: Selected Writings, 1965–1990,* ed. by Paul Wilson (New York: Vintage Books, 1991) pp. 127–214.

34. "Civil society" thus came to the attention of international donors anxious to promote democratization and development in the Third World, Eastern Europe, and the former Soviet states in the form of an emerging sector of nongovernmental organizations. Despite some striking successes, critiques have multiplied over the last several years. See, for example, Michael Edwards and David Hulme, eds., *Making a Difference: NGOs and Development in a Changing World* (London: Earthscan, 1992) and *Beyond the Magic Bullet: NGO Performance and Accountability in the Post–Cold War World* (West Hartford, Conn.: Kumarian Press, 1996); and Marina Ottaway and Thomas Carothers, eds., *Funding Virtue: Civil Society Aid and Democracy Promotion* (Washington, D.C.: Carnegie Endowment for International Peace, 2000).

Civil Society and Citizenship in the United States

In the United States talk of civil society did not emerge until the 1980s; and, while civil society in this debate is often set off against the state, the oppositionist overtones of the Eastern European and Latin American movements find little place in American political discourse, where much of the emphasis is on civil society as an alternative to state action or a basis for a more "civil" politics.

One strand of the distinctly American version of contemporary civil society discourse emerges clearly in a work that does not use the term, but that invoked a renewed appreciation of the role of "mediating structures" in democratic life—Peter Berger's and Richard John Neuhaus's *To Empower People*. Berger and Neuhaus called for a rethinking of the welfare state to use mediating institutions such as neighborhood, family, church, and voluntary associations "wherever possible" for the realization of social purposes. Carefully noting that theirs was not a call for dismantling the welfare state, they nevertheless insisted that institutions outside the state should be the arenas for empowering individuals and communities and democratizing the delivery of welfare services. Their work thus crystallized, and to a large extent anticipated, what would become a conservative counterrevolution in American public policy. At the same time, it introduced a notion (represented most clearly among the earlier authors surveyed here in the thinking of Tom Paine) of civil society as a functional substitute for (or supplement to) government.

Michael Walzer's thoughtful contribution to the debate echoes this vision to some extent. For Walzer, civil society is the realm of "uncoerced human associations" and "the set of relational networks—formed for the sake of family, faith, interest, and ideology—that fill this space." The new attention to civil society, in Walzer's view, stems from use of the term in the Eastern European struggles against tyranny, but it responds to longstanding dissatisfactions with competing visions of the basis for the good life—democratic citizenship, socialist citizenship, free markets, nationalism. What Walzer calls "the civil society argument" is a corrective to the narrow focus of these visions of humankind as active citizen, worker and maker, consumer, and patriot, respectively, and to the neglect of human relationships outside these narrow spheres. Yet civil society alone does not provide a lasting solution to the organization of modern life, in Walzer's view, because civil society itself depends upon a functioning political community. In the end, "there is no escape from power and coercion, no possibility of choosing, like the old anarchists, civil society alone."

Benjamin Barber's *Strong Democracy,* on the other hand, sees civil society precisely as a key ingredient in reviving the Aristotelian and Tocquevillian notion of active citizenship nurtured in "strong democratic community." By the latter, Barber means a community characterized by active participation grounded in ongoing civic education, open arenas for participation, and real decision-making possibilities for ordinary citizens. In an Aristotelian vein, Barber argues that civic virtue grows out of civic practice, not the reverse. At the same time, he points out that certain structures, particularly those that encourage active citizenship, are more conducive to civic practice than others; political association, not voluntary association in general, nurtures citizenship. Sara Evans and Harry Boyte make a similar point in *Free Spaces,* but they emphasize the importance of "communal spaces" created by organizers of all sorts and drawing on existing community resources. In both these versions, civil society is not so much a functional substitute for the state as a launching ground for new social initiatives, many of them directed at changing state policy, and for the generation of civic activism.

Jean Cohen and Andrew Arato, drawing on earlier work by German social theorist Jürgen Habermas, take a similar tack in their attempt to incorporate the notion of civil society into political and social theory. Autonomous institutions outside the state and the market, they argue, provide scope for independent voice and initiative in modern societies and are essential to the constitution of a genuine "public sphere." Cohen and Arato emphasize the co-responsibility of the interventionist modern state and the modern corporate economy in undermining the ability of citizens to frame independent judgments, assert their authority over their lives, and re-encounter community among themselves. They insist that only an autonomous and vigorous civil society can reinvigorate public communication and public life and see social movements as important expressions of such autonomy. Habermas himself, taking up many of their ideas, has stressed the difference between groups that are anchored in civil society and those that play a role (as organized interests, spokespeople for this or that point of view, or political actors) but have their base of support in the corporate or political system. Only the former, in Habermas's view, can contribute to a genuine expression of autonomous citizen action.[35]

A final set of authors looks to civil society as a source of attitudes, norms, and values that can "make democracy work" (in Robert Putnam's phrase). Edward Shils, for instance, builds on the notion that civil society is somehow the realm of "civility," of public spiritedness, of tolerance and civic virtue. More profoundly, for Shils civil society corresponds to a liberal democracy in which societal constraints, perhaps more than Madisonian institutions, serve to protect minorities from the self-interested majority. For civility is fundamentally "an attitude and a pattern of conduct," equivalent, according to Shils, to Montesquieu's notion of virtue: love of the republic. Thus, it includes an attachment to the institutions that characterize civil society and an attitude of concern for the common good. Civil manners make cooperation among divergent interests possible and thus contribute to the successful working of democratic institutions.[36]

35. See Jürgen Habermas, *Between Parts and Norms: Contributions to a Discourse Theory of Law and Democracy* (Cambridge, Mass.: MIT Press, 1998), pp. 362–384.

36. For a subtle assessment of the contributions of associational life to the moral dispositions of citizens, see Nancy L. Rosenblum, *Membership and Morals: The Personal Uses of Pluralism in America* (Princeton, N.J.: Princeton University Press, 1998).

Robert Putnam's (1994) study of local institutions in modern Italy made a similar argument. Institutions may partially shape human behavior, Putnam argued, but, more importantly, the cultural context in which institutions have to operate profoundly determine their chances for success or failure. In the Italian case, Putnam found that the efficiency and legitimacy of the regional governments introduced throughout the country in 1971 differed markedly from region to region. His analysis traced those differences to underlying differences in what he called "civic community," or the degree of civic engagement displayed by citizens in the various regions. Strongest in the Northern Italian states and weakest in the South, civic engagement—as measured by membership in voluntary associations, newspaper reading, and other indicators—seemed to account for major differences in how the respective regional governments worked, what citizens thought of them, and how effective they were. In the light of the Italian evidence, Putnam went on to argue that "social capital"—defined as social networks and the social trust and norms of reciprocity that sustained them—was crucial to a healthy democracy and a healthy economy. Looking now at the United States, Putnam argued in a series of articles (1994, 1995) capped by a major book (2000) that social capital was in decline in the United States, as people abandoned the sorts of voluntary associations that had been popular in the 1950s and 1960s and the sorts of everyday social interactions that had characterized that same period. Though roundly criticized by a variety of authors,[37] Putnam's arguments have been tremendously influential in the social sciences and the popular press.

Robert Bellah and his associates' earlier study of American attitudes had stressed the conflict between individualistic ways of talking about civic responsibility and togetherness and long-standing commitments to community and public service. Important undercurrents in American tradition, from the biblical language of faith in Jewish and Christian communities to civic republicanism, continue to challenge the dominant discourse without gaining the upper hand. In their 1996 introduction to the updated edition of their book, Bellah and his coauthors call attention to what they call a "crisis of civic membership." Following Robert Putnam's lead, they argue that American "social capital" is depleted, but that, more profoundly, the decline in connectedness and social trust they and others detect threatens Americans' personal identities, as well. Without a sense of belonging, without a notion of communal purpose, contemporary Americans, in their view, lose confidence in their own sense of selfhood. Unlike other authors who express similar concerns, however, Bellah and company trace these effects to the dramatic economic changes that have taken place over the last twenty-five years: globalization, growing disparities between the rich and everyone else, and a declining sense of civic obligation among the wealthy.

37. See for example, Bob Edwards, Michael Foley, and Mario Diani, *Beyond Tocqueville: Civil Society and the Social Capital Debate in Comparative Perspectives* (Hanover, N.H.: University Press

Conclusion

The readings in this volume trace a complex history of thinking about the conditions of citizenship and the character of the good society. From Aristotle, Western thinkers and the societies they helped mold have inherited perennial questions about what shapes citizens and contributes to civic virtue and civic engagement. But the consolidation of the modern state as the predominant form of political organization and the increasing division of labor and social complexity that went with it not only raised that question anew but provoked new questions about what role the ordinary occupations and preoccupations of citizens play in the public sphere and in building the good society. While some worried that the increasing complexity of modern society undermined concern for the common good and even the possibility of talking about a public good, others saw the multiple associations that make up modern societies and represent the diverse interests and initiatives of citizens as vital instruments of citizenship. These debates are still very much unresolved, as the selections in this volume testify; but they continue to sustain and nurture thinking about the character of our common life and the project, to use Michael Walzer's term, of building the good life.

The Civil Society Reader

from The Politics

BOOK I

1. Every state is a community of some kind, and every community is established with a view to some good; for everyone always acts in order to obtain that which they think good. But, if all communities aim at some good, the state or political community *[polis]*, which is the highest of all, and which embraces all the rest, aims at good in a greater degree than any other, and at the highest good.

Some people think that the qualifications of a statesman, king, householder, and master are the same, and that they differ, not in kind, but only in the number of their subjects. For example, the ruler over a few is called a master; over more, the manager of a household; over a still larger number, a statesman or king, as if there were no difference between a great household and a small state. The distinction which is made between the king and the statesman is as follows: When the government is personal, the ruler is a king; when, according to the rules of the political science, the citizens rule and are ruled in turn, then he is called a statesman.

But all this is a mistake, as will be evident to any one who considers the matter according to the method which has hitherto guided us. As in other departments of science, so in politics, the compound should always be resolved into the simple elements or least parts of the whole. We must therefore look at the elements of which the state is composed, in order that we may see in what the different kinds of rule differ from one another, and whether any scientific result can be attained about each one of them.

2. He who thus considers thing in their first growth and origin, whether a state or anything else, will obtain the clearest view of them. In the first place there must be a union of those who cannot exist without each other; namely, of male and female, that the race may continue (and this is a union which is formed, not of choice, but because, in common with other animals and with plants, mankind have a natural desire to leave behind them an image of themselves), and of natural ruler and subject, that both may be preserved. For that which can foresee by the exercise of mind is by nature lord and master, and that which can with its body give effect to such foresight is a subject, and by nature a slave; hence master and slave have the same interest. Now nature has distinguished between the female and slave. For she is not niggardly, like the smith who fashions the Delphian knife for many uses; she makes each thing for a single use, and every instrument is best made when intended for one and not for many uses. But among barbarians no distinction is made between women and slaves, because there is no natural ruler among them: they are a community of slaves, male and female. That is why the poets say,

It is meet that Hellenes should rule over barbarians;[1]

as if they thought that the barbarian and the slave were by nature one.

Out of these two relationships the first thing to arise is the family, and Hesiod is right when he says,

First house and wife and an ox for the plough,[2]

for the ox is the poor man's slave. The family is the association established by nature for the supply of men's everyday wants, and the members of it are called by Charondas, "companions of the cupboard," and by Epimenides the Cretan, "companions of the manager." But when several families are united, and the association aims at something more than the supply of daily needs, the first society to be formed is the village. And the most natural form of the village appears to be that of a colony from the family, composed of the children and grandchildren, who are said to be "suckled with the same milk." And this is the reason why Hellenic states were originally governed by kings; because the Hellenes were under royal rule before they came together, as the barbarians still are. Every family is ruled by the eldest, and therefore in the colonies of the family the kingly form of government prevailed because they were of the same blood. As Homer says:

Each one gives law to his children and to his wives.[3]

For they lived dispersedly, as was the manner in ancient times. That is why men say that the Gods have a king, because they themselves either are or were in ancient times under the rule of a king. For they imagine not only the forms of the Gods but their ways of life to be like their own.

1. Euripides, *Iphigeneia in Aulis,* 1400.
2. Hesiod, *Works and Days,* 405.
3. Homer, *Odyssey,* IX 114–15.

When several villages are united in a single complete community, large enough to be nearly or quite self-sufficing, the state comes into existence, originating in the bare needs of life, and continuing in existence for the sake of a good life. And therefore, if the earlier forms of society are natural, so is the state, for it is the end of them, and the nature of a thing is its end. For what each thing is when fully developed, we call its nature, whether we are speaking of a man, a horse, or a family. Besides, the final cause and end of a thing is the best, and to be self-sufficing is the end and the best.

Hence it is evident that the state is a creation of nature, and that man is by nature a political animal. And he who by nature and not by mere accident is without a state, is either a bad man or above humanity; he is like the

Tribeless, lawless, heartless one,[4]

whom Homer denounces—the natural outcast is forthwith a lover of war; he may be compared to an isolated piece at draughts.

Now, that man is more of a political animal than bees or any other gregarious animals is evident. Nature, as we often say, makes nothing in vain, and man is the only animal who has the gift of speech. And whereas mere voice is but an indication of pleasure or pain, and is therefore found in other animals (for their nature attains to the perception of pleasure and pain and the intimation of them to one another, and no further), the power of speech is intended to set forth the expedient and inexpedient, and therefore likewise the just and the unjust. And it is a characteristic of man that he alone has any sense of good and evil, of just and unjust, and the like, and the association of living beings who have this sense makes a family and a state.

Further, the state is by nature clearly prior to the family and to the individual, since the whole is of necessity prior to the part; for example, if the whole body be destroyed, there will be no foot or hand, except homonymously, as we might speak of a stone hand; for when destroyed the hand will be no better than that. But things are defined by their function and power; and we ought not to say that they are the same when they no longer have their proper quality, but only that they are homonymous. The proof that the state is a creation of nature and prior to the individual is that the individual, when isolated, is not self-sufficing; and therefore he is like a part in relation to the whole. But he who is unable to live in society, or who has no need because he is sufficient for himself, must be either a beast or a god: he is no part of a state. A social instinct is implanted in all men by nature, and yet he who first founded the state was the greatest of benefactors. For man, when perfected, is the best of animals, but, when separated from law and justice, he is the worst of all; since armed injustice is the more dangerous, and he is equipped at birth with arms, meant to be used by intelligence and excellence,

4. Homer, *Iliad,* IX 63.

which he may use for the worst ends. That is why, if he has not excellence, he is the most unholy and the most savage of animals, and the most full of lust and gluttony. But justice is the bond of men in states; for the administration of justice, which is the determination of what is just, is the principle of order in political society.

. . .

BOOK II

5. Next let us consider what should be our arrangements about property: should the citizens of the perfect state have their possessions in common or not? This question may be discussed separately from the enactments about women and children. Even supposing that the women and children belong to individuals, according to the custom which is at present universal, may there not be an advantage in having and using possessions in common? E.g. (1) the soil may be appropriated, but the produce may be thrown for consumption into the common stock; and this is the practice of some nations. Or (2), the soil may be common, and may be cultivated in common, but the produce divided among individuals for their private use; this is a form of common property which is said to exist among certain foreigners. Or (3), the soil and the produce may be alike common.

When the husbandsmen are not the owners, the case will be different and easier to deal with; but when they till the ground for themselves the question of ownership will give a world of trouble. If they do not share equally in enjoyment and toils, those who labor much and get little will necessarily complain of those who labor little and receive or consume much. But indeed there is always a difficulty in men living together and having all human relations in common, but especially in their having common property. The partnerships of fellow-travellers are an example to the point; for they generally fall out over everyday matters and quarrel about any trifle which turns up. So with servants: we are most liable to take offense at those with whom we most frequently come into contact in daily life.

These are only some of the disadvantages which attend the community of property; the present arrangement, if improved as it might be by good customs and laws, would be far better, and would have the advantages of both systems. Property should be in a certain sense common, but, as a general rule, private; for, when everyone has a distinct interest, men will not complain of one another, and they will make more progress, because everyone will be attending to his own business. And yet by reason of goodness, and in respect of use, "Friends," as the proverb says, "will have all things common." Even now there are traces of such a principle, showing that is it not impracticable, but, in well-ordered states, exists already to a certain extent and may be carried further. For, although every man has his own property, some things he will place at the disposal of his friends, while of others he shares the use with them. The Lacedaemonians, for example, use one another's slaves, and horses, and dogs, as if they were their own; and when they lack provisions on a journey, they appropriate what they find in the fields throughout the country. It is clearly better that property should be private, but the use of it common; and the special business of the legislator is to create in men this benevolent disposition. Again, how immeasurably greater is the pleasure, when a man feels a thing to be his own; for surely the love of self is a feeling implanted by nature and not given in vain, although selfishness is rightly censured; this, however, is not the mere love of self, but the love of self in excess, like the miser's love of money; for all, or almost all, men love money and other such objects in a measure. And further, there is the greatest pleasure in doing a kindness or service to friends or guests or companions, which can only be rendered when a man has private property. These advantages are lost by excessive unification of the state. The exhibition of two excellences, besides, is visibly annihilated in such a state: first, temperance towards women (for it is an honorable action to abstain from another's wife for temperance sake); secondly, liberality in the matter of property. No one, when men have all things in common, will any longer set an example of liberality or do any liberal action; for liberality consists in the use which is made of property.

Such legislation may have a specious appearance of benevolence; men readily listen to it, and are easily induced to believe that in some wonderful manner everybody will become everybody's friend—especially when someone is heard denouncing the evils now existing in states, suits about contracts, convictions for perjury, flatteries of rich men and the like, which are said to arise out of the possession of private property. These evils, however, are due not to the absence of communism but to wickedness. Indeed, we see that there is much more quarreling among those who have all things in common, though there are not many of them when compared with the vast numbers who have private property.

Again, we ought to reckon not only the evils from which the citizens will be saved, but also the advantages which they will lose. The life which they are to lead appears to be quite impracticable. The error of Socrates must be attributed to the false supposition from which he starts. Unity there should be, both of the family and of the state, but in some respects only. For there is a point at which a state may attain such a degree of unity as to be no longer a state, or at which, without actually ceasing to exist, it will become an inferior state, like harmony, passing into unison, or rhythm which has been reduced to a single foot. The state, as I was saying, is a plurality, which should be united and made into a community by education; and it is strange that the author of a system of education which he thinks will make the state virtuous, should expect to improve his citizens by regulations of this sort, and not by philosophy or by customs and laws, like those which prevail at Sparta and Crete respecting common meals, whereby the legislator has made property common. Let us remember that we should not disregard the experience of ages; in the multitude of years these things, if they were good, would certainly not have been unknown; for almost everything has been found out, although sometimes they are not put together; in other cases men do not use the knowledge which they have. Great light would be thrown on this subject if we could see such a form of government in the actual process of construction; for the legislator could not form a state at all without distributing and dividing its constituents into associations for common meals, and into phratries and tribes. But all this legislation ends only in forbidding agriculture to the guardians, a prohibition which the Lacedaemonians try to enforce already.

But, indeed, Socrates has not said, nor is it easy to decide, what in such a community will be the general form of the state. The citizens who are not guardians are the majority, and about them nothing has been determined: are the husbandmen, too, to have their property in common? Or is each individual to have his own? and are their wives and children to be individual or common? If, like the guardians, they are to have all things in common, in what do they differ from them, or what will they gain by submitting to their government? Or upon what principle would they submit, unless indeed the governing class adopt the ingenious policy of the Cretans, who give their slaves the same institutions as their own, but forbid them gymnastic exercises and the possession of arms. If, on the other hand, the inferior classes are to be like other cities in respect to marriage and property, what will be the form of the community? Must it not contain two states in one, each hostile to the other? He makes the guardians into a mere occupying garrison, while the husbandmen and artisans and the rest are real citizens. But if so the suits and quarrels, and all the evils which Socrates affirms to exist in other states, will exist equally among them. He says indeed that, having so good an education, the citizens will not need many laws, for example laws about the city or about the markets; but then he confines his education to the guardians. Again, he makes the husbandmen owners of the property upon condition of their paying a tribute. But in that case they are likely to be much more unmanageable and conceited than the Helots, or Penestae, or slaves in general. And whether community of wives and property be necessary for the lower equally with the higher class or not, and the questions akin to this, what will be the education, form of government, laws of the lower class, Socrates has nowhere determined: neither is it easy to discover this, nor is their character of small importance if the common life of the guardians is to be maintained.

Again, if Socrates makes the women common, and retains private property, the men will see to the fields, but who will see to the house? And who will do so if the agricultural class have both their property and their wives in common? Once more: it is absurd to argue, from the analogy of animals, that men and women should follow the same pursuits, for animals have not to manage a household. The government, too, as constituted by Socrates, contains elements of danger; for he makes the same person always rule. And if this is often a cause of disturbance among the meaner sort, how much more among high-spirited warriors? But that the persons whom he makes rulers must be the same is evident; for the gold which the God mingles in the souls of men is not at one time given to one, at another time to another, but always to the same: as he says, God mingles gold in some, and

silver in others, from their very birth; but brass and iron in those who are meant to be artisans and husbandmen. Again, he deprives the guardians even of happiness, and says that the legislator ought to make the whole state happy. But the whole cannot be happy unless most, or all, or some of its parts enjoy happiness. In this respect happiness is not like the even principle in numbers, which may exist only in the whole, but in neither of the parts; not so happiness. And if the guardians are not happy, who are? Surely not the artisans, or the common people. The Republic of which Socrates discourses has all these difficulties, and others quite as great.
6. Having determined these questions, we have next to consider whether there is only one form of government or many, and if many, what they are, and how many, and what are the differences between them.

A constitution is the arrangement of magistracies in a state, especially of the highest of all. The government is everywhere sovereign in the state, and the constitution is in fact the government.

· · ·

BOOK III

1. He who would inquire into the essence and attributes of various kinds of government must first of all determine what a state is. At present this is a disputed question. Some say that the state has done a certain act; others, not the state, but the oligarchy or the tyrant. And the legislator or statesman is concerned entirely with the state, a government being an arrangement of the inhabitants of a state. But a state is a composite, like any other whole made up of many parts—these are the citizens, who compose it. It is evident, therefore, that we must begin by asking, Who is the citizen, and what is the meaning of the term? For here again there may be a difference of opinion. He who is a citizen in a democracy will often not be a citizen in an oligarchy. Leaving out of consideration those who have been made citizens, or who have obtained the name of citizen in any other accidental manner, we may say, first, that a citizen is not a citizen because he lives in a certain place, for resident aliens and slaves share in the place; nor is he a citizen who has legal rights to the extent of suing and being sued; for this right may be enjoyed under the provisions of a treaty. Resident aliens in many places do not possess even such rights completely, for they are obliged to have a patron, so that they do but imperfectly participate in the community, and we call them citizens only in a qualified sense, as we might apply the term to children who are too young to be on the register, or to old men who have been relieved from state duties. Of these we do not say quite simply that they are citizens, but add in the one case that they are not of age, and in the other, that they are past the age, or something of that sort; the precise expression is immaterial, for our meaning is clear. Similar difficulties to those which I have mentioned may be raised and answered about disfranchised citizens and about exiles. But the citizen whom we are seeking to define is a citizen in the strictest sense, against whom no such exception can be taken, and his special characteristic is that he shares in the administration of justice, and in offices. Now of offices some are discontinuous, and the same persons are now allowed to hold them twice, or can only hold them after a fixed interval; others have no limit of time—for example, the office of juryman or member of the assembly. It may, indeed, be argued that these are not magistrates at all, and that their functions give them no share in the government. But surely it is ridiculous to say that those who have the supreme power do not govern. Let us not dwell further upon this, which is a purely verbal question; what we want is a common term including both juryman and member of the assembly. Let us for the sake of distinction, call it "indefinite office," and we will assume that those who share in such office are citizens. This is the most comprehensive definition of a citizen, and best suits all those who are generally so called.

But we must not forget that things of which the underlying principles differ in kind, one of them being first, another second, another third, have, when regarded in this relation, nothing, or hardly anything, worth mentioning in common. Now we see that governments differ in kind, and those some of them are prior and that others are posterior; those which are faulty or perverted are necessarily posterior to those which are perfect. (What we mean by perversion will be hereafter explained.) The citizen then of necessity differs under each form of government; and our definition is best adapted to the citizen of a democracy; but not necessarily to other states. For in some states the people are not acknowledged, nor have they any regular assembly, but only extraordinary ones; and law-suits are distributed by sections among the magistrates. At Lacedaemon, for instance, the Ephors determine suits about contracts, which they distribute among themselves, while the elders are judges of homicide, and other causes are decided by other magistrates. A similar principle prevails at Carthage; there certain magistrates decide all causes. We may, indeed, modify our definition of the citizen so as to include these states. In them it is the holder of a definite, not an indefinite office, who is juryman and member of the assembly, and to some or all such holders of definite offices is reserved the right of deliberating or judging about some thing or about all things. The conception of the citizen now begins to clear up.

He who has the power to take part in the deliberative or judicial administration of any state is said by us to be a citizen of that state; and, speaking generally, a state is a body of citizens sufficing for the purposes of life.

. . .

For example, in democracies the people are supreme, but in oligarchies, the few; and, therefore, we say that these two constitutions also are different: and so in other cases.

First, let us consider what is the purpose of a state, and how many forms of rule there are by which human society is regulated. We have already said, in the first part of this treatise, when discussing household management and the rule of a master, that man is by nature a political animal. And therefore, men, even when they do not require one another's help, desire to live together; not but that they are also brought together by their common interests in so far as they each attain to any measure of well-being. This is certainly the chief end, both of individuals and of states. And mankind meet together and maintain the political community also for the sake of mere life (in which there is possibly some noble element so long as the evils of existence do not greatly overbalance the good). And we all see that men cling to life even at the cost of enduring great misfortune, seeming to find in life a natural sweetness and happiness.

There is no difficulty in distinguishing the various kinds of rule; they have been often defined already in our popular discussions. The rule of a master, although the slave by nature and the master by nature have in reality the same interests, is nevertheless exercised primarily with a view to the interest of the master, but accidentally considers the slave, since, if the slave perish, the rule of the master perishes with him. On the other hand, the government of a wife and children and of a household, which we have called household management, is exercised in the first instance for the good of the governed or for the common good of both parties, but essentially for the good of the governed, as we see to be the case in medicine, gymnastic, and the arts in general, which are only accidentally concerned with the good of the artists themselves. For there is no reason why the trainer may not sometimes practice gymnastics, and the helmsman is always one of the crew. The trainer or the helmsman considers the good of those committed to his care. But, when he is one of the persons taken care of, he accidentally participates in the advantage, for the helmsman is also a sailor, and the trainer becomes one of those in training. And so in politics: when the state is framed upon the principle of equality and likeness, the citizens think that they ought to hold office by turns. Formerly, as is natural, everyone would take his turn of service; and then again, somebody else would look after his interest, just as he, while in office, had looked after theirs. But nowadays, for the sake of the advantage which is to gained from the public revenues and from office, men want to be always in office. One might imagine that the rulers, being sickly, were only kept in health while they continued in office; in that case we may be sure that they would be hunting after places. The conclusion is evident: that governments which have a regard to the common interest are constituted in accordance with strict principles of justice, and are therefore true forms; but those which regard only the interest of the rulers are all defective and perverted forms, for they are despotic, whereas a state is a community of freemen.

7. Having determined these points, we have next to consider how many forms of government there are, and what they are; and in the first place what are the true forms, for when they are determined the perversions of them will at once be apparent. The words constitution and government have the same meaning, and the government, which is the supreme authority in states, must be in the hands of one, or of a few, or of the many. The true forms of government, therefore, are those in which the one, or the few, or the many, govern with a view to the common interest; but governments which rule with a view to the private interest, whether of the one,

or the few, or of the many, are perversions. For the members of a state, if they are truly citizens, ought to participate in its advantages. Of forms of government in which one rules, we call that which regards the common interest, kingship; that in which more than one, but not many, rule, aristocracy; and it is so called, either because the rulers are the best men, or because they have at heart the best interests of the state and of the citizens. But when the many administer the state for the common interest, the government is called by the generic name—a constitution. And there is a reason for this use of language. One man or a few may excel in excellence; but as the number increases it becomes more difficult for them to attain perfection in every kind of excellence, though they may in military excellence, for this is found in the masses. Hence in a constitutional government the fighting-men have the supreme power, and those who possess arms are the citizens.

Of the above-mentioned forms, the perversions are as follows:—of kingship, tyranny; of aristocracy, oligarchy; of constitutional government, democracy. For tyranny is a kind of monarchy which has in view the interest of the monarch only; oligarchy has in view the interest of the wealthy; democracy, of the needy; none of them the common good of all.

8. But there are difficulties about these forms of government, and it will therefore be necessary to state a little more at length the nature of each of them. For he who would make a philosophical study of the various sciences, and is not only concerned with practice, ought not to overlook or omit anything, but to set forth the truth in every particular. Tyranny, as I was saying, is monarchy exercising the rule of a master over the political society; oligarchy is when men of property have the government in their hands; democracy, the opposite, when the indigent, and not the men of property, are the rulers. And here arises the first of our difficulties, and it relates to the distinction just drawn. For democracy is said to be the government of the many. But what if the many are men of property and have the power in their hands? In like manner oligarchy is said to be the government of the few; but what if the poor are fewer than the rich, and have the power in their hands because they are stronger? In these cases the distinction which we have drawn between these different forms of government would no longer hold good.

Suppose, once more, that we add wealth to the few and poverty to the many, and name the governments accordingly—an oligarchy is said to be that in which the few and the wealthy, and a democracy that in which the many and the poor are the rulers—there will still be a difficulty. For, if the only forms of government are the ones already mentioned, how shall we describe those other governments also just mentioned by us, in which the rich are the more numerous and the poor are the fewer, and both govern in their respective states?

The argument seems to show that, whether in oligarchies or in democracies, the number of the governing body, whether the greater number, as in a democracy, or the smaller number, as in an oligarchy, is an accident due to the fact that the rich everywhere are few, and the poor numerous. But if so, there is a misapprehension of the causes of the difference between them. For the real difference between democracy and oligarchy is poverty and wealth. Wherever men rule by reason of their wealth, whether they be few or many, that is an oligarchy, and where the poor rule, that is a democracy. But in fact the rich are few and the poor many, for few are well-to-do, whereas freedom is enjoyed by all, and wealth and freedom are the grounds on which the two parties claim power in the state.

9. Let us begin by considering the common definitions of oligarchy and democracy, and what is oligarchical and democratic justice. For all men cling to justice of some kind, but their conceptions are imperfect and they do not express the whole idea. For example, justice is thought by them to be, and is, equality—not, however, for all, but only for equals. And the inequality is thought to be, and is, justice; neither is this for all, but only for unequals. When the persons are omitted, then men judge erroneously. The reason is that they are passing judgment on themselves, and most people are bad judges in their own case. And whereas justice implies a relation to persons as well to things, and a just distribution, as I have already said in the *Ethics,* implies the same ratio between the persons and between the things, they agree about the equality of the things, but dispute about the equality of the persons, chiefly for the reason which I have just given—because they are bad judges in their own affairs; and secondly, because both the parties to the argument are speaking of a limited and partial justice, but imagine themselves to be speaking of absolute justice. For the one party, if they are unequal in one respect, for example wealth, consider themselves to be unequal in all; and the other party, if they are equal in one respect, for example free birth, consider themselves to be equal in all. But they leave out the capital point. For if men met and associated out of regard to wealth only, their share in the state would be proportioned to their property, and the oligarchical doctrine would then seem to carry the day. It would not be just that he who paid one mina should have the same share of a hundred minae, whether of the principal or of the profits, as he who paid the remaining ninety-nine. But a state exists for the sake of a good life, and not for the sake of life only: if life only were the object, slaves and brute animals might form a state, but they cannot, for they have no share in happiness or in a life based on choice. Nor does a state exist for the sake of alliance and security from injustice, nor yet for the sake of exchange and mutual intercourse; for then the Tyrrhenians and the Carthaginians, and all who have commercial treaties with one another, would be the citizens of one state. True, they have agreements about imports, and engagements that they will do no wrong to one another, and written articles of alliance. But there are no magistracies common to the contracting parties; different states have each their own magistracies. Nor does one state take care that the citizens of the other are such as they ought to be, nor see that those who come under the terms of the treaty do no wrong or wickedness at all, but only that they do no injustice to one another. Whereas, those who care for good government take into consideration political excellence and defect. Whence it may be further inferred that excellence must be the care of a state which is truly so called, and not merely enjoys the name: for without this end the community becomes a mere alliance which differs

only in place from alliances of which the members live apart; and law is only a convention, "a surety to one another of justice," as the sophist Lycophron says, and has no real power to make the citizens good and just.

This is obvious; for suppose distinct places, such as Corinth and Megara, to be brought together so that their walls touched, still they would not be one city, not even if the citizens had the right to intermarry, which is one of the rights peculiarly characteristic of states. Again, if men dwelt at a distance from one another, but not so far off as to have no intercourse, and there were laws among them that they should not wrong each other in their exchanges, neither would this be a state. Let us suppose that one man is a carpenter, another a farmer, another a shoemaker, and so on, and that their number is ten thousand: nevertheless if they have nothing in common but exchange, alliance, and the like, that would not constitute a state. Why is this? Surely not because they are at a distance from one another; for even supposing that such a community were to meet in one place, but that each man had a house of his own, which was in a manner his state, and that they made alliance with one another, but only against evil-doers; still an accurate thinker would not deem this to be a state, if their intercourse with one another was of the same character after as before their union. It is clear then that a state is not a mere society, having a common place, established for the prevention of mutual crime and for the sake of exchange. These are conditions without which a state cannot exist; but all of them together do not constitute a state, which is a community of families and aggregations of families in well-being, for the sake of a perfect and self-sufficing life. Such a community can only be established among those who live in the same place and intermarry. Hence there arise in cities family connections, brotherhoods, common sacrifices, amusements which draw men together. But these are created by friendship, for to choose to live together is friendship. The end of the state is the good life, and these are the means toward it. And the state is the union of families and villages in a perfect and self-sufficing life, by which we mean a happy and honorable life.

Our conclusion, then, is that political society exists for the sake of noble actions, and not of living together. Hence they who contribute most to such a society have a greater share in it than those who have the same or a greater freedom or nobility of birth but are inferior to them in political excellence; or than those who exceed them in wealth but are surpassed by them in excellence.

From what has been said it will be clearly seen that all the partisans of different forms of government speak of a part of justice only.

· · ·

BOOK IV

11. We have now to inquire what is the best constitution for most states, and the best life for most men, neither assuming a standard of excellence which is above ordinary persons, nor an education which is exceptionally favored by nature and circumstances, nor yet an ideal state which is an aspiration only, but having regard to the life in which the majority are able to share, and to the form of government which states in general can attain. As to those aristocracies, as they are called, of which we were just now speaking, they either lie beyond the possibilities of the greater number of states, or they approximate to the so-called constitutional government, and therefore need no separate discussion. And in fact the conclusion at which we arrive respecting all these forms rests upon the same grounds. For if what was said in the *Ethics* is true, that the happy life is the life according to excellence lived without impediment, and that excellence is a mean, then the life which is in a mean, and in a mean attainable by everyone, must be the best. And the same principles of excellence and badness are characteristic of cities and of constitutions; for the constitution is so to speak the life of the city.

Now in all states there are three elements: one class is very rich, another very poor, and a third in a mean. It is admitted that moderation and the mean are best, and therefore it will clearly be best to possess the gifts of fortune in moderation; for in that condition of life men are most ready to follow rational principle. But he who greatly excels in beauty, strength, birth, or wealth, or on the other hand who is very poor, or very weak, or of very low status, finds it difficult to follow rational principle. Of these two the one sort grow into violent and great criminals, the others into rogues and petty rascals. And two sorts of offenses correspond to them, the one committed from violence, the other from roguery [Again, the middle class is least likely to shrink from rule, or to be over-ambitious for it],[5] both of which are injuries to the state. Again, those who have too much of the goods of fortune, strength, wealth, friends, and the like, are neither willing nor able to submit to authority. The evil begins at home; for when they are boys, by reason of the luxury in which they are brought up, they never learn, even at school, the habit of obedience. On the other hand, the very poor, who are in the opposite extreme, are too degraded. So that the one class cannot obey, and can only rule despotically; the other knows not how to command and must be ruled like slaves. Thus arises a city, not of freemen, but of masters and slaves, the one despising, the other envying; and nothing can be more fatal to friendship and good fellowship in states than this: for good fellowship springs from friendship; when men are at enmity with one another, they would rather not even share the same path. But a city ought to be composed, as far as possible, of equals and similars; and these are generally the middle classes. Wherefore the city which is composed of middle-class citizens is necessarily best constituted in respect to the elements of which we say the fabric of the state naturally consists. And this is the class of citizens which is most secure in a state, for they do not, like the poor, covet other men's goods; nor do others covet theirs, as the poor covet the goods of the rich; and as they neither plot against others, nor are themselves plotted against, they pass through life safely. Wisely then did Phocylides pray—"Many things are best in the mean; I desire to be of a middle condition in my city."

5. Excised by one editor.

Thus it is manifest that the best political community is formed by citizens of the middle class, and that those states are likely to be well-administered in which the middle class is large, and stronger if possible than both the other classes, or at any rate than either singly; for the addition of the middle class turns the scale, and prevents either of the extremes from being dominant. Great then is the good fortune of a state in which the citizens have a moderate and sufficient property; for where some possess much, and the others nothing, there may arise an extreme democracy, or a pure oligarchy; or a tyranny may grow of either extreme — either out of the most rampant democracy, or out of an oligarchy; but it is not so likely to arise out of the middle constitutions and those akin to them. I will explain the reason for this hereafter, when I speak of the revolutions of states. The mean condition of states is clearly best, for no other is free from faction; and where the middle class is large, there are least likely to be factions and dissensions. For a similar reason large states are less liable to faction than small ones, because in them the middle class is large; whereas in small states it is easy to divide all the citizens into two classes who are either rich or poor, and to leave nothing in the middle. And democracies are safer and more permanent than oligarchies, because they have a middle class, which is more numerous and has a greater share in the government; for when there is no middle class, and the poor are excessive in number, troubles arise, and the state soon comes to an end. A proof of the superiority of the middle class is that the best legislators have been of a middle condition; for example, Solon, as his own verses testify; and Lycurgus, for he was not a king; and Charondas, and almost all legislators.

These considerations will help us to understand why most governments are either democratic or oligarchical. The reason is that the middle class is seldom numerous in them, and whichever party, whether the rich or the common people, transgresses the mean and predominates; draws the constitution its own way, and thus arises either oligarchy or democracy. There is another reason — the poor and the rich quarrel with one another, and whichever side gets the better, instead of establishing a just or popular government, regards political supremacy as the prize of victory, and the one party sets up a democracy and the other an oligarchy. Further, both the parties which had the supremacy in Greece looked only to the interest of their own form of government, and established in states, the one, democracies, and the other, oligarchies; they thought of their own advantage, and of the advantage of the other states not at all. For these reasons the middle form of government has rarely, if ever, existed, and among a very few only. One man alone of all who ever ruled in Greece has induced to give this middle constitution to states. But it has now become a habit among the citizens of states not even to care about equality; all men are seeking for dominion, or, if conquered, are willing to submit.

What then is the best form of government, and what makes it the best, is evident; and of other constitutions, since we say that there are many kinds of democracy and many of oligarchy, it is not difficult to see which has the first and which the second or any other place in the order of excellence, now that we have determined which is the best. For that which is nearest to the best must of necessity be better, and that which is further from the mean worse, if we are judging absolutely and not relatively to given conditions: I say "relatively to given conditions," since a particular government may be preferable, but another form may be better for some people.

· · ·

BOOK VII

1. He who would duly inquire about the best form of a state ought first to determine which is the most eligible life; while this remains uncertain the best form of the state must also be uncertain; for, in the natural order of things, those men may be expected to lead the best life who are governed in the best manner of which their circumstances admit. We ought therefore to ascertain, first of all, which is the most generally eligible life, and then whether the same life is or is not best for the state and for individuals.

Assuming that enough has been already said in discussions outside the school concerning the best life, we will now only repeat what is contained in them. Certainly no one will dispute the propriety of that partition of goods which separates them into three classes, *viz.* external goods, goods of the body, and goods of the soul, or deny that the happy man must have all three. For no one would maintain that he is happy who has not in him a particle of courage or temperance or justice or practical wisdom, who is afraid of every insect which flutters past him, and will commit any crime, however great, in order to gratify his lust for meat or drink, who will sacrifice his dearest friend for the sake of half a farthing, and is as feeble and false in mind as a child or a madman. These propositions are almost universally acknowledged as soon as they are uttered, but men differ about the degree or relative superiority of this or that good. Some think that a very moderate amount of excellence is enough, but set no limit to their desires for wealth, property, power, reputation, and the like. To them we shall reply by an appeal to facts, which easily prove that mankind does not acquire or preserve the excellences by the help of external goods, but external goods by the help of the excellences, and that happiness, whether consisting in pleasure or excellence, or both, is more often found with those who are most highly cultivated in their mind and in their character, and have only a moderate share of external goods, than among those who possess external goods to a useless extent but are deficient in higher qualities; and this is not only a matter of experience, but, if reflected upon, will easily appear to be in accordance with reason. For, whereas external goods have a limit, like any other instrument, and all things useful are useful for a purpose, and where there is too much of them they must either do harm, or at any rate be of no use, to their possessors, every good of the soul, the greater it is, is also of greater use, if the epithet useful as well as noble is appropriate to such subjects. No proof is required to show that the best state of one thing in relation to another corresponds in degree of excellence to the interval between the natures of which we say that these very states are states: so that, if the soul is more noble than our possessions or our bodies, both absolutely and in relation to us, it must be admitted that the best state of either has a similar ratio to the other. Again, it is for the sake of the soul that goods external and goods of the body are desirable at all, and all wise men ought to choose them for the sake of the soul, and not the soul for the sake of them.

Let us acknowledge then that each one has just so much of happiness as he has of excellence and wisdom, and of excellent and wise action. The gods are a witness to us of this truth, for they are happy and blessed, not by reason of any external good, but in themselves and by reason of their own nature. And herein of necessity lies the difference between good fortune and happiness; for external goods come of themselves, and chance is the author of them, but no one is just or temperate by or through chance. In like manner, and by a similar train of argument, the happy state may be shown to be that which is best and which acts rightly; and it cannot act rightly without doing right actions, and neither individual nor state can do right actions without excellence and wisdom. Thus, the courage, justice, and wisdom of a state have the same form and nature as the qualities which give the individual who possesses them the name of just, wise or temperate.

Thus much may suffice by way of preface: for I could not avoid touching upon these questions, neither could I go through all the arguments affecting them; these are the business of another science.

Let us assume then that the best life, both for individuals and states, is the life of excellence, when excellence has external goods enough for the performance of good actions. If there are any who dispute our assertion, we will in this treatise pass them over, and consider their objections hereafter.

2. There remains to be discussed the question, whether the happiness of the individual is the same as that of the state, or different. Here again there can be no doubt—no one denies that they are the same. For those who hold that the well-being of the individual consists in his wealth, also think that riches make the happiness of the whole state, and those who value most highly the life of a tyrant deem that city the happiest which rules over the greatest number; while they who approve an individual for his excellence say that the more excellent a city is, the happier it is. Two points here present themselves for consideration: first, which is the more desirable life, that of a citizen who is a member of a state, or that of an alien who has no political ties; and again, which is the best form of constitution or the best condition of a state, either on the supposition that political privileges are desirable for all, or for a majority only? Since the good of the state and not of the individual is the proper subject of political thought and speculation, and we are engaged in a political discussion, while the first of these two points has a secondary interest for us, the latter will be the main subject of our inquiry.

Now it is evident that that form of government is best in which every man, whoever he is, can act best and live happily. But even those who agree in thinking that the life of excellence is the most desirable raise a question, whether the life of business and politics is or is not more desirable than one which is wholly independent of external goods, I mean than a contemplative life, which by some is maintained to be the only one worthy of a philosopher. For these two lives—the life of the philosopher and the life of the statesman—appear to have been preferred by those who have been most keen in the pursuit of excellence, both in our own and in other ages. Which is the better is a question of no small account; for the wise man, like the wise state, will necessarily regulate his life according to the best end. There are some who think that while a despotic rule over others is the greatest injustice, to exercise a constitutional rule over them, even though not unjust, is a great impediment to a man's individual well-being. Others take an opposite view; they maintain that the true life of man is the practical and political, and that every excellence admits of being practiced, quite as much by statesman and rulers as by private individuals. Others, again, are of the opinion that arbitrary and tyrannical rule alone makes for happiness; indeed, in some states the entire aim both of the laws and of the constitution is to give men despotic power over their neighbors. And, therefore, although in most cities the laws may be said generally to be in a chaotic state, still, if they aim at anything, they aim at the maintenance of power: thus in Lacedaemon and Crete the system of education and the greater part of the laws are framed with a view to war. And in all nations which are able to gratify their ambition military power is held in esteem, for example among the Scythians and Persians and Thracians and Celts. In some nations there are even laws tending to stimulate the warlike virtues, as at Carthage, where we are told that men obtain the honor of wearing as many armlets as they have served campaigns. There was once a law in Macedonia that he who had not killed an enemy should wear a halter, and among the Scythians no one who had not slain his man was allowed to drink out of the cup which was handed round at a certain feast. Among the Iberians, a warlike nation, the number of enemies whom a man has slain is indicated by the number of obelisks which are fixed in the earth round his tomb; and there are numerous practices among other nations of a like kind, some of them established by law and others by custom. Yet to a reflecting mind it must appear very strange that the statesman should be always considering how he can dominate and tyrannize over others, whether they are willing or not. How can that which is not even lawful be the business of the statesman or the legislator? Unlawful it certainly is to rule without regard to justice, for there may be might where there is no right. The other arts and sciences offer no parallel; a physician is not expected to persuade or coerce his patients, nor a pilot the passengers in his ship. Yet most men appear to think that the art of despotic government is statesmanship, and what men affirm to be unjust and inexpedient in their own case they are not ashamed of practicing towards others; they demand just rule for themselves, but where other men are concerned they care nothing about it. Such behavior is irrational; unless the one party is, and the other is not, born to serve, in which case men have a right to command, not indeed all their fellows, but only those who are intended to be subjects; just as we ought not to hunt men, whether for food or sacrifice, but only those animals which may be hunted for food or sacrifice, that is to say, such wild animals as are eatable. And surely there may be a city happy in isolation, which we will assume to be well-governed (for it is quite possible that a city thus isolated might be well-administered and have good laws); but such a city would not be constituted with any view to war or the conquest of enemies—all that sort of thing must be excluded. Hence we see very plainly that warlike pursuits, although generally to be deemed honorable, are not the supreme end of all things, but only means. And the good lawgiver should inquire how states and races of men and communities may participate in a good life, and in the happiness which is attainable by them. His enactments will not be always the same; and where there are neighbors he will have to see what sort of studies should be practiced in relation to their several characters, or how the measures appropriate in relation to each are to be adopted. The end at which the best form of government should aim may be properly made a matter of future considerations.

[tr. 1988 ed.]

from "Idea for a Universal History with a Cosmopolitan Purpose"

Fourth Proposition

The means which nature employs to bring about the development of innate capacities is that of antagonism within society, in so far as this antagonism becomes in the long run the cause of a law-governed social order. By antagonism, I mean in this context the *unsocial sociability* of men, that is, their tendency to come together in society, coupled, however, with a continual resistance which constantly threatens to break this society up. This propensity is obviously rooted in human nature. Man has an inclination to *live in society,* since he feels in this state more like a man, that is, he feels able to develop his natural capacities. But he also has a great tendency to *live as an individual,* to isolate himself, since he also encounters in himself the unsocial characteristic of wanting to direct everything in accordance with his own ideas. He therefore expects resistance all around, just as he knows of himself that he is in turn inclined to offer resistance to others. It is this very resistance which awakens all man's powers and induces him to overcome his tendency to laziness. Through the desire for honor, power or property, it drives him to seek status among his fellows, whom he cannot *bear* yet cannot *bear to leave.* Then the first true steps are taken from barbarism to culture, which in fact consists in the social worthiness of man. All man's talents are now gradually developed, his taste cultivated, and by a continued process of enlightenment, a beginning is made towards establishing a way of thinking which can with time transform the primitive natural capacity for moral discrimination into definite practical principles; and thus a *pathologically* enforced social union is transformed into a *moral* whole. Without these asocial qualities (far from admirable in themselves) which cause the resistance inevitably encountered by each individual as he furthers his self-seeking pretensions, man would live an Arcadian, pastoral existence of perfect concord, self-sufficiency and mutual love. But all human talents would remain hidden for ever in a dormant state, and men, as good-natured as the sheep they tended, would scarcely render their existence more valuable than that of their animals. The end for which they were created, their rational nature, would be an unfilled void. Nature should thus be thanked for fostering social incompatibility, enviously competitive vanity, and insatiable desires for possession or even power. Without these desires, all man's excellent natural capacities would never be roused to develop. Man wishes concord, but nature, knowing better what is good for his species, wishes discord. Man wishes to live comfortably and pleasantly, but nature intends that he should abandon idleness and inactive self-sufficiency and plunge instead into labor and hardships, so that he may by his own adroitness find means of liberating himself from them in turn. The natural impulses which make this possible, the sources of the very unsociableness and continual resistance which cause so many evils, at the same time encourage man towards new exertions of his powers and thus towards further development of his natural capacities. They would thus seem to indicate the design of a wise creator—not, as it might seem, the hand of a malicious spirit who had meddled in the creator's glorious work or spoiled it out of envy.

Fifth Proposition

The greatest problem for the human species, the solution of which nature compels him to seek, is that of attaining a civil society which can administer justice universally.

The highest purpose of nature—that is, the development of all natural capacities—can be fulfilled for mankind only in society, and nature intends that man should accomplish this, and indeed all his appointed ends, by his own efforts. This purpose can be fulfilled only in a society which has not only the greatest freedom, and therefore a continual antagonism among its members, but also the most precise specification and preservation of the limits of this freedom in order that it can coexist with the freedom of others. The highest task which nature has set for mankind must therefore be that of establishing a society in which *freedom under external laws* would be combined to the greatest possible extent with irresistible force, in other words of establishing a perfectly *just civil constitution*. For only through the solution and fulfillment of this task can nature accomplish its other intentions with our species. Man, who is otherwise so enamored with unrestrained freedom, is forced to enter this state of restriction by sheer necessity. And this is indeed the most stringent of all forms of necessity, for it is imposed by men upon themselves, in that their inclinations make it impossible for them to exist side by side for long in a state of wild freedom. But once enclosed within a precinct like that of civil union, the same inclinations have the most beneficial effect. In the same way, trees in a forest, by seeking to deprive each other of air and sunlight, compel each other to find these by upward growth, so that they grow beautiful and straight—whereas those which put out branches at will, in freedom and in isolation from others, grow stunted, bent and twisted. All the culture and art which adorn mankind and the finest social order man creates are fruits of his unsociability. For it is compelled by its own nature to discipline itself, and thus, by enforced art, to develop completely the germs which nature implanted.

Sixth Proposition

This problem is both the most difficult and the last to be solved by the human race. The difficulty (which the very idea of this problem clearly presents) is this: if he lives among others of his own species, man is *an animal who needs a master.* For he certainly abuses his freedom in relation to others of his own kind. And even although, as a rational creature, he desires a law to impose limits on the freedom of all, he is still misled by his self-seeking animal inclinations into exempting himself from the law where he can. He thus requires a *master* to break his self-will and force him to obey a universally valid will under which everyone can be free. But where is he to find such a master? Nowhere else but in the human species. But this master will also be an animal who needs a master. Thus while man may try as he will, it is hard to see how he can obtain for public justice a supreme authority which would itself be just, whether he seeks this authority in a single person or in a group of many persons selected for this purpose. For each one of them will always misuse his freedom if he does not have anyone above him to apply force to him as the laws should require it. Yet the highest authority has to be just *in itself* and yet also a *man.* This is therefore the most difficult of all tasks, and a perfect solution is impossible. Nothing straight can be constructed from such warped wood as that which man is made of. Nature only requires of us that we should approximate to this idea.[1] A further reason why this task must be the last to be accomplished is that man needs for it a correct conception of the nature of a possible constitution, great experience tested in many affairs of the world, and above all else a good will prepared to accept the findings of this experience. But three factors such as these will not easily be found in conjunction, and if they are, it will happen only at a late stage and after many unsuccessful attempts.

Seventh Proposition

The problem of establishing a perfect civil constitution is subordinate to the problem of a law-governing external relationship with other states, and cannot be

---

1. Man's role is thus a highly artificial one. We do not know how it is with the inhabitants of other planets and with their nature, but if we ourselves execute this commission of nature well, we may surely flatter ourselves that we occupy no mean status among our neighbors in the cosmos. Perhaps their position is such that each individual can fulfill his destiny completely within his own lifetime. With us it is otherwise; only the species as a whole can hope for this.

solved unless the latter is also solved. What is the use of working for a law-governed civil constitution among individual men, that is, of planning a *commonwealth?* The same unsociability which forced men to do so gives rise in turn to a situation whereby each commonwealth, in its external relations (i.e. as a state in relation to other states), is in a position of unrestricted freedom. Each must accordingly expect from any other precisely the same evils which formerly oppressed individual men and forced them into a law-governed civil state. Nature has thus again employed the unsociableness of men, and even of the large societies and states which human beings construct, as a means of arriving at a condition of calm and security through their inevitable *antagonism.* Wars, tense and unremitting military preparations, and the resultant distress which every state must eventually feel within itself, even in the midst of peace—these are the means by which nature drives nations to make initially imperfect attempts, but finally, after many devastations, upheavals and even complete inner exhaustion of their powers, to take the step which reason could have suggested to them even without so many sad experiences—that of abandoning a lawless state of savagery and entering a federation of peoples in which every state, even the smallest, could expect to derive its security and rights not from its own power or it own legal judgment, but solely from this great federation *(Fœdus Amphictyonum),* from a united power and the law-governed decisions of a united will. However wild and fanciful this idea may appear—and it has been ridiculed as such when put forward by the Abbé St Pierre and Rousseau (perhaps because they thought that its realization was so imminent)—it is nonetheless the inevitable outcome of the distress in which men involve one another. For this distress must force the states to make exactly the same decision (however difficult it may be for them) as that which man was forced to make, equally unwillingly, in his savage state—the decision to renounce his brutish freedom and seek calm and security within a law-governed constitution. All wars are accordingly so many attempts (not indeed by the intention of men, but by the intention of nature) to bring about new relations between states, and, by the destruction or at least the dismemberment of old entities, to create new ones. But these new bodies, either in themselves or alongside one another, will in turn be unable to survive, and will thus necessarily undergo further revolutions of a similar sort, till finally, partly by an optimal internal arrangement of the civil constitution, and partly by common external agreement and legislation, a state of affairs is created which, like a civil commonwealth, can maintain itself *automatically.*

Whether we should firstly expect that the states, by an Epicurean concourse of efficient causes, should enter by random collisions (like those of small material particles) into all kinds of formations which are again destroyed by new collisions, until they arrive *by chance* at a formation which can survive in its existing form (a lucky accident which is hardly likely ever to occur); or whether we should assume as a second possibility that nature in this case follows a regular course in leading our species gradually upwards from the lower level of animality to the highest level of humanity through forcing man to employ an art which is nonetheless his own, and hence that nature develops man's original capacities by a perfectly regular process within this apparently disorderly arrangement; or whether we should rather accept the third possibility that nothing at all, or at least nothing rational, will anywhere emerge from all these actions and counter-actions among men as a whole, that things will remain as they have always been, and that it would thus be impossible to predict whether the discord which is so natural to our species is not preparing the way for a hell of evils to overtake us, however civilized our condition, in that nature, by barbaric devastation, might perhaps again destroy this civilized state and all the cultural progress hitherto achieved (a fate against which it would be impossible to guard under a rule of blind chance, with which the state of lawless freedom is in fact identical, unless we assume that the latter is secretly guided by the wisdom of nature)—these three possibilities boil down to the question of whether it is rational to assume that the order of nature is *purposive* in its parts but *purposeless* as a whole.

While the purposeless state of savagery did hold up the development of all the natural capacities of human beings, it nonetheless finally forced them, through the evils in which it involved them, to leave this state and enter into a civil constitution in which all their dormant capacities could be developed. The same applies to the barbarous freedom of established states. For while the full development of natural capacities is here likewise held up by the expenditure of each commonwealth's whole resources on armaments against the others, and by the depredations caused by war (but most of all by the necessity of constantly remaining in readiness for war), the resultant evils still have a beneficial effect. For they compel our species to discover a law of equilibrium to regulate the essentially healthy hostility which prevails among the states and is produced by their freedom. Men are compelled to reinforce this law by introducing a system of united power, hence a cosmopolitan system of general political security. This state of affairs is not completely free from *danger,* lest human energies should lapse into inactivity, but it is also not without a principle of *equality* governing the *actions and counter-actions* of these energies, lest they should destroy one another. When it is little beyond the half-way mark in its development, human nature has to endure the hardest of evils under the guise of outward prosperity before this final step (i.e., the union of states) is taken; and Rousseau's preference for the state of savagery does not appear so very mistaken if only we leave out of consideration this last stage which our species still has to surmount. We are *cultivated* to a high degree by art and science. We are *civilized* to the point of excess in all kinds of social courtesies and proprieties. But we are still a long way from the point where we could consider ourselves *morally* mature. For while the idea of morality is indeed present in culture, an application of this idea which only extends to the semblances of morality, as in love of honor and outward propriety, amounts merely to civilization. But as long as states apply all their resources to their vain and violent schemes of expansion, thus incessantly obstructing the slow and laborious efforts of their citizens to cultivate their minds, and even deprive them of all support in these efforts, no progress in this direction can be expected. For a long internal process of careful work on the part of each commonwealth is necessary for the education of its citizens. But all good enterprises which are not grafted on to a morally good attitude of mind are nothing but illusion and outwardly glittering misery. The human race will no doubt remain in this condition until it has worked itself out of the chaotic state of its political relations in the way I have described.

Eighth Proposition

The history of the human race as a whole can be regarded as the realization of a hidden plan of nature to bring about an internally—and for this purpose also externally—perfect political constitution as the only possible state within which all natural capacities of mankind can be developed completely. This proposition follows from the previous one. We can see that philosophy too may have its *chiliastic* expectations; but they are of such a kind that their fulfillment can be hastened, if only indirectly, by a knowledge of the idea they are based on, so that they are anything but over-fanciful. The real test is whether experience can discover anything to indicate a purposeful natural process of this kind. In my opinion, it can discover *a little;* for this cycle of events seems to take so long a time to complete, that the small part of it traversed by mankind up till now does not allow us to determine with certainty the shape of the whole cycle, and the relation of its parts to the whole. It is no easier than it is to determine, from all hitherto available astronomical observations, the path which our sun with its whole swarm of satellites is following within the vast system of the fixed stars; although from the general premise that the universe is constituted as a system and from the little which has been learned by observation, we can conclude with sufficient certainty that a movement of this kind does exist in reality. Nevertheless, human nature is such that it cannot be indifferent even to the most remote epoch which may eventually affect our species, so long as this epoch can be expected with certainty. And in the present case, it is especially hard to be indifferent, for it appears that we might by our own rational projects accelerate the coming of this period which will be so welcome to our descendants. For this reason, even the faintest signs of its approach will be extremely important to us. The mutual relationships between states are already so sophisticated that none of them can neglect its internal culture without losing power and influence in relation to the others. Thus the purpose of nature is at least fairly well safeguarded (if not actually furthered) even by the ambitious schemes of the various states. Furthermore, civil freedom can no longer be so easily infringed without disadvantage to all trades and industries, and especially to commerce, in the event of which the state's power in its external relations will also decline. But this freedom is gradually increasing. If the citizen is deterred from seeking his personal welfare in any way he chooses which is consistent with the freedom of others, the vitality of business in general and hence also the strength of the whole are held in check. For this reason, restrictions placed upon personal activities are increasingly relaxed, and general freedom of religion is granted. And thus, although folly and caprice creep in at times, *enlightenment* gradually arises. It is a great benefit which the human race must reap even from its rulers' self-seeking schemes of expansion, if only they realize what is to their own advantage. But this enlightenment, and with it a certain sympathetic interest which the enlightened man inevitably feels for anything good which he comprehends fully, must gradually spread upwards towards the thrones and even influence their principles of government. But while, for example, the world's present rulers have no money to spare for public educational institutions or indeed for anything which concerns the world's best interests (for everything has already been calculated out in advance for the next war), they will nonetheless find that it is to their own advantage at least not to hinder their citizens' private efforts in this direction, however weak and slow they may be. But eventually, war itself gradually becomes not only a highly artificial undertaking, extremely uncertain in its outcome for both parties, but also a very dubious risk to take, since its aftermath is felt by the state in the shape of a constantly increasing national debt (a modern invention) whose repayment becomes interminable. And in addition, the effects which an upheaval in any state produces upon all the others in our continent, where all are so closely linked by trade, are so perceptible that these other states are forced by their own insecurity to offer themselves as arbiters, albeit without legal authority, so that they indirectly prepare the way for a great political body of the future, without precedent in the past. Although this political body exists for the present only in the roughest of outlines, it nonetheless seems as if a feeling is beginning to stir in all its members, each of which has an interest in maintaining the whole. And this encourages the hope that, after many revolutions, with all their transforming effects, the highest purpose of nature, a universal *cosmopolitan existence,* will at last be realized as the matrix within which all the original capacities of the human race may develop.

Ninth Proposition

A philosophical attempt to work out a universal history of the world in accordance with a plan of nature aimed at a perfect civil union of mankind, must be regarded as possible and even as capable of furthering the purpose of nature itself. It is admittedly a strange and at first sight absurd proposition to write a *history* according to an idea of how world events must develop if they are to conform to certain rational ends; it would seem that only a *novel* could result from such premises. Yet if it may be assumed that nature does not work without a plan and purposeful end, even amidst the arbitrary play of human freedom, this idea might nevertheless prove useful. And although we are too short-sighted to perceive the hidden mechanism of nature's scheme, this idea may yet serve as a guide to us in representing an otherwise planless *aggregate* of human actions as conforming, at least when considered as a whole, to a *system*. For if we start out from *Greek* history as that in which all other earlier or contemporary histories are preserved or at least authenticated,[2] if we next trace the influence of the Greeks upon the shaping and mis-shaping of the body politic of *Rome,* which engulfed the Greek state, and follow down to our own times the influence of Rome upon the *Barbarians* who in turn destroyed it, and if we finally add the political history of other peoples *episodically,* in so far as knowledge of them has gradually come down to us through these enlightened nations, we shall discover a regular process of improvement in the political constitutions of our continent (which will probably legislate eventually for all other continents). Furthermore, we must always concentrate our attention on civil constitutions, their laws, and the mutual relations among states, and notice how these factors, by virtue of the good they contained, served for a time to elevate and glorify nations (and with them the arts and sciences). Conversely, we should observe how their inherent defects led to their overthrow, but in such a way that a germ of enlightenment always survived, developing further with each revolution, and prepared the way for a subsequent higher level of improvement.

All this, I believe, should give us some guidance in explaining the thoroughly confused interplay of human affairs and in prophesying future political changes. Yet the same use has already been made of human history even when it was regarded as the disjointed product of unregulated freedom. But if we assume a plan of nature, we have grounds for greater hopes. For such a plan opens up the comforting prospect of a future in which we are shown from afar how the human race eventually works its way upward to a situation in which all the germs implanted by nature can be developed fully, and in which man's destiny can be fulfilled here on earth. Such a *justification* of nature—or rather perhaps of *providence*—is no mean motive for adopting a particular point of view in considering the world. For what is the use of lauding and holding up for contemplation the glory and wisdom of creation in the non-rational sphere of nature, if the history of mankind, the very part of this great display of supreme wisdom which contains the purpose of all the rest, is to remain a constant reproach to everything else? Such a spectacle would force us to turn away in revulsion, and, by making us despair of ever finding any completed rational aim behind it, would reduce us to hoping for it only in some other world.

It would be a misinterpretation of my intention to contend that I meant this idea of a universal history, which to some extent follows an *a priori* rule, to supersede

2. Only an *educated public* which has existed uninterruptedly from its origin to our times can authenticate ancient history. Beyond that, all is *terra incognita;* and the history of peoples who lived outside this public can begin only from the time at which they entered it. This occurred with the *Jewish* people at the time of the Ptolemies through the Greek translation of the Bible, without which their *isolated* reports would meet with little belief. From this point, once it has been properly ascertained, their narratives can be followed backwards. And it is the same with all other peoples. The first page of Thucydides, as Hume puts it, is the only beginning of all true history.

the task of history proper, that of *empirical* composition. My idea is only a notion of what a philosophical mind, well acquainted with history, might be able to attempt from a different angle. Besides, the otherwise praiseworthy detail in which each age now composes its history must naturally cause everyone concern as to how our remote descendants will manage to cope with the burden of history which we shall bequeath to them a few centuries from now. No doubt they will value the history of the oldest times, of which the original documents would long since have vanished, only from the point of view of what interests *them*, that is, the positive and negative achievements of nations and governments in relation to the cosmopolitan goal. We should bear this in mind, and we should likewise observe the ambitions of rulers and their servants, in order to indicate to them the only means by which they can be honorably remembered in the most distant ages. And this may provide us with another *small* motive for attempting a philosophical history of this kind.

[1784]

from "Perpetual Peace"

SECOND SECTION
Which Contains the Definitive Articles of a Perpetual Peace between States

A state of peace among men living together is not the same as the state of nature, which is rather a state of war. For even if it does not involve active hostilities, it involves a constant threat of their breaking out. Thus the state of peace must be *formally instituted,* for a suspension of hostilities is not in itself a guarantee of peace. And unless one neighbor gives a guarantee to the other at his request (which can happen only in a *lawful* state), the latter may treat him as an enemy.[1]

1. It is usually assumed that one cannot take hostile action against anyone unless one has already been actively *injured* by them. This is perfectly correct if both parties are living in a *legal civil state.* For the fact that the one has entered such a state gives the required guarantee to the other, since both are subject to the same authority. But man (or an individual person) in a mere state of nature robs me of any such security and injures me by virtue of this very state in which he coexists with me. He may not have injured me actively *(facto),* but he does injure me by the very lawlessness of his state *(statu iniusto),* for he is a permanent threat to me, and I can require him either to enter into a common lawful state along with me or to move away from my vicinity. Thus the postulate on which all the following articles are based is that all men who can at all influence one another must adhere to some kind of civil constitution. But any legal constitution, as far as the persons who live under it are concerned, will conform to one of the three following types:

    (1) a constitution based on the *civil right* of individuals within a nation *(ius civitatis).*

    (2) a constitution based on the *international right* of states in their relationships with one another *(ius gentium).*

    (3) a constitution based on *cosmopolitan right,* in so far as individuals and states, coexisting in an external relationship of mutual influences, may be regarded as citizens of a universal state of mankind *(ius cosmopoliticum).* This classification with respect to the idea of a perpetual peace, is not arbitrary, but necessary. For if even one of the parties were able to influence the others physically and yet itself remained in a state of nature, there would be a risk of war, which it is precisely the aim of the above articles to prevent.

First Definitive Article of a Perpetual Peace:
The Civil Constitution of Every State Shall Be Republican

A *republican constitution* is founded upon three principles: firstly, the principle of *freedom* for all members of a society (as men); secondly, the principle of the *dependence* of everyone upon a single common legislation (as subjects); and thirdly, the principle of legal *equality* for everyone (as citizens).[2] It is the only constitution which can be derived from the idea of an original contract, upon which all rightful legislation of a people must be founded. Thus as far as right is concerned, republicanism is in itself the original basis of every kind of civil constitution, and it only remains to ask whether it is the only constitution which can lead to a perpetual peace.

    2. *Rightful (i.e. external) freedom* cannot, as is usually thought, be defined as a warrant to do whatever one wishes unless it means doing injustice to others. For what is meant by a *warrant?* It means a possibility of acting in a certain way so long as this action does not do any injustice to others. Thus the definition would run as follows: freedom is the possibility of acting in ways which do no injustice to others. That is, we do no injustice to others (no matter what we may actually do) if we do no injustice to others. Thus the definition is an empty tautology. In fact, my external and rightful *freedom* should be defined as a warrant to obey no external laws except those to which I have been able to give my own consent. Similarly, external and rightful *equality* within a state is that relationship among the citizens whereby no one can put anyone else under a legal obligation without submitting simultaneously to a law which requires that he can himself be put under the same kind of obligation by the other person. (And we do not need to define the principle of *legal* dependence, since it is always implied in the concept of a political constitution). The validity of these innate and inalienable rights, the necessary property of mankind, is confirmed and enhanced by the principle that man may have lawful relations even with higher beings (if he believes in the latter). For he may consider himself as a citizen of a transcendental world, to which the same principles apply. And as regards my freedom, I am not under any obligation even to divine laws (which I can recognize by reason alone), except in so far as I have been able to give my own consent to them; for I can form a conception of the divine will only in terms of the law of freedom of my own reason. As for the principle of equality in relation to the most exalted being I can conceive of, apart from God (e.g. a power such as Aeon), there is no reason, if I and this higher being are both doing our duty in our own stations, why it should be my duty to obey while he should enjoy the right to command. But the reason why this principle of equality (unlike that of freedom) does not apply to a relationship towards God, is that God is the only being for whom the concept of duty ceases to be valid.

    But as for the right of equality of all citizens as subjects, we may ask whether a *hereditary aristocracy* is admissible. The answer to this question will depend entirely on whether more importance is attached to the superior *rank* granted by the state to one subject over another than is attached to *merit,* or vice versa. Now it is obvious that if rank is conferred according to birth, it will be quite uncertain whether merit (skill and devotion within one's office) will accompany it; it will be tantamount to conferring a position of command upon a favored individual without any merit on his part, and this could never be approved by the general will of the people in an original contract, which is, after all, the principle behind all rights. For it does not necessarily follow that a nobleman is also a *noble man.* And as for a nobility of office, i.e. the rank of a *higher magistracy* which can be attained by merit, the rank does not attach as a possession to the person, but to the post occupied by the person, and this does not violate the principle of equality. For when a person lays down his office, he simultaneously resigns his rank and again becomes one of the people.

The republican constitution is not only pure in its origin (since it springs from the pure concept of right); it also offers a prospect of attaining the desired result, that is, a perpetual peace, and the reason for this is as follows: If, as is inevitably the case under this constitution, the consent of the citizens is required to decide whether or not war is to be declared, it is very natural that they will have great hesitation in embarking on so dangerous an enterprise. For this would mean calling down on themselves all the miseries of war, such as doing the fighting themselves, supplying the costs of the war from their own resources, painfully making good the ensuing devastation, and, as the crowning evil, having to take upon themselves a burden of debt which will embitter peace itself and which can never be paid off on account of the constant threat of new wars. But under a constitution where the subject is not a citizen, and which is therefore not republican, it is the simplest thing in the world to go to war. For the head of state is not a fellow citizen, but the owner of the state, and a war will not force him to make the slightest sacrifice so far as his banquets, hunt, pleasure palaces and court festivals are concerned. He can thus decide on war, without any significant reason, as a kind of amusement, and unconcernedly leave it to the diplomatic corps (who are always ready for such purposes) to justify the war for the sake of propriety.

The following remarks are necessary to prevent the republican constitution from being confused with the democratic one, as commonly happens. The various forms of state *(civitas)* may be classified either according to the different persons who exercise supreme authority, or according to the way in which the nation is governed by its ruler, whoever he may be. The first classification goes by the form of sovereignty *(forma imperii),* and only three such forms are possible, depending on whether the ruling power is in the hands of an *individual,* of *several persons* in association, or of *all* those who together constitute civil society (i.e. *autocracy, aristocracy* and *democracy*—the power of a prince, the power of a nobility, and the power of the people). The second classification depends on the form of government *(forma regiminis),* and relates to the way in which the state, setting out from its constitution (i.e. an act of the general will whereby the mass becomes a people), makes use of its plenary power. The form of government, in this case, will be either *republican* or *despotic. Republicanism* is that political principle whereby the executive power (the government) is separated from the legislative power. Despotism prevails in a state if the laws are made and arbitrarily executed by one and the same power, and it reflects the will of the people only in so far as the ruler treats the will of the people as his own private will. Of the three forms of sovereignty, *democracy,* in the truest sense of the word, is necessarily a *despotism* because it establishes an executive power through which all the citizens may make decisions about (and indeed against) the single individual without his consent, so that decisions are made by all the people and yet not by all the people; and this means that the general will is in contradiction with itself, and thus also with freedom.

For any form of government which is not *representative* is essentially an *anomaly,* because one and the same person cannot at the same time be both the legislator and the executor of his own will, just as the general proposition in logical reasoning cannot at the same time be a secondary proposition subsuming the particular within the general. And even if the other two political constitutions (i.e. autocracy and aristocracy) are always defective in as much as they leave room for a despotic form of government, it is at least possible that they will be associated with a form of government which accords with the *spirit* of a representative system. Thus Frederick II at least *said* that he was merely the highest servant of the state,[3] while a democratic constitution makes this attitude impossible, because everyone under it wants to be a ruler. We can therefore say that the smaller the number of ruling persons in a state and the greater their powers of representation, the more the constitution will approximate to its republican potentiality, which it may hope to realize eventually by gradual reforms. For this reason, it is more difficult in an aristocracy than in a monarchy to reach this one and only perfectly lawful kind of constitution, while it is possible in a democracy only by means of violent revolution. But the people are immensely more concerned with the mode of government[4] than with the form of the constitution, although a great deal also depends on the degree to which the constitution fits the purpose of the government. But if the mode of government is to accord with the concept of right, it must be based on the representative system. This system alone makes possible a republican state, and without it, despotism and violence will result, no matter what kind of constitution is in force. None of the so-called "republics" of antiquity employed such a system, and they thus inevitably ended in despotism, although this is still relatively bearable under the rule of a single individual.

Second Definitive Article of a Perpetual Peace: The Right of Nations Shall Be Based on a Federation of Free States

Peoples who have grouped themselves into nation states may be judged in the same way as individual men living in a state of nature, independent of external laws; for they are a standing offense to one another by the very fact that they are

3. Many have criticized the high-sounding appellations which are often bestowed on a ruler (e.g. "the divine anointed," or "the executor and representative of the divine will on earth") as gross and extravagant flatteries, but it seems to me without reason. Far from making the ruler of the land arrogant, they ought rather to fill his soul with humility. For if he is a man of understanding (which we must certainly assume), he will reflect that he has taken over an office which is too great for a human being, namely that of administering God's most sacred institution on earth, the rights of man; he will always live in fear of having in any way injured God's most valued possession.

4. Mallet due Pan, in his flamboyant but hollow and empty style, boasts of having at last, after many years of experience, become convinced of the truth of Pope's famous saying: "For forms of government let fools contest; Whate'er is best administered is best." If this means that the best administered government is the best administered, he has cracked a nut (as Swift puts it) and been rewarded

neighbors. Each nation, for the sake of its own security, can and ought to demand of the others that they should enter along with it into a constitution, similar to the civil one, within which the rights of each could be secured. This would mean establishing a *federation of peoples*. But a federation of this sort would not be the same thing as an international state. For the idea of an international state is contradictory, since every state involves a relationship between a superior (the legislator) and an inferior (the people obeying the laws), whereas a number of nations forming one state would constitute a single nation. And this contradicts our initial assumption, as we are here considering the right of nations in relation to one another in so far as they are a group of separate states which are not to be welded together as a unit.

We look with profound contempt upon the way in which savages cling to their lawless freedom. They would rather engage in incessant strife than submit to a legal constraint which they might impose upon themselves, for they prefer the freedom of folly to the freedom of reason. We regard this as barbarism, coarseness, and brutish debasement of humanity. We might thus expect that civilized peoples, each united within itself as a state, would hasten to abandon so degrading a condition as soon as possible. But instead of doing so, each *state* sees its own majesty (for it would be absurd to speak to the majesty of a *people*) precisely in not having to submit to any external legal constraint, and the glory of its ruler consists in his power to order thousands of people to immolate themselves for a cause which does not truly concern them, while he need not himself incur any danger whatsoever.[5] And the main difference between the savage nations of Europe and those of America is that while some American tribes have been entirely eaten up by their enemies, the Europeans know how to make better use of those they have defeated than merely by making a meal of them. They would rather use them to increase the number of their own subjects, thereby augmenting their stock of instruments for conducting even more extensive wars.

Although it is largely concealed by governmental constraints in law-governed civil society, the depravity of human nature is displayed without disguise in the unrestricted relations which obtain between the various nations. It is therefore to be wondered at that the word *right* has not been completely banished from military politics as superfluous pedantry, and that no state has been bold enough to declare itself publicly in favor of doing so. For Hugo Grotius, Pufendorf, Vattel

---

with a worm. But if it means that the best administered government is also the best kind of government (i.e. the best constitution), it is completely false, for examples of good governments prove nothing whatsoever about kinds of government. Who, indeed, governed better than a Titus or a Marcus Aurelius, and yet the one left a Domitian as his successor, and the other a Commodus. And this could not have happened under a good constitution, since their unsuitability for the post of ruler was known early enough, and the power of their predecessors was great enough to have excluded them from the succession.

5. Thus a Bulgarian prince, replying to the Greek Emperor who had kindly offered to settle his dispute with him by a duel, declared: "A smith who possesses tongs will not lift the glowing iron out of the coals with his own hands."

and the rest (sorry comforters as they are) are still dutifully quoted in *justification* of military aggression, although their philosophically or diplomatically formulated codes do not and cannot have the slightest *legal* force, since states as such are not subject to a common external constraint. Yet there is no instance of a state ever having been moved to desist from its purpose by arguments supported by the testimonies of such notable men. This homage which every state pays (in words at least) to the concept of right proves that man possesses a greater moral capacity, still dormant at present, to overcome eventually the evil principle within him (for he cannot deny that it exists), and to hope that others will do likewise. Otherwise the word *right* would never be used by states which intend to make war on one another, unless in a derisory sense, as when a certain Gallic prince declared: "Nature has given to the strong the prerogative of making the weak obey them." The way in which states seek their rights can only be by war, since there is no external tribunal to put their claims to trial. But rights cannot be decided by military victory, and a *peace treaty* may put an end to the current war, but not to that general warlike condition within which pretexts can always be found for a new war. And indeed, such a state of affairs cannot be pronounced completely unjust, since it allows each party to act as judge in its own cause. Yet while natural right allows us to say to men living in a lawless condition that they ought to abandon it, the right of nations does not allow us to say the same of states. For as states, they already have a lawful internal constitution, and have thus outgrown the coercive right of others to subject them to a wider legal constitution in accordance with their conception of right. On the other hand, reason, as the highest legislative moral power, absolutely condemns war as a test of rights and sets up peace as an immediate duty. But peace can neither be inaugurated nor secured without a general agreement between the nations; thus a particular kind of league, which we might call a *pacific federation (foedus pacificum),* is required. It would differ from a *peace treaty (pactum pacis)* in that the latter terminates *one* war, whereas the former would seek to end *all* wars for good. This federation does not aim to acquire any power like that of a state, but merely to preserve and secure the *freedom* of each state in itself, along with that of the other confederated states, although this does not mean that they need to submit to public laws and to a coercive power which enforces them, as do men in a state of nature. It can be shown that this idea of *federalism,* extending gradually to encompass all states and thus leading to perpetual peace, is practicable and has objective reality. For if by good fortune one powerful and enlightened nation can form a republic (which is by its nature inclined to seek perpetual peace), this will provide a focal point for federal association among other states. These will join up with the first one, thus securing the freedom of each state in accordance with the idea of international right, and the whole will gradually spread further and further by a series of alliances of this kind.

It would be understandable for a people to say: "There shall be no war among us; for we will form ourselves into a state, appointing for ourselves a supreme legislative, executive, and juridical power to resolve our conflicts by peaceful means." But if this state says: "There shall be no war between myself and other states, although I do not recognize any supreme legislative power which could secure my rights and whose rights I should in turn secure," it is impossible to understand what justification I can have for placing any confidence in my rights, unless I can rely on some substitute for the union of civil society, that is, on a free federation. If the concept of international right is to retain any meaning at all, reason must necessarily couple it with a federation of this kind.

The concept of international right becomes meaningless if interpreted as a right to go to war. For this would make it a right to determine what is lawful not by means of universally valid external laws, but by means of one-sided maxims backed up by physical force. It could be taken to mean that it is perfectly just for men who adopt this attitude to destroy one another, and thus to find perpetual peace in the vast grave where all the horrors of violence and those responsible for them would be buried. There is only one rational way in which states coexisting with other states can emerge from the lawless condition of pure warfare. Just like individual men, they must renounce their savage and lawless freedom, adapt themselves to public coercive laws, and thus form an *international state (civitas gentium),* which would necessarily continue to grow until it embraced all the peoples of the earth. But since this is not the will of the nations, according to their present conception of international right (so that they reject *in hypothesi* what is true *in thesi*), the positive idea of a *world republic* cannot be realized. If all is not to be lost, this can at best find a negative substitute in the shape of an enduring and gradually expanding *federation* likely to prevent war. The latter may check the current of man's inclination to defy the law and antagonize his fellows, although there will always be a risk of it bursting forth anew. *Furor impius intus—fremit horridus ore cruento* (Virgil).[6]

Third Definitive Article of a Perpetual Peace: Cosmopolitan Right Shall Be Limited to Conditions of Universal Hospitality

As in the foregoing articles, we are here concerned not with philanthropy, but with *right.* In this context, *hospitality* means the right of a stranger not to be treated with

6. At the end of a war, when peace is concluded, it would not be inappropriate for a people to appoint a day of atonement after the festival of thanksgiving. Heaven would be invoked in the name of the state to forgive the human race for the great sin of which it continues to be guilty, since it will not accommodate itself to a lawful constitution in international relations. Proud of its independence, each state prefers to employ the barbarous expedient of war, although war cannot produce the desired decision on the rights of particular states. The thanksgivings for individual victories during a war, the hymns which are sung (in the style of the Israelites) to the *Lord of Hosts,* contrast no less markedly with the moral conception of a father of mankind. For besides displaying indifference to the way in which nations pursue their mutual rights (deplorable though it is), they actually rejoice at having annihilated numerous human beings or their happiness.

hostility when he arrives on someone else's territory. He can indeed be turned away, if this can be done without causing his death, but he must not be treated with hostility, so long as he behaves in a peaceable manner in the place he happens to be in. The stranger cannot claim the *right of a guest* to be entertained, for this would require a special friendly agreement whereby he might become a member of the native household for a certain time. He may only claim a *right of resort,* for all men are entitled to present themselves in the society of others by virtue of their right to communal possession of the earth's surface. Since the earth is a globe, they cannot disperse over an infinite area, but must necessarily tolerate one another's company. And no one originally has any greater right than anyone else to occupy any particular portion of the earth. The community of man is divided by uninhabitable parts of the earth's surface such as oceans and deserts, and even then, the *ship* or the *camel* (the ship of the desert) make it possible for them to approach their fellows over these ownerless tracts, and to utilize as a means of social intercourse that *right to the earth's surface* which the human race shares in common. The inhospitable behavior of coastal dwellers (as on the Barbary coast) in plundering ships on the adjoining seas or enslaving stranded seafarers, or that of inhabitants of the desert (as with the Arab Bedouins), who regard their proximity to nomadic tribes as a justification for plundering them, is contrary to natural right. But this natural right of hospitality, that is, the right of strangers, does not extend beyond those conditions which make it possible for them to *attempt* to enter into relations with the native inhabitants. In this way, continents distant from each other can enter into peaceful mutual relations which may eventually be regulated by public laws, thus bringing the human race nearer and nearer to a cosmopolitan constitution.

If we compare with this ultimate end the *inhospitable* conduct of the civilized states of our continent, especially the commercial states, the injustice which they display in *visiting* foreign countries and peoples (which in their case is the same as *conquering* them) seems appallingly great. America, the negro countries, the Spice Islands, the Cape, et cetera, were looked upon at the time of their discovery as ownerless territories; for the native inhabitants were counted as nothing. In East India (Hindustan), foreign troops were brought in under the pretext of merely setting up trading posts. This led to oppression of the natives, incitement of the various Indian states to widespread wars, famine, insurrection, treachery and the whole litany of evils which can afflict the human race.

China[7] and Japan (Nippon), having had experience of such guests, have wisely placed restrictions on them. China permits contact with her territories, but not entrance into them, while Japan only allows contact with a single European people,

---

7. If we wish to give this great empire the name by which it calls itself (i.e. *China,* not *Sina* or any similar form), we need only consult Georgi's *Alphabetum Tibetanum,* pp. 651–654, note b in particular. According to Professor Fischer of Petersburg, it actually has no fixed name which it might apply to itself; the commonest one is still the word *Kin,* which means gold (the Tibetans, however, called this *Ser*), which explains why the emperor is called King of Gold (i.e. of the fairest land in the world). The word is apparently pronounced *Chin* in the land itself, but expressed as *Kin* by the Italian missionaries,

the Dutch, although they are still segregated from the native community like prisoners. The worse (or from the point of view of moral judgments, the best) thing about all this is that the commercial states do not even benefit by their violence, for all their trading companies are on the point of collapse. The Sugar Islands, that stronghold of the cruelest and most calculated slavery, do not yield any real profit; they serve only the indirect (and not entirely laudable) purpose of training sailors for warships, thereby aiding the prosecution of wars in Europe. And all this is the work of powers who make endless ado about their piety, and who wish to be considered as chosen believers while they live on the fruits of iniquity.

The peoples of the earth have thus entered in varying degrees into a universal community, and it has developed to the point where a violation of rights in *one* part of the world is felt *everywhere*. The idea of a cosmopolitan right is therefore not fantastic and overstrained; it is a necessary complement to the unwritten code of political and international right, transforming it into a universal right of humanity. Only under this condition can we flatter ourselves that we are continually advancing towards a perpetual peace.

First Supplement: On the Guarantee of a Perpetual Peace

Perpetual peace is *guaranteed* by no less an authority than the great artist *Nature* herself *(natura daedala rerum)*. The mechanical process of nature visibly exhibits

---

who cannot pronounce the correct guttural sound. It can also be seen that what the Romans called the land of the people of *Ser* was in fact China, and silk was brought from there to Europe via Greater Tibet (probably crossing Lesser Tibet, Bukhara and Persia). This led to numerous speculations on the antiquity of this extraordinary state as compared with that of Hindustan, and on its relations with Tibet as well as with Japan. But the name Sina or Tschina, which neighbouring countries allegedly use of it, leads nowhere.

Perhaps the ancient but hitherto obscure community between Europe and Tibet can be explained from what Hesychius has recorded of the hierophant's cry κονξ 'Ομπαξ *(Konx Ompax)* in the Eleusinian Mysteries (cf. *Journey of the Younger Anacharsis*, part V, p. 447 *et seq*). For according to Georgi's *Alphabetum Tibetanum*, the word *Concioa* means god, and it markedly resembles *Konx*, while *Pah-cio* (*ibid.* p. 520), which the Greeks might easily have pronounced *pax*, means *promulgator legis*, the divinity which pervades the whole of nature (also called *Cencresi*, p. 177). But *Om*, which La Croze translates as *benedictus* (blessed), can scarcely mean anything other than *beatific* if applied to the deity (p. 507). When P. Francisco Orazio asked the Tibetan lamas how they conceived of god *(Concioa)*, he always received the answer: *"God is the community of all the holy ones"* (i.e. the community of blessed souls, at last reunited in the deity by being reborn as lamas after numerous migrations through all kinds of bodies, and thereby transformed into beings worthy of adoration—p. 223). Thus the mysterious name *Konx Ompax* might designate that *holy (Konx), heavenly (Om)* and *wise (Pax)* supreme being who pervades the whole world, i.e. nature personified. As used in the Greek mysteries, it may well have signified *monotheism* to the epopts, as distinct from the *polytheism* of the uninitiated mass, although it savored of atheism to P. Orazio *(loc. cit.)*. Our earlier considerations should help to explain how this mysterious name reached the Greeks from Tibet; conversely, this influence makes it appear probable that Europe at an early date had contact with China by way of Tibet, perhaps even earlier than with India.

the purposive plan of producing concord among men, even against their will and indeed by means of their very discord. This design, if we regard it as a compelling cause whose laws of operation are unknown to us, is called *fate*. But if we consider its purposive function within the world's development, whereby it appears as the underlying wisdom of a higher cause, showing the way towards the objective goal of the human race and predetermining the world's evolution, we call it *providence*.[8] We cannot actually observe such an agency in the artifices of nature, nor can we even *infer* its existence from them. But as with all relations between the form of things and their ultimate purposes, we can and must *supply it mentally* in order to conceive of its possibility by analogy with human artifices. Its relationship to and conformity with the end which reason directly prescribes to us (i.e. the end of morality) can only be conceived of as an idea. Yet while this idea is indeed far-fetched in *theory*, it does possess dogmatic validity and has a very real foundation in *practice*, as with the concept of *perpetual peace*, which makes it our duty to promote it by using the natural mechanism described above. But in contexts such as this, where we are concerned purely with theory and not with religion, we should also note that it is more in keeping with the limitations of human reason to speak of *nature* and not of *providence*, for reason, in dealing with cause and effect relationships, must keep within the bounds of possible experience. *Modesty* forbids us to speak of providence as something we can recognize, for this would mean donning the wings of Icarus and presuming to approach the mystery of its inscrutable intentions.

8. In the mechanism of nature, of which man (as a sensory being) is a part, there is evident a fundamental form on which its very existence depends. This form becomes intelligible to us only if we attribute it to the design of a universal creator who has determined it in advance. We call this predetermining influence divine *providence*, and further define it as *original providence* in so far as it is active from the earliest times onwards (*providentia conditrix; semel iussit, semper parent*—Augustine). In as much as it sustains the course of nature in accordance with purposive universal laws, we call it *ruling providence (providentia gubernatrix)*. If it realizes particular ends which man could not have foreseen and whose existence can only be guessed at from the results, it is termed *guiding providence (providentia directrix)*. And finally, if individual events are regarded as divinely intended, we no longer speak of providence but of a *special dispensation (directio extraordinaria)*. But it is foolish presumption for man to claim that he can recognize this as such, since it implies that a miracle has taken place, even if the events are not specifically described as miraculous. For however pious and humble it may sound, it is absurd and self-conceited for anyone to conclude from a single event that the efficient cause is governed by a special principle, or that the event in question is an end in itself and not just the natural and mechanical consequence of another end which is completely unknown to us. Similarly, it is false and self-contradictory to classify providence in terms of worldly objects *(materialiter)*, dividing it up into *general* and *particular*, as occurs in the doctrine that providence takes care to preserve the various species of creatures, but leaves chance to look after the individuals; for the whole point of saying that providence applies in general is that no single object should be excepted from it. This classification, however, was probably meant to indicate that the intentions of providence are carried out *in different ways (formaliter)*. These might be *ordinary* (e.g. the annual death and revival of nature with the changes of seasons) or *extraordinary* (e.g. the transporting of wood by Ocean currents to Arctic coasts where it cannot grow, thus providing for the native inhabitants, who could not live without it). In the latter case, while we can well explain the physico-mechanical cause of the phenomena in question (e.g.

But before we define this guarantee more precisely, we must first examine the situation in which nature has placed the actors in her great spectacle, for it is this situation which ultimately demands the guarantee of peace. We may next enquire in what manner the guarantee is provided.

Nature's provisional arrangement is as follows. Firstly, she has taken that war itself is invested with an inherent *dignity;* for even philosophers have eulogized it as a kind of ennobling influence on man, forgetting the Greek saying that "war is bad in that it produces more evil people than it destroys." So much, then, for what nature does to further *her own end* with respect to the human race as an animal species.

We now come to the essential question regarding the prospect of perpetual peace. What does nature do in relation to the end which man's own reason prescribes to him as a duty, that is, how does nature help to promote his *moral purpose?* And how does nature guarantee that what man *ought* to do by the laws of his freedom (but does not do) will in fact be done through nature's compulsion, without prejudice to the free agency of man? This question arises, moreover, in all three areas of public right—in *political, international* and *cosmopolitan right.* For if I say that nature *wills* that this or that should happen, this does not mean that nature imposes on us a *duty* to do it, for duties can only be imposed by practical reason, acting without any external constraint. On the contrary, nature does it herself, whether we are willing or not: *fata volentem ducunt, nolentem trahunt.*

1. Even if people were not compelled by internal dissent to submit to the coercion of public laws, war would produce the same effect from outside. For in accordance with the natural arrangement described above, each people would find itself

---

by the fact that the riverbanks in temperate lands are covered in forests, so that the trees may fall into the rivers and be carried further afield by currents like the Gulf Stream), we must not on the other hand overlook teleology, which indicates the foresight of a wise agency governing nature. But the conception, current in the academic world, of a divine *participation* or *collaboration (concursus)* in effects experienced in the world of the senses, is superfluous. For *firstly,* it is self-contradictory to try to harness disparates together *(gryphes iungere equis),* and to imply that a being who is himself the complete cause of the world's developments has to *supplement* his own predetermining providence during the course of world events (so that it must originally have been inadequate); for example, it is absurd to say that after God, the doctor acted as an assistant in curing the patient—*causa solitaria non iuvat.* God is the creator of the doctor and of all his medicaments, so that the effect must be ascribed *entirely* to him if we are to ascend to that supreme original cause which is theoretically beyond our comprehension. Alternatively, it can be ascribed *entirely* to the doctor, in so far as we treat the event in question as belonging to the order of nature and as capable of explanation within the causal series of earthly occurrences. And *secondly,* if we adopt such attitudes, we are deprived of all definite principles by which we might judge effects. But the concept of a divine *concursus* is completely acceptable and indeed necessary in the moral and practical sense, which refers exclusively to the transcendental world. For example, we may say that we should never cease to strive towards goodness, for we believe that God, even by means which we cannot comprehend, will make up for our own lack of righteousness so long as our attitude is sincere. It is, however, self-evident that no one should use such arguments to *explain* a good deed, regarded as a secular event, for this would presuppose theoretical knowledge of the transcendental, which it is absurd for us to claim.

confronted by another neighboring people pressing it upon it, thus forcing it to form itself internally into a *state* in order to encounter the other as an armed *power.* Now the *republican* constitution is the only one which does complete justice to the rights of man. But it is also the most difficult to establish, and even more so to preserve, so that many maintain that it would only be possible within a state of *angels,* since men, with their self-seeking inclinations, would be incapable of adhering to a constitution of so sublime a nature. But in fact, nature comes to the aid of the universal and rational human will, so admirable in itself but so impotent in practice, and makes use of precisely those self-seeking inclinations in order to do so. It only remains for men to create a good organization for the state, a task which is well within their capability, and to arrange it in such a way that their self-seeking energies are opposed to one another, each thereby neutralizing or eliminating the destructive effects of the rest. And as far as reason is concerned, the result is the same as if man's selfish tendencies were non-existent, so that man, even if he is not morally good in himself, is nevertheless compelled to be a good citizen. As hard as it may sound, the problem of setting up a state can be solved even by a nation of devils (so long as they possess understanding). It may be stated as follows: "In order to organize a group of rational beings who together require universal laws for their survival, but of whom each separate individual is secretly inclined to exempt himself from them, the constitution must be so designed that, although the citizens are opposed to one another in their private attitudes, these opposing views may inhibit one another in such a way that the public conduct of the citizens will be the same as if they did not have such evil attitudes." A problem of this kind must be soluble. For such a task does not involve the moral improvement of man; it only means finding out how the mechanism of nature can be applied to men in such a manner that the antagonism of their hostile attitudes will make them compel one another to submit to coercive laws, thereby producing a condition of peace within which the laws can be enforced. We can see this principle at work among the actually existing (although as yet very imperfectly organized) states. For in their external relations, they have already approached what the idea of right prescribes, although the reason for this is certainly not their internal moral attitudes. In the same way, we cannot expect their moral attitudes to produce a good political constitution; on the contrary, it is only through the latter than the people can be expected to attain a good level of moral culture. Thus that mechanism of nature by which selfish inclinations are naturally opposed to one another in their external relations can be used by reason to facilitate the attainment of its own end, the reign of established right. Internal and external peace are thereby furthered and assured, so far as it lies within the power of the state itself to do so. We may therefore say that nature *irresistibly wills* that right should eventually gain the upper hand. What men have neglected to do will ultimately happen of its own accord, albeit with much inconvenience. As Bouterwek puts it: "If the reed is bent too far, it breaks; and he who wants too much gets nothing."

[1795]

from *An Essay on the History of Civil Society*

PART FOURTH. OF CONSEQUENCES THAT RESULT FROM THE ADVANCEMENT OF CIVIL AND COMMERCIAL ARTS.
Section I.
Of the Separation of Arts and Professions

It is evident, that, however urged by a sense of necessity, and a desire of convenience, or favored by any advantages of situation and policy, a people can make no great progress in cultivating the arts of life, until they have separated, and committed to different persons, the several tasks, which require a peculiar skill and attention. The savage, or the barbarian, who must build and plant, and fabricate for himself, prefers, in the interval of great alarms and fatigues, the enjoyments of sloth to the improvement of his fortune: he is, perhaps, by the diversity of his wants, discouraged from industry; or, by his divided attention, prevented from acquiring skill in the management of any particular subject.

The enjoyment of peace, however, and the prospect of being able to exchange one commodity for another, turns, by degrees, the hunter and the warrior into a tradesman and a merchant. The accidents which distribute the means of subsistence unequally, inclination, and favorable opportunities, assign the different occupations of men; and a sense of utility leads them, without end, to subdivide their professions.

The artist finds, that the more he can confine his attention to a particular part of any work, his productions are the more perfect, and grow under his hands in the greater quantities. Every undertaker in manufacture finds, that the more he can subdivide the tasks of his workmen, and the more hands he can employ on separate articles, the more are his expenses diminished, and his profits increased. The consumer too requires, in every kind of commodity, a workmanship more perfect than hands employed on a variety of subjects can produce; and the progress of commerce is but a continued subdivision of the mechanical arts.

Every craft may engross the whole of a man's attention, and has a mystery which must be studied or learned by a regular apprenticeship. Nations of tradesmen come to consist of members who, beyond their own particular trade, are ignorant of all human affairs, and who may contribute to the preservation and enlargement of their commonwealth, without making its interest an object of their regard or attention. Every individual is distinguished by his calling, and has a place to which he is fitted. The savage, who knows no distinction but that of his merit, of his sex, or of his species, and to whom his community is the sovereign object of affection, is astonished to find, that in a scene of this nature, his being a man does not qualify him for any station whatever: he flies to the woods with amazement, distaste, and aversion.

By the separation of arts and professions, the sources of wealth are laid open; every species of material is wrought up to the greatest perfection, and every commodity is produced in the greatest abundance. The state may estimate its profits and its revenues by the number of its people. It may produce, by its treasure, that national consideration and power, which the savage maintains at the expense of his blood.

The advantage gained in the inferior branches of manufacture by the separation of their parts, seem to be equalled by those which arise from a similar device in the higher departments of policy and war. The soldier is relieved from every care but that of his service; statesmen divide the business of civil government into shares; and the servants of the public, in every office, without being skillful in the affairs of state, may succeed, by observing forms which are already established on the experience of others. They are made, like the parts of an engine, to concur to a purpose, without any concert of their own; and, equally blind with the trader to any general combination, they unite with him, in furnishing to the state its resources, its conduct, and its force.

. . .

It may even be doubted, whether the measure of national capacity increases with the advancement of arts. Many mechanical arts, indeed, require no capacity; they succeed best under a total suppression of sentiment and reason; and ignorance is the mother of industry as well as of superstition. Reflection and fancy are subject to err; but a habit of moving the hand, or the foot, is independent of either. Manufactures, accordingly, prosper most, where the mind is least consulted, and where the workshop may, without any great effort of imagination, be considered as an engine, the parts of which are men.

The forest has been felled by the savage without the use of the axe, and weights have been raised without the aid of the mechanical powers. The merit of the inventor, in every branch, probably deserves a preference to that of the performer; and he who invented a tool, or could work without its assistance, deserved the praise of ingenuity in a much higher degree than the mere artist, who, by its assistance, produced a superior work.

But if many parts in the practice of every art, and in the detail of every department, require no abilities, or actually tend to contract and to limit the views of the mind, there are others which lead to general reflections, and to enlargement of thought. Even in manufacture, the genius of the master, perhaps, is cultivated, while that of the inferior workman lies waste. The statesman may have a wide comprehension of human affairs, while the tools he employs are ignorant of the system in which they are themselves combined. The general officer may be a great proficient in the knowledge of war, while the soldier is confined to a few motions of the hand and the foot. The former may have gained, what the latter has lost; and being occupied in the conduct of disciplined armies, may practice on a larger scale, all the arts of preservation, of deception, and of stratagem, which the savage exerts in leading a small party, or merely in defending himself.

The practitioner of every act and profession may afford matter of general speculation to the man of science; and thinking itself, in this age of separations, may become a peculiar craft. In the bustle of civil pursuits and occupations, men appear in a variety of lights, and suggest matter of inquiry and fancy, by which conversation is enlivened, and greatly enlarged. The productions of ingenuity are brought to the market; and men are willing to pay for whatever has a tendency to inform or amuse. By this means the idle, as well as the busy, contribute to forward the progress of arts, and bestow on polished nations that air of superior ingenuity, under which they appear to have gained the ends that were pursued by the savage in his forest, knowledge, order, and wealth.

Section II.
Of the Subordination Consequent to the Separation of Arts and Professions

There is one ground of subordination in the difference of natural talents and dispositions; a second in the unequal division of property; and a third, not less sensible, in the habits which are acquired by the practice of different arts.

Some employments are liberal, others mechanic. They require different talents, and inspire different sentiments; and whether or not this be the cause of the preference we actually give, it is certainly reasonable to form our opinion of the rank that is due to men of certain professions and stations, from the influence of their manner of life in cultivating the powers of the mind, or in preserving the sentiments of the heart.

There is an elevation natural to man, by which he would be thought, in his rudest state, however urged by necessity, to rise above the consideration of mere subsistence, and the regards of interest: He would appear to act only from the heart, in its engagements of friendship, or opposition; he would show himself only upon occasions of danger or difficulty, and leave ordinary cares to the weak or the servile.

The same apprehensions, in every situation, regulate his notions of meanness or dignity. In that of polished society, his desire to avoid the character of sordid, makes him conceal his regard for what relates merely to his preservation or his livelihood. In his estimation, the beggar, who depends upon charity; the laborer, who toils that he may eat; the mechanic, whose art requires no exertion of genius, are degraded by the object they pursue, and by the means they employ to attain it. Professions requiring more knowledge and study; proceeding on the exercise of fancy, and the love of perfection; leading to applause as well as to profit, place the artist in a superior class, and bring him nearer to that station in which men are supposed to be highest; because in it they are bound to no task; because they are left to follow the disposition of the mind, and to take that part in society, to which they are led by the sentiments of the heart, or by the calls of the public.

This last was the station, which, in the distinction between freemen and slaves, the citizens of every ancient republic strove to gain, and to maintain for themselves. Women, or slaves, in the earliest ages, had been set apart for the purposes of domestic care, or bodily labor; and in the progress of lucrative arts, the latter were bred to mechanical professions, and were even entrusted with merchandise for the benefit of their masters. Freemen would be understood to have no object beside those of politics and war. In this manner, the honors of one half of the species were sacrificed to those of the other; as stones from the same quarry are buried in the foundation, to sustain the blocks which happen to be hewn for the superior parts of the pile. In the midst of our encomiums bestowed on the Greeks and Romans, we are, by this circumstance, made to remember, that no human institution is perfect.

In many of the Grecian states, the benefits arising to the free from this cruel distinction, were not conferred equally on all the citizens. Wealth being unequally divided, the rich alone were exempted from labor; the poor were reduced to work for their own subsistence: interest was a reigning passion in both, and the possession of slaves, like that of any other lucrative property, became an object of avarice, not an exemption from sordid attentions. The entire effects of the institution were obtained, or continued to be enjoyed for any considerable time, at Sparta alone. We feel its injustice; we suffer for the helot, under the severities and unequal treatment to which he was exposed: but when we think only of the superior order of men in this state; when we attend to that elevation and magnanimity of spirit, for which danger had no terror, interest no means to corrupt; when we consider them as friends, or as citizens, we are apt to forget, like themselves, that slaves have a title to be treated like men.

We look for elevation of sentiment, and liberality of mind, among those orders of citizens, who, by their condition, and their fortunes, are relieved from sordid cares and attentions. This was the description of a free man at Sparta; and if the lot of a slave among the ancients was really more wretched than that of the indigent laborer and the mechanic among the moderns, it may be doubted, whether the superior orders, who are in possession of consideration and honors, do not proportionally fail in the dignity which befits their condition. If the pretensions to equal justice and freedom should terminate in rendering every class equally servile and mercenary, we make a nation of helots, and have no free citizens.

In every commercial state, notwithstanding any pretension to equal rights, the exaltation of a few must depress the many. In this arrangement, we think that the extreme meanness of some classes must arise chiefly from the defect of knowledge, and of liberal education; and we refer to such classes, as to any image of what our species must have been in its rude and uncultivated state. But we forget how many circumstances, especially in populous cities, tend to corrupt the lowest orders of men. Ignorance is the least of their failings. An admiration of wealth unpossessed, becoming a principle of envy, or of servility; a habit of acting perpetually with a view in profit, and under a sense of subjection; the crimes to which they are allured, in order to feed their debauch, or to gratify their avarice, are examples, not of ignorance, but of corruption and baseness. If the savage has not received our instructions, he is likewise unacquainted with our vices. He knows no superior, and cannot be servile; he knows no distinctions of fortune, and cannot be envious; he acts from his talents in the highest station which human society can offer, that of the counselor, and the soldier of his country. Toward forming his sentiments, he knows all that the heart requires to be known; he can distinguish the friend whom he loves, and the public interest which awakens his zeal.

The principal objections to democratical or popular government, are taken from the inequalities which arise among men in the result of commercial arts. And it must be confessed, that popular assemblies, when composed of men whose dispositions are sordid, and whose ordinary applications are illiberal, however they may be entrusted with the choice of their masters and leaders, are certainly, in their own persons, unfit to command. How can he who has confined his views to his own subsistence or preservation, be entrusted with the conduct of nations? Such men, when admitted to deliberate on matters of state, bring to its councils confusion and tumult, or servility and corruption; and seldom suffer it to repose from ruinous factions, or the effect of resolutions ill formed or ill conducted.

The Athenians retained their popular government under all these defects. The mechanic was obliged, under a penalty, to appear in the public market-place, and to hear debates on the subjects of war, and of peace. He was tempted by pecuniary rewards, to attend on the trial of civil and criminal causes. But notwithstanding an exercise tending so much to cultivate their talents, the indigent came always with minds intent upon profit, or with the habits of an illiberal calling. Sunk under the sense of their personal disparity and weakness, they were ready to resign themselves entirely to the influence of some popular leader, who flattered their passions, and wrought on their fears; or, actuated by envy, they were ready to banish from the state whomsoever was respectable and eminent in the superior order of citizens: and whether from their neglect of the public at one time, or their mal-administration at another, the sovereignty was every moment ready to drop from their hands.

The people, in this case, are, in fact, frequently governed by one, or a few, who know how to conduct them. Pericles possessed a species of princely authority at Athens; Crassus, Pompey, and Caesar, either jointly or successively, possessed for a considerable period the sovereign direction of Rome.

Whether in great or in small states, democracy is preserved with difficulty, under the disparities of condition, and the unequal cultivation of the mind, which attend the variety of pursuits, and applications, that separate mankind in the advanced state of commercial arts. In this, however, we do not plead against the form of democracy, after the principle is removed; and see the absurdity of pretensions to equal influence and consideration, after the characters of men have ceased to be similar.

Section III.
Of the Manners of Polished and Commercial Nations

Mankind, when in their rude state, have a great uniformity of manners; but when civilized, they are engaged in a variety of pursuits; they tread on a larger field, and separate to a greater distance. If they be guided, however, by similar dispositions, and by like suggestions of nature, they will probably, in the end, as well as in the beginning of their progress, continue to agree in many particulars; and while communities admit, in their members, that diversity of ranks and professions which we have already described, as the consequence or the foundation of commerce, they will resemble each other in many effects of this distribution, and of other circumstances in which they nearly concur.

Under every form of government, statesmen endeavor to remove the dangers by which they are threatened from abroad, and the disturbances which molest them at home. By this conduct, if successful, they in a few ages gain an ascendant for their country; establish a frontier at a distance from its capital; they find, in the mutual desires of tranquility, which come to possess mankind, and in those public establishments which tend to keep the peace of society, a respite from foreign wars, and a relief from domestic disorders. They learn to decide every contest without tumult, and to secure, by the authority of law, every citizen in the possession of his personal rights.

. . .

Many such differences may arise among polished nations, from the effects of climate, or from sources of fashion, that are still more unaccountable and obscure; but the principal distinctions on which we can rest, are derived from the part a people are obliged to act in their national capacity; from the objects placed in their view by the state; or from the constitution of government, which prescribing the terms of society to its subjects, has a great influence in forming their apprehensions and habits.

The Roman people, destined to acquire wealth by conquest, and by the spoil of provinces; the Carthaginians, intent on the returns of merchandise, and the produce of commercial settlements, must have filled the streets of their several capitals with men of a different disposition and aspect. The Roman laid hold of his sword when he wished to be great, and the state found her armies prepared in the dwellings of her people. The Carthaginian retired to his counter on a similar project; and, when the state was alarmed, or had resolved on a war, lent of his profits to purchase an army abroad.

The member of a republic, and the subject of a monarchy, must differ, because they have different parts assigned to them by the forms of their country: the one destined to live with his equals, or, by his personal talents and character, to contend for pre-eminence; the other, born to a determinate station, where any pretense to equality creates a confusion, and where nought but precedence is studied. Each, when the institutions of his country are mature, may find in the laws a protection to his personal rights; but those rights themselves are differently understood, and with a different set of opinions, give rise to a different temper of mind. The republican must act in the state, to sustain his pretensions; he must join a party, in order to be safe; he must form one, in order to be great. The subject of monarchy refers to his birth for the honor he claims; he waits on a court, to show his importance; and holds out the ensigns of dependence and favor, to gain him esteem with the public.

If national institutions, calculated for the preservation of liberty, instead of calling upon the citizen to act for himself, and to maintain his rights, should give a security, requiring, on his part, no personal attention or effort; this seeming perfection of government might weaken the bands of society, and, upon maxims of independence, separate and estrange the different ranks it was meant to reconcile. Neither the parties formed in republics, nor the courtly assemblies which meet in monarchical governments, could take place, where the sense of a mutual dependence should cease to summon their members together. The resorts for commerce might be frequented, and mere amusement might be pursued in the crowd, while the private dwelling became a retreat for reserve, averse to the trouble arising from regards and attentions, which it might be part of the political creed to believe of no consequence, and a point of honor to hold in contempt.

This humor is not likely to grow either in republics or monarchies: it belongs more properly to a mixture of both; where the administration of justice may be better secured; where the subject is tempted to look for equality, but where he finds only independence in its place; and where he learns, from a spirit of equality, to hate the very distinctions to which, on account of their real importance, he pays a remarkable deference.

In either of the separate forms of republic or monarchy, or in acting on the principles of either, men are obliged to court their fellow citizens, and to employ parts and address to improve their fortunes, or even to be safe. They find in both a school for discernment and penetration; but in the one, are taught to overlook the merits of a private character, for the sake of abilities that have weight with the public; and in the other, to overlook great and respectable talents, for the sake of qualities engaging or pleasant in the scene of entertainment, and private society. They are obliged, in both, to adapt themselves with care to the fashion and manners of their country. They find no place for caprice or singular humors. The republican must be popular, and the courtier polite. The first must think himself well placed in every company; the other must choose his resorts, and desire to be distinguished only where the society itself is esteemed. With his inferiors, he takes an air of protection; and suffers, in his turn, the same air to be taken with himself.

. . .

The ancient states of Greece and Italy derived their manners in war from the nature of their republican government; those of modern Europe, from the influence of monarchy, which, by its prevalence in this part of the world, has a great effect on nations, even where it is not the form established. Upon the maxims of this government, we apprehend a distinction between the state and its members, as that between the King and the people, which renders war an operation of policy, not of popular animosity. While we strike at the public interest, we would spare the private, and we carry a respect and consideration for individuals, which often stops the issues of blood in the ardor of victory, and procures to the prisoner of war a hospitable reception in the very city which he came to destroy. These practices are so well established, that scarcely any provocation on the part of an enemy, or any exigence of service, can excuse a trespass on the supposed rules of humanity, or save the leader who commits it from becoming an object of detestation and horror.

To this, the general practice of the Greeks and the Romans was opposite. They endeavored to wound the state by destroying its members, by desolating its territory, and by ruining the possessions of its subjects. They granted quarter only to enslave, or to bring the prisoner to a more solemn execution; and an enemy, when disarmed, was, for the most part, either sold in the market, or killed, that he might never return to strengthen his party. When this was the issue of war, it was no wonder, that battles were fought with desperation, and that every fortress was defended to the last extremity. The game of human life went upon a high stake, and was played with a proportional zeal.

The term *barbarian,* in this state of manners, could not be employed by the Greeks or the Romans in that sense in which we use it; to characterize a people regardless of commercial arts; profuse of their own lives, and of those of others; vehement in their attachment to one society, and implacable in their antipathy to another. This, in a great and shining part of their history, was their own character, as well as that of some other nations, whom, upon this very account, we distinguish by the appellations of *barbarous* or *rude.*

It has been observed, that those celebrated nations are indebted, for a great part of their estimation, not to the matter of their history, but to the manner in which it has been delivered, and to the capacity of their historians, and other writers. Their story has been told by men who knew how to draw our attention on the proceedings of the understanding and of the heart, more than on the detail of facts; and who could exhibit characters to be admired and loved, in the midst of actions which we should now universally hate or condemn. Like Homer, the model of Grecian literature, they could make us forget the horrors of a vindictive, cruel, and remorseless proceeding towards an enemy, in behalf of the strenuous conduct, the courage, and vehement affections, with which the hero maintained the cause of his friend and of his country.

Our manners are so different, and the system upon which we regulate our apprehensions, in many things, so opposite, that no less could make us endure the practice of ancient nations. Were that practice recorded by the mere journalist, who retains only the detail of events, without throwing any light on the character of the actors; who, like the Tartar historian, tells only what blood was spilled in the field, and how many inhabitants were massacred in the city; we should never have distinguished the Greeks from their barbarous neighbors, nor have thought, that the character of civility pertained even to the Romans, till very late in their history, and in the decline of their empire.

. . .

To form a judgment of the character from which they acted in the field, and in their competitions with neighboring nations, we must observe them at home. They were bold and fearless in their civil dissensions; ready to proceed to extremities, and to carry their debates to the decision of force. Individuals stood distinguished by their personal spirit and vigor, not by the valuation of their estates, or the rank of their birth. They had a personal elevation founded on the sense of equality, not of precedence. The general of one campaign was, during the next, a private soldier, and served in the ranks. They were solicitous to acquire bodily strength; because, in the use of their weapons, battles were a trial of the soldier's strength, as well as of the leader's conduct. The remains of their statuary, shows a manly grace, an air of simplicity and ease, which being frequent in nature, were familiar to the artist. The mind, perhaps, borrowed a confidence and force, from the vigor and address of the body; their eloquence and style bore a resemblance to the carriage of the person. The understanding was chiefly cultivated in the practice of affairs. The most respectable personages were obliged to mix with the crowd, and derived their degree of ascendancy, only from their conduct, their eloquence, and personal vigor. They had no forms of expression, to mark a ceremonious and guarded respect. Invective proceeded to railing, and the grossest terms were often employed by the most admired and accomplished orators. Quarreling had no rules but the immediate dictates of passion, which ended in words of reproach, in violence, and blows. They fortunately went always unarmed; and to wear a sword in times of peace, was among them the mark of a barbarian. When they took arms in the divisions of faction, the prevailing party supported itself by expelling their opponents, by proscriptions, and bloodshed. The usurper endeavored to maintain his station by the most violent and prompt executions. He was opposed, in his turn, by conspiracies and assassinations, in which the most respectable citizens were ready to use the dagger.

Such was the character of their spirit, in its occasional ferments at home; and it burst commonly with a suitable violence and force, against their foreign rivals and enemies. The amiable plea of humanity was little regarded by them in the operations of war. Cities were razed, or enslaved; the captive sold, mutilated, or condemned to die.

When viewed on this side, the ancient nations have but a sorry plea for esteem with the inhabitants of modern Europe, who profess to carry the civilities of peace into the practice of war; and who value the praise of indiscriminate lenity at a higher rate than even that of military prowess, or the love of their country. And yet they have, in other respects, merited and obtained our praise. Their ardent attachment to their country; their contempt of suffering, and of death, in its cause; their manly apprehensions of personal independence, which rendered every individual, even under tottering establishments, and imperfect laws, the guardian of freedom to his fellow citizens; their activity of mind; in short, their penetration, the ability of their conduct, and force of their spirit, have gained them the first rank among nations.

If their animosities were great, their affections were proportionate: they, perhaps, loved, where we only pity; and were stern and inexorable, where we are not merciful, but only irresolute. After all, the merit of a man is determined by his candor and generosity to his associates, by his zeal for national objects, and by his vigor in maintaining political rights; not by moderation alone, which proceeds frequently from indifference to national and public interests, and which serves to relax the nerves on which the force of a private as well as a public character depends.

When under the Macedonian and the Roman monarchies, a nation came to be considered as the estate of a prince, and the inhabitants of a province to be regarded as a lucrative property, the possession of territory, not the destruction of its people, became the object of conquest. The pacific citizen had little concern in the quarrels of sovereigns; the violence of the soldier was restrained by discipline. He fought, because he was taught to carry arms, and to obey: he sometimes shed unnecessary blood in the ardor of victory; but, except in the case of civil wars, had no passions to excite his animosity beyond the field and the day of battle. Leaders judged of the objects of an enterprise, and they arrested the sword when these were obtained.

In the modern nations of Europe, where extent of territory admits of a distinction between the state and its subjects, we are accustomed to think of the individual with compassion, seldom of the public with zeal. We have improved on the laws of war, and on the lenitives which have been devised to soften its rigors; we have mingled politeness with the use of the sword; we have learned to make war under the stipulation of treaties and cartels, and trust to the faith of an enemy whose ruin was meditate. Glory is more successfully obtained by saving and protecting, than by destroying the vanquished: and the most amiable of all objects is, in appearance, attained; the employing of force, only for the obtaining of justice, and for the preservation of national rights.

. . .

The term *polished,* if we may judge from its etymology, originally referred to the state of nations in respect to their laws and government.[1] In its later applications, it refers no less to their proficiency in the liberal and mechanical arts, in literature, and in commerce. But whatever may be its application, it appears, that if there were a name still more respectable than this, every nation, even the most barbarous, or the most corrupted, would assume it; and bestow its reverse where they conceived a dislike, or apprehended a difference. The names of *alien,* or *foreigner,* are seldom pronounced without some degree of intended reproach. That of *barbarian,* in use with one arrogant people, and that of *gentil,* with another, only served to distinguish the stranger, whose language and pedigree differed from theirs.

Even where we pretend to found our opinions on reason, and to justify our preference of one nation to another, we frequently bestow our esteem on circumstances which do not relate to national character, and which have little tendency to promote the welfare of mankind. Conquest, or great extent of territory, however peopled, and great wealth, however distributed or employed, are titles upon which we indulge our own, and the vanity of other nations, as we do that of private men on the score of their fortunes and honors. We even sometimes contend, whose capital is the most overgrown; whose king has the most absolute power; and at whose court the bread of the subject is consumed in the most senseless riot. These indeed are the notions of vulgar minds; but it is impossible to determine, how far the notions of vulgar minds may lead mankind.

There have certainly been very few examples of states, who have, by arts and policy, improved the original dispositions of human nature, or endeavored, by wise and effectual precautions, to prevent its corruption. Affection, and force of mind, which are the band and the strength of communities, were the inspiration of God, and original attributes in the nature of man. The wisest policy of nations, except in a very few instances, has tended, we may suspect, rather to maintain the peace of society, and to repress the external effects of bad passions, than to strengthen the disposition of the heart itself to justice and goodness. It has tended, by introducing a variety of arts, to exercise the ingenuity of men, and by engaging them in a variety of pursuits, inquiries, and studies, to inform, but frequently to corrupt the mind. It has tended to furnish matter of distinction and vanity; and by incumbering the individuals with new subjects of personal care, to substitute the anxiety he entertains for himself, instead of the confidence and the affection he should entertain for his fellow creatures.

Whether this suspicion be just or not, we are come to point at circumstances tending to verify, or to disprove it: and if to understand the real felicity of nations be of importance, it is certainly so likewise, to know what are those weaknesses, and those vices, by which men not only mar this felicity, but in one age forfeit all the external advantages they had gained in a former.

---

1. The 1768 edition adds here: "and men civilized were men practised in the duty of citizens." The next sentence ends with the addition: "and men civilized are scholars, men of fashion and traders."

The wealth, the aggrandizement and power of nations, are commonly the effects of virtue; the loss of these advantages, is often a consequence of vice.

Were we to suppose men to have succeeded in the discovery and application of every art by which states are preserved, and governed; to have attained, by efforts of wisdom and magnanimity, the admired establishments and advantages of a civilized and flourishing people; the subsequent part of their history, containing, according to vulgar apprehension, a full display of those fruits in maturity, of which they had till then carried only the blossom, and the first formation, should, still more than the former, merit our attention, and excite our admiration.

The event, however, has not corresponded to this expectation. The virtues of men have shone most during their struggles, not after the attainment of their ends. Those ends themselves, though attained by virtue, are frequently the causes of corruption and vice. Mankind, in aspiring to national felicity, have substituted arts which increase their riches, instead of those which improve their nature. They have entertained admiration of themselves, under the titles of *civilized* and of *polished,* where they should have been affected with shame; and even where they have for a while acted on maxims tending to raise, to invigorate, and to preserve the national character, they have, sooner or later, been diverted from their object, and fallen a prey to misfortune, or to the neglects which prosperity itself had encouraged.

War, which furnishes mankind with a principal occupation of their restless spirit, serves, by the variety of its events, to diversify their fortunes. While it opens to one tribe or society, the way to eminence, and leads to dominion, it brings another to subjection, and closes the scene of their national efforts. The celebrated rivalship of Carthage and Rome was, in both parties, the natural exercise of an ambitious spirit, impatient of opposition, or even of equality. The conduct and the fortune of leaders, held the balance for some time in suspense; but to whichever side it had inclined, a great nation was to fall; a seat of empire, and of policy, was to be removed from its place; and it was then to be determined, whether the Syriac or the Latin should contain the erudition that was, in future ages, to occupy the studies of the learned.

States have been thus conquered from abroad, before they gave any signs of internal decay, even in the midst of prosperity, and in the period of their greatest ardor for national objects. Athens, in the height of her ambition, and of her glory, received a fatal wound, in striving to extend her maritime power beyond the Grecian seas. And nations of every description, formidable by their rude ferocity, respected for their discipline and military experience, when advancing, as well as when declining, in their strength, fell a prey, by turns, to the ambition and arrogant spirit of the Romans. Such examples may excite and alarm the jealousy and caution of states; the presence of similar dangers may exercise the talents of politicians and statesmen; but mere reverses of fortune are the common materials of history, and must long since have ceased to create our surprise.

Did we find, that nations advancing from small beginnings, and arrived at the possession of arts which lead to dominion, became secure of their advantages, in proportion as they were qualified to gain them; that they proceeded in a course of uninterrupted felicity, till they were broke by external calamities; and that they retained their force, till a more fortunate or vigorous power arose to depress them; the subject in speculation could not be attended with many difficulties, nor give rise to many reflections. But when we observe among nations a kind of spontaneous return to obscurity and weakness; when, in spite of perpetual admonitions of the danger they run, they suffer themselves to be subdued, in one period, by powers which could not have entered into competition with them in a former, and by forces which they had often baffled and despised; the subject becomes more curious, and its explanation more difficult.

. . .

Section III.
Of Relaxations in the National Spirit Incident to Polished Nations

Improving nations, in the course of their advancement, have to struggle with foreign enemies, to whom they bear an extreme animosity, and with whom, in many conflicts, they contend for their existence as a people. In certain periods too, they feel in their domestic policy inconveniences and grievances, which beget an eager impatience; and they apprehend reformations and new establishments, from which they have sanguine hopes of national happiness. In early ages, every art is imperfect, and susceptible of many improvements. The first principles of every science are yet secrets to be discovered, and to be successively published with applause and triumph.

We may fancy to ourselves, that in ages of progress, the human race, like scouts gone abroad on the discovery of fertile lands, having the world open before them, are presented at every step with the appearance of novelty. They enter on every new ground with expectation and joy: They engage in every enterprise with the ardor of men, who believe they are going to arrive at national felicity, and permanent glory; and forget past disappointments amidst the hopes of future success. From mere ignorance, rude minds are intoxicated with every passion; and partial to their own condition, and to their own pursuits, they think that every scene is inferior to that in which they are placed. Roused alike by success, and by misfortune, they are sanguine, ardent, and precipitant; and leave to the more knowing ages which succeed them, monuments of imperfect skill, and of rude execution in every art; but they leave likewise the marks of a vigorous and ardent spirit, which their successors are not always qualified to sustain, or to imitate.

This may be admitted, perhaps, as a fair description of prosperous societies, at least during certain periods of their progress. The spirit with which they advance may be unequal, in different ages, and may have its paroxysms, and intermissions, arising from the inconstancy of human passions, and from the casual appearance or removal of occasions that excite them. But does this spirit, which for a time continues to carry on the project of civil and commercial arts, find a natural pause in the termination of its own pursuits? May the business of civil society be accomplished, and may the occasion of farther exertion be removed? Do continued disappointments reduce sanguine hopes, and familiarity with objects blunt the edge of novelty? Does experience itself cool the ardor of the mind? May the society be again compared to the individual? And may it be suspected, although the vigor of a nation, like that of a natural body, does not waste by a physical decay, that yet it may sicken for want of exercise, and die in the close of its own exertions? May societies, in the completion of all their designs, like men in years, who disregard the amusements, and are insensible to the passions, of youth, become cold and indifferent to objects that used to animate in a ruder age? And may a polished community be compared to a man, who having executed his plan, built his house, and made his settlement; who having, in short, exhausted the charms of every subject, and wasted all his ardor, sinks into languor and listless indifference? If so, we have found at least another simile to our purpose. But it is probable, that here too, the resemblance is imperfect; and the inference that would follow, like that of most arguments drawn from analogy, tends rather to amuse the fancy, than to give any real information on the subject to which it refers.

The materials of human art are never entirely exhausted, and the applications of industry are never at an end. The national ardor is not, at any particular time, proportioned to the occasion there is for activity; nor curiosity, to the extent of subject that remains to be studied.

. . .

Among the occupations that may be enumerated, as tending to exercise the invention, and to cultivate the talents of men, are the pursuits of accommodation and wealth, including all the different contrivances which serve to increase manufactures, and to perfect the mechanical arts. But it must be owned, that as the materials of commerce may continue to be accumulated without any determinate limit, so the arts which are applied to improve them, may admit of perpetual refinements. No measure of fortune, or degree of skill, is found to diminish the supposed necessities of human life, refinement and plenty foster new desires, while they furnish the means, or practice the methods, to gratify them.

. . .

The commercial and lucrative arts may continue to prosper, but they gain an ascendant at the expense of other pursuits. The desire to profit stifles the love of perfection. Interest cools the imagination, and hardens the heart; and, recommending employments in proportion as they are lucrative, and certain in their gains, it drives ingenuity, and ambition itself, to the counter and the workshop.

But apart from these considerations, the separation of professions, while it seems to promise improvement of skill, and is actually the cause why the productions of every art become more perfect as commerce advances; yet in its termination, and ultimate effects, serves, in some measure, to break the bands of society, to substitute form[2] in place of ingenuity, and to withdraw individuals from the common sense of occupation, on which the sentiments of the heart, and the mind, are most happily employed.

Under the *distinction* of callings, by which the members of polished society are separated from each other, every individual is supposed to possess his species of talent, or his peculiar skill, in which the others are confessedly ignorant; and society is made to consist of parts, of which none is animated with the spirit of society itself.[3] "We see in the same persons," said Pericles, "an equal attention to private and to public affairs; and in men who have turned to separate professions, a competent knowledge of what relates to the community; for we alone consider those who are inattentive to the state, as perfectly insignificant." This encomium on the Athenians, was probably offered under an apprehension, that the contrary was likely to be charged by their enemies, or might soon take place. It happened accordingly, that the business of state, as well as of war, came to be worse administered at Athens, when these, as well as other applications, became the objects of separate professions, and the history of this people abundantly showed, that men ceased to be citizens, even to be good poets and orators, in proportion as they came to be distinguished by the profession of these, and other separate crafts.

Animals less honored than we, have sagacity enough to procure their food, and to find the means of their solitary pleasures; but it is reserved for man to consult, to persuade, to oppose, to kindle in the society of his fellow creatures, and to lose the sense of his personal interest or safety, in the ardor of his friendships and his oppositions.

When we are involved in any of the divisions into which mankind are separated, under the denominations of a country, a tribe, or an order of men any way affected by common interests, and guided by communicating passions, the mind recognizes its natural station; the sentiments of the heart, and the talents of the understanding, find their natural exercise. Wisdom, vigilance, fidelity, and fortitude, are the characters requisite in such a sense, and the qualities which it tends to improve.

In simple or barbarous ages, when nations are weak, and beset with enemies, the love of a country, of a party, or a faction, are the same. The public is a knot of friends, and its enemies are the rest of mankind. Death, or slavery, are the ordinary evils which they are concerned to ward off; victory and dominion, the objects to which they aspire. Under the sense of what they may suffer from foreign invasions, it is one object, in every prosperous society, to increase its force, and to extend its limits. In proportion as this object is gained, security increases. They who possess the interior districts, remote from the frontier, are unused to alarms from abroad. They who are placed on the extremities, remote from the seats of government, are unused to hear of political interests; and the public becomes an object perhaps too extensive, for the conceptions of either. They enjoy the protection of

2. From the 1768 edition: "substitute mere forms and rules of art."
3. From the 1768 edition: "with the spirit that ought to prevail in the conduct of nations."

its laws, or of its armies; and they boast of its splendor, and its power; but the glowing sentiments of public affection, which, in small states, mingle with the tenderness of the parent and the lover, of the friend and the companion, merely by having their object enlarged, lose great part of their force.

The manners of rude nations require to be reformed. Their foreign quarrels, and domestic dissensions, are the operations of extreme and sanguinary passions. A state of greater tranquility hath many happy effects. But if nations pursue the plan of enlargement and pacification, till their members can no longer apprehend the common ties of society, nor be engaged by affection in the cause of their country, they must err on the opposite side, and by leaving too little to agitate the spirits of men, bring on ages of languor, if not of decay.

The members of a community may, in this manner, like the inhabitants of a conquered province, be made to lose the sense of every connection, but that of kindred or neighborhood; and have no common affairs to transact, but those of trade: Connections, indeed, or transactions, in which probity and friendship may still take place; but in which the national spirit, whose ebbs and flows we are now considering, cannot be exerted.

. . .

Whatever be the national extent, civil order, and regular government, are advantages of the greatest importance; but it does not follow, that every arrangement made to obtain these ends, and which may, in the making, exercise and cultivate the best qualities of men, is therefore of a nature to produce permanent effects, and to secure the preservation of that national spirit from which it arose.

We have reason to dread the political refinements of ordinary men, when we consider, that repose, or inaction itself, is in a great measure their object; and that they would frequently model their governments, not merely to prevent injustice and error, but to prevent agitation and bustle; and by the barriers they raise against the evil actions of men, would prevent them from acting at all. Every dispute of a free people, in the opinion of such politicians, amounts to disorder, and a breach of the national peace. What heart-burnings? What delay to affairs? What want of secrecy and dispatch? What defect of police? Men of superior genius sometimes seem to imagine, that the vulgar have no title to act, or to think. A great prince is pleased to ridicule the precaution by which judges in a free country are confined to the strict interpretation of law.[4]

We easily learn to contract our opinions of what men may, in consistence with public order, be safely permitted to do. The agitations of a republic, and the license of its members, strike the subjects of monarchy with aversion and disgust. The freedom with which the European is left to traverse the streets and the fields, would appear to a Chinese a sure prelude to confusion and anarchy. "Can men behold their superior and not tremble? Can they converse without a precise and written ceremonial? What hopes of peace, if the streets are not barricaded at an

---

4. [Frederick the Great,] *Memoirs of Brandenburg* [English translation 1752].

hour? What wild disorder, if men are permitted in any thing to do what they please?"

If the precautions which men thus take against each other be necessary to repress their crimes, and do not arise from a corrupt ambition, or from cruel jealousy in their rulers, the proceeding itself must be applauded, as the best remedy of which the vices of men will admit. The viper must be held at a distance, and the tiger chained. But if a rigorous policy, applied to enslave, not to restrain from crimes, has an actual tendency to corrupt the manners, and to extinguish the spirit of nations; if its severities be applied to terminate the agitations of a free people, not to remedy their corruptions; if forms be often applauded as salutary, because they tend merely to silence the voice of mankind, or be condemned as pernicious, because they allow this voice to be heard; we may expect that many of the boasted improvements of civil society, will be mere devices to lay the political spirit at rest, and will chain up the active virtues more than the restless disorders of men.

If to any people it be the avowed object of policy, in all its internal refinements, to secure the person and the property of the subject, without any regard to his political character, the constitution indeed may be free, but its members may likewise become unworthy of the freedom they possess, and unfit to preserve it. The effects of such a constitution may be to immerse all orders of men in their separate pursuits of pleasure, which they may now enjoy with little disturbance; or of gain, which they may preserve without any attention to the commonwealth.

If this be the end of political struggles, the design, when executed, in securing to the individual his estate, and the means of subsistence, may put an end to the exercise of those very virtues that were required in conducting its execution. A man who, in concert with his fellow subjects, contends with usurpation in defense of his estate or his person, may find an exertion of great generosity, and of a vigorous spirit; but he who, under political establishments, supposed to be fully confirmed, betakes him, because he is safe, to the mere enjoyment of fortune, has in fact turned to a source of corruption the very advantages which the virtues of the other procured. Individuals, in certain ages, derive their protection chiefly from the strength of the party to which they adhere; but in times of corruption, they flatter themselves, that they may continue to derive from the public that safety which, in former ages, they must have owed to their own vigilance and spirit, to the warm attachment of their friends, and to the exercise of every talent which could render them respected, feared, or beloved. In one period, therefore, mere circumstances serve to excite the spirit, and to preserve the manners of men; in another, great wisdom and zeal for the good of mankind on the part of their leaders, are required for the same purposes.

. . .

The dangers to liberty are not the subject of our present consideration; but they can never be greater from any cause than they are from the supposed remissness of a people, to whose personal vigor every constitution, as it owed its establishment, so must continue to owe its preservation. Nor is this blessing ever less secure than it is in the possession of men who think that they enjoy it in safety, and who therefore consider the public only as it presents to their avarice a number of lucrative employments; for the sake of which they may sacrifice those very rights which render themselves objects of management or consideration.

From the tendency of these reflections, then, it should appear, that a national spirit is frequently transient, not on account of any incurable distemper in the nature of mankind, but on account of their voluntary neglects and corruptions. This spirit subsisted solely, perhaps, in the execution of a few projects, entered into for the acquisition of territory or wealth; it comes, like a useless weapon, to be laid aside after its end is attained.

Ordinary establishments terminate in a relaxation of vigor, and are ineffectual to the preservation of states; because they lead mankind to rely on their arts, instead of their virtues, and to mistake for an improvement of human nature, a mere accession of accommodation, or of riches.[5] Institutions that fortify the mind, inspire courage, and promote national felicity, can never tend to national ruin.

Is it not possible, amidst our admiration of arts, to find some place for these? Let statesmen, who are entrusted with the government of nations, reply for themselves. It is their business to shew, whether they climb into stations of eminence, merely to display a passion for interest, which they had better indulge in obscurity; and whether they have capacity to understand the happiness of a people, the conduct of whose affairs they are so willing to undertake.

Section IV.
The Same Subject Continued

Men frequently, while they study to improve their fortunes,[6] neglect themselves; and while they reason for their country, forget the considerations that most deserve their attention. Numbers, riches, and the other resources of war, are highly important: but nations consist of men; and a nation consisting of degenerate and cowardly men, is weak; a nation consisting of vigorous, public-spirited, and resolute men, is strong. The resources of war, where other advantages are equal, may decide a contest; but the resources of war, in hands that cannot employ them, are of no avail.

Virtue is a necessary constituent of national strength: capacity, and a vigorous understanding, are no less necessary to sustain the fortune of states. Both are improved by discipline, and by the exercises in which men are engaged. We

5. New footnote from the 1768 edition: "Adeo is quae laboramus sola crevimus Divitis luxuriamque. [So strictly has our growth been limited to the only things for which we strive, wealth and luxury] Liv[y]. lib. vii. c. 25."

6. From the 1768 edition: "while they are engaged in what is accounted the most selfish of all pursuits, the improvement of fortune, then most."

despise, or we pity, the lot of mankind, while they lived under uncertain establishments, and were obliged to sustain in the same person, the character of the senator, the statesman, and the soldier. Polished nations[7] discover, that any one of these characters is sufficient in one person; and that the ends of each, when disjoined, are more easily accomplished. The first, however, were circumstances under which nations advanced and prospered; the second were those in which the spirit relaxed, and the nation went to decay.

We may, with good reason, congratulate our species on their having escaped from a state of barbarous disorder and violence, into a state of domestic peace and regular policy; when they have sheathed the dagger, and disarmed the animosities of civil contention; when the weapons with which they contend are the reasonings of the wise, and the tongue of the eloquent. But we cannot, meantime, help to regret, that they should ever proceed, in search of perfection, to place every branch of administration behind the counter, and come to employ, instead of the statesman and warrior, the mere clerk and accountant.

By carrying this system to its height, men are educated, who could copy for Caesar his military instructions, or even execute a part of his plans; but none who could act in all the different scenes for which the leader himself must be qualified, in the state and in the field, in times of order or of tumult, in times of division or of unanimity; none who could animate the council when deliberating on ordinary occasions, or when alarmed by attacks from abroad.

The policy of China is the most perfect model of an arrangement, at which the ordinary refinements of government are aimed; and the inhabitants of this empire possess, in the highest degree, those arts on which vulgar minds make the felicity and greatness of nations to depend. The state has acquired, in a measure unequaled in the history of mankind, numbers of men, and the other resources of war. They have done what we are very apt to admire; they have brought national affairs to the level of the meanest capacity; they have broken them into parts, and thrown them into separate departments; they have clothed every proceeding with splendid ceremonies, and majestical forms; and where the reverence of forms cannot repress disorder, a rigorous and severe police, armed with every species of corporal punishment, is applied to the purpose. The whip, and the cudgel, are held up to all orders of men; they are at once employed, and they are dreaded by every magistrate. A mandarin is whipped, for having ordered a pickpocket to receive too few or too many blows.

Every department of state is made the object of a separate profession, and every candidate for office must have passed through a regular education; and, as in the graduations of the university, must have obtained by his proficiency, or his standing, the degree to which he aspires. The tribunals of state, of war, and of the revenue, as well as of literature, are conducted by graduates in their different studies: but while learning is the great road to preferment, it terminates, in being able to

7. From the 1768 edition: "Commercial nations."

read, and to write; and the great object of government consists in raising, and in consuming the fruits of the earth. With all these resources, and this learned preparation, which is made to turn these resources to use, the state is in reality weak; has repeatedly given the example which we seek to explain; and among the doctors of war or of policy, among the millions who are set apart for the military profession, can find none of its members who are fit to stand forth in the dangers of their country, or to form a defense against the repeated inroads of an enemy reputed to be artless and mean.

It is difficult to tell how long the decay of states might be suspended by the cultivation of arts on which their real felicity and strength depend; by cultivating in the higher ranks those talents for the council and the field, which cannot, without great disadvantage, be separated; and in the body of a people, that zeal for their country, and that military character, which enable them to take a share in defending its rights.

Times may come, when every proprietor must defend his own possessions, and every free people maintain their own independence. We may imagine, that against such an extremity, an army of hired troops is a sufficient precaution; but their own troops are the very enemy against which a people is sometimes obliged to fight. We may flatter ourselves, that extremities of this sort, in any particular case, are remote; but we cannot, in reasoning on the general fortunes of mankind, avoid putting the case, and referring to the examples in which it has happened. It has happened in every instance where the polished have fallen a prey to the rude, and where the pacific inhabitant has been reduced to subjection by military force.

. . .

The subdivision of arts and professions, in certain examples, tends to improve the practice of them, and to promote their ends. By having separated the arts of the clothier and the tanner, we are the better supplied with shoes and with cloth. But to separate the arts which form the citizen and the statesman, the arts of policy and war, is an attempt to dismember the human character, and to destroy those very arts we mean to improve. By this separation, we in effect deprive a free people of what is necessary to their safety; or we prepare a defense against invasions from abroad, which gives a prospect of usurpation, and threatens the establishment of military government at home.

We may be surprised to find the beginning of certain military instructions at Rome, referred to a time no earlier than that of the Cimbric War. It was then, we are told by Valerius Maximus, that Roman soldiers were made to learn from gladiators the use of a sword: and the antagonists of Phyrrhus and of Hannibal were, by the account of this writer, still in need of instruction in the first rudiments of their trade. They had already, by the order and chance of their encampments, impressed the Grecian invader with awe and respect; they had already, not by their victories, but by their national vigor and firmness, under repeated defeats, induced him to sue for peace. But the haughty Roman, perhaps, knew the advantage of order and of union, without having been broke to the inferior arts of the mercenary soldier; and had the courage to face the enemies of his country, without having practiced the use of his weapon under the fear of being whipped. He could ill be persuaded, that a time might come, when refined and intelligent nations would make the art of war to consist in a few technical forms; that citizens and soldiers might come to be distinguished as much as women and men; that the citizen would become possessed of a property which he would not be able, or required, to defend; that the soldier would be appointed to keep for another what he would be taught to desire, and what he would be enabled to seize for himself; that, in short, one set of men were to have an interest in the preservation of civil establishments, without the power to defend them; that the other were to have this power, without either the inclination or the interest.

This people, however, by degrees came to put their military force on the very footing to which this description alludes. Marius made a capital change in the manner of levying soldiers at Rome: He filled his legions with the mean and the indigent, who depended on military pay for subsistence; he created a force which rested on mere discipline alone, and the skill of the gladiator; he taught his troops to employ their swords against the constitution of their country, and set the example of a practice which was soon adopted and improved by his successors.

The Romans only meant by their armies to encroach on the freedom of other nations, while they preserved their own. They forgot, that in assembling soldiers of fortune, and in suffering any leader to be master of a disciplined army, they actually resigned their political rights, and suffered a master to arise for the state. This people, in short, whose ruling passion was depredations and conquest, perished by the recoil of an engine which they themselves had erected against mankind.

The boasted refinements, then, of the polished age, are not divested of danger. They open a door, perhaps, to disaster, as wide and accessible as any of those they have shut. If they build walls and ramparts, they enervate the minds of those who are placed to defend them; if they form disciplined armies, they reduce the military spirit of entire nations; and by placing the sword where they have given a distaste to civil establishments, they prepare for mankind the government of force.

· · ·

If men must go wrong, there is a choice of their very errors, as well as of their virtues. Ambition, the love of personal eminence, and the desire of fame, although they sometimes lead to the commission of crimes, yet always engage men in pursuits that require to be supported by some of the greatest qualities of the human soul; and if eminence is the principal object of pursuit, there is, at least, a probability, that those qualities may be studied on which a real elevation of mind is raised. But when public alarms have ceased, and contempt of glory is recommended as an article of wisdom, the sordid habits, and mercenary dispositions, to which, under a general indifference to national objects, the members of a polished or commercial state are exposed, must prove at once the most effectual suppression of every liberal sentiment, and the most fatal reverse of all those principles from which communities derive their hopes of preservation, and their strength.

It is noble to possess happiness and independence, either in retirement, or in public life. The characteristic of the happy, is to acquit themselves well in every condition; in the court, or in the village; in the senate, or in the private retreat. But if they affect any particular station, it is surely that in which their actions may be rendered most extensively useful. Our considering mere retirement, therefore, as a symptom of moderation, and of virtue, is either a remnant of that system, under which monks and anchorets, in former ages, have been canonized; or proceeds from a habit of thinking, which appears equally fraught with moral corruption, from our considering public life as a scene for the gratification of mere vanity, avarice, and ambition; never as furnishing the best opportunity for a just and a happy engagement of the mind and the heart.

Emulation, and the desire of power, are but sorry motives to public conduct; but if they have been, in any case, the principal inducements from which men have taken part in the service of their country, any diminution of their prevalence or force is a real corruption of national manners; and the pretended moderation assumed by the higher orders of men, has a fatal effect in the state. The disinterested love of the public, is a principle without which some constitutions of government cannot subsist: but when we consider how seldom this has appeared a reigning passion, we have little reason to impute the prosperity or preservation of nations, in every case, to its influence.

It is sufficient, perhaps, under one form of government, that men should be fond of their independence; that they should be ready to oppose usurpation, and to repel personal indignities: under another, it is sufficient, that they should be tenacious of their rank, and of their honors; and instead of a zeal for the public, entertain a vigilant jealousy of the rights which pertain to themselves. When numbers of men retain a certain degree of elevation and fortitude, they are qualified to give a mutual check to their several errors, and are able to act in that variety of situations which the different constitutions of government have prepared for their members: but, under the disadvantages of a feeble spirit, however directed, and however informed, no national constitution is safe; nor can any degree of enlargement to which a state has arrived, secure its political welfare.

In states where property, distinction, and pleasure, are thrown out as baits to the imagination, and incentives to passion, the public seems to rely for the preservation of its political life, on the degree of emulation and jealousy with which parties mutually oppose and restrain each other. The desires of preferment and profit in the breast of the citizen, are the motives from which he is excited to enter on public affairs, and are the considerations which direct his political conduct. The suppression, therefore, of ambition, of party-animosity, and of public envy, is probably, in every such case, not a reformation, but a symptom of weakness, and a prelude to more sordid pursuits, and ruinous amusements.

On the eve of such a revolution in manners, the higher ranks, in every mixed or monarchical government, have need to take care of themselves. Men of business, and of industry, in the inferior stations of life, retain their occupations, and are secured, by a kind of necessity, in the possession of those habits on which they rely for their quiet, and for the moderate enjoyments of life. But the higher orders of men, if they relinquish the state, if they cease to possess that courage and elevation of mind, and to exercise those talents which are employed in its defense, and its government, are, in reality, by the seeming advantages of their station, become the refuse of that society of which they once were the ornament; and from being the most respectable, and the most happy, of its members, are become the most wretched and corrupt. In their approach to this condition, and in the absence of every manly occupation, they feel a dissatisfaction and languor which they cannot explain: They pine in the midst of apparent enjoyments; or, by the variety and caprice of their different pursuits and amusements, exhibit a state of agitation, which, like the disquiet of sickness, is not a proof of enjoyment or pleasure, but of suffering and pain. The care of his buildings, his equipage, or his table, is chosen by one; literary amusement, or some frivolous study, by another. The sports of the country, and the diversions of the town; the gaming-table,[8] dogs, horses, and wine, are employed to fill up the blank of a listless and unprofitable life. They speak of human pursuits, as if the whole difficulty were to find something to do: They fix on some frivolous occupation, as if there were nothing that deserved to be done: They consider what tends to the good of their fellow creatures, as a disadvantage to themselves: They fly from every scene, in which any efforts of vigor are required, or in which they might be allured to perform any service to their country. We misapply our compassion in pitying the poor; it were much more justly applied to the rich, who become the first victims of that wretched insignificance, into which the members of every corrupted state, by the tendency of their weaknesses, and their vices, are in haste to plunge themselves.

It is in this condition, that the sensual invent all those refinements on pleasure, and devise those incentives to a satiated appetite, which tend to foster the corruptions of a dissolute age. The effects of brutal appetite, and the mere debauch, are more flagrant, and more violent, perhaps, in rude ages, than they are in the later periods of commerce and luxury: but that perpetual habit of searching for animal pleasure where it is not to be found, in the gratifications of an appetite that is cloyed, and among the ruins of an animal constitution, is not more fatal to the virtues of the soul, than it is even to the enjoyment of sloth, or of pleasure; it is not a more certain avocation from public affairs, or a surer prelude to national decay, than it is a disappointment to our hopes of private felicity.

[1767]

8. These different occupations differ from each other, in respect to their dignity, and their innocence; but none of them are the schools from which men are brought to sustain the tottering fortune of nations; they are equally avocations from what ought to be the principal pursuit of man, the good of mankind.

from *Rights of Man*

OF SOCIETY AND CIVILIZATION

Great part of that order which reigns among mankind is not the effect of government. It has its origin in the principles of society and the natural constitution of man. It existed prior to government, and would exist if the formality of government was abolished. The mutual dependence and reciprocal interest which man has upon man, and all the parts of a civilized community upon each other, create that great chain of connection which holds it together. The landholder, the farmer, the manufacturer, the merchant, the tradesman, and every occupation, prospers by the aid which each receives from the other, and from the whole. Common interest regulates their concerns, and forms their law; and the laws which common usage ordains, have a greater influence than the laws of government. In fine, society performs for itself almost everything which is ascribed to government.

To understand the nature and quantity of government proper for man, it is necessary to attend to his character. As Nature created him for social life, she fitted him for the station she intended. In all cases she made his natural wants greater than his individual powers. No one man is capable, without the aid of society, of supplying his own wants; and those wants, acting upon every individual, impel the whole of them into society, as naturally as gravitation acts to a center.

But she has gone further. She has not only forced man into society, by a diversity of wants, which the reciprocal aid of each other can supply, but she has implanted in him a system of social affections, which, though not necessary to his existence, are essential to his happiness. There is no period in life when this love for society ceases to act. It begins and ends with our being.

If we examine, with attention, into the composition and constitution of man, the diversity of his wants, and the diversity of talents in different men for reciprocally accommodating the wants of each other, his propensity to society, and consequently to preserve the advantages resulting from it, we shall easily discover, that a great part of what is called government is mere imposition.

Government is no farther necessary than to supply the few cases to which society and civilization are not conveniently competent; and instances are not wanting to show, that everything which government can usefully add thereto, has been performed by the common consent of society, without government.

For upwards of two years from the commencement of the American war, and to a longer period in several of the American States, there were no established forms of government. The old governments had been abolished, and the country was too much occupied in defense, to employ its attention in establishing new governments; yet during this interval, order and harmony were preserved as inviolate as in any country in Europe. There is a natural aptness in man, and more so in society, because it embraces a greater variety of abilities and resource, to accommodate itself to whatever situation it is in. The instant formal government is abolished, society begins to act. A general association takes place, and common interest produces common security.

So far it is from being true, as has been pretended, that the abolition of any formal government is the dissolution of society, that it acts by a contrary impulse, and brings the latter the closer together. All that part of its organization which it had committed to its government, devolves again upon itself, and acts through its medium. When men, as well from natural instinct, as from reciprocal benefits, have habituated themselves to social and civilized life, there is always enough of its principles in practice to carry them through any changes they may find necessary or convenient to make in their government. In short, man is so naturally a creature of society, that it is almost impossible to put him out of it.

Formal government makes but a small part of civilized life; and when even the best that human wisdom can devise is established, it is a thing more in name and idea, than in fact. It is to the great and fundamental principles of society and civilization—to the common usage universally consented to, and mutually and reciprocally maintained—to the unceasing circulation of interest, which, passing through its million channels, invigorates the whole mass of civilized man—it is to these things, infinitely more than to anything which even the best instituted government can perform, that the safety and prosperity of the individual and of the whole depends.

The more perfect civilization is, the less occasion has it for government, because the more does it regulate its own affairs, and govern itself; but so contrary is the practice of old governments to the reason of the case, that the expenses of them increase in the proportion they ought to diminish. It is but few general laws that civilized life requires, and those of such common usefulness, that whether they are enforced by the forms of government or not, the effect will be nearly the same. If we consider what the principles are that first condense men into society, and what the motives that regulate their mutual intercourse afterwards, we shall find, by the time we arrive at what is called government, that nearly the whole of the business is performed by the natural operation of the parts upon each other.

Man, with respect to all those matters, is more a creature of consistency than he is aware, or than governments would wish him to believe. All the great laws of society are laws of nature. Those of trade and commerce, whether with respect to the intercourse of individuals, or of nations, are laws of mutual and reciprocal interest. They are followed and obeyed, because it is the interest of the parties so to do, and not on account of any formal laws their governments may impose or interpose.

But how often is the natural propensity to society disturbed or destroyed by the operations of government! When the latter, instead of being ingrafted on the principles of the former, assumes to exist for itself, and acts by partialities of favor and oppression, it becomes the cause of the mischiefs it ought to prevent.

If we look back to the riots and tumults, which at various times have happened in England, we shall find, that they did not proceed from the want of a government, but that government was itself the generating cause; instead of consolidating society it divided it; it deprived it of its natural cohesion, and engendered discontents and disorders, which otherwise would not have existed. In those associations which men promiscuously form for the purpose of trade, or of any concern, in which government is totally out of the question, and in which they act merely on the principles of society, we see how naturally the various parties unite; and this shows, by comparison, that governments, so far from being always the cause or means of order, are often the destruction of it. The riots of 1780 had no other source than the remains of those prejudices, which the government itself had encouraged. But with respect to England there are also other causes.

Excess and inequality of taxation, however disguised in the means, never fail to appear in their effects. As a great mass of the community are thrown thereby into poverty and discontent, they are constantly on the brink of commotion; and deprived, as they unfortunately are, of the means of information, are easily heated to outrage. Whatever the apparent cause of any riots may be, the real one is always want of happiness. It shows that something is wrong in the system of government, that injures the felicity by which society is to be preserved.

But as fact is superior to reasoning, the instance of America presents itself to confirm these observations.—If there is a country in the world, where concord, according to common calculation, would be least expected, it is America. Made up, as it is, of people from different nations,[1] accustomed to different forms and habits of government, speaking different languages, and more different in their modes of

1. That part of America which is generally called New England, including New Hampshire, Massachusetts, Rhode Island, and Connecticut, is peopled chiefly by English descendants. In the state of New York, about half are Dutch, the rest English, Scottish, and Irish. In New Jersey, a mixture of English and Dutch, with some Scottish and Irish. In Pennsylvania, about one third are English, another Germans, and the remainder Scottish and Irish, with some Swedes. The States to the southward have a greater proportion of English than the middle States, but in all of them there is a mixture; and besides those enumerated, there are a considerable number of French, and some few of all the European nations lying on the coast. The most numerous religious denomination are the Presbyterians; but no one sect is established above another, and all men are equally citizens.

worship, it would appear that the union of such a people was impracticable; but by the simple operation of constructing government on the principles of society and the rights of man, every difficulty retires, and all the parts are brought into cordial unison. There, the poor are not oppressed, the rich are not privileged. Industry is not mortified by the splendid extravagance of a court rioting at its expense. Their taxes are few, because their government is just; and as there is nothing to render them wretched, there is nothing to engender riots and tumults.

A metaphysical man, like Mr Burke, would have tortured his invention to discover how such a people could be governed. He would have supposed that some must be managed by fraud, others by force, and all by some contrivance; that genius must be hired to impose upon ignorance, and show and parade to fascinate the vulgar. Lost in the abundance of his researches, he would have resolved and re-resolved, and finally overlooked the plain and easy road that lay directly before him.

One of the great advantages of the American Revolution has been, that it led to a discovery of the principles, and laid open the imposition, of governments. All the revolutions till then had been worked within the atmosphere of a court, and never on the great floor of a nation. The parties were always of the class of courtiers; and whatever was their rage for reformation, they carefully preserved the fraud of the profession.

In all cases they took care to represent government as a thing made up of mysteries, which only themselves understood; and they hid from the understanding of the nation, the only thing that was beneficial to know, namely, *That government is nothing more than a national association acting on the principles of society.*

Having thus endeavored to show, that the social and civilized state of man is capable of performing within itself, almost everything necessary to its protection and government, it will be proper, on the other hand, to take a review of the present old governments, and examine whether their principles and practice are correspondent thereto.

. . .

WAYS AND MEANS
of improving the condition of Europe, interspersed with Miscellaneous Observations

In contemplating a subject that embraces with equatorial magnitude the whole region of humanity, it is impossible to confine the pursuit in one single direction. It takes ground on every character and condition that appertains to man, and blends the individual, the nation, and the world.

From a small spark, kindled in America, a flame has arisen, not to be extinguished. Without consuming, like the *Ultima Ratio Regum,* it winds its progress from nation to nation, and conquers by a silent operation. Man finds himself changed, he scarcely perceives how. He acquires a knowledge of his rights by attending justly to his interest, and discovers in the event that the strength and powers of despotism consist wholly in the fear of resisting it, and that, in order *"to be free, it is sufficient that he wills it."*

Having in all the preceding parts of this work endeavored to establish a system of principles as a basis, on which governments ought to be erected, I shall proceed in this, to the ways and means of rendering them into practice. But in order to introduce this part of the subject with more propriety, and stronger effect, some preliminary observation, deducible from, or connected with, those principles, are necessary.

Whatever the form or constitution of government may be, it ought to have no other object than the *general* happiness. When, instead of this, it operates to create and increase wretchedness in any of the parts of society, it is on a wrong system, and reformation is necessary.

Customary language has classed the condition of man under the two descriptions of civilized and uncivilized life. To the one it has ascribed felicity and affluence; to the other hardship and want. But however our imagination may be impressed by painting and comparison, it is nevertheless true, that a great portion of mankind, in what are called civilized countries, are in a state of poverty and wretchedness, far below the condition of an Indian. I speak not of one country, but of all. It is so in England, it is so all over Europe. Let us enquire into the cause.

It lies not in any natural defect in the principles of civilization, but in preventing those principles having a universal operation; the consequence of which is, a perpetual system of war and expense, that drains the country, and defeats the general felicity of which civilization is capable.

All the European governments (France now excepted) are constructed not on the principle of universal civilization, on the reverse of it. So far as those governments relate to each other, they are in the same condition as we conceive of savage uncivilized life; they put themselves beyond the law as well of GOD as of man, and are, with respect to principle and reciprocal conduct, like so many individuals in a state of nature.

The inhabitants of every country, under the civilization of laws, easily civilize together, but governments being yet in an uncivilized state, and almost continually at war, they pervert the abundance which civilized life produces to carry on the uncivilized part to a greater extent. By thus engrafting the barbarism of government upon the internal civilization of a country, it draws from the latter, and more especially from the poor, a great portion of those earnings, which should be applied to their own subsistence and comfort.—Apart from all reflections of morality and philosophy, it is a melancholy fact, that more than one fourth of the labor of mankind is annually consumed by this barbarous system.

What has served to continue this evil, is the pecuniary advantage which all the governments of Europe have found in keeping up this state of uncivilization. It affords to them pretenses for power, and revenue, for which there would be neither occasion nor apology, if the circle of civilization were rendered complete. Civil government alone, or the government of laws, is not productive of pretenses for many taxes; it operates at home, directly under the eye of the country, and precludes the possibility of much imposition. But when the scene is laid in the uncivilized contention of governments, the field of pretenses is enlarged, and the country, being no longer a judge, is open to every imposition, which governments please to act.

Not a thirtieth, scarcely a fortieth, part of the taxes which are raised in England are either occasioned by, or applied to, the purposes of civil government. It is not difficult to see, that the whole which the actual government does in this respect, is to enact laws, and that the country administers and executes them, at its own expense, by means of magistrates, juries, sessions, and assize, over and above the taxes which it pays.

In this view of the case, we have two distinct characters of government; the one the civil government, or the government of laws, which operates at home, the other the court or cabinet government, which operates abroad, on the rude plan of uncivilized life; the one attended with little charge, the other with boundless extravagance; and so distinct are the two, that if the latter were to sink, as it were by a sudden opening of the earth, and totally disappear, the former would not be deranged. It would still proceed, because it is the common interest of the nation that it should, and all the means are in practice.

Revolutions, then, have for their object, a change in the moral condition of governments, and with this change the burden of public taxes will lessen, and civilization will be left to the enjoyment of that abundance, of which it is now deprived.

In contemplating the whole of this subject, I extend my views into the department of commerce. In all my publications, where the matter would admit, I have been an advocate for commerce, because I am a friend to its effects. It is a pacific system, operating to cordialize mankind, by rendering nations, as well as individuals, useful to each other. As to mere theoretical reformation, I have never preached it up. The most effectual process is that of improving the condition of man by means of his interest; and it is on this ground that I take my stand.

If commerce were permitted to act to the universal extent it is capable, it would extirpate the system of war, and produce a revolution in the uncivilized state of governments. The invention of commerce has arisen since those governments began, and is the greatest approach towards universal civilization, that has yet been made by any means not immediately flowing from moral principles.

Whatever has a tendency to promote the civil intercourse of nations, by an exchange of benefits, is a subject as worthy of philosophy as of politics. Commerce is no other than the traffic of two individuals, multiplied on a scale of numbers; and by the same rule that nature intended the intercourse of two, she intended that of all. For this purpose she has distributed the materials of manufactures and commerce, in various and distant parts of a nation and of the world; and as they cannot be procured by war so cheaply or so commodiously as by commerce, she has rendered the latter the means of extirpating the former.

As the two are nearly the opposites of each other, consequently, the uncivilized state of European governments is injurious to commerce. Every kind of destruction or embarrassment serves to lessen the quantity, and it matters but little in what part of the commercial world the reduction begins. Like blood, it cannot be taken from any of the parts, without being taken from the whole mass in circulation, and all partake of the loss. When the ability in any nation to buy is destroyed, it equally involves the seller. Could the government of England destroy the commerce of all other nations, she would most effectually ruin her own.

It is possible that a nation may be the carrier for the world, but she cannot be the merchant. She cannot be the seller and the buyer of her own merchandize. The ability to buy must reside out of herself; and, therefore, the prosperity of any commercial nation is regulated by the prosperity of the rest. If they are poor she cannot be rich, and her condition, be it what it may, is an index of the height of the commercial tide in other nations.

[1791]

The Federalist, No. 10

To the People of the State of New York:

Among the numerous advantages promised by a well constructed Union, none deserve to be more accurately developed than its tendency to break and control the violence of faction. The friend of popular governments never finds himself so much alarmed for their character and fate, as when he contemplates their propensity to this dangerous vice. He will not fail, therefore, to set a due value on any plan which, without violating the principles to which he is attached, provides a proper cure for it.

The instability, injustice, and confusion introduced into the public councils, have, in truth, been the mortal diseases under which popular governments have ever here perished; as they continue to be the favorite and fruitful topics from which the adversaries to liberty derive their most specious declamations.

The valuable improvements made by the American constitutions on the popular models, both ancient and modern, cannot certainly be too much admired; but it would be an unwarrantable partiality, to contend that they have as effectually obviated the danger on this side, as was wished and expected. Complaints are everywhere heard from our most considerate and virtuous citizens, equally the friends of public and private faith, and of public and personal liberty, that our governments are too unstable, that the public good is disregarded in the conflicts of rival parties, and that the measures are too often decided, not according to the rules of justice and the rights of the minor party, but by the superior force of an interested and overbearing majority.

However anxiously we may wish that these complaints had no foundation, the evidence of known facts will not permit us to deny that they are in some degree true. It will be found, indeed, on a candid review of our situation, that some of the distresses under which we labor have been erroneously charged on the operation of our governments; but it will be found, at the same time, that other causes will not alone account for many of our heaviest misfortunes; and, particularly, for that prevailing and increasing distrust of public engagements, and alarm for private rights, which are echoed from one end of the continent to the other. These must be chiefly, if not wholly, effects of the unsteadiness and injustice with which a factious spirit has tainted our public administrations.

By a faction, I understand a number of citizens, whether amounting to a majority or minority of the whole, who are united and actuated by some common impulse of passion, or of interest, adverse to the rights of other citizens, or to the permanent and aggregate interests of the community.

There are two methods of curing the mischiefs of faction: the one, by removing its causes; the other, by controlling its effects.

There are again two methods of removing the cause of faction: the one, by destroying the liberty which is essential to its existence; the other, by giving to every citizen the same opinions, the same passions, and the same interests.

It could never be more truly said than of the first remedy, that it was worse than the disease. Liberty is to faction what air is to fire, an aliment without which instantly expires. But it could not be less folly to abolish liberty, which is essential to political life, because it nourishes faction, than it would be to wish the annihilation of air, which is essential to animal life, because it imparts to fire its destructive agency.

The second expedient is as impracticable as the first would be unwise. As long as the reason of man continues fallible, and he is at liberty to exercise it, different opinions will be formed. As long as the connection subsists between his reason and his self-love, his opinions and his passions will have a reciprocal influence on each other and the former will be objects to which the latter will attach themselves.

The diversity in the faculties of men from which the rights of property originate, is not an insuperable obstacle to a uniformity of interests. The protection of these faculties is the first object of government. From the protection of different and unequal faculties of acquiring property, the possession of different degrees and kinds of property immediately results; and from the influence of these on the sentiments and views of the respective proprietors, ensues a division of the society into different interests and parties.

The latent causes of faction are thus sown in the nature of man; and we see them everywhere brought in different degrees of activity, according to the different circumstances of civil society. A zeal for different opinion concerning religion, concerning government, and many other points, as well of speculation as of practice; an attachment to different leaders ambitiously contending for preeminence and power; or to persons of other descriptions whose fortunes have been interesting to the human passions, have, in turn, divided mankind into parties, inflamed them with mutual animosity, and rendered them much more disposed to vex and oppress each other than to co-operate for their common good.

So strong is this propensity of mankind to fall into mutual animosities, that where no substantial occasion presents itself, the most frivolous and fanciful distinctions have been sufficient to kindle their unfriendly passions and excite their most violent conflicts. But the most common and durable source of factions has been the various and unequal distribution of property. Those who hold and those who are without property have ever formed distinct interests in society. Those who are creditors, and those who are debtors, fall under a like discrimination. A landed interest, a manufacturing interest, a mercantile interest, a moneyed interest, with many lesser interests, grow up of necessity in civilized nations, and divide them into different classes, actuated by different sentiments and views. The regulation of these various and interfering interests forms the principal task of modern legislation, and involves the spirit of party and faction in the necessary and ordinary operations of the government.

No man is allowed to be a judge in his own cause, because his interest would certainly bias his judgment, and, not improbably, corrupt his integrity. With equal, nay with greater reason a body of men are unfit to be both judges and parties at the same time; yet what are many of the most important acts of legislation, but so many judicial determinations, not indeed concerning the rights of single persons, but concerning the rights of large bodies of citizens? And what are the different classes of legislators but advocates and parties to the causes which they determine? Is a law proposed concerning private debts? It is a question to which the creditors are parties on one side and the debtors on the other. Justice ought to hold the balance between them. Yet the parties are, and must, be, themselves the judges; and the most numerous party, or, in other words, the most powerful faction must be expected to prevail.

Shall domestic manufactures be encouraged, and in what degree, by restrictions on foreign manufactures? are questions which would be differently decided by the landed and the manufacturing classes, and probably by neither with a sole regard to justice and the public good. The apportionment of taxes on the various descriptions of property is an act which seems to require the most exact impartiality; yet there is, perhaps, no legislative act in which greater opportunity and temptation are given to a predominant party to trample on the rules of justice. Every shilling with which they overburden the inferior number, is shilling saved to their own pockets.

It is in vain to say that enlightened statesmen will be able to adjust these clashing interests, and render them all subservient to the public good. Enlightened statesmen will not always be at the helm. Nor, in many cases, can such an adjustment be made at all without taking into view indirect and remote considerations, which will rarely prevail over the immediate interest which one party may find in disregarding the rights of another or the good of the whole.

The inference to which we are brought is, that the *causes* of faction cannot be removed, and that relief is only to be sought in the means of controlling its *effects*.

If a faction consists of less than a majority, relief is supplied by the republican principle, which enables the majority to defeat its sinister views by regular vote. It may clog the administration, it may convulse the society; but it will be unable to execute and mask its violence under the forms of the Constitution.

When a majority is included in a faction, the form of popular government, on the other hand, enables it to sacrifice to its ruling passion or interest both the public good and the rights of other citizens. To secure the public good and private rights against the danger of such a faction, and at the same time to preserve the spirit and the form of popular government, is then the great object to which our inquiries are directed. Let me add that it is the great desideratum by which this form of government can be rescued from the opprobrium under which it has so long labored, and be recommended to the esteem and adoption of mankind.

By what means is this object attainable? Evidently by one or two only. Either the existence of the same passion or interest in a majority at the same time must be prevented, or the majority, having such coexistent passion or interest, must be rendered, by their number and local situation, unable to concert and carry into effect schemes of oppression. If the impulse and the opportunity be suffered to coincide, we well know that neither moral nor religious motives can be relied on as an adequate control. They are not found to be such on the injustice and violence of individuals, and lose their efficacy in proportion to the number combined together, that is, in proportion as their efficacy becomes needful.

From this view of the subject it may be concluded that a pure democracy, by which I mean a society consisting of a small number of citizens, who assemble and administer the government in person, can admit of no cure for the mischiefs of faction. A common passion or interest will, in almost every case, be felt by a majority of the whole; a communication and concert result from the form of government itself; and there is nothing to check the inducements to sacrifice the weaker party or an obnoxious individual. Hence it is that such democracies have ever been spectacles of turbulence and contention; have ever been found incompatible with personal security of the rights of property; and have in general been as short in their lives as they have been violent in their deaths. Theoretic politicians, who have patronized this species of government, have erroneously supposed that by reducing mankind to a perfect equality in their political rights, they would, at the same time, be perfectly equalized and assimilated in their possessions, their opinions, and their passions.

A republic, by which I mean a government in which the scheme of representation takes place, opens a different prospect, and promises the cure for which we are seeking. Let us examine the points in which it varies from pure democracy, and we shall comprehend both the nature of the cure and the efficacy which it must derive from the Union.

The two great points of difference between a democracy and a republic are: first, the delegation of the government, in the latter, to a small number of citizens elected by the rest; secondly, the greater number of citizens, and greater sphere of country, over which the latter may be extended.

The effect of the first difference is, on the one hand, to, refine and enlarge the public views, by passing them through the medium of a chosen body of citizens, whose wisdom may best discern the true interest of their country, and whose patriotism and love of justice will be least likely to sacrifice it to temporary or partial considerations. Under such a regulation, it may well happen that the public voice, pronounced by the representatives of the people, will be more consonant to the public good than if pronounced by the people themselves, convened for the purpose. On the other hand, the effect may be inverted. Men of factious tempers, of local prejudices, or of sinister designs, may, by intrigue, by corruption, or by other means, first obtain the suffrages, and then betray the interests, of the people. The question resulting is, whether small or extensive republics are more favorable to the election of proper guardians of the public weal; and it is clearly decided in favor of the latter by two obvious considerations:

In the first place, it is to be remarked that, however small the republic may be, the representatives must be raised to a certain number, in order to guard against the cabals of a few; and that, however large it may be, they must be limited to a certain number, in order to guard against the confusion of a multitude. Hence, the number of representatives in the two cases not being in proportion to that of the two constituents, and being proportionally greater in the small republic, it follows that, if the proportion of fit characters be not less in the large than in the small republic, the former will present a greater option, and consequently a greater probability of a fit choice.

In the next place, as each representative will be chosen by a greater number of citizens in the large than in the small republic, it will be more difficult for unworthy candidates to practice with success the vicious arts by which elections are too often carried; and the suffrages of the people being more free, will be more likely to center in men who possess the most attractive merit and the most diffusive and established characters.

It must be confessed that in this, as in most other cases, there is a mean, on both sides of which inconveniences will be found to lie. By enlarging too much the number of electors, you render the representative too little acquainted with all their local circumstances and lesser interests; as by reducing it too much, you render him unduly attached to these, and too little fit to comprehend and pursue great and national objects. The federal Constitution forms a happy combination in this respect; the great and aggregate interests being referred to the national, the local and particular to the State legislatures.

The other point of difference is, the greater number of citizens and extent of territory which may be brought within the compass of republican than of democratic government; and it is this circumstance principally which renders factious combinations less to be dreaded in the former than in the latter. The smaller the society, the fewer probably will be the distinct parties and interests composing it; the fewer the distinct parties and interests, the more frequently will a majority be found of the same party; and the smaller the number of individuals composing a majority, and the smaller the compass within which they are placed, the more easily will they concert and execute their plans of oppression. Extend the sphere, and you take a greater variety of parties and interests; you make it less probable that a majority of the whole will have a common motive to invade the rights of other citizens; or if such a common motive exists, it will be more difficult for all who feel it to discover their own strength, and to act in unison with each other. Besides other impediments, it may be remarked that, where there is a consciousness of unjust or dishonorable purposes, communication is always checked by distrust in proportion to the number whose concurrence is necessary.

Hence, it clearly appears, that the same advantage which a republic has over a democracy, in controlling the effects of faction, is enjoyed by a large over a small republic,—is enjoyed by the Union over the States composing it. Does the advantage consist in the substitution of representatives whose enlightened views and virtuous sentiments render them superior to local prejudices and to schemes of injustice? It will not be denied that the representation of the Union will be most likely to possess these requisite endowments. Does it consist in the greater security afforded by a greater variety of parties, against the event of any one party being able to outnumber and oppress the rest? In an equal degree does the increase variety of parties comprised within the Union, increase this security? Does it, in fine, consist in the greater obstacles opposed to the concert and accomplishment of the secret wishes of an unjust and interested majority? Here, again, the extent of the Union gives it the most palpable advantage.

The influence of factious leaders may kindle a flame within their particular States, but will be unable to spread a general conflagration through the other States. A religious sect may degenerate into a political faction in part of the Confederacy; but the variety of sects dispersed over the entire face of it must secure the national councils against any danger from that source. A rage for paper money, for an abolition of debts, for an equal division of property, or for any other improper or wicked project, will be less apt to pervade the whole body of the Union than a particular member of it; in the same proportion as such a malady is more likely to taint a particular county or district, than an entire State.

In the extent and proper structure of the Union, therefore, we behold a republican remedy for the diseases most incident to republican government. And according to the degree of pleasure and pride we feel in being republicans, ought to be our zeal in cherishing the spirit and supporting the character of Federalists.

PUBLIUS

[1787]

from Philosophy of Right

CIVIL SOCIETY

182. The concrete person, who is himself the object of his particular aims, is, as a totality of wants and a mixture of caprice and physical necessity, one principle of civil society. But the particular person is essentially so related to other particular persons that each establishes himself and finds satisfaction by means of the others, and at the same time purely and simply by means of the form of universality, the second principle here.

183. In the course of the actual attainment of selfish ends—an attainment conditioned in this way by universality—there is formed a system of complete interdependence, wherein the livelihood, happiness, and legal status of one man is interwoven with the livelihood, happiness, and rights of all. On this system, individual happiness, et cetera, depend, and only in this connected system are they actualized and secured. This system may be prima facie regarded as the external state, the state based on need, the state as the Understanding envisages it.

184. The Idea in this its stage of division imparts to each of its moments a characteristic embodiment; to particularity it gives the right to develop and launch forth in all directions; and to universality the right to prove itself not on the ground and necessary form of particularity, but also the authority standing over it and its final end. It is the system of the ethical order, split into its extremes and lost, which constitutes the Idea's abstract moment, its moment of reality. Here the Idea is present only as a relative totality and as the inner necessity behind this outward appearance.

185. Particularity by itself, given free rein in every direction to satisfy its needs, accidental caprices, and subjective desires, destroys itself and its substantive concept in this process of gratification. At the same time, the satisfaction of need, necessary and accidental alike, is accidental because it breeds new desires without end, is in thoroughgoing dependence on caprice and external accident, and is held in check by the power of universality. In these contrasts and their complexity, civil society affords a spectacle of extravagance and wants as well as of the physical and ethical degeneration common to them both.

. . .

186. But in developing itself independently to totality, the principle of particularity passes over into universality, and only there does it attain its truth and the right to which its positive actuality is entitled. This unity is not the identity which the ethical order requires, because at this level, that of division (see Paragraph 184), both principles are self-subsistent. It follows that this unity is present here not as freedom but as necessity, since it is by compulsion that the particular rises to the form of universality and seeks and gains its stability in that form.

187. Individuals in their capacity as burghers in this state are private persons whose end is their own interest. This end is *mediated* through the universal which thus *appears* as a *means* to its realization. Consequently, individuals can attain their ends only in so far as they themselves determine their knowing, willing, and acting in a universal way and make themselves links in this chain of social connections. In these circumstances, the interest of the Idea—an interest of which these members of civil society are as such unconscious—lies in the process whereby their singularity and their natural condition are raised, as a result of the necessities imposed by nature as well as of arbitrary needs, to formal freedom and formal universality of knowing and willing—the process whereby their particularity is educated up to subjectivity.

. . .

188. Civil society contains three moments:

(A) The mediation of need and one man's satisfaction through his work and the satisfaction of the needs of all others—the System of Needs.
(B) The actuality of the universal principle of freedom therein contained—the protection of property through the *Administration of Justice.*
(C) Provision against contingencies still lurking in systems (A) and (B), and care for particular interests as a common interest, by means of the *Police* and the *Corporation.*

A. The System of Needs

189. Particularity is in the first instance characterized in general by its contrast with the universal principle of the will and thus is subjective need. This attains its objectivity, i.e. its satisfaction, by means of (α) external things, which at this stage are likewise the property and product of the needs and wills of others, and (β) work and effort, the middle term between the subjective and the objective. The aim here is the satisfaction of subjective particularity, but the universal asserts itself in the bearing which this satisfaction has on the needs of others and their free arbitrary wills. The show of rationality thus produced in this sphere of finitude is the Understanding, and this is the aspect which is of most importance in considering this sphere and which itself constitutes the reconciling element within it.

Political economy is the science which starts from this view of needs and labor but then has the task of explaining mass-relationships and mass-movements in their complexity and their qualitative and quantitative character. This is one of the sciences which have arisen out of the conditions of the modern world. Its development affords the interesting spectacle (as in Smith, Say, and Ricardo) of thought working upon the endless mass of details which confront it at the outset and extracting therefrom the simple principles of the thing, the Understanding effective in the thing and directing it. It is to find reconciliation here to discover in the sphere of needs this show of rationality lying in the thing and effective there; but if we look at it from the opposite point of view, this is the field in which the Understanding with its subjective aims and moral fancies vents its discontent and moral frustration.

(a) The Kind of Need and Satisfaction [typical of civil society]

190. An animal's needs and its ways and means of satisfying them are both alike restricted in scope. Though man is subject to this restriction too, yet at the same time he evinces his transcendence of it and his universality, first by the multiplication of needs and means of satisfying them, and secondly by the differentiation and division of concrete need into single parts and aspects which in turn become different needs, particularized and so more abstract.

In [abstract] right, what we had before us was the person; in the sphere of morality, the subject; in the family, the family-member; in civil society as a whole, the burgher or *bourgeois*. Here at the standpoint of need . . . what we have before us is the composite idea which we call *man*. Thus this is the first time, and indeed properly the only time, to speak of *man* in this sense.

191. Similarly, the means to particularized needs and all the various ways of satisfying these are themselves divided and multiplied and so in turn become proximate ends and abstract needs. This multiplication goes on *ad infinitum;* taken as a whole, it is refinement, i.e. a discrimination between these multiplied needs, and judgment on the suitability of means to their ends.

192. Needs and means, as things existent *realiter,* become something which has being for others by whose needs and work satisfaction for all alike is conditioned. When needs and means become abstract in quality, abstraction is also a character of the reciprocal relation of individuals to one another. This abstract character, universality, is the character of being recognized and is the moment which makes concrete, i.e. social, the isolated and abstract needs and their ways and means of satisfaction.

193. This social moment thus becomes a particular end-determinant for means in themselves and their acquisition, as well as for the manner in which needs are satisfied. Further, it directly involves the demand for equality of satisfaction with others. The need for this equality and for the emulation, which is the equalizing of oneself with others, as well as the other need also present here, the need of the particular to assert itself in some distinctive way, become themselves a fruitful source of the multiplication of needs and their expansion.

194. Since in social needs, as the conjunction of immediate or natural needs with mental needs arising from ideas, it is needs of the latter type which because of their universality make themselves preponderant, this social moment has in it the aspect of liberation, i.e. the strict natural necessity of need is obscured and man is concerned with his own opinion, indeed with an opinion which is universal, and with a necessity of his own making alone, instead of with an external necessity, an inner contingency, and mere caprice.

The idea has been advanced that in respect of his needs man lived in freedom in the so-called "state of nature" when his needs were supposed to be confined to what are known as the simple necessities of nature, and when he required for their satisfaction only the means which the accidents of nature directly assured to him. This view takes no account of the moment of liberation intrinsic to work, on which see the following Paragraphs. And apart from this, it is false, because to be confined to mere physical needs as such and their direct satisfaction would simply be the condition in which the mental is plunged in the natural and so would be one of savagery and unfreedom, while freedom itself is to be found only in the reflection of mind into itself, in mind's distinction from nature, and in the reflex of mind in nature.

195. This liberation is abstract since the particularity of the ends remains their basic content. When social conditions tend to multiply and subdivide needs, means, and enjoyments indefinitely—a process which, like the distinction between natural and refined needs, has no qualitative limits—this is luxury. In this same process, however, dependence and want increase *ad infinitum,* and the material to meet these is permanently barred to the needy man because it consists of external objects with the special character of being property, the embodiment of the free will of others, and hence from his point of view its recalcitrance is absolute.

(b) The Kind of Work [typical of civil society]

196. The means of acquiring and preparing the particularized means appropriate to our similarly particularized needs is work. Through work the raw material directly supplied by nature is specifically adapted to these numerous ends by all sorts of different processes. Now this formative change confers value on means and gives them their utility, and hence man in what he consumes is mainly concerned with the products of men. It is the products of human effort which man consumes.

197. The multiplicity of objects and situations which excite interest is the stage on which theoretical education develops. This education consists in possessing not simply a multiplicity of ideas and facts, but also a flexibility and rapidity of mind, ability to pass from one idea to another, to grasp complex and general relations, and so on. It is the education of the understanding in every way, and so also the building up of language. Practical education, acquired through working, consists first in the automatically recurrent need for something to do and the habit of simply being busy; next, in the strict adaptation of one's activity according not only to the nature of the material worked on, but also, and especially, to the pleasure of other workers; and finally, in a habit, produced by this discipline, of objective activity and universally recognized aptitudes.

198. The universal and objective element in work, on the other hand, lies in the abstracting process which effects the subdivision of needs and means and thereby *eo ipso* subdivides production and brings about the division of labor. By this division, the work of the individual becomes less complex, and consequently his skill at his section of the job increases, like his output. At the same time, this abstraction of one man's skill and means of production from another's completes and makes necessary everywhere the dependence of men on one another and their reciprocal relation in the satisfaction of their other needs. Further, the abstraction of one man's production from another's makes work more and more mechanical, until finally man is able to step aside and install machines in his place.

(c) Capital [and class-divisions]

199. When men are thus dependent on one another and reciprocally related to one another in their work and the satisfaction of their needs, subjective self-seeking turns into a contribution to the satisfaction of the needs of everyone else. That is to say, by a dialectical advance, subjective self-seeking turns into the mediation of the particular through the universal, with the result that each man in earning, producing, and enjoying on his own account is *eo ipso* producing and earning for the enjoyment of everyone else. The compulsion which brings this about is rooted in the complex interdependence of each on all, and it now presents itself to each as the universal permanent capital which gives each the opportunity, by the exercise of his education and skill, to draw a share from it and so be assured of his livelihood, while what he thus earns by means of his work maintains and increases the general capital.

200. A particular man's resources, or in other words his opportunity of sharing in the general resources, are conditioned, however, partly by his own unearned principal (his capital), and partly by his skill; this in turn is itself dependent not only on his capital, but also on accidental circumstances whose multiplicity introduces differences in the development of natural, bodily, and mental characteristics, which were already in themselves dissimilar. In this sphere of particularity, these differences are conspicuous in every direction and on every level, and, together with the arbitrariness and accident which this sphere contains as well, they have as their inevitable consequence disparities of individual resources and ability.

The objective right of the particularity of mind is contained in the Idea. Men are made unequal by nature, where inequality is in its element, and in civil society the right of particularity is so far from annulling this natural inequality that it produces it out of mind and raises it to an inequality of skill and resources, and even to one of moral and intellectual attainment. To oppose to this right a demand for equality is a folly of the Understanding which takes as real and rational its abstract equality and its "ought-to-be."

This sphere of particularity, which fancies itself the universal, is still only relatively identical with the universal, and consequently it still retains in itself the particularity of nature, i.e. arbitrariness, or in other words the relics of the state of nature. Further, it is reason, immanent in the restless system of human needs, which articulates it into an organic whole with different members (see the following Paragraph).

201. The infinitely complex, criss-cross, movements of reciprocal production and exchange, and the equally infinite multiplicity of means therein employed, become crystallized, owing to the universality inherent in their content, and distinguished into general groups. As a result, the entire complex is built up into particular systems of needs, means, and types of work relative to these needs, modes of satisfaction and of theoretical and practical education, i.e. into systems, to one or other of which individuals are assigned—in other words, into class-divisions.

202. The classes are specifically determined in accordance with the concept as *(a)* the *substantial* or immediate [or agricultural] class; *(b)* the reflecting or *formal* [or business] class; and finally *(c)* the *universal* class [the class of civil servants].

203. *(a)* The substantial or [agricultural] class has its capital in the natural products of the soil which it cultivates—soil which is capable of exclusively private ownership and which demands formation in an objective way and not mere haphazard exploitation. In face of the connection of [agricultural] work and its fruits with separate and fixed times of the year, and the dependence of harvests on the variability of natural processes, the aim of need in this class turns into provision for the future; but owing to the conditions here, the agricultural mode of subsistence remains one which owes comparatively little to reflection and independence of will, and this mode of life is in general such that this class has the substantial disposition of an ethical life which is immediate, resting on family relationship and trust.

The real beginning and original foundation of states has been rightly ascribed to the introduction of agriculture along with marriage, because the principle of agriculture brings with it the formation of the land and consequentially exclusively private property; the nomadic life of savages, who seek their livelihood from place to place, it brings back to the tranquility of private rights and the assured satisfaction of their needs. Along with these changes, sexual love is restricted to marriage, and this bond in turn grows into an enduring league, inherently universal, while needs expand into care for a family, and personal possessions into family goods. Security, consolidation, lasting satisfaction of needs, and so forth—things which are the most obvious recommendations of marriage and agriculture—are nothing but forms of universality, modes in which rationality, the final end and aim, asserts itself in these spheres.

In this matter, nothing is of more interest than the ingenious and learned explanations which my distinguished friend, Herr Creuzer, has given[1] of the agrarian festivals, images, and sanctuaries of the ancients. He shows that it was because the ancients themselves had become conscious of the divine origin of agriculture and other institutions associated with it that they held them in such religious veneration.

In course of time, the character of this class as "substantial" undergoes modifications through the working of the civil law, in particular the administration of justice, as well as through the working of education, instruction, and religion. These modifications, which occur in the other classes also, do not affect the substantial content of the class but only its form and the development of its power of reflection.

204. (*b*) The business class has for its task the adaptation of raw materials, and for its means of livelihood it is thrown back on its work, on reflection and intelligence, and essentially on the mediation of one man's needs and work with those of others. For what this class produces and enjoys, it has mainly itself, its own industry, to thank. The task of this class is subdivided into

(A) work to satisfy single needs in a comparatively concrete way and to supply single orders—craftsmanship;
(B) work of a more abstract kind, mass-production to satisfy single needs, but needs in more universal demand—manufacture;
(C) the business of exchange, whereby separate utilities are exchanged the one for the other, principally through the use of the universal medium of exchange, money, which actualizes the abstract value of all commodities—trade.

205. (*c*) The universal class [the class of civil servants] has for its task the universal interests of the community. It must therefore be relieved from direct labor to supply its needs, either by having private means or by receiving an allowance from the state which claims its industry, with the result that private interest finds its satisfaction in its work for the universal.

206. It is in accordance with the concept that class-organization, as particularity become objective to itself, is split in this way into its general divisions. But the question of the particular class to which an individual is to belong is one on which natural capacity, birth, and other circumstances have their influence, though the essential and final determining factors are subjective opinion and the individual's arbitrary will, which win in this sphere their right, their merit, and their dignity.

---

1. Notably in the fourth volume of his *Mythologie und Symbolik.*

Hence what happens here by inner necessity occurs at the same time by the mediation of the arbitrary will, and to the conscious subject it has the shape of being the work of his own will.

207. A man actualizes himself only in becoming something definite, i.e. something specifically particularized; this means restricting himself exclusively to one of the particular spheres of need. In this class-system, the ethical frame of mind therefore is rectitude and *esprit de corps,* i.e. the disposition to make oneself a member of one of the moments of civil society by one's own act, through one's energy, industry, and skill, to maintain oneself in this position, and to fend for oneself only through this process of mediating oneself with the universal, while in this way gaining recognition both in one's own eyes and in the eyes of others. Morality has its proper place in this space where the paramount thing is reflection on one's doings, and the quest of happiness and private wants, and where the contingency in satisfying these makes into a duty even a single and contingent act of assistance.

. . .

208. As the private particularity of knowing and willing, the principle of this system of needs contains absolute universality, the universality of freedom, only abstractly and therefore as the right of property. At this point, however, this right is no longer merely implicit but has attained its recognized actuality as the protection of property through the administration of justice.

B. The Administration of Justice

209. The relatedness arising from the reciprocal bearing on one another of needs and work to satisfy these is first of all reflected into itself as infinite personality, as abstract right. But it is this very sphere of relatedness—a sphere of education—which gives abstract right the determinate existence of being something universally recognized, known, and willed, and having a validity and an objective actuality mediated by this known and willed character.

It is part of education, of thinking as the consciousness of the single in the form of universality, that the ego comes to be apprehended as a universal person in which all are identical. A man counts as a man in virtue of his manhood alone, not because he is a Jew, Catholic, Protestant, German, Italian, et cetera. This is an assertion which thinking ratifies and to be conscious of it is of infinite importance. It is defective only when it is crystallized, e.g. as a cosmopolitanism in opposition to the concrete life of the state.

210. The objective actuality of the right consists, first, in its existence for consciousness, in its being known in some way or other; secondly, in its possessing the power which the actual possesses, in its being valid, and so also in its becoming known as universally valid.

(a) Right as Law

211. The principle of rightness becomes the law *(Gesetz)* when, in its objective existence, it is posited *(gesetzt),* i.e. when thinking makes it determinate for consciousness and makes it known as what is right and valid; and in acquiring this determinate character, the right becomes positive law in general.

To posit something as universal, i.e. to bring it before consciousness as universal, is, I need hardly say, to think. Thereby its content is reduced to its simplest form and so is given its final determinacy. In becoming law, what is right acquires for the first time not only the form proper to its universality, but also its true determinacy. Hence making a law is not to be represented as merely the expression of a rule of behavior valid for everyone, though that is one moment in legislation; the more important moment, the inner essence of the matter, is knowledge of the content of the law in its determinate universality.

Since it is only animals which have their law as instinct, while it is man alone who has law as custom, even systems of customary law contain the moment of being thoughts and being known. Their difference from positive law consists solely in this, that they are known only in a subjective and accidental way, with the result that in themselves they are less determinate and the universality of thought is less clear in them. (And apart from this, knowledge of a system of law either in general or in its details, is the accidental possession of a few.) The supposition that it is customary law, on the strength of its character as custom, which possesses the privilege of having become part of life is a delusion, since the valid laws of a nation do not cease to be its customs by being written and codified— and besides, it is as a rule precisely those versed in the deadest of topics and the deadest of thoughts who talk nowadays of "life" and of "becoming part of life." When a nation begins to acquire even a little culture, its customary law must soon come to be collected and put together. Such a collection is a legal code, but one which, as a mere collection, is markedly formless, indeterminate, and fragmentary. The main difference between it and a code properly so-called is that in the latter the principles of jurisprudence in their universality, and so in their determinacy, have been apprehended in terms of thought and expressed. English national law or municipal law is contained, as is well known, in statutes (written laws) and in so-called "unwritten" laws. This unwritten law, however, is as good as written, and knowledge of it may, and indeed must, be acquired simply by reading the numerous quartos which it fills. The monstrous confusion, however, which prevails both in English law and its administration is graphically portrayed by those acquainted with the matter. In particular, they comment on the fact that, since this unwritten law is contained in court verdicts and judgments, the judges are continually legislators. The authority of precedent is binding on them, since their predecessors have done nothing but give expression to the unwritten law; and yet they are just as much exempt from its authority, because they are themselves repositories of the unwritten law and so have the right to criticize previous judgments and pronounce whether they accorded with the unwritten law or not.

A similar confusion might have arisen in the legal system of the later Roman Empire owing to the different but authoritative judgments of all the famous jurists. An Emperor met the situation, however, by a sensible expedient when, by what was called the Law of Citations, he set up a kind of College of the jurists who were longest deceased. There was a President, and the majority vote was accepted.[2]

No greater insult could be offered to a civilized people or to its lawyers than to deny them ability to codify their law; for such ability cannot be that of constructing a legal system with a novel content, but only that of apprehending, i.e. grasping in thought, the content of existing laws in its determinate universality and then applying them to particular cases.

212. It is only because of this identity between its implicit and its posited character that positive law has obligatory force in virtue of its rightness. In being posited in positive law, the right acquires determinate existence. Into such existence there may enter the contingency of self-will and other particular circumstances and hence there may be a discrepancy between the content of the law and the principle of rightness.

In positive law, therefore, it is the legal which is the source of our knowledge of what is right, or, more exactly, of our legal rights *(Rechtens)*. Thus the science of positive law is to that extent an historical science with authority as its guiding principle. Anything over and above this historical study is matter for the Understanding and concerns the collection of laws, their classification on external principles, deductions from them, their application to fresh details, et cetera. When the Understanding meddles with the nature of the thing itself, its theories, e.g. of criminal law, show what its deductive argumentation can concoct.

The science of positive law has not only the right, but even the inescapable duty, to study given laws, to deduce from its positive data their progress in history, their applications and subdivisions, down to the last detail, and to exhibit their implications. On the other hand, if, after all these deductions have been proved, the further question about the rationality of a specific law is still raised, the question may seem perverse to those who are busied with these pursuits, but their astonishment at it should be at least stop short of dismay. . . .

213. Right becomes determinate in the first place when it has the form of being posited as positive law; it also becomes determinate in content by being applied both to the material of civil society (i.e. to the endlessly growing complexity and subdivision of social ties and the different species of property and contract within the society) and also to ethical ties based on the heart, on love and trust, though only in so far as these involve abstract right as one of their aspects. Morality and moral commands concern the will on its most private, subjective, and particular side, and so cannot be a matter for positive legislation. Further material for the

2. Hugo: *Lehrbuch der Geschichte des römischen Rechts,* Pgr. 354 [Pgr. 385 in the 7th ed.].

determinate content of law is provided by the rights and duties which have their source in the administration of justice itself, in the state, and so forth.

. . .

(b) Law determinately existent

215. If laws are to have a binding force, it follows that, in view of the right of self-consciousness they must be made universally known.

To hang the laws so high that no citizen could read them (as Dionysius the Tyrant did) is injustice of one and the same kind as to bury them in row upon row of learned tomes, collections of dissenting judgments and opinions, records of customs, et cetera, and in a dead language too, so that knowledge of the law of the land is accessible only to those who have made it their professional study. Rulers who have given a national law to their peoples in the form of a well-arranged and clear-cut legal code — or even a mere formless collection of laws, like Justinian's — have been the greatest benefactors of their peoples and have received thanks and praise for their beneficence. But the truth is that their work was at the same time a great act of justice.

216. For a public legal code, simple general laws are required, and yet the nature of the *finite* material to which law is applied leads to the further determining of general laws *ad infinitum.* On the one hand, the law ought to be a comprehensive whole, closed and complete; and yet, on the other hand, the need for further determinations is continual. But since this antinomy arises only when universal principles, which remain fixed and unchanged, are applied to particular types of case, the right to a complete legal code remains unimpaired, like the right that these simple general principles should be capable of being laid down and understood apart and in distinction from their application to such particular types.

217. The principle of rightness passes over in civil society into law. My individual right, whose embodiment has hitherto been immediate and abstract, now similarly becomes embodied in the existent will and knowledge of everyone, in the sense that it becomes recognized. Hence property acquisitions and transfers must now be undertaken and concluded only in the form which that embodiment gives to them. In civil society, property rests on contract and on the formalities which make ownership capable of proof and valid in law.

. . .

218. Since property and personality have legal recognition and validity in civil society, wrongdoing now becomes an infringement, not merely of what is subjectively infinite, but of the universal thing which is existent with inherent stability and strength. Hence a new attitude arises: the action is seen as a danger to society and thereby the magnitude of the wrongdoing is increased. On the other hand, however, the fact that society has become strong and sure of itself diminishes the external importance of the injury and so leads to a mitigation of its punishment.

(c) The Court of Justice

. . .

219. By taking the form of law, right steps into a determinate mode of being. It is then something on its own account, and in contrast with particular willing and opining of the right, it is self-subsistent and has to vindicate itself as something universal. This is achieved by recognizing it and making it actual in a particular case without the subjective feeling of private interest; and this is the business of a public authority—the court of justice.

. . .

222. In court the specific character which rightness acquires is that it must be demonstrable. When parties go to law, they are put in the position of having to make good their evidence and their claims and to make the judge acquainted with the facts. These steps in a legal process are themselves rights, and their course must therefore be fixed by law. They also constitute an essential part of jurisprudence.

223. These steps in a legal process are subdivided continually within no fixed limits into more and more actions, each being distinct in itself and a right. Hence a legal process, in itself in any case a means, now begins to be something external to its end and contrasted with it. This long course of formalities is a right of the parties at law and they have the right to traverse it from beginning to end. Still, it may be turned into an evil, and even an instrument of wrong, and for this reason it is by law made the duty of the parties to submit themselves to the simple process of arbitration (before a tribunal of arbitrators) and to the attempt to reconcile their differences out of court, in order that they—and right itself, as the substance of the thing and so the thing really at issue—may be protected against legal processes and their misuse.

. . .

229. In civil society, the Idea is lost in particularity and has fallen asunder with the separation of inward and outward. In the administration of justice, however, civil society returns to its concept, to the unity of the implicit universal with the subjective particular, although here the latter is only that present in single cases and the universality in question is that of *abstract* right. The actualization of this unity through its extension to the whole ambit of particularity is (i) the specific function of the Police, though the unification which it effects is only relative; (ii) it is the Corporation which actualizes the unity completely, though only in a whole which, while concrete, is restricted.

C. The Police and the Corporation

230. In the system of needs, the livelihood and welfare of every single person is a possibility whose actual attainment is just as much conditioned by his caprices and particular endowment as by the objective system of needs. Through the administration of justice, offenses against property or personality are annulled. But the right actually present in the particular requires, first, that accidental hindrances to one aim or another be removed, and undisturbed safety of person and property be attained; and secondly, that the securing of every single person's livelihood and welfare be treated and actualized as a right, i.e. that particular welfare as such be so treated.

. . .

235. In the indefinite multiplication and interconnection of day-to-day needs, (*a*) the acquisition and exchange of the means to their satisfaction—a satisfaction which everyone confidently expects to be possible of attainment without hindrance, and (*b*) the endeavours made and the transactions carried out in order to shorten the process of attainment as much as possible, give rise to factors which are a common interest, and when one man occupies himself with these his work is at the same time done for all. The situation is productive too of contrivances and organizations which may be of use to the community as a whole. These universal activities and organizations of general utility call for the oversight and care of the public authority.

236. The differing interests of producers and consumers may come into collision with each other; and although a fair balance between them on the whole may be brought about automatically, still their adjustment also requires a control which stands above both and is consciously undertaken. The right to the exercise of such control in a single case (e.g. in the fixing of the prices of the commonest necessaries of life) depends on the fact that, by being publicly exposed for sale, goods in absolutely universal daily demand are offered not so much to an individual as such but rather to a universal purchaser, the public; and thus both the defense of the public's right not to be defrauded, and also the management of goods inspection, may lie, as a common concern, with a public authority. But public care and direction are most of all necessary in the case of the larger branches of industry, because these are dependent on conditions abroad and on combinations of distant circumstances which cannot be grasped as a whole by the individuals tied to these industries for their living.

At the other extreme to freedom of trade and commerce in civil society is public organization to provide for everything and determine everyone's labor—take for example in ancient times the labor on the pyramids and the other huge monuments in Egypt and Asia which were constructed for pubic ends, and the worker's task was not mediated through his private choice and particular interest. This interest invokes freedom of trade and commerce against control from above; but the more blindly it sinks into self-seeking aims, the more it requires such control to bring it back to the universal. Control is also necessary to diminish the danger of upheavals arising from clashing interests and to abbreviate the period in which their tension should be eased through the working of a necessity of which they themselves know nothing.

237. Now while the possibility of sharing in the general wealth is open to individuals and is assured to them by the public authority, still it is subject to contingencies on the subjective side (quite apart from the fact that this assurance must remain incomplete), and the more it presupposes skill, health, capital, and so forth as its conditions, the more is it so subject.

238. Originally the family is the substantive whole whose function it is to provide for the individual on his particular side by giving him either the means and the skill necessary to enable him to earn his living out of the resources of society, or else subsistence and maintenance in the event of his suffering a disability. But civil society tears the individual from his family ties, estranges the members of the family from one another, and recognizes them as self-subsistent persons. Further, for the paternal soil and the external inorganic resources of nature from which the individual formerly derived his livelihood, it substitutes its own soil and subjects the permanent existence of even the entire family to dependence on itself and to contingency. Thus the individual becomes a son of civil society which has as many claims upon him as he has rights against it.

239. In its character as a universal family, civil society has the right and duty of superintending and influencing education, inasmuch as education bears upon the child's capacity to become a member of society. Society's right here is paramount over the arbitrary and contingent preferences of parents, particulary in cases where education is to be completed not by the parents but by others. To the same end, society must provide public educational facilities so far as is practicable.

240. Similarly, society has the right and duty of acting as trustee to those whose extravagance destroys the security of their own subsistence or their families.' It must substitute for extravagance the pursuit of the ends of society and the individuals concerned.

241. Not only caprice, however, but also contingencies, physical conditions, and factors grounded in external circumstances (see Paragraph 200) may reduce men to poverty. The poor still have the needs common to civil society, and yet since society has withdrawn from them the natural means of acquisition (see Paragraph 217) and broken the bond of the family—in the wider sense of the clan—their poverty leaves them more or less deprived of all the advantages of society, of the opportunity or acquiring skill or education of any kind, as well as of the administration of justice, the public health services, and often even of the consolations of religion, and so forth. The public authority takes the place of the family where the poor are concerned in respect not only of their immediate want but also of laziness of disposition, malignity, and the other vices which arise out of their plight and their sense of wrong.

242. Poverty and, in general, the distress of every kind to which every individual is exposed from the start in the cycle of his natural life has a subjective side which demands similarly subjective aid, arising both from the special circumstances of a particular case and also from love and sympathy. This is the place where morality

finds plenty to do despite all public organization. Subjective aid, however, both in itself and in its operation, is dependent on contingency and consequently society struggles to make it less necessary, by discovering the general causes of penury and general means of its relief, and by organizing relief accordingly.

Casual almsgiving and casual endowments, for example, for the burning of lamps before holy images, et cetera, are supplemented by public almshouses, hospitals, street-lighting, and so forth. There is still quite enough left over and above these things for charity to do on its own account. A false view is implied both when charity insists on having this poor relief reserved solely to private sympathy and the accidental occurrence of knowledge and a charitable disposition, and also when it feels injured or mortified by universal regulations and ordinances which are *obligatory*. Public social conditions are on the contrary to be regarded as all the more perfect the less (in comparison with what is arranged publicly) is left for an individual to do by himself as his private inclination directs.

243. When civil society is in a state of unimpeded activity, it is engaged in expanding internally in population and industry. The amassing of wealth is intensified by generalizing (*a*) the linkage of men by their needs, and (*b*) the methods of preparing and distributing the means to satisfy these needs, because it is from this double process of generalization that the largest profits are derived. That is one side of the picture. The other side is the subdivision and restriction of particular jobs. This results in the dependence and distress of the class tied to work of that sort, and these again entail inability to feel and enjoy the broader freedoms and especially the intellectual benefits of civil society.

244. When the standard of living of a large mass of people falls below a certain subsistence level—a level regulated automatically as the one necessary for a member of the society—and when there is a consequent loss of the sense of right and wrong, of honesty and the self-respect which makes a man insist on maintaining himself by his own work and effort, the result is the creation of a rabble of paupers. At the same time this brings with it, at the other end of the social scale, conditions which greatly facilitate the concentration of disproportionate wealth in a few hands.

245. When the masses begin to decline into poverty, (*a*) the burden of maintaining them at their ordinary standard of living might be directly laid on the wealthier classes, or they might receive the means of livelihood directly from other public sources of wealth (e.g. from the endowments of rich hospitals, monasteries, and other foundations). In either case, however, the needy would receive subsistence directly, not by means of their work, and this would violate the principle of civil society and the feeling of individual independence and self-respect in its individual members. (*b*) As an alternative, they might be given subsistence indirectly through being given work, i.e. the opportunity to work. In this event the volume of production would be increased, but the evil consists precisely in an excess of production and in the lack of a proportionate number of consumers who are themselves also producers, and thus it is simply intensified by both of

the methods *(a)* and *(b)* by which it is sought to alleviate it. It hence becomes apparent that despite an excess of wealth civil society is not rich enough, i.e. its own resources are insufficient to check excessive poverty and the creation of a penurious rabble.

In the example of England we may study these phenomena on a large scale and also in particular the results of poor-rates, immense foundations, unlimited private beneficence, and above all the abolition of the Guild Corporations. In Britain, particularly in Scotland, the most direct measure against poverty and especially against the loss of shame and self-respect—the subjective bases of society—as well as against laziness and extravagance, et cetera, the begetters of the rabble, has turned out to be to leave the poor to their fate and instruct them to beg in the streets.

246. This inner dialectic of civil society thus drives it—or at any rate drives a specific civil society—to push beyond its own limits and seek markets, and so its necessary means of subsistence, in other lands which are either deficient in the goods it has overproduced, or else generally backward in industry, et cetera.

247. The principle of family life is dependence on the soil, on land, *terra firma.* Similarly, the natural element for industry, animating its outward movement, is the sea. Since the passion for gain involves risk, industry though bent on gain yet lifts itself above it; instead of remaining rooted to the soil and the limited circle of civil life with its pleasures and desires, it embraces the element of flux, danger, and destruction. Further, the sea is the greatest means of communication, and trade by sea creates commercial connections between distant countries and so relations involving contractual rights. At the same time, commerce of this kind is the most potent instrument of culture, and through it trade acquires its significance in the history of the world.

. . .

248. This far-flung connecting link affords the means for the colonizing activity—sporadic or systematic—to which the mature civil society is driven and by which it supplies to a part of its population a return to life on the family basis in a new land and so also supplies itself with a new demand and field for its industry.

249. While the public authority must also undertake the higher directive function of providing for the interests which lead beyond the borders of its society (see Paragraph 246), its primary purpose is to actualize and maintain the universal contained within the particularity of civil society, and its control takes the form of an external system and organization for the protection and security of particular ends and interests *en masse,* inasmuch as these interests subsist only in this universal. This universal is immanent in the interests of particularity itself and, in accordance with the Idea, particularity makes it the end and object of its own willing and activity. In this way ethical principles circle back and appear in civil society as a factor immanent in it; this consistutes the specific character of the Corporation.

(b) The Corporation

250. In virtue of the substantiality of its natural and family life, the agricultural class has directly within itself the concrete universal in which it lives. The class of civil servants is universal in character and so has the universal explicitly as its ground and as the aim of its activity. The class between them, the business class, is essentially concentrated on the particular, and hence it is to it that Corporations are specially appropriate.

251. The labor organization of civil society is split, in accordance with the nature of its particulars, into different branches. The implicit likeness of such particulars to one another becomes really existent in an association, as something common to its members. Hence a selfish purpose, directed towards its particular self-interest, apprehends and evinces itself at the same time as universal; and a member of civil society is in virtue of his own particular skill a member of a Corporation, whose universal purpose is thus wholly concrete and no wider in scope than the purpose involved in business, its proper task and interest.

252. In accordance with this definition of its functions, a Corporation has the right, under the surveillance of the public authority (*a*) to look after its own interests within its own sphere, (*b*) to co-opt members, qualified objectively by the requisite skill and rectitude, to a number fixed by the general structure of society, (*c*) to protect its members against particular contingencies, (*d*) to provide the education requisite to fit others to become members. In short, its right is to come on the scene like a second family for its members, while civil society can only be an indeterminate sort of family because it comprises everyone and so is farther removed from individuals and their special exigencies.

. . .

253. In the Corporation, the family has its stable basis in the sense that its livelihood is assured there, conditionally upon capability, i.e. it has a stable capital. In addition, this nexus of capability and livelihood is a *recognized* fact, with the result that the Corporation member needs no external marks beyond his own membership as evidence of his skill and his regular income and subsistence, i.e. as evidence that he is a somebody. It is also recognized that he belongs to a whole which is itself an organ of the entire society, and that he is actively concerned in promoting the comparatively distinterested end of this whole. Thus he commands the respect due to one in his social position.

. . .

255. As the family was the first, so the Corporation is the second ethical root of the state, the one planted in civil society. The former contains the moments of subjective particularity and objective universality in a substantial unity. But these moments are sundered in civil society to begin with; on the one side there is the particularity of need and satisfaction, reflected into itself, and on the other side the universality of abstract rights. In the Corporation these moments are united in an inward fashion, so that in this union particular welfare is present as a right and is actualized.

The sanctity of marriage and the dignity of Corporation membership are the two fixed points round which the unorganized atoms of civil society revolve.

256. The end of the Corporation is restricted and finite, while the public authority was an external organization involving a separation and a merely relative identity of controller and controlled. The end of the former and the externality and relative identity of the latter find their truth in the absolutely universal end and its absolute actuality. Hence the sphere of civil society passes over into the state.

The town is the seat of the civil life of business. There reflection arises, turns in upon itself, and pursues its atomizing task; each man maintains himself in and through his relation to others who, like himself, are persons possessed of rights. The country, on the other hand, is the seat of an ethical life resting on nature and the family. Town and country thus constitute the two moments, still ideal moments, whose true ground is the state, although it is from them that the state springs.

The philosophic proof of the concept of the state is this development of ethical life from its immediate phase through civil society, the phase of division, to the state, which then reveals itself as the true ground of these phases. A proof in philosophic science can only be a development of this kind.

. . .

THE STATE

257. The state is the actuality of the ethical Idea. It is ethical mind *qua* the substantial will manifest and revealed to itself, knowing and thinking itself, accomplishing what it knows and in so far as it knows it. The state exists immediately in custom, mediately in individual self-consciousness, knowledge, and activity, while self-consciousness in virtue of its sentiment towards the state finds in the state, as its essence and the end and product of its activity, its substantive freedom.

. . .

258. The state is absolutely rational inasmuch as it is the actuality of the substantial will which it possesses in the particular self-consciousness once that consciousness has been raised to consciousness of its universality. This substantial unity is an absolute unmoved end in itself, in which freedom comes into its supreme right. On the other hand this end has supreme right against the individual, whose supreme duty is to be a member of the state.

If the state is confused with civil society, and if its specific end is laid down as the security and protection of property and personal freedom, then the interest of the individuals as such becomes the ultimate end of their association, and it follows that membership of the state is something optional. But the state's relation to the individual is quite different from this. Since the state is mind objectified, it is only as one of its members that the individual himself has objectivity, genuine individuality, and an ethical life. Unification pure and simple is the true content and aim of the individual, and the individual's destiny is the living of a universal life. His further particular satisfaction, activity, and mode of conduct have this substantive and universally valid life as their starting point and their result.

Rationality, taken generally and in the abstract, consists in the thorough-going unity of the universal and the single. Rationality, concrete in the state, consists *(a)* so far as its content is concerned, in the unity of objective freedom (i.e. freedom of the universal or substantial will) and subjective freedom (i.e. freedom of everyone in his knowing and in his volition of particular ends); and consequently, *(b)* so far as its form is concerned, in self-determining action on laws and principles which are thoughts and so universal. This Idea is the absolutely eternal and necessary being of mind.

But if we ask what is or has been the historical origin of the state in general, still more if we ask about the origin of any particular state, of its rights and institutions, or again if we inquire whether the state originally arose out of patriarchal conditions or out of fear or trust, or out of Corporations, et cetera, or finally if we ask in what light the basis of the state's rights has been conceived and consciously established, whether this basis has been supposed to be positive divine right, or contract, custom, et cetera—all these questions are no concern of the Idea of the state. We are here dealing exclusively with the philosophic science of the state, and from that point of view all these things are mere appearance and therefore matters for history. So far as the authority of any existing state has anything to do with reasons, these reasons are culled from the forms of the law authoritative within it.

The philosophical treatment of these topics is concerned only with their inward side, with the thought of their concept.

. . .

A. Constitutional Law

260. The state is the actuality of concrete freedom. But concrete freedom consists in this, that personal individuality and its particular interests not only achieve their complete development and gain explicit recognition for their right (as they do in the sphere of the family and civil society) but, for one thing, they also pass over of their own accord into the interest of the universal, and, for another thing, they know and will the universal; they even recognize it as their own substantive mind; they take it as their end and aim and are active in its pursuit. The result is that the universal does not prevail or achieve completion except along with particular interests and through the co-operation of particular knowing and willing; and individuals likewise do not live as private persons for their own ends alone, but in the very act of willing these they will the universal in the light of the universal, and their activity is consciously aimed at none but the universal end. The principle of modern states has prodigious strength and depth because it allows the principle of subjectivity to progress to its culmination in the

extreme of self-subsistent personal particularity, and yet at the same time brings it back to the substantive unity and so maintains this unity in the principle of subjectivity itself.

261. In contrast with the spheres of private rights and private welfare (the family and civil society), the state is from one point of view an external necessity and their higher authority; its nature is such that their laws and interests are subordinate to it and dependent on it. On the other hand, however, it is the end immanent within them, and its strength lies in the unity of its own universal end and aim with the particular interest of individuals, in the fact that individuals have duties to the state in proportion as they have rights against it.

[1821]

from "On the Jewish Question"

I. BRUNO BAUER, DIE JUDENFRAGE[1]

The German Jews seek emancipation. What kind of emancipation do they want? *Civic, political* emancipation.

Bruno Bauer replies to them: In Germany no one is politically emancipated. We ourselves are not free. How then could we liberate you? You Jews are *egoists* if you demand for yourselves, as Jews, a special emancipation. You should work, as Germans, for the political emancipation of Germany, and as men, for the emancipation of mankind. You should feel the particular kind of oppression and shame which you suffer, not as an exception to the rule but rather as a confirmation of the rule.

Or do the Jews want to be placed on a footing of equality with the *Christian subjects?* If they recognize the *Christian state* as legally established they also recognize the régime of general enslavement. Why should their particular yoke be irksome when they accept the general yoke? Why should the German be interested in the liberation of the Jew, if the Jew is not interested in the liberation of the German?

The *Christian* state recognizes nothing but *privileges.* The Jew himself, in this state, has the privilege of being a Jew. As a Jew he possesses rights which the Christians do not have. Why does he want rights which he does not have but which the Christians enjoy?

In demanding his emancipation from the Christian state he asks the Christian state to abandon its *religious* prejudice. But does he, the Jew, give up *his* religious prejudice? Has he then the right to insist that someone else should forswear his religion?

The *Christian* state, *by its very nature,* is incapable of emancipating the Jew. But, adds Bauer, the Jew, by his very nature, cannot be emancipated. As long as

---

1. *The Jewish Question* [Braunschweig, 1843.—*Marx*]

the state remains Christian, and as long as the Jew remains a Jew, they are equally incapable, the one of conferring emancipation, the other of receiving it.

With respect to the Jews the Christian state can only adopt the attitude of a Christian state. That is, it can permit the Jew, as a matter of privilege, to isolate himself from its other subjects; but it must then allow the pressures of all the other spheres of society to bear upon the Jew, and all the more heavily since he is in *religious* opposition to the dominant religion. But the Jew likewise can only adopt a Jewish attitude, i.e. that of a foreigner, towards the state, since he opposes his illusory nationality to actual nationality, his illusory law to actual law. He considers it his right to separate himself from the rest of humanity; as a matter of principle he takes no part in the historical movement and looks to a future which has nothing in common with the future of mankind as a whole. He regards himself as a member of the Jewish people, and the Jewish people as the chosen people.

On what grounds, then, do you Jews demand emancipation? On account of your religion? But it is the mortal enemy of the state religion. As citizens? But there are no citizens in Germany. As men? But you are not men any more than those to whom you appeal.

Bauer, after criticizing earlier approaches and solutions, formulates the question of Jewish emancipation in a new way. What, he asks, is the nature of the Jew who is to be emancipated, and the *nature* of the Christian state which is to emancipate him? He replies by a critique of the Jewish religion, analyses the religious opposition between Judaism and Christianity, explains the essence of the Christian state; and does all this with dash, clarity, wit and profundity, in a style which is as precise as it is pithy and vigorous.

How then does Bauer resolve the Jewish question? What is the result? To formulate a question is to resolve it. The critical study of the Jewish question is the answer to the Jewish question. Here it is in brief: we have to emancipate ourselves before we can emancipate others.

The most stubborn form of the opposition between Jew and Christian is the *religious* opposition. How is an opposition resolved? By making it impossible. And how is *religious* opposition made impossible? By abolishing *religion*. As soon as Jew and Christian come to see in their respective religions nothing more than *stages in the development of the human mind*—snake skins which have been cast off by *history,* and *man* as the snake who clothed himself in them—they will no longer find themselves in religious opposition, but in a purely critical, *scientific* and human relationship. *Science* will then constitute their unity. But scientific oppositions are resolved by science itself.

The *German* Jew, in particular, suffers from the general lack of political freedom and the pronounced Christianity of the state. But in Bauer's sense the Jewish question has a general significance, independent of the specifically German conditions. It is the question of the relations between religion and the state, of the *contradiction between religious prejudice and political emancipation.* Emancipation from religion is posited as a condition, both for the Jew who wants political emancipation, and for the state which should emancipate him and itself be emancipated.

"Very well, it may be said (and the Jew himself says it) but the Jew should not be emancipated because he is a Jew, because he has such an excellent and universal moral creed; the *Jew* should take second place to the citizen, and he will be a *citizen* although he is and desires to remain a Jew. In other words, he is and remains a *Jew,* even though he is a *citizen* and as such lives in a universal human condition; his restricted Jewish nature always finally triumphs over his human and political obligations. The bias persists even though it is overcome by general principles. But if it persists, it would be truer to say that it overcomes all the rest." "It is only in a sophistical and superficial sense that the Jew could remain a Jew in political life. Consequently, if he wanted to remain a Jew, this would mean that the superficial became the essential and thus triumphed. In other words, his life *in the state* would be only a semblance, or a momentary exception to the essential and normal."[2]

Let us see also how Bauer establishes the role of the state.

"France," he says, "has provided us recently,[3] in connection with the Jewish question (and for that matter all other *political* questions), with the spectacle of a life which is free but which revokes its freedom by law and so declares it to be merely an appearance; and which, on the other hand, denies its free laws by its acts."[4]

"In France, universal liberty is not yet established by law, nor is the *Jewish question as yet resolved,* because legal liberty, i.e. the equality of all citizens, is restricted in actual life, which is still dominated and fragmented by religious privileges, and because the lack of liberty in actual life influences law in its turn and obliges it to sanction the division of citizens who are by nature free into oppressors and oppressed."[5]

When, therefore, would the Jewish question be resolved in France?

"The Jew would really have ceased to be Jewish, for example, if he did not allow his religious code to prevent his fulfillment of his duties towards the state and his fellow citizens; if he attended and took part in the public business of the Chamber of Deputies on the sabbath. It would be necessary, further, to abolish all *religious privilege,* including the monopoly of a privileged church. If, thereafter, some or many or *even the overwhelming majority felt obliged to fulfil their religious duties,* such practices should be left *to them as an absolutely* private matter."[6] "There is no longer any religion when there is no longer a privileged religion. Take away from

---

2. Bauer, "Die Fähigkeit der heutigen Juden und Christen, frei zu werden," *Einundzwanzig Bogen,* p. 57. *[Marx]* Emphases added by Marx.

3. Chamber of Deputies. Debate of 26th December, 1840. *[Marx]*

4. Bauer, *Die Judenfrage,* p. 64. *[Marx]*

5. Ibid., p. 65. *[Marx]*

6. Loc. cit. *[Marx]*

religion its power to excommunicate and it will no longer exist."[7] "Mr. Martin du Nord has seen, in the suggestion to omit any mention of Sunday in the law, a proposal to declare that Christianity has ceased to exist. With equal right (and the right is well founded) the declaration that the law of the sabbath is no longer binding upon the Jew would amount to proclaiming the end of Judaism."[8]

Thus Bauer demands, on the one hand, that the Jew should renounce Judaism, and in general that man should renounce religion, in order to be emancipated as a citizen. On the other hand, he considers, and this follows logically, that the political abolition of religion is the abolition of all religion. The state which presupposes religion is not yet a true or actual state. "Clearly, the religious idea gives some assurances to the state. But to what state? *To what kind of state?*"[9]

At this point we see that the Jewish question is considered only from one aspect.

It was by no means sufficient to ask: who should emancipate? who should be emancipated? The critic should ask a third question: *what kind of emancipation is involved?* What are the essential conditions of the emancipation which is demanded? The criticism of *political emancipation* itself was only the final criticism of the Jewish question and its genuine resolution into the *"general question of the age."*

Bauer, since he does not formulate the problem at this level, falls into contradictions. He establishes conditions which are not based upon the nature of *political* emancipation. He raises questions which are irrelevant to his problem, and he resolves problems which leave his question unanswered. When Bauer says of the opponents of Jewish emancipation that "Their error was simply to assume that the Christian state was the only true one, and not to subject it to the same criticism as Judaism,"[10] we see his own error in the fact that he subjects *only* the "Christian state," and not the "state as such" to criticism, that he does not examine *the relation between political emancipation and human emancipation,* and that he, therefore, poses conditions which are only explicable by his lack of critical sense in confusing political emancipation and universal human emancipation. Bauer asks the Jews: Have you, from your standpoint, the right to demand *political emancipation?* We ask the converse question: from the standpoint of *political* emancipation can the Jew be required to abolish Judaism, or man be asked to abolish religion?

The Jewish question presents itself differently according to the state in which the Jew resides. In Germany, where there is no political state, no state as such, the Jewish question is purely *theological.* The Jew finds himself in *religious* opposition to the state, which proclaims Christianity as its foundation. This state is a theologian *ex professo.* Criticism here is criticism of theology. And so we move always in the domain of theology, however *critically* we may move therein.

---

7. Ibid., p. 71. *[Marx]*
8. Bauer, *Die Judenfrage,* p. 66. *[Marx]*
9. Ibid., p. 97. *[Marx]*
10. Bauer, *Die Judenfrage,* p. 3. *[Marx]*

In France, which is a *constitutional* state, the Jewish question is a question of constitutionalism, of the incompleteness *of political emancipation.* Since the *semblance* of a state religion is maintained here, if only in the insignificant and self-contradictory formula of a *religion of the majority,* the relation of the Jews to the state also retains a semblance of religious, theological opposition.

It is only in the free states of North America, or at least in some of them, that the Jewish question loses its *theological* significance and becomes a truly *secular* question. Only where the state exists in its completely developed form can the relation of the Jew, and of the religious man in general, to the political state appear in a pure form, with its own characteristics. The criticism of this relation ceases to be theological criticism when the state ceases to maintain a *theological* attitude towards religion, that is, when it adopts the attitude of a state, i.e. a *political* attitude. Criticism then becomes *criticism of the political state.* And at this point, where the question ceases to be *theological,* Bauer's criticism ceases to be critical.

"There is not, in the United States, either a state religion or a religion declared to be that of a majority, or a predominance of one religion over another. The state remains aloof from all religions."[11] There are even some states in North America in which "the constitution does not impose any religious belief or practice as a condition of political rights."[12] And yet, "no one in the United States believes that a man without religion can be an honest man."[13] And North America is pre-eminently the country of religiosity, as Beaumont,[14] Tocqueville[15] and the Englishman, Hamilton,[16] assure us in unison. However, the states of North America only serve as an example. The question is: what is the relation between *complete* political emancipation and religion? If we find in the country which has attained full political emancipation, that religion not only continues to *exist* but is *fresh* and *vigorous,* this is proof that the existence of religion is not at all opposed to the perfection of the state. But since the existence of religion is the existence of a defect, the source of this defect must be sought in the *nature* of the state itself. Religion no longer appears as the basis, but as the *manifestation* of secular narrowness. That is why we explain the religious constraints upon the free citizens by the secular constraints upon them. We do not claim that they must transcend their religious narrowness in order to get rid of their secular limitations. We claim that they will transcend their religious narrowness once they have overcome their secular limitations. We do not turn secular questions into theological questions; we turn theological questions into secular ones. History has for long

---

11. Gustave de Beaumont, *Marie ou l'esclavage aux États-Unis,* Bruxelles, 1835, 2 vols., II, p. 207. *[Marx]* Marx refers to another edition, Paris, 1835.

12. Ibid., p. 216. Beaumont actually refers to *all* the States of North America.

13. Ibid., p. 217. *[Marx]*

14. G. de Beaumont, op. cit. *[Marx]*

15. A. de Tocqueville, *De la démocratie en Amérique. [Marx]*

16. Thomas Hamilton, *Men and Manners in North America,* Edinburgh, 1833, 2 vols. *[Marx]* Marx quotes from the German translation, Mannheim, 1834.

enough been resolved into superstition; but we now resolve superstition into history. The question of the *relation between political emancipation and religion* becomes for us a question of the *relation between political emancipation and human emancipation.* We criticize the religious failings of the political state by criticizing the political state in its *secular* form, disregarding its religious failings. We express in human terms the contradiction between the state and a *particular religion,* for example *Judaism,* by showing the contradiction between the state and particular *secular elements,* between the state and *religion in general* and between the state and its general *presuppositions.*

The *political* emancipation of the Jew or the Christian—of the *religious* man in general—is the *emancipation* of the state from Judaism, Christianity, and *religion* in general. The *state* emancipates itself from religion in its own particular way, in the mode which corresponds to its nature, by emancipating itself from the *state religion;* that is to say, by giving recognition to no religion and affirming itself purely and simply as a state. To be *politically* emancipated from religion is not to be finally and completely emancipated from religion, because political emancipation is not the final and absolute form of *human* emancipation.

The limits of political emancipation appear at once in the fact that the *state* can liberate itself from a constant without man himself being *really* liberated; that a state may be a *free state* without man himself being a *free man.* Bauer himself tacitly admits this when he makes political emancipation depend upon the following condition—

"It would be necessary, moreover, to abolish all religious privileges, including the monopoly of a privileged church. If some people, or even the *immense majority, still felt obliged to fulfill their religious duties,* this practice should be left to them as a *completely private matter.*" Thus the state may have emancipated itself from religion, even though the *immense majority* of people continue to be religious. And the immense majority do not cease to be religious by virtue of being religious *in private.*

The attitude of the state, especially the *free state,* towards religion is only the attitude towards religion of the individuals who compose the state. It follows that man frees himself from a constraint in a *political* way, through the state, when he transcends his limitations, in contradiction with himself, and in an *abstract, narrow* and partial way. Furthermore, by emancipating himself politically, man emancipates himself in a *devious way,* through an intermediary, however *necessary* this intermediary may be. Finally, even when he proclaims himself an atheist through the intermediary of the state, that is, when he declares the state to be an atheist, he is still engrossed in religion, because he only recognizes himself as an atheist in a roundabout way, through an intermediary. Religion is simply the recognition of man in a roundabout fashion; that is, through an intermediary. The state is the intermediary between man and human liberty. Just as Christ is the intermediary to whom man attributes all his own divinity and all his religious *bonds,* so the state is the intermediary to which man confides all his non-divinity and all his *human freedom.*

The *political* elevation of man above religion shares the weaknesses and merits of all such political measures. For example, the state as a state abolishes *private property* (i.e. man decrees by *political* means the *abolition* of private property) when it abolishes the *property qualification* for electors and representatives, as has been done in many of the North American States. Hamilton interprets this phenomenon quite correctly from the political standpoint: *The masses have gained a victory over property owners and financial wealth.*[17] Is not private property ideally abolished when the non-owner comes to legislate for the owner of property? The *property qualification* is the last *political* form in which private property is recognized.

But the political suppression of private property not only does not abolish private property; it actually presupposes its existence. The state abolishes, after its fashion, the distinctions established by *birth, social rank, education, occupation,* when it decrees that birth, social rank, education, occupation are *non-political* distinctions; when it proclaims, without regard to these distinctions, that every member of society is an *equal* partner in popular sovereignty, and treats all the elements which compose the real life of the nation from he standpoint of the state. But the state, none the less, allows private property, education, occupation, to *act* after *their* own fashion, namely as private property, education, occupation, and to manifest their *particular* nature. Far from abolishing these *effective* differences, it only exists so far as they are presupposed; it is conscious of being a *political* state and it manifests its *universality* only in opposition to these elements. Hegel, therefore, defines the relation of the political state to religion quite correctly when he says: "In order for the state to come in to existence as the *self-knowing* ethical actuality of spirit, it is essential that it should be distinct from the forms of authority and of faith. But this distinction emerges only in so far as divisions occur within the ecclesiastical sphere itself. It is only in this way that the state, above the *particular* churches, has attained to the universality of thought—its formal principle—and is bringing this universality into existence."[18] To be sure! Only in this manner, *above* the *particular* elements, can the state constitute itself as universality.

The perfected political state is, by its nature, the *species*-life[19] of man as *opposed* to his material life. All the presuppositions of this egoistic life continue to exist in *civil society outside* the political sphere, as qualities of civil society.

17. Hamilton, op. cit., I, pp. 288, 306, 309. *[Marx]*

18. Hegel, *Grundlinien der Philosophie des Rechts,* Ier Aufgabe, 1821, p. 346. *[Marx]* See the English translation by T. M. Knox, *Hegel's Philosophy of Right,* Oxford, 1942, p. 173.

19. The terms "species-life" *(Gattungsleben)* and "species-being" *(Gattungswesen)* are derived from Feuerbach. In the first chapter of *Das Wesen des Christentums [The Essence of Christianity],* Leipzig, 1841, Feuerbach discusses the nature of man, and argues that man is to be distinguished from animals not by "consciousness" as such, but by a particular kind of consciousness. Man is not only conscious of himself as an individual; he is also conscious of himself as a member of the human species, and so he apprehends a "human essence" which is the same in himself and in other men. According to

Where the political state has attained to its full development, man leads, not only in thought, in consciousness, but in *reality,* in *life,* a double existence—celestial and terrestrial. He lives in the *political community,* where he regards himself as a *communal being,* and in *civil society* where he acts simply as a *private individual,* treats other men as means, degrades himself to the role of a mere means, and becomes the plaything of alien powers. The political state, in relation to civil society, is just as spiritual as is heaven in relation to earth. It stands in the same opposition to civil society, and overcomes it in the same manner as religion overcomes the narrowness of the profane world; that is, it has always to acknowledge it again, reestablish it, and allow itself to be dominated by it. Man, in his *most intimate* reality, in civil society, is a profane being. Here, where he appears both to himself and to others as a real individual he is an *illusory* phenomenon. In the state, on the contrary, where he is regarded as a species-being,[20] man is the imaginary member of an imaginary sovereignty, divested of his real, individual life, and infused with an unreal universality.

The conflict in which the individual, as the professor of a *particular* religion, finds himself involved with his own quality of citizenship and with other men as members of the community, may be resolved into the *secular* schism between the *political* state and *civil society.* For man as a *bourgeois*[21] "life in the state is only an appearance or a fleeting exception to the normal and essential." It is true that the *bourgeois,* like the Jew, participates in political life only in a sophistical way, just as the *citoyen*[22] is a Jew or a *bourgeois* only in a sophistical way. But this sophistry is not personal. It is the *sophistry of the political state* itself. The difference between the religious man and the citizen is the same as that between the shopkeeper and the citizens, between the day-labourer and the citizen, between the landed proprietor and the citizen, between the *living individual* and the *citizen.* The contradiction in which the religious man finds himself with the political man, is the same contradition in which the *bourgeois* finds himself with the citizen, and the member of society with his *political lion's skin.*

This secular opposition, to which the Jewish question reduces itself—the relation between the political state and its presuppositions, whether the latter are material elements such as private property, etc., or spiritual elements such as culture or religion, the conflict between the *general interest* and *private interest,* the schism between the *political* state and *civil society*—these profane contradictions,

---

Feuerbach this ability to conceive of "species" is the fundamental element in the human power of reasoning: "Science is the consciousness of species." Marx, while not departing from this meaning of the terms, employs them in other contexts; and he insists more strongly than Feuerbach that since this "species-consciousness" defines the nature of man, man is only living and acting authentically (i.e. in accordance with his nature) when he lives and acts deliberately as a "species-being," that is, as a *social* being.

20. See previous note.
21. I.e. as a member of civil society.
22. I.e. the individual with political rights.

Bauer leaves intact, while he directs his polemic against their *religious* expression. "It is precisely this basis—that is, the needs which assure the existence of *civil society* and *guarantee its necessity*—which exposes its existence to continual danger, maintains an element of uncertainty in civil society, produces this continually changing compound of wealth and poverty, of prosperity and distress, and above all generates change."[23] Compare the whole section entitled "Civil society,"[24] which follows closely the distinctive features of Hegel's philosophy of right. Civil society, in its opposition to this political state, is recognized as necessary because the political state is recognized as necessary.

Political emancipation certainly represents a great progress. It is not, indeed, the final form of human emancipation, but it is the final form of human emancipation *within* the framework of the prevailing social order. It goes without saying that we are speaking here of real, practical emancipation.

Man emancipates himself *politically* from religion by expelling it from the sphere of public law to that of private law. Religion is no longer the spirit of the *state,* in which man behaves, albeit in a specific and limited way and in a particular sphere, as a species-being, in community with other men. It has become the spirit of *civil society,* of the sphere of egoism and of the *bellum omnium contra omnes.* It is no longer the essence of *community,* but the essence of *differentiation.* It has become what it was at the *beginning,* an expression of the fact that man is *separated* from the *community,* from himself and from other men. It is now only the abstract avowal of an individual folly, a private whim or caprice. The infinite fragmentation of religion in North America, for example, already gives it the *external* form of a strictly private affair. It has been relegated among the numerous private interests and exiled from the life of the community as such. But one should have no illusions about the scope of political emancipation. The division of man into the *public person* and the *private person,* the *displacement* of religion from the state to civil society—all this is not a stage in political emancipation but its consummation. Thus political emancipation does not abolish, and does not even strive to abolish, man's *real* religiosity.

The *decomposition* of man into Jew and citizen, Protestant and citizen, religious man and citizen, is not a deception practiced *against* the political system nor yet an evasion of political emancipation. It is *political emancipation itself,* the *political* mode of emancipation from religion. Certainly, in periods when the political state as such comes violently to birth in civil society, and when men strive to liberate themselves through political emancipation, the state can, and must, proceed to *abolish and destroy religion;* but only in the same way as it proceeds to abolish private property, by declaring a maximum, by confiscation, or by progressive taxation, or in the same way as it proceeds to abolish life, by the *guillotine.* At those times when the state is most aware of itself, political life seeks to stifle its

23. Bauer, *Die Judenfrage,* p. 8. *[Marx]*
24. Ibid., pp. 8–9. *[Marx]*

own prerequisites—civil society and its elements—and to establish itself as the genuine and harmonious species-life of man. But it can only achieve this end by setting itself in *violent* contradiction with its own conditions of existence, by declaring a *permanent* revolution. Thus the political drama ends necessarily with the restoration of religion, of private property, of all the elements of civil society, just as war ends with the conclusion of peace.

The members of the political state are religious because of the dualism between individual life and species-life, between the life of civil society and political life. They are religious in the sense that man treats political life, which is remote from his own individual existence, as if it were his true life; and in the sense that religion is here the spirit of civil society, and expresses the separation and withdrawal of man from man. Political democracy is Christian in the sense that man, not merely one man but every man, is there considered a sovereign being, a supreme being; but it is uneducated, unsocial man, man just as he is in his fortuitous existence, man as he has been corrupted, lost to himself, alienated, subjected to the rule of inhuman conditions and elements, by the whole organization of our society—in short man who is not yet a *real* species-being. Creations of fantasy, dreams, the postulates of Christianity, the sovereignty of man—but of man as an alien being distinguished from the real man—all these become, in democracy, the tangible and present reality, secular maxims.

In the perfected democracy, the religious and theological consciousness appears to itself all the more religious and theological in that it is apparently without any political significance or terrestrial aims, is an affair of the heart withdrawn from the world, an expression of the limitations of reason, a product of arbitrariness and fantasy, a veritable life in the beyond. Christianity here attains the *practical* expression of its universal religious significance, because the most varied views are brought together in the form of Christianity, and still more because Christianity does not ask that anyone should profess Christianity, but simply that he should have some kind of religion (*see* Beaumont, op. cit.). The religious consciousness runs riot in a wealth of contradictions and diversity.

We have shown, therefore, that political emancipation from religion leaves religion in existence, although this is no longer a privileged religion. The contradiction in which the adherent of a particular religion finds himself in relation to his citizenship is only *one aspect* of the universal *secular contradiction between the political state and* civil society. The consummation of the Christian state is a state which acknowledges itself simply as a state and ignores the religion of its members. The emancipation of the state from religion is not the emancipation of the real man from religion.

We do not say to the Jews, therefore, as does Bauer: you cannot be emancipated politically without emancipating yourselves completely from Judaism. We say rather: it is because you can be emancipated politically, without renouncing Judaism completely and absolutely, that *political emancipation* itself is not *human* emancipation. If you want to be politically emancipated, without emancipating yourselves humanly, the inadequacy and the contradiction is not entirely in yourselves but in the *nature* and the *category* of political emancipation. If you are preoccupied with this category you share the general prejudice. Just as the state *evangelizes* when, although it is a state, it adopts a Christian attitude towards the Jews, the Jew *acts politically* when, though a Jew, he demands civil rights.

But if a man, though a Jew, can be emancipated politically and acquire civil rights, can he claim and acquire what are called the *rights of man?* Bauer *denies* it. "The question is whether the Jew as such, that is, the Jew who himself avows that he is constrained by his true nature to live eternally separate from men, is able to acquire and to concede to others the *universal rights of man.*"

"The idea of the rights of man was only discovered in the Christian world, in the last century. It is not an innate idea; on the contrary, it is acquired in a struggle against the historical traditions in which man has been educated up to the present time. The rights of man are not, therefore, a gift of nature, nor a legacy from past history, but the reward of a struggle against the accident of birth and against the privileges which history has hitherto transmitted from generation to generation. They are the results of culture, and only he can possess them who has merited and earned them."

"But can the Jew really take possession of them? As long as he remains Jewish the limited nature which makes him a Jew must prevail over the human nature which should associate him, as a man, with other men; and it will isolate him from everyone who is not a Jew. He declares, by this separation, that the particular nature which makes him Jewish is his true and supreme nature, before which human nature has to efface itself."

"Similarly, the Christian as such cannot grant the rights of man."[25]

According to Bauer man has to sacrifice the *"privilege of faith"* in order to acquire the general rights of man. Let us consider for a moment the so-called rights of man; let us examine them in their most authentic form, that which they have among those who *discovered* them, the North Americans and the French! These rights of man are, in part, *political rights,* which can only be exercised if one is a member of a community. Their content is *participation* in the *community* life, in the *political* life of the community, the life of the state. They fall in the category of *political liberty,* of *civil rights,* which as we have seen do not at all presuppose the consistent and positive abolition of religion; nor consequently, of Judaism. It remains to consider the other part, namely the *rights of man* as distinct from the *rights of citizen.*

Among them is to be found the freedom of conscience, the right to practice a chosen religion. The *privilege of faith* is expressly recognized, either as a *right of man* or as a consequence of a right of man, namely liberty. *Declaration of the Rights of Man and of the Citizen,* 1791, Article 10: "No one is to be disturbed on

25. *Bauer,* Die Judenfrage, *pp. 19–20. [Marx]*

account of his opinions, even religious opinions." There is guaranteed, as one of the rights of man, "the liberty of every man to practice the *religion* to which he adheres."

The *Declaration of the Rights of Man, etc.* 1793, enumerates among the rights of man (Article 7): "The liberty of religious observance." Moreover, it is even stated, with respect to the right to express ideas and opinions, to hold meetings, to practise a religion, that: "The necessity of enunciating these *rights* presupposes either the existence or the recent memory of despotism." Compare the Constitution of 1795, Section XII, Article 354.

Constitution of Pennsylvania, Article 9, § 3: "All men have received from nature the imprescriptible *right* to worship the Almighty according to the dictates of their conscience, and no one can be legally compelled to follow, establish or support against his will any religion or religious ministry. No human authority can, in any circumstances, intervene in a matter of conscience or control the forces of the soul."

Constitution of New Hampshire, Articles 5 and 6: "Among these natural rights some are by nature inalienable since nothing can replace them. The rights of conscience are among them."[26]

The incompatibility between religion and the rights of man is so little manifest in the concept of the rights of man that the *right to be religious,* in one's own fashion, and to practice one's own particular religion, is expressly included among the rights of man. The privilege of faith is a *universal right of man.*

A distinction is made between the rights of man and the rights of the citizen. Who is this *man* distinct from the *citizen?* No one but the *member of civil society.* Why is the member of civil society called "man," simply man, and why are his rights called the "rights of man"? How is this fact to be explained? By the relation between the political state and civil society, and by the nature of political emancipation.

Let us notice first of all that the so-called *rights of man,* as distinct from the *rights of the citizen,* are simply the rights of a *member of civil society,* that is, of egoistic man, of man separated from other men and from the community. The most radical constitution, that of 1793, says: *Declaration of the Rights of Man and of the Citizen:* Article 2. "These rights, etc. (the natural and imprescriptible rights) are: *equality, liberty, security, property.*"

What constitutes liberty?

Article 6. "Liberty is the power which man has to do everything which does not harm the rights of others."

Liberty is, therefore, the right to do everything which does not harm others. The limits within which each individual can act without harming others are determined by law, just as the boundary between two fields is marked by a stake. It is a question of the liberty of man regarded as an isolated monad, withdrawn into

26. Beaumont, op. cit., II, pp. 206–7. *[Marx]*

himself. Why, according to Bauer, is the Jew not fitted to acquire the rights of man? "As long as he remains Jewish the limited nature which makes him a Jew must prevail over the human nature which should associate him, as a man, with other men; and it will isolate him from everyone who is not a Jew." But liberty as a right of man is not founded upon the relations between man and man, but rather upon the separation of man from man. It is the right of such separation. The right of the *circumscribed* individual, withdrawn into himself.

The practical application of the right of liberty is the right of private property. What constitutes the right of private property?

Article 16 (*Constitution* of 1793). "The right of *property* is that which belongs to every citizen of enjoying and disposing *as he will* of his goods and revenues, of the fruits of his work and industry."

The right of property is, therefore, the right to enjoy one's fortune and to dispose of it as one will; without regard for other men and independently of society. It is the right of self-interest. This individual liberty, and its application, form the basis of civil society. It leads every man to see in other men, not the *realization,* but rather the *limitation* of his own liberty. It declares above all the right "to enjoy and to dispose *as one will,* one's goods and revenues, the fruits of one's work and industry."

There remain the other rights of man, equality and security.

The term "equality" has here no political significance. It is only the equal right to liberty as defined above; namely that every man is equally regarded as a self-sufficient monad. The Constitution of 1795 defines the concept of liberty in this sense.

Article 5 (*Constitution* of 1795). "Equality consists in the fact that the law is the same for all, whether it protects or punishes."

And security?

Article 8 (*Constitution* of 1793). "Security consists in the protection afforded by society to each of its members for the preservation of his person, his rights, and his property."

Security is the supreme social concept of civil society; the concept of the police. The whole society exists only in order to guarantee for each of its members the preservation of his person, his rights and his property. It is in this sense that Hegel calls civil society "the state of need and of reason."

The concept of security is not enough to raise civil society above its egoism. Security is, rather, the *assurance* of its egoism.

None of the supposed rights of man, therefore, go beyond the egoistic man, man as he is, as a member of civil society; that is, an individual separated from the community, withdrawn into himself, wholly preoccupied with his private interest and acting in accordance with his private caprice. Man is far from being considered, in the rights of man, as a species-being; on the contrary, species-life itself—society—appears as a system which is external to the individual and as a limitation of his original independence. The only bond between men is natural necessity, need and private interest, the preservation of their property and their egoistic persons.

It is difficult enough to understand that a nation which has just begun to liberate itself, to tear down all the barriers between different sections of the people and to establish a political community should solemnly proclaim (*Declaration* of 1791) the rights of the egoistic man, separated from his fellow men and from the community, and should renew this proclamation at a moment when only the most heroic devotion can save the nation (and, is, therefore, urgently called for), and when the sacrifice of all the interests of civil society is in question and egoism should be punished as a crime. (*Declaration of the Rights of Man, etc.* 1793). The matter becomes still more incomprehensible when we observe that the political liberators reduce citizenship, the *political community*, to a mere *means* for preserving these so-called rights of man; and consequently, that the citizen is declared to be the servant of egoistic "man," that the sphere in which man functions as a species-being is degraded to a level below the sphere where he functions as a partial being, and finally that it is man as a bourgeois and not man as a citizen who is considered the *true* and *authentic* man.

"The end of every *political association* is the *preservation* of the natural and imprescriptible rights of man." (*Declaration of the Rights of Man, etc.* 1791, Article 2.) "Government is instituted in order to guarantee man's enjoyment of his natural and imprescriptible rights." (*Declaration, etc.* 1793, Article 1.) Thus, even in the period of its youthful enthusiasm, which is raised to fever pitch by the force of circumstances, political life declares itself to be only a *means,* whose end is the life of civil society. It is true that its revolutionary practice is in flagrant contradiction with its theory. While, for instance, security is declared to be one of the rights of man, the violation of the privacy of correspondence is openly considered. While the "unlimited freedom of the Press" (*Constitution* of 1793, Article 122), as a corollary of the right of individual liberty, is guaranteed, the freedom of the Press is completely destroyed, since "the freedom of the Press should not be permitted when it endangers public liberty."[27] This amounts to saying: the right to liberty ceases to be a right as soon as it comes into conflict with *political* life, whereas in theory political life is no more than the guarantee of the rights of man—the rights of the individual man—and should, therefore, be suspended as soon as it comes into contradiction with its *end,* these rights of man. But practice is only the exception, while theory is the rule. Even if one decided to regarded revolutionary practice as the correct expression of this relation, the problem would remain as to why it is that in the minds of political liberators the relation is inverted, so that the ends appears as the means and the means as the end? This optical illusion of their consciousness would always remain a problem, though a psychological and theoretical one.

27. Buchez et Roux, "Robespierre jeune," *Histoire parlementaire de la Révolution française,* Tome XXVIII, p. 159. *[Marx]*

But the problem is easily solved.

Political emancipation is at the same time the *dissolution* of the old society, upon which the sovereign power, the alienated political life of the people, rests. Political revolution is a revolution of civil society. What was the nature of the old society? It can be characterized in one word: *feudalism*. The old civil society had a *directly political* character; that is, the elements of civil life such as property, the family, and types of occupation had been raised, in the form of lordship, caste and guilds, to elements of political life. They determined, in this form, the relation of the individual to the *state as a whole;* that is, his *political* situation, or in other words, his separation and exclusion from the other elements of society. For this organization of national life did not constitute property and labour as social elements; it rather succeeded in *separating* them from the body of the state, and made them *distinct* societies within society. Nevertheless, at least in the feudal sense, the vital functions and conditions of civil society remained political. They excluded the individual from the body of the state, and transformed the *particular* relation which existed between his corporation and the state into a general relation between the individual and social life, just as they transformed his specific civil activity and situation into a general activity and situation. As a result of this organization, the state as a whole and its consciousness, will and activity—the general political power—also necessarily appeared as the *private* affair of a ruler and his servants, separated from the people.

The political revolution which overthrew this power of the ruler, which made state affairs the affairs of the people, and the political state a matter of *general* concern, i.e. a real state, necessarily shattered everything—estates, corporations, guilds, privileges—which expressed the separation of the people from community life. The political revolution therefore *abolished* the *political character of civil society*. It dissolved civil society into its basic elements, on the one hand *individuals,* and on the other hand the *material and cultural elements* which formed the life experience and the civil situation of these individuals. It set free the political spirit which had, so to speak, been dissolved, fragmented and lost in the various culs-de-sac of feudal society; it reassembled these scattered fragments, liberated the political spirit from its connexion with civil life and made of it the community sphere, the *general* concern of the people, in principle independent of these particular elements of civil life. A *specific* activity and situation in life no longer had any but an individual significance. They no longer constituted the general relation between the individual and the state as a whole. Public affairs as such became the general affair of each individual, and political functions became general functions.

But the consummation of the idealism of the state was at the same time the consummation of the materialism of civil society. The bonds which had restrained the egoistic spirit of civil society were removed along with the political yoke. Political emancipation was at the same time an emancipation of civil society from politics and from even the *semblance* of a general content.

Feudal society was dissolved into its basic element, *man;* but into *egoistic* man who was its real foundation.

Man in this aspect, the member of civil society, is now the foundation and presupposition of the *political* state. He is recognized as such in the rights of man.

But the liberty of egoistic man, and the recognition of this liberty, is rather the recognition of the *frenzied* movement of the cultural and material elements which form the content of his life.

Thus man was not liberated from religion; he received religious liberty. He was not liberated from property; he received the liberty to own property. He was not liberated from the egoism of business; he received the liberty to engage in business.

The *formation of the political state,* and the dissolution of civil society into independent *individuals* whose relations are regulated by *law,* as the relations between men in the corporations and guilds were regulated by *privilege,* are accomplished by *one and the same act.* Man as a member of civil society—*non-political* man—necessarily appears as the *natural* man. The rights of man appear as natural rights because *conscious* activity is concentrated upon political *action. Egoistic* man is the *passive, given* result of the dissolution of society, an object of *direct apprehension* and consequently a *natural* object. The *political revolution* dissolves civil society into its elements without *revolutionizing* these elements themselves or subjecting them to criticism. This revolution regards civil society, the sphere of human needs, labor, private interests and civil law, as the *basis of its own existence,* as a self-subsistent *precondition,* and thus as its *natural basis.* Finally, man as a member of civil society is identified with *authentic man,* man as distinct from citizen, because he is man in his sensuous, individual and *immediate* existence, whereas *political* man is only abstract, artificial man, man as an *allegorical, moral* person. Thus man as he really is, is seen only in the form of *egoistic* man, and man in his *true* nature only in the form of the *abstract citizen.*

The abstract notion of political man is well formulated by Rousseau: "Whoever dares undertake to establish a people's institutions must feel himself capable of *changing,* as it were, *human nature* itself, of *transforming* each individual who, in isolation, is a complete but solitary whole, into a *part* of something greater than himself, from which in a sense, he derives his life and his being; [of changing man's nature in order to strengthen it;] of substituting a limited and moral existence for the physical and independent life [with which all of us are endowed by nature]. His task, in short, is to take from *a man his own powers,* and to give him in exchange alien powers which he can only employ with the help of other men."[28]

28. J. J. Rousseau, *Du contrat social,* Book II. Chapter VII, "The Legislator." Marx quoted this passage in French, and added the emphases; he omitted the portions enclosed in square brackets.

Every emancipation is a *restoration* of the human world and of human relationships to *man himself.*

Political emancipation is a reduction of man, on the one hand to a member of civil society, an *independent* and *egoistic* individual, and on the other hand, to a *citizen,* to a moral person.

Human emancipation will only be complete when the real, individual man has absorbed into himself the abstract citizen; when as an individual man, in his everyday life, in his work and in his relationships, he has become a *species-being;* and when he has recognized and organized his own powers *(forces propres)* as *social* powers so that he no longer separates this social power from himself as *political* power.

[1843]

from Democracy in America

POLITICAL ASSOCIATION IN THE UNITED STATES

> *Everyday use that the Anglo-Americans make of the right of association.*
> *Three types of political associations. How the Americans apply the represen-*
> *tative system to associations. Dangers resulting therefrom to the state. Great*
> *convention of 1831 concerned with tariffs. Legislative character of that con-*
> *vention. Why the unlimited exercise of the right of association is not as dan-*
> *gerous in the United States as elsewhere. Why it may be considered neces-*
> *sary. Utility of associations in democratic nations.*

Better use has been made of association and this powerful instrument of action
has been applied to more varied aims in America than anywhere else in the world.

Apart from permanent associations such as townships, cities, and counties
created by law, there are a quantity of others whose existence and growth are
solely due to the initiative of individuals.

The inhabitant of the United States learns from birth that he must rely on himself to combat the ills and trials of life; he is restless and defiant in his outlook toward the authority of society and appeals to its power only when he cannot do
without it. The beginnings of this attitude first appear at school, where the children, even in their games, submit to rules settled by themselves and punish offenses which they have defined themselves. The same attitude turns up again in all
the affairs of social life. If some obstacle blocks the public road halting the circulation of traffic, the neighbors at once form a deliberative body; this improvised
assembly produces an executive authority which remedies the trouble before anyone has thought of the possibility of some previously constituted authority beyond
that of those concerned. Where enjoyment is concerned, people associate to make
festivities grander and more orderly. Finally, associations are formed to combat
exclusively moral troubles: intemperance is fought in common. Public security,

trade and industry, and morals and religion all provide the aims for associations in the United States. There is no end which the human will despairs of attaining by the free action of the collective power of individuals.

Later I shall have occasion to speak of the effects of association on civil life. For the moment I must stick to the world of politics.

The right of association being recognized, citizens can use it in different ways. An association simply consists in the public and formal support of specific doctrines by a certain number of individuals who have undertaken to cooperate in a stated way in order to make these doctrines prevail. Thus the right of association can almost be identified with freedom to write, but already associations are more powerful than the press. When some view is represented by an association, it must take clearer and more precise shape. It counts its supporters and involves them in its cause; these supporters get to know one another, and numbers increase zeal. An association unites the energies of divergent minds and vigorously directs them toward a clearly indicated goal.

Freedom of assembly marks the second stage in the use made of the right of association. When a political association is allowed to form centers of action at certain important places in the country, its activity becomes greater and its influence more widespread. There men meet, active measures are planned, and opinions are expressed with that strength and warmth which the written word can never attain.

But the final stage is the use of association in the sphere of politics. The supporters of an agreed view may meet in electoral colleges and appoint mandatories to represent them in a central assembly. That is, properly speaking, the application of the representative system to one party.

So, in the first of these cases, men sharing one opinion are held together by a purely intellectual tie; in the second case, they meet together in small assemblies representing only a fraction of the party; finally, in the third case, they form something like a separate nation within the nation and a government within the government. Their mandatories, like those of the majority, represent by themselves all the collective power of their supporters, and, like them in this too, they appear as national representatives with all the moral prestige derived therefrom. It is true that, unlike the others, they have no right to make laws, but they do have the power to attack existing laws and to formulate, by anticipation, laws which should take the place of the present ones.

Imagine some people not perfectly accustomed to the use of freedom, or one in which profound political passions are seething. Suppose that, besides the majority that makes the laws, there is a minority which only deliberates and which gets laws ready for adoption; I cannot help but think that then public order would be exposed to great risks.

There is certainly a great gap between proving that one law is in itself better than another and establishing that it ought to be substituted for it. But where trained minds may still see a wide gap, the hasty imagination of the crowd may be unaware of this. Moreover, there are times when the nation is divided into two almost equal parties, each claiming to represent the majority. If, besides the ruling power, another power is established with almost equal moral authority, can one suppose that in the long run it will just talk and not act?

Will it always stop short in front of the metaphysical consideration that the object of associations is to direct opinions and not to constrain them, and to give advice about the law but not to make it?

The more I observe the main effects of a free press, the more convinced am I that, in the modern world, freedom of the press is the principal and, so to say, the constitutive element in freedom. A nation bent on remaining free is therefore right to insist, at whatever cost, on respect for this freedom. But *unlimited* freedom of association must not be entirely identified with freedom to write. The former is both less necessary and more dangerous than the latter. A nation may set limits there without ceasing to be its own master; indeed, in order to remain its own master, it is sometimes necessary to do so.

In America there is no limit to freedom of association for political ends.

One example will show better than anything I could say just how far it is tolerated.

One remembers how excited the Americans were by the free-trade-tariff controversy. Not opinions only, but very powerful material interests stood to gain or lose by a tariff. The North thought that some of its prosperity was due thereto, while the South blamed it for almost all its woes. One may say that over a long period the tariff question gave rise to the only political passions disturbing the Union.

In 1831, when the quarrel was most envenomed, an obscure citizen of Massachusetts thought of suggesting through the newspapers that all opponents of the tariff should send deputies to Philadelphia to concert together measures to make trade free. Thanks to the invention of printing, this suggestion passed in but a few days from Maine to New Orleans. The opponents of the tariff took it up ardently. They assembled from all sides and appointed deputies. Most of the latter were known men, and some of them had risen to celebrity. South Carolina, which was later to take up arms in this cause, sent sixty-three people as its delegates. On October 1, 1831, the assembly, which in American fashion styled itself a convention, was constituted at Philadelphia; it counted more than two hundred members. The discussions were public, and from the very first day it took on an altogether legislative character; discussion covered the extent of the powers of Congress, theories of free trade, and finally the various provisions of the tariff. After ten days the assembly broke up, having issued an address to the American people. In that address it declared first that Congress had not the right to impose a tariff and that the existing tariff was unconstitutional, and second that it was against the interest of any people, in particular the American people, that trade should not be free.

It must be admitted that unlimited freedom of association in the political sphere has not yet produced in America the fatal results that one might anticipate from it elsewhere. The right of association is of English origin and always existed in America. Use of this right is now an accepted part of customs and mores.

In our own day freedom of association has become a necessary guarantee against the tyranny of the majority. In the United States, once a party has become predominant, all public power passes into its hands; its close supporters occupy all offices and have control of all organized forces. The most distinguished men of the opposite party, unable to cross the barrier keeping them from power, must be able to establish themselves outside it; the minority must use the whole of its moral authority to oppose the physical power oppressing it. Thus the one danger has to be balanced against a more formidable one.

The omnipotence of the majority seems to me such a danger to the American republics that the dangerous expedient used to curb it is actually something good.

Here I would repeat something which I have put in other words when speaking of municipal freedom: no countries need associations more—to prevent either despotism of parties or the arbitrary rule of a prince—than those with a democratic social state. In aristocratic nations secondary bodies form natural associations which hold abuses of power in check. In countries where such associations do not exist, if private people did not artificially and temporarily create something like them, I see no other dike to hold back tyranny of whatever sort, and a great nation might with impunity be oppressed by some tiny faction or by a single man.

The meeting of a great political convention (for conventions are of all kinds), though it may often be a necessary measure, is always, even in America, a serious event and one that good patriots cannot envisage without alarm.

That came out clearly during the convention of 1831, when all the men of distinction taking part therein tried to moderate its language and limit its objective. Probably the convention of 1831 did greatly influence the attitude of the malcontents and prepared them for the open revolt of 1832 against the commercial laws of the Union.

One must not shut one's eyes to the fact that unlimited freedom of association for political ends is, of all forms of liberty, the last that a nation can sustain. While it may not actually lead it into anarchy, it does constantly bring it to the verge, thereof. But this form of freedom, howsoever dangerous, does provide guarantees in one direction; in countries where associations are free, secret societies are unknown. There are factions in America, but no conspirators.

Concerning the different ways in which the right of association is understood
in Europe and in America, and the different uses made of it.

The most natural right of man, after that of acting on his own, is that of combining his efforts with those of his fellows and acting together. Therefore the right of association seems to me by nature almost as inalienable as individual liberty. Short of attacking society itself, no lawgiver can wish to abolish it. However, though for some nations freedom to unite is purely beneficial and a source of prosperity, there are other nations who pervert it by their excesses and turn a fount of life into a cause of destruction. So I think it will be thoroughly useful both for governments and for political parties if I make a comparison between the different ways in which associations are used in those nations that understand what freedom is and in those where this freedom turns into license.

Most Europeans still regard association as a weapon of war to be hastily improvised and used at once on the field of battle.

An association may be formed for the purpose of discussion, but everybody's mind is preoccupied by the thought of impending action. An association is an army; talk is needed to count numbers and build up courage, but after that they march against the enemy. Its members regard legal measures as possible means, but they are never the only possible means of success.

The right of association is not understood like that in the United States. In America the citizens who form the minority associate in the first place to show their numbers and to lessen the moral authority of the majority, and secondly, by stimulating competition, to discover the arguments most likely to make an impression on the majority, for they always hope to draw the majority over to their side and then to exercise power in its name.

Political associations in the United States are therefore peaceful in their objects and legal in the means used; and when they say that they only wish to prevail legally, in general they are telling the truth.

There are several reasons for this difference between the Americans and ourselves. In Europe there are parties differing so much from the majority that they can never hope to win its support, and yet these parties believe themselves strong enough to struggle against it on their own. When such a party forms an association it intends not to convince but to fight. In America those whose opinions make a wide gap between them and the majority can do nothing to oppose its power; all others hope to win it over.

So the exercise of the right of association becomes dangerous when great parties see no possibility of becoming the majority. In a country like the United States, where differences of view are only matters of nuance, the right of association can remain, so to say, without limits.

It is our inexperience of liberty in action which still leads us to regard freedom of association as no more than a right to make war on the government. The first idea which comes into a party's mind, as into that of an individual, when it gains some strength is that of violence; the thought of persuasion only comes later, for it is born of experience.

The English, though the divisions between them are so deep, seldom abuse the right of associations, because they have had long experience of it.

Furthermore, we have such a passionate taste for war that there is no enterprise so reckless or dangerous to the state, but it is thought glorious to die for it with arms in one's hand.

But perhaps universal suffrage is the most powerful of all the elements tending to moderate the violence of political associations in the United States. In a country with universal suffrage the majority is never in doubt, because no party can reasonably claim to represent those who have not voted at all. Therefore associations know, and everyone knows, that they do not represent the majority. The very fact of their existence proves this, for if they did represent the majority, they themselves would change the law instead of demanding reforms.

Thereby the moral strength of the government they attack is greatly increased and their own correspondingly weakened.

Almost all associations in Europe believe or claim that they represent the wishes of the majority. This belief or claim greatly increases their strength and wonderfully serves to legitimize their acts. For what is more excusable than violence to bring about the triumph of the oppressed cause of right?

Thus in the immense complication of human laws it sometimes comes about that extreme freedom corrects the abuse of freedom, and extreme democracy forestalls the dangers of democracy.

In Europe associations regard themselves in a way as the legislature and executive council of the nation which cannot raise its own voice; starting from this conception, they act and they command. In America, where everyone sees that they represent only a minority in the nation, they talk and petition.

The means used by associations in Europe are in accord with the aim proposed.

The main aim of these associations being to act and not to talk, to fight and not to convince, there is naturally nothing civilian about their organization, and indeed military ways and maxims are introduced therein; one also finds them centralizing control of their forces as much as they can and placing the whole authority in very few hands.

Members of these associations answer to a word of command like soldiers on active service; they profess the dogma of passive obedience, or rather, by the single act of uniting, have made a complete sacrifice of their judgment and free will; hence within associations, there often prevails a tyranny more intolerant than that exercised over society in the name of the government they attack.

This greatly diminishes their moral strength. They lose the sacred character belonging to the struggle of the oppressed against the oppressor. For how can a man claim that he wants to be free when in certain cases he consents servilely to obey some of his fellow men, yielding up his will and submitting his very thoughts to them?

The Americans too have provided a form of government within their associations, but it is, if I may put it so, a civil government. There is a place for individual independence there; as in society, all the members are advancing at the same time toward the same goal, but they are not obliged to follow exactly the same path. There has been no sacrifice of will or of reason, but rather will and reason are applied to bring success to a common enterprise.

[1835]

. . .

HOW INDIVIDUALISM IS MORE PRONOUNCED AT THE END OF A DEMOCRATIC REVOLUTION THAN AT ANY OTHER TIME

It is just at the moment when a democratic society is establishing itself on the ruins of an aristocracy that this isolation of each man from the rest and the egoism resulting therefrom stand out clearest.

Not only are there many independent people in such a society, but their number is constantly increasing with more and more of those who have just attained independence and are drunk with their new power. These latter have a presumptuous confidence in their strength, and never imagining that they could ever need another's help again, they have no inhibition about showing that they care for nobody but themselves.

There is usually a prolonged struggle before an aristocracy gives way, and in the course of that struggle implacable hatreds have been engendered between the classes. Such passions last after victory, and one can see traces of them in the ensuing democratic confusion.

Those who once held the highest ranks in the subverted hierarchy cannot forget their ancient greatness at once and for a long time feel themselves strangers in the new society. They regard all those whom society now makes their equals as oppressors whose fate could not concern them; they have lost sight of their former equals and no longer feel tied by common interests to their lot; each of them, in his separate retreat, feels reduced to taking care of himself alone. But those formerly at the bottom of the social scale and now brought up to the common level by a sudden revolution cannot enjoy their new-found independence without some secret uneasiness: there is a look of fear mixed with triumph in their eyes if they do meet one of their former superiors, and they avoid them.

Therefore it is usually at the time when democratic societies are taking root that men are most disposed to isolate themselves.

There is a tendency in democracy not to draw men together, but democratic revolutions make them run away from each other and perpetuate, in the midst of equality, hatreds originating in inequality.

The Americans have this great advantage, that they attained democracy without the sufferings of a democratic revolution and they were born equal instead of becoming so.

HOW THE AMERICANS COMBAT THE EFFECTS OF INDIVIDUALISM BY FREE INSTITUTIONS

Despotism, by its very nature suspicious, sees the isolation of men as the best guarantee of its own permanence. So it usually does all it can to isolate them. Of all the vices of the human heart egoism is that which suits it best. A despot will lightly forgive his subjects for not loving him, provided they do not love one another. He does not ask them to help him guide the state; it is enough if they do not claim to manage it themselves. He calls those who try to unite their efforts to create a general prosperity "turbulent and restless spirits," and twisting the natural meaning of words, he calls those "good citizens" who care for none but themselves.

Thus vices originating in despotism are precisely those favored by equality. The two opposites fatally complete and support each other.

Equality puts men side by side without a common link to hold them firm. Despotism raises barriers to keep them apart. It disposes them not to think of their fellows and turns indifference into a sort of public virtue.

Despotism, dangerous at all times, it is therefore particularly to be feared in ages of democracy.

It is easy to see that in such ages men have a peculiar need for freedom.

Citizens who are bound to take part in public affairs must turn from the private interests and occasionally take a look at something other than themselves.

As soon as common affairs are treated in common, each man notices that he is not as independent of his fellows as he used to suppose and that to get their help he must often offer his aid to them.

When the public governs, all men feel the value of public goodwill and all try to win it by gaining the esteem and affection of those among whom they must live.

Those frigid passions that keep hearts asunder must then retreat and hide at the back of consciousness. Pride must be disguised; contempt must not be seen. Egoism is afraid of itself.

Under a free government most public officials are elected, so men whose great gifts and aspirations are too closely circumscribed in private life daily feel that they cannot do without the people around them.

It thus happens that ambition makes a man care for his fellows, and, in a sense, he often finds his self-interest in forgetting about himself. I know that one can point to all the intrigues caused by an election, the dishonorable means often used by candidates, and the calumnies spread by their enemies. These do give rise to feelings of hatred, and the more frequent the elections, the worse they are.

Those are great ills, no doubt, but passing ones, whereas the benefits that attend them remain.

Eagerness to be elected may, for the moment, make particular men fight each other, but in the long run this same aspiration induces mutual helpfulness on the part of all; and while it may happen that the accident of an election estranges two friends, the electoral system forges permanent links between a great number of citizens who might otherwise have remained forever strangers to one another. Liberty engenders particular hatreds, but despotism is responsible for general indifference.

The Americans have used liberty to combat the individualism born of equality, and they have won.

The lawgivers of America did not suppose that a general representation of the whole nation would suffice to ward off a disorder at once so natural to the body social of a democracy and so fatal. They thought it also right to give each part of the land its own political life so that there should be an infinite number of occasions for the citizens to act together and so that every day they should feel that they depended on one another.

That was wise conduct.

The general business of a country keeps only the leading citizens occupied. It is only occasionally that they come together in the same places, and since they often lose sight of one another, no lasting bonds form between them. But when the people who live there have to look after the particular affairs of a district, the same people are always meeting, and they are forced, in a manner, to know and adapt themselves to one another.

It is difficult to force a man out of himself and get him to take an interest in the affairs of the whole state, for he has little understanding of the way in which the fate of the state can influence his own lot. But if it is a question of taking a road past his property, he sees at once that this small public matter has a bearing on his greatest private interests, and there is no need to point out to him the close connection between his private profit and the general interest.

Thus, far more may be done by entrusting citizens with the management of minor affairs than by handing over control of great matters, toward interesting them in the public welfare and convincing them that they constantly stand in need of one another in order to provide for it.

Some brilliant achievement may win a people's favor at one stroke. But to gain the affection and respect of your immediate neighbors, a long succession of little services rendered and of obscure good deeds, a constant habit of kindness and an established reputation for disinteretedness, are required.

Local liberties, then, which induce a great number of citizens to value the affection of their kindred and neighbors, bring men constantly into contact, despite the instincts which separate them, and force them to help one another.

In the United States the most opulent citizens are at pains not to get isolated from the people. On the contrary, they keep in constant contact, gladly listen and themselves talk any and every day. They know that the rich in democracies always need the poor and that good manners will draw them to them more than benefits conferred. For benefits by their very greatness spotlight the difference in conditions and arouse a secret annoyance in those who profit from them. But the charm of simple good manners is almost irresistible. Their affability carries men away, and even their vulgarity is not always unpleasant.

The rich do not immediately appreciate this truth. They generally stand out against it as long as a democratic revolution is in progress and do not admit it at once even after the revolution is accomplished. They will gladly do good to the people, but they still want carefully to keep their distance from them. They think that that is enough, but they are wrong. They could ruin themselves in that fashion without warming their neighbors' hearts. What is wanted is not the sacrifice of their money but of their pride.

It would seem as if in the United States every man's power of invention was on the stretch to find new ways of increasing the wealth and satisfying the needs of the public. The best brains in every neighborhood are constantly employed in searching for new secrets to increase the general prosperity, and any that they find are at once at the service of the crowd.

If one takes a close look at the weaknesses and vices of many of those who bear sway in America, one is surprised at the growing prosperity of the people, but it is a mistake to be surprised. It is certainly not the elected magistrate who makes the American democracy prosper, but the fact that the magistrates are elected.

It would not be fair to assume that American patriotism and the universal zeal for the common good have no solid basis. Though private interest, in the United States as elsewhere, is the driving force behind most of men's actions, it does not regulate them all.

I have often seen Americans make really great sacrifices for the common good, and I have noticed a hundred cases in which, when help was needed, they hardly ever failed to give each other trusty support.

The free institutions of the United States and the political rights enjoyed their provide a thousand continual reminders to every citizen that he lives in society. At every moment they bring his mind back to this idea, that it is the duty as well as the interest of men to be useful to their fellows. Having no particular reason to hate others, since he is neither their slave nor their master, the American's heart easily inclines toward benevolence. At first it is of necessity that men attend to the public interest, afterward by choice. What had been calculation becomes instinct. By dint of working for the good of his fellow citizens, he in the end acquires a habit and taste for serving them.

There are many men in France who regard equality of conditions as the first of evils and political liberty as the second. When forced to submit to the former, they strive at least to escape the latter. But for my part, I maintain that there is only one effective remedy against the evils which equality may cause, and that is political liberty.

ON THE USE WHICH THE AMERICANS MAKE OF ASSOCIATIONS IN CIVIL LIFE

I do not propose to speak of those political associations by means of which men seek to defend themselves against the despotic action of the majority or the encroachments of royal power. I have treated that subject elsewhere. It is clear that unless each citizen learned to combine with his fellows to preserve his freedom at a time when he individually is becoming weaker and so less able in isolation to defend it, tyranny would be bound to increase with equality. But here I am only concerned with those associations in civil life which have no political object.

In the United States, political associations are only one small part of the immense number of different types of associations found there.

Americans of all ages, all stations in life, and all types of disposition are forever forming associations. There are not only commercial and industrial associations in which all take part, but others of a thousand different types—religious, moral, serious, futile, very general and very limited, immensely large and very minute. Americans combine to give fêtes, found seminaries, build churches, distribute books, and send missionaries to the antipodes. Hospitals, prisons, and schools take shape in that way. Finally, if they want to proclaim a truth or propagate some feeling by the encouragement of a great example, they form an association. In every case, at the head of any new undertaking, where in France you would find the government or in England some territorial magnate, in the United States you are sure to find an association.

I have come across several types of association in America of which, I confess, I had not previously the slightest concept, and I have often admired the extreme skill they show in proposing a common object for the exertions of very many and in inducing them voluntarily to pursue it.

Since that time I have traveled in England, a country from which the Americans took some of their laws and many of their customs, but it seemed to me that the principle of association was not used nearly so constantly or so adroitly there.[1]

A single Englishman will often carry through some great undertaking, whereas Americans form associations for no matter how small a matter. Clearly the former regard association as a powerful means of action, but the latter seem to think of it as the only one.

Thus the most democratic country in the world now is that in which men have in our time carried to the highest perfection the art of pursuing in common the objects of common desires and have applied this new technique to the greatest number of purposes. Is that just an accident, or is there really some necessary connection between associations and equality?

In aristocratic societies, while there is a multitude of individuals who can do nothing on their own, there is also a small number of very rich and powerful men, each of whom can carry out great undertakings on his own.

In aristocratic societies men have no need to unite for action, since they are held firmly together.

Every rich and powerful citizen is in practice the head of a permanent and enforced association composed of all those whom he makes help in the execution of his designs.

---

1. See Alexis de Tocqueville, *Journeys to England and Ireland,* edited by J. P. Mayer (New Haven, Conn.: Yale, 1958).

But among democratic peoples all the citizens are independent and weak. They can do hardly anything for themselves, and none of them is in a position to force his fellows to help him. They would all therefore find themselves helpless if they did not learn to help each other voluntarily.

If the inhabitants of democratic countries had neither the right nor the taste for uniting for political objects, their independence would run great risks, but they could keep both their wealth and their knowledge for a long time. But if they did not learn some habits of acting together in the affairs of daily life, civilization itself would be in peril. A people in which individuals had lost the power of carrying through great enterprises by themselves without acquiring the faculty of doing them together, would soon fall back into barbarism.

Unhappily, the same social conditions that render associations so necessary to democratic nations also make their formation more difficult there than elsewhere.

When several aristocrats want to form an association, they can easily do so. As each of them carries great weight in society, a very small number of associates may be enough. So, being few, it is easy to get to know and understand one another and agree on rules.

But that is not so easy in democratic nations, where, if the association is to have any power, the associates must be very numerous.

I know that many of my contemporaries are not the least embarrassed by this difficulty. They claim that as the citizens become weaker and more helpless, the government must become proportionately more skillful and active, so that society should do what is no longer possible for individuals. They think that answers the whole problem, but I think they are mistaken.

A government could take the place of some of the largest associations in America, and some particular states of the Union have already attempted that. But what political power could ever carry on the vast multitude of lesser undertakings which associations daily enable American citizens to control?

It is easy to see the time coming in which men will be less and less able to produce, by each alone, the commonest bare necessities of life. The tasks of government must therefore perpetually increase, and its efforts to cope with them must spread its net ever wider. The more government takes the place of associations, the more will individuals lose the idea of forming associations and need the government to come to their help. That is a vicious circle of cause and effect. Must the public administration cope with every industrial undertaking beyond the competence of one individual citizen? And if ultimately, as a result of the minute subdivision of landed property, the land itself is so infinitely parceled out that it can only be cultivated by associations of laborers, must the head of the government leave the helm of state to guide the plow?

The morals and intelligence of a democratic people would be in as much danger as its commerce and industry if ever a government wholly usurped the place of private associations.

Feelings and ideas are renewed, the heart enlarged, and the understanding developed only by the reciprocal action of men one upon another.

I have shown how these influences are reduced almost to nothing in democratic countries; they must therefore be artificially created, and only associations can do that.

When aristocrats adopt a new idea or conceive a new sentiment, they lend it something of the conspicuous station they themselves occupy, and so the mass is bound to take notice of them, and they easily influence the minds and hearts of all around.

In democratic countries only the governing power is naturally in a position so to act, but it is easy to see that its action is always inadequate and often dangerous.

A government, by itself, is equally incapable of refreshing the circulation of feelings and idea among a great people, as it is of controlling every industrial undertaking. Once it leaves the sphere of politics to launch out on this new track, it will, even without intending this, exercise an intolerable tyranny. For a government can only dictate precise rules. It imposes the sentiments and ideas which it favors, and it is never easy to tell the difference between its advice and its commands.

This will be even worse if the government supposes that its real interest is to prevent the circulation of ideas. It will then stand motionless and let the weight of its deliberate somnolence lie heavy on all.

It is therefore necessary that it should not act alone.

Among democratic peoples associations must take the place of the powerful private persons whom equality of conditions has eliminated.

As soon as several Americans have conceived a sentiment or an idea that they want to produce before the world, they seek each other out, and when found, they unite. Thenceforth they are no longer isolated individuals, but a power conspicuous from the distance whose actions serve as an example; when it speaks, men listen.

The first time that I heard in America that one hundred thousand men had publicly promised never to drink alcoholic liquor, I thought it more of a joke than a serious matter and for the moment did not see why these very abstemious citizens could not content themselves with drinking water by their own firesides.

In the end I came to understand that these hundred thousand Americans, frightened by the progress of drunkenness around them, wanted to support sobriety by their patronage. They were acting in just the same way as some great territorial magnate who dresses very plainly to encourage a contempt of luxury among simple citizens. One may fancy that if they had lived in France each of these hundred thousand would have made individual representations to the government asking it to supervise all the public houses throughout the realm.

Nothing, in my view, more deserves attention than the intellectual and moral associations in America. American political and industrial associations easily catch our eyes, but the others tend not to be noticed. And even if we do notice them we tend to misunderstand them, hardly ever having seen anything similar before. However, we should recognize that the latter are as necessary as the former to the American people; perhaps more so.

In democratic countries knowledge of how to combine is the mother of all other forms of knowledge; on its progress depends that of all the others.

Among laws controlling human societies there is one more precise and clearer, it seems to me, than all the others. If men are to remain civilized or to become civilized, the art of association must develop and improve among them at the same speed as equality of conditions spreads.

ON THE CONNECTIONS BETWEEN ASSOCIATIONS AND NEWSPAPERS

When no firm and lasting ties any longer unite men, it is impossible to obtain the cooperation of any great number of them unless you can persuade every man whose help is required that he serves his private interests by voluntarily uniting his efforts to those of all the others.

That cannot be done habitually and conveniently without the help of a newspaper. Only a newspaper can put the same thought at the same time before a thousand readers.

A newspaper is an adviser that need not be sought out, but comes of its own accord and talks to you briefly every day about the commonweal without distracting you from your private affairs.

So the more equal men become and more individualism becomes a menace, the more necessary are newspapers. We should underrate their importance if we thought they just guaranteed liberty; they maintain civilization.

I am far from denying that newspapers in democratic countries lead citizens to do very ill-considered things in common; but without newspapers there would be hardly any common action at all. So they mend many more ills than they cause.

A newspaper is not only able to suggest a common plan to many men; it provides them with the means of carrying out in common the plans that they have thought of for themselves.

The leading citizens living in an aristocratic country can see each other from afar, and if they want to unite their forces they go to meet one another, bringing a crowd in their train.

But in democratic countries it often happens that a great many men who both want and need to get together cannot do so, for all being very small and lost in the crowd, they do not see one another at all and do not know where to find one another. Then a newspaper gives publicity to the feeling or idea that had occurred to them all simultaneously but separately. They all at once aim toward that light, and these wandering spirits, long seeking each other in the dark, at last meet and unite.

The newspaper brought them together and continues to be necessary to hold them together.

In a democracy an association cannot be powerful unless it is numerous. Those composing it must therefore be spread over a wide area, and each of them is anchored to the place in which he lives by the modesty of his fortune and a crowd of small necessary cares. They need some means of talking every day without seeing one another and of acting together without meeting. So hardly any democratic association can carry on without a newspaper.

There is therefore a necessary connection between associations and newspapers. Newspapers make associations, and associations make newspapers; and if it were true to say that associations must multiply as quickly as conditions become equal, it is equally certain that the number of papers increases in proportion as associations multiply.

Thus, of all countries on earth, it is in America that one finds both the most associations and the most newspapers.

This connection between the multiplicity of newspapers and associations leads on to the discovery of another relation between the state of the ephemeral press and the form of administration of the country. We find that the number of newspapers among a democratic people must diminish or increase according to the greater or lesser centralization of the administration. For in democracies it is not possible to entrust the exercise of local powers to the leading citizens as is done in aristocracies. Either such powers must be abolished or be placed in the hands of a very large number of men. The latter form a true association permanently established by law to administer a part of the country, and they feel the need for a newspaper which will reach them daily in the midst of their petty business and keep them informed about the state of public affairs. The more numerous these local authorities are, the greater the number of people legally required to exercise these powers, and so, the need for them being felt continually, the more profusely do newspapers abound.

The extraordinary subdivision of administrative power has much more to do with the enormous number of American newspapers than has the great political freedom of the country and the absolute independence of the press. If all the inhabitants of the Union were electors, but the suffrage only involved the choice of members of Congress, they would only need a few newspapers, for the occasions on which they had to act together, though important, would be very rare. But within the great association which is the nation, the law has established in each province, each city, and, one may almost say, each village little associations responsible for local administration. The legislature has thus compelled each American to cooperate every day of his life with some of his fellow citizens for a common purpose, and each one of them needs a newspaper to tell him what the others are doing.

I think that a democratic people[2] without any national representative assembly

2. I say a "democratic people." The administration might be very much decentralized in an aristocracy without the need for newspapers being felt, since in that case the local powers are in the hands of

but with a great number of small local powers would in the end have more newspapers than would another people governed by a centralized administration and an elected legislature. I find the best explanation for the prodigious growth of the daily press in the United States in the fact that there the greatest national freedom is combined with all manner of local liberties.

It is generally believed in France and in England that to abolish the taxes weighing down the press would be enough to increase the number of newspapers indefinitely. That greatly exaggerates the effect of such a reform. Newspapers do not multiply simply because they are cheap, but according to the more or less frequent need felt by a great number of people to communicate with one another and to act together.

I should also attribute the increasing influence of the daily press to causes more general than those by which it is commonly explained.

A newspaper can only survive if it gives publicity to feelings or principles common to a large number of men. A newspaper therefore always represents an association whose members are its regular readers.

This association may be more or less strictly defined, more or less closed, more or less numerous, but there must at least be the seed of it in men's minds, for otherwise the paper would not survive.

That leads me to the final reflection with which I will end this chapter.

As equality spreads and men individually become less strong, they ever increasingly let themselves glide with the stream of the crowd and find it hard to maintain alone an opinion abandoned by the rest.

The newspaper represents the association; one might say that it speaks to each of its readers in the name of all the rest, and the feebler they are individually, the easier it is to sweep them along.

The power of newspapers must therefore grow as equality spreads.

RELATIONSHIPS BETWEEN CIVIL AND POLITICAL ASSOCIATIONS

There is one country in the world which, day in, day out, makes use of an unlimited freedom of political association. And the citizens of this same nation, alone in the world, have thought of using the right of association continually in civil life, and by this means have come to enjoy all the advantages which civilization can offer.

In all countries where political associations are forbidden, civil associations are rare.

It is hardly likely that this is due to accident, and it is wiser to conclude that there must be some natural, perhaps inevitable connection between the two types of association.

---

a very small number of men who either act on their own or know one another and can easily meet and come to an understanding.

Men chance to have a common interest in a certain matter. It may be a trading enterprise to direct or an industrial undertaking to bring to fruition; those concerned meet and combine; little by little in this way they get used to the idea of association.

The more there are of these little business concerns in common, the more do men, without conscious effort, acquire a capacity to pursue great aims in common.

Thus civil associations pave the way for political ones, but on the other hand, the art of political association singularly develops and improves this technique for civil purpose.

In civil life each man can, at a stretch, imagine that he is in a position to look after himself. In politics he could never fancy that. So when a people has a political life, the idea of associations and eagerness to form them are part of everybody's everyday life. Whatever natural distaste men may have for working in common, they are always ready to do so for the sake of a party.

In this way politics spread a general habit and taste for association. A whole crowd of people who might otherwise have lived on their own are taught both to want to combine and how to do so.

Politics not only brings many associations into being, it also creates extensive ones.

The common interests of civil life seldom naturally induce great numbers to act together. A great deal of artifice is required to produce such a result.

But in politics opportunities for this are continually offering themselves of their own accord. Moreover, it is only large associations which make the general value of this method plain. Individually weak citizens form no clear conception in advance of the power they might gain by combining; to understand that, they must be shown it. Hence it is often easier to get a multitude to work together than just a few people; where one thousand do not see the advantage in combining, ten thousand do see it. In politics men combine for great ends, and the advantages gained in important matters give them a practical lesson in the value of helping one another even in lesser affairs.

A political association draws a lot of people at the same time out of their own circle; however much differences in age, intelligence, or wealth may naturally keep them apart, it brings them together and puts them in contact. Once they have met, they always know how to meet again.

One cannot take part in most civil associations without risking some of one's property; this is the case with all manufacturing and trading companies. Men who have as yet little skill in the technique of association and do not understand the main rules thereof are afraid, the first time they combine in this way, that they may pay dearly for their experience. They may therefore prefer not to use a powerful means toward success because of the risks involved. But they have less hesitation in joining political associations, which do not strike them as dangerous because they do not risk losing their money. But they cannot belong to such associations for long without discovering how to maintain order among large numbers and what procedures enable men to advance in methodical agreement toward a common aim. They thus learn to submit their own will to that of all the rest and to make their own exertions subordinate to the common action, all things which are as necessary to know, whether the association be political or civil.

So one may think of political associations as great free schools to which all citizens come to be taught the general theory of association.

But even if political association did not directly contribute to the progress of civil association, to destroy the former would harm the latter.

When citizens can only combine for certain purposes, they regard association as a strange and unusual procedure and hardly consider the possibility thereof.

When they are allowed to combine freely for all purposes, they come in the end to think of association as the universal, one might also say the only, means by which men can attain their various aims. Every new want at once revives that idea. Thus, as I have said before, the technique of association becomes the mother of every other technique; everyone studies and applies it.

When some types of association are forbidden and others allowed, it is hard to tell in advance the difference between the former and the latter. Being in doubt, people steer clear of them altogether, and in some vague way public opinion tends to consider any association whatsoever as a rash and almost illicit enterprise.[3]

It is therefore a delusion to suppose that the spirit of association, if suppressed in one place, will nevertheless display the same vigor in all other directions, and that if only men are allowed to prosecute certain undertakings in common, that is enough to ensure that they will eagerly do so. When citizens have the faculty and habit of associating for everything, they will freely associate for little purposes as well as great. But if they are only allowed to associate for trivial purposes, they will have neither the will nor the power to do so. To leave them entire liberty to combine in matters of trade will be in vain; they will hardly feel the slightest interest in using the rights granted; and having exhausted your strength in keeping them from forbidden associations, you will be surprised to find that you cannot persuade them to form those that are allowed.

---

3. This is more especially true when the executive power has the responsibility for allowing or forbidding associations by its arbitrary prerogative.

When the law forbids certain associations and leaves the courts to punish those who disobey, the ill is much less; in that cause every citizen knows beforehand more or less how things stand; in a sense he can judge the matter for himself before it gets to the courts, and keeping clear of those forbidden, joins those permitted. All free peoples have always understood that limits may thus be set to the right of association. But if the legislature should entrust a man with the power of deciding beforehand which associations are dangerous and which are useful, and left him free either to destroy any and every association in the bud or to let it grow, because no one would be able to see beforehand in what cases associations would be permitted and in what other cases it was best to avoid them, the movement toward association would be completely paralyzed. Laws of the former type are directed only against certain associations; those of the latter type are directed against society itself and inflict damage on it. I can conceive that a just government might have recourse to the former, but I do not admit the right of any government to introduce the latter.

I do not assert that there can be no civil associations in a country in which political associations are forbidden, for men cannot live in society without undertakings some things in common. But I maintain that in such a country civil associations will always be few, feebly conceived, and unskillfully managed and either will never form any vast designs or will fail in the execution of them.

This naturally leads me to think that freedom of political association is not nearly as dangerous to public peace as is supposed and that it could happen that it might give stability to a state which for some time it had shaken.

In democratic countries political associations are, if one may put it so, the only powerful people who aspire to rule the state. Hence the governments of today look upon associations of this type much as medieval kings regarded the great vassals of the Crown; they feel a sort of instinctive abhorrence toward them and combat them whenever they meet.

But they bear a natural goodwill toward civil associations because they easily see that they, far from directing public attention to public affairs, serve to turn men's minds away therefrom, and getting them more and more occupied with projects for which public tranquillity is essential, discourage thoughts of revolution. But they do not take the point that the multiplication of political associations is an immense help for civil associations and that in avoiding one dangerous ill they deprive themselves of an efficacious remedy. When you see the Americans every day freely combining to make some political opinion triumph, to get some politician into the government, or to snatch power from another, it is hard to conceive that men of such independence will not often fall into the abuse of license.

But if, on the other hand, you come to think of the infinite number of industrial undertakings which are run in partnership in the United States, if you notice how on every side the Americans are working without relaxation on important and difficult designs which would be thrown into confusion by the slightest revolution, you will easily understand why these people who are so well occupied have no temptation to disturb the state or to upset the public calm by which they profit.

It is enough to see things separately, or should we discover the hidden link connecting them? It is through political associations that Americans of every station, outlook, and age day by day acquire a general taste for association and get familiar with the way to use the same. Through them large numbers see, speak, listen, and stimulate each other to carry out all sorts of undertakings in common. Then they carry these conceptions with them into the affairs of civil life and put them to a thousand uses.

In this way, by the enjoyment of a dangerous liberty, the Americans learn the art of rendering the dangers of freedom less formidable.

By picking on one moment in the history of a nation it is easy to prove that political associations disturb the state and paralyze industry. But if you take the life of a people as one complete whole it may prove easy to show that freedom of political association favors the welfare and even the tranquillity of the citizens.

I said in the first part of this book: "Unlimited freedom of association should not be confused with freedom to write; the one is both less necessary and more dangerous than the other. A country can set limits there without ceasing to be its own master; it must sometimes do so in order to continue to control its fate." And later on I added: "One must understand that unlimited political freedom of association is of all forms of liberty the last which a people can sustain. If it does not topple them over into anarchy, it brings them continually to the brink thereof."

For these reasons I certainly do not think that a nation is always in a position to allow its citizens an absolute right of political association, and I even doubt whether there has even been at any time a nation in which it was wise not to put any limits to the freedom of association.

One hears it said that such and such a nation could not maintain internal peace, inspire respect for its laws, or establish a stable government if it did not set strict limits to the right of association. These are undoubtedly great benefits, and one can understand why, to gain or keep them, a nation may agree for a time to impose galling restrictions on itself; but still a nation should know what price it pays for these blessings.

To save a man's life, I can understand cutting off his arm. But I don't want anyone to tell me that he will be as dexterous without it.

[1848]

from The Public and Its Problems

THE ECLIPSE OF THE PUBLIC

Optimism about democracy is today under a cloud. We are familiar with denunciation and criticism which, however, often reveal their emotional source in their peevish and undiscriminating tone. Many of them suffer from the same error into which earlier laudations fell. They assume that democracy is the product of an idea, of a single and consistent intent. Carlyle was no admirer of democracy, but in a lucid moment he said: "Invent the printing press and democracy is inevitable." Add to this: Invent the railway, the telegraph, mass manufacture and concentration of population in urban centres, and some form of democratic government is, humanly speaking, inevitable. Political democracy as it exists today calls for adverse criticism in abundance. But the criticism is only an exhibition of querulousness and spleen or of a superiority complex, unless it takes cognizance of the conditions out of which popular government has issued. All intelligent political criticism is comparative. It deals not with all-or-none situations, but with practical alternatives; an absolutistic indiscriminate attitude, whether in praise or blame, testifies to the heat of feeling rather than the light of thought.

American democratic polity was developed out of genuine community life, that is, association in local and small centres where industry was mainly agricultural and where production was carried on mainly with hand tools. It took form when English political habits and legal institutions worked under pioneer conditions. The forms of association were stable, even though their units were mobile and migratory. Pioneer conditions put a high premium upon personal work, skill, ingenuity, initiative and adaptability, and upon neighborly sociability. The township or some not much larger area was the political unit, the town meeting the political medium, and roads, schools, the peace of the community, were the political objectives. The state was a sum of such units, and the national state a federation—unless perchance a confederation—of states. The imagination of the founders did not travel far beyond what could be accomplished and understood in a congeries of self-governing communities. The machinery provided for the selection of the chief executive of the federal union is illustrative evidence. The electoral college assumed that citizens would choose men locally known for their high standing; and that these men when chosen would gather together for consultation to name some one known to them for his probity and public spirit and knowledge. The rapidity with which the scheme fell into disuse is evidence of the transitoriness of the state of affairs that was predicated. But at the outset there was no dream of the time when the very names of the presidential electors would be unknown to the mass of the voters, when they would plump for a "ticket" arranged in a more or less private caucus, and when the electoral college would be an impersonal registering machine, such that it would be treachery to employ the personal judgment which was originally contemplated as the essence of the affair.

The local conditions under which our institutions took shape is well indicated by our system, apparently so systemless, of public education. Any one who has tried to explain it to a European will understand what is meant. One is asked, say, what method of administration is followed, what is the course of study and what the authorized methods of teaching. The American member to the dialogue replies that in this state, or more likely county, or town, or even some section of a town called a district, matters stand thus and thus; somewhere else, so and so. The participant from this side is perhaps thought by the foreigner to be engaged in concealing his ignorance; and it would certainly take a veritable cyclopedic knowledge to state the matter in its entirety. The impossibility of making any moderately generalized reply renders it almost indispensable to resort to a historical account in order to be intelligible. A little colony, the members of which are probably mostly known to one another in advance, settle in what is almost, or quite, a wilderness. From belief in its benefits and by tradition, chiefly religious, they wish their children to know at least how to read, write and figure. Families can only rarely provide a tutor; the neighbors over a certain area, in New England an area smaller even than the township, combine in a "school district." They get a schoolhouse built, perhaps by their own labor, and hire a teacher by means of a committee, and the teacher is paid from the taxes. Custom determines the limited course of study, and tradition the methods of the teacher, modified by whatever personal insight and skill he may bring to bear. The wilderness is gradually subdued; a network of highways, then of railways, unite the previously scattered communities. Large cities grow up; studies grow more numerous and methods more carefully scrutinized. The larger unit, the state, but not the federal state, provides schools for training teachers and their qualifications are more carefully looked into and tested. But subject to certain quite general conditions imposed by the state-legislature, but not the national state, local maintenance and control remain the rule. The community pattern is more complicated, but is not destroyed. The instance seems richly instructive as to the state of affairs under which our borrowed, English, political institutions were reshaped and forwarded.

We have inherited, in short, local town-meeting practices and ideas. But we live and act and have our being in a continental national state. We are held together by non-political bonds, and the political forms are stretched and legal institutions patched in an *ad hoc* and improvised manner to do the work they have to do. Political structures fix the channels in which non-political, industrialized currents flow. Railways, travel and transportation, commerce, the mails, telegraph and telephone, newspapers, create enough similarity of ideas and sentiments to keep the thing going as a whole, for they create interaction and interdependence. The unprecedented thing is that states, as distinguished from military empires, can exist over such a wide area. The notion of maintaining a unified state, even nominally self-governing, over a country as extended as the United States and consisting of a large and racially diversified population would once have seemed the wildest of fancies. It was assumed that such a state could be found only in territories hardly larger than a city-state and with a homogeneous population. It seemed almost self-evident to Plato—as to Rousseau later—that a genuine state could hardly be larger than the number of persons capable of personal acquaintance with one another. Our modern state-unity is due to the consequences of technology employed so as to facilitate the rapid and easy circulation of opinions and information, and so as to generate constant and intricate interaction far beyond the limits of face-to-face communities. Political and legal forms have only piecemeal and haltingly, with great lag, accommodated themselves to the industrial transformation. The elimination of distance, at the base of which are physical agencies, has called into being the new form of political association.

The wonder of the performance is the greater because of the odds against which it has been achieved. The stream of immigrants which has poured in is so large and heterogeneous that under conditions which formerly obtained it would have disrupted any semblance of unity as surely as the migratory invasion of alien hordes once upset the social equilibrium of the European continent. No deliberately adopted measures would have accomplished what has actually happened. Mechanical forces have operated, and it is no cause for surprise if the effect is more mechanical than vital. The reception of new elements of population in large number from heterogeneous peoples, often hostile to one another at home, and the welding them into even an outward show of unity is an extraordinary feat. In many respects, the consolidation has occurred so rapidly and ruthlessly that much of value has been lost which different peoples might have contributed. The creation of political unity has also promoted social and intellectual uniformity, a standardization favorable to mediocrity. Opinion has been regimented as well as outward behavior. The temper and flavor of the pioneer have evaporated with extraordinary rapidity; their precipitate, as is often noted, is apparent only in the wild-west romance and the movie. What Bagehot called the cake of custom formed with increasing acceleration, and the cake is too often flat and soggy. Mass production is not confined to the factory.

The resulting political integration has confounded the expectations of earlier critics of popular government as much as it must surprise its early backers if they are gazing from on high upon the present scene. The critics predicted disintegration, instability. They foresaw the new society falling apart, dissolving into mutually repellent animated grains of sand. They, too, took seriously the theory of "Individualism" as the basis of democratic government. A stratification of society into immemorial classes within which each person performed his stated duties according to his fixed position seemed to them the only warrant of stability. They had no faith that human beings released from the pressure of this system could hold together in any unity. Hence they prophesied a flux of governmental régimes, as individuals formed factions, seized power, and then lost it as some newly improvised faction proved stronger. Had the facts conformed to the theory of Individualism, they would doubtless have been right. But, like the authors of the theory, they ignored the technological forces making for consolidation.

In spite of attained integration, or rather perhaps because of its nature, the Public seems to be lost; it is certainly bewildered.[1] The government, officials and their activities, are plainly with us. Legislatures make laws with luxurious abandon; subordinate officials engage in a losing struggle to enforce some of them; judges on the bench deal as best they can with the steadily mounting pile of disputes that come before them. But where is the public which these officials are supposed to represent? How much more is it than geographical names and official titles? The United States, the state of Ohio or New York, the county of this and the city of that? Is the public much more than what a cynical diplomat once called Italy: a geographical expression? Just as philosophers once imputed a substance to qualities and traits in order that the latter might have something in which to inhere and thereby gain a conceptual solidity and consistency which they lacked on their face, so perhaps our political "common-sense" philosophy imputes a public only to support and substantiate the behavior of officials. How can the latter be public officers, we despairingly ask, unless there is a public? If a public exists, it is surely as uncertain about its own whereabouts as philosophers since Hume have been about the residence and make-up of the self. The number of voters who take advantage of their majestic right is steadily decreasing in proportion to those who might use it. The ratio of actual to eligible voters is now about one-half. In spite of somewhat frantic appeal and organized effort, the endeavor to bring voters to a sense of their privileges and duties has so far been noted for failure. A few preach the impotence of all politics; the many nonchalantly practice abstinence and indulge in indirect action. Skepticism regarding the efficacy of voting is openly expressed, not only in the theories of intellectuals, but in the words of lowbrow masses: "What difference does it make whether I vote or not? Things go on just the same anyway. My vote never changed anything." Those somewhat more reflective add: "It is nothing but a fight between the ins and the outs. The only

1. See Walter Lippmann's *The Phantom Public.* To this as well as to his *Public Opinion,* I wish to acknowledge my indebtedness, not only as to this particular point, but for ideas involved in my entire discussion even when it reaches conclusions diverging from his.

difference made by an election is as to who get the jobs, draw the salaries and shake down the plum tree."

Those still more inclined to generalization assert that the whole apparatus of political activities is a kind of protective coloration to conceal the fact that big business rules the governmental roost in any case. Business is the order of the day, and the attempt to stop or deflect its course is as futile as Mrs. Partington essaying to sweep back the tides with a broom. Most of those who hold these opinions would profess to be shocked if the doctrine of economic determinism were argumentatively expounded to them, but they act upon a virtual belief in it. Nor is acceptance of the doctrine limited to radical socialists. It is implicit in the attitude of men of big business and financial interests, who revile the former as destructive "Bolshevists." For it is their firm belief that "prosperity"—a word which has taken on religious color—is the great need of the country, that they are its authors and guardians, and hence by right the determiners of polity. Their denunciations of the "materialism" of socialists is based simply upon the fact that the latter want a different distribution of material force and well-being than that which satisfies those now in control.

The unfitness of whatever public exists, with respect to the government which is nominally its organ, is made manifest in the extra-legal agencies which have grown up. Intermediary groups are closest to the political conduct of affairs. It is interesting to compare the English literature of the eighteenth century regarding factions with the status actually occupied by parties. Factionalism was decried by all thinkers as the chief enemy to political stability. Their voice of condemnation is reechoed in the writing of early nineteenth-century American writers on politics. Extensive and consolidated factions under the name of parties are now not only a matter of course, but popular imagination can conceive of no other way by which officials may be selected and governmental affairs carried on. The centralizing movement has reached a point where even a third party can lead only a spasmodic and precarious existence. Instead of individuals who in the privacy of their consciousness make choices which are carried into effect by personal volition, there are citizens who have the blessed opportunity to vote for a ticket of men mostly unknown to them, and which is made up for them by an undercover machine in a caucus whose operations constitute a kind of political predestination. There are those who speak as if ability to choose between two tickets were a high exercise of individual freedom. But it is hardly the kind of liberty contemplated by the authors of the individualistic doctrine. "Nature abhors a vacuum." When the public is as uncertain and obscure as it is today, and hence as remote from government, bosses with their political machines fill the void between government and the public. Who pulls the strings which move the bosses and generates power to run the machines is a matter of surmise rather than of record, save for an occasional overt scandal.

Quite aside, however, from the allegation that "Big Business" plays the tune and pulls the strings to which bosses dance, it is true that parties are not creators of policies to any large extent at the present time. For parties yield in piece-meal accommodation to social currents, irrespective of professed principles. As these lines are written a weekly periodical remarks: "Since the end of the Civil War practically all the more important measures which have been embodied in federal legislation have been reached without a national election which turned upon the issue and which divided the two major parties." Reform of civil service, regulation of railways, popular election of senators, national income tax, suffrage for women, and prohibition are supported to substantiate the statement. Hence its other remark appears justified: "American party politics seem at times to be a device for preventing issues which may excite popular feeling and involve bitter controversies from being put up to the American people."

These scattered comments are not made in the belief that they convey any novel truth. Such things are familiar; they are the common-places of the political scene. They could be extended indefinitely by any careful observer of the scene. The significant thing is that familiarity has bred indifference if not contempt. Indifference is the evidence of current apathy, and apathy is testimony to the fact that the public is so bewildered that it cannot find itself. The remarks are not made with a view to drawing a conclusion. They are offered with a view to outlining a problem: What is the public? If there is a public, what are the obstacles in the way of its recognizing and articulating itself? Is the public a myth? Or does it come into being only in periods of marked social transition when crucial alternative issues stand out, such as that between throwing one's lot in with the conservation of established institutions or with forwarding new tendencies? In a reaction against dynastic rule which has come to be felt as despotically oppressive? In a transfer of social power from agrarian classes to industrial?

Is not the problem at the present time that of securing experts to manage administrative matters, other than the framing of policies? It may be urged that the present confusion and apathy are due to the fact that the real energy of society is now directed in all non-political matters by trained specialists who manage things, while politics are carried on with a machinery and ideas formed in the past to deal with quite another sort of situation. There is no particular public concerned in finding expert school instructors, competent doctors, or business managers. Nothing called a public intervenes to instruct physicians in the practice of the healing art or merchants in the art of salesmanship. The conduct of these callings and others characteristic of our time are decided by science and pseudo-science. The important governmental affairs at present, it may be argued, are also technically complicated matters to be conducted properly by experts. And if at present people are not educated to the recognition of the importance of finding experts and of entrusting administration to them, it may plausibly be asserted that the prime obstruction lies in the superstitious belief that there is a public concerned to determine the formation and execution of general social policies. Perhaps the apathy of the electorate is due to the irrelevant artificiality of the issues with which it is attempted to work up factitious excitement. Perhaps this artificiality is in turn mainly due to the survival of political beliefs and machinery from a period when science and technology were so immature as not to permit of a definite technique for handling definite social situations and meeting specific social needs. The attempt to decide by law that the legends of a primitive Hebrew people regarding the genesis of man are more authoritative than the results of scientific inquiry might be cited as a typical example of the sort of thing which is bound to happen when the accepted doctrine is that a public organized for political purposes, rather than experts guided by specialized inquiry, is the final umpire and arbiter of issues.

The questions of most concern at present may be said to be matters like sanitation, public health, healthful and adequate housing, transportation, planning of cities, regulation and distribution of immigrants, selection and management of personnel, right methods of instruction and preparation of competent teachers, scientific adjustment of taxation, efficient management of funds, and so on. These are technical matters, as much so as the construction of an efficient engine for purposes of traction or locomotion. Like it they are to be settled by inquiry into facts; and as the inquiry can be carried on only by those especially equipped, so the results of inquiry can be utilized only by trained technicians. What has counting heads, decision by majority and the whole apparatus of traditional government to do with such things? Given such considerations, and the public and its organization for political ends is not only a ghost, but a ghost which walks and talks, and obscures, confuses and misleads governmental action in a disastrous way.

Personally I am far from thinking that such considerations, pertinent as they are to administrative activities, cover the entire political field. They ignore forces which have to be composed and resolved before technical and specialized action can come into play. But they aid in giving definiteness and point to a fundamental question: What, after all, is the public under present conditions? What are the reasons for its eclipse? What hinders it from finding and identifying itself? By what means shall its inchoate and amorphous estate be organized into effective political action relevant to present social needs and opportunities? What has happened to the Public in the century and a half since the theory of political democracy was urged with such assurance and hope?

Previous discussion has brought to light some conditions out of which the public is generated. It has also set forth some of the causes through which a "new age of human relationships" has been brought into being. These two arguments form the premises which, when they are related to each other, will provide our answer to the questions just raised. Indirect, extensive, enduring and serious consequences of conjoint and interacting behavior call a public into existence having a common interest in controlling these consequences. But the machine age has so enormously expanded, multiplied, intensified and complicated the scope of the indirect consequences, has formed such immense and consolidated unions in action, on an impersonal rather than a community basis, that the resultant public cannot identify and distinguish itself. And this discovery is obviously an antecedent condition of any effective organization on its part. Such is our thesis regarding the eclipse which the public idea and interest have undergone. There are too many publics and too much of public concern for our existing resources to cope with. The problem of a democratically organized public is primarily and essentially an intellectual problem, in a degree to which the political affairs of prior ages offer no parallel.

Our concern at this time is to state how it is that the machine age in developing the Great Society has invaded and partially disintegrated the small communities of former times without generating a Great Community. The facts are familiar enough; our especial affair is to point out their connections with the difficulties under which the organization of a democratic public is laboring. For the very familiarity with the phenomena conceals their significance and blinds us to their relation to immediate political problems.

There was a time when a man might entertain a few general political principles and apply them with some confidence. A citizen believed in states' rights or in a centralized federal government; in free trade protection. It did not involve much mental strain to imagine that by throwing in his lot with one party or another he could so express his views that his belief would count in government. For the average voter today the tariff question is a complicated medley of infinite detail, schedules of rates specific and *ad valorem* on countless things, many of which he does not recognize by name, and with respect to which he can form no judgment. Probably not one voter in a thousand even reads the scores of pages in which the rates of toll are enumerated and he would not be much wiser if he did. The average man gives it up as a bad job. At election time, appeal to some time-worn slogan may galvanize him into a temporary notion that he has convictions on an important subject, but except for manufacturers and dealers who have some interest at stake in this or that schedule, belief lacks the qualities which attach to beliefs about matters of personal concern. Industry is too complex and intricate.

Political apathy, which is a natural product of the discrepancies between actual practices and traditional machinery, ensues from inability to identify one's self with definite issues. These are hard to find and locate in the vast complexities of current life. When traditional war-cries have lost their import in practical policies which are consonant with them, they are readily dismissed as bunk. Only habit and tradition, rather than reasoned conviction, together with a vague faith in doing one's civic duty, send to the polls a considerable percentage of the fifty per cent who still vote. And of them it is a common remark that a large number vote against something or somebody rather than for anything or anybody, except when powerful agencies create a scare. The old principles do not fit contemporary life as it is lived, however well they may have expressed the vital interests of the times in which they arose. Thousands feel their hollowness even if they cannot make their feeling articulate. The confusion which has resulted from the size and ramifications of social activities has rendered men skeptical of the efficiency of political action. Who is sufficient unto these things? Men feel that they are caught in the sweep of forces too vast to understand or master. Thought is brought to a standstill and action paralyzed. Even the specialist finds it difficult to trace the chain of "cause and effect"; and even he operates only after the event, looking backward, while meantime social activities have moved on to effect a new state of affairs.

. . . The ramification of the issues before the public is so wide and intricate, the technical matters involved are so specialized, the details are so many and so shifting, that the public cannot for any length of time identify and hold itself. It is not that there is no public, no large body of persons having a common interest in the consequences of social transactions. There is too much public, a public too diffused and scattered and too intricate in composition. And there are too many publics, for conjoint actions which have indirect, serious and enduring consequences are multitudinous beyond comparison, and each one of them crosses the others and generates its own group of persons especially affected with little to hold these different publics together in an integrated whole.

The picture is not complete without taking into account the many competitors with effective political interest. Political concerns have, of course, always had strong rivals. Persons have always been, for the most part, taken up with their more immediate work and play. The power of "bread and the circus" to divert attention from public matters is an old story. But now the industrial conditions which have enlarged, complicated and multiplied public interests have also multiplied and intensified formidable rivals to them. In countries where political life has been most successfully conducted in the past, there was a class specifically set aside, as it were, who made political affairs their special business. Aristotle could not conceive a body of citizens competent to carry on politics consisting of others than those who had leisure, that is, of those who were relieved from all other preoccupations, especially that of making a livelihood. Political life, till recent times, bore out his belief. Those who took an active part in politics were "gentlemen," persons who had had property and money long enough, and enough of it, so that its further pursuit was vulgar and beneath their station. Today, so great and powerful is the sweep of the industrial current, the person of leisure is usually an idle person. Persons have had their own business to attend to, and "business" has its own precise and specialized meaning. Politics thus tends to become just another "business": the especial concern of bosses and the managers of the machine.

The increase in the number, variety and cheapness of amusements represents a powerful diversion from political concern. The members of an inchoate public have too many ways of enjoyment, as well as of work, to give much thought to organization into an effective public. Man is a consuming and sportive animal as well as a political one. What is significant is that access to means of amusement has been rendered easy and cheap beyond anything known in the past. The present era of "prosperity" may not be enduring. But the movie, radio, cheap reading matter and motor car with all they stand for have come to stay. That they did not originate in deliberate desire to divert attention from political interests does not lessen their effectiveness in that direction. The political elements in the constitution of the human being, those having to do with citizenship, are crowded to one side. In most circles it is hard work to sustain conversation on a political theme; and once initiated, it is quickly dismissed with a yawn.

One phase of the workings of a technological age, with its unprecedented command of natural energies, while it is implied in what has been said, needs explicit attention. The older publics, in being local communities, largely homogeneous with one another, were also, as the phrase goes, static. They changed, of course, but barring war, catastrophe and great migrations, the modifications were gradual. They proceeded slowly and were largely unperceived by those undergoing them. The newer forces have created mobile and fluctuating associational forms. The common complaints of the disintegration of family life may be placed in evidence. The movement from rural to urban assemblies is also the result and proof of this mobility. Nothing stays long put, not even the associations by which business and industry are carried on. The mania for motion and speed is a symptom of the restless instability of social life, and it operates to intensify the causes from which it springs. Steel replaces wood and masonry for buildings; ferro-concrete modifies steel, and some invention may work a further revolution. Muscle Shoals was acquired to produce nitrogen, and new methods have already made antiquated the supposed need of great accumulation of water power. Any selected illustration suffers because of the heterogeneous mass of cases to select from. How can a public be organized, we may ask, when literally it does not stay in place? Only deep issues or those which can be made to appear such can find a common denominator among all the shifting and unstable relationships. Attachment is a very different function of life from affection. Affections will continue as long as the heart beats. But attachment requires something more than organic causes. The very things which stimulate and intensify affections may undermine attachments. For these are bred in tranquil stability; they are nourished in constant relationships. Acceleration of mobility disturbs them at their root. And without abiding attachments associations are too shifting and shaken to permit a public readily to locate and identify itself.

The new era of human relationships in which we live is one marked by mass production for remote markets, by cable and telephone, by cheap printing, by railway and steam navigation. Only geographically did Columbus discover a new world. The actual new world has been generated in the last hundred years. Steam and electricity have done more to alter the conditions under which men associate together than all the agencies which affected human relationships before our time. There are those who lay the blame for all the evils of our lives on steam, electricity and machinery. It is always convenient to have a devil as well as a savior to bear the responsibilities of humanity. In reality, the trouble springs rather from the

ideas and absence of ideas in connection with which technological factors operate. Mental and moral beliefs and ideals change more slowly than outward conditions. If the ideals associated with the higher life of our cultural past have been im-
paired, the fault is primarily with them. Ideals and standards formed without
regard to the means by which they are to be achieved and incarnated in flesh are
bound to be thin and wavering. Since the aims, desires and purposes created by a
machine age do not connect with tradition, there are two sets of rival ideals, and
those which have actual instrumentalities at their disposal have the advantage. Because the two are rivals and because the older ones retain their glamor and sentimental prestige in literature and religion, the newer ones are perforce harsh and
narrow. For the older symbols of ideal life still engage thought and command loyalty. Conditions have changed, but every aspect of life, from religion and education to property and trade, shows that nothing approaching a transformation has
taken place in ideas and ideals. Symbols control sentiment and thought, and the
new age has no symbols consonant with its activities. Intellectual instrumentalities for the formation of an organized public are more inadequate than its overt
means. The ties which hold men together in action are numerous, tough and subtle. But they are invisible and intangible. We have the physical tools of communication as never before. The thoughts and aspirations congruous with them are not
communicated, and hence are not common. Without such communication the
public will remain shadowy and formless, seeking spasmodically for itself, but
seizing and holding its shadow rather than its substance. Till the Great Society is
converted into a Great Community, the Public will remain in eclipse. Communication can alone create a great community. Our Babel is not one of tongues but of
the signs and symbols without which shared experience is impossible.

SEARCH FOR THE GREAT COMMUNITY

. . . That government exists to serve its community, and that this purpose cannot be
achieved unless the community itself shares in selecting its governors and determining their policies, are a deposit of fact left, as far as we can see, permanently in
the wake of doctrines and forms, however transitory the latter. They are not the
whole of the democratic idea, but they express it in its political phase. Belief in
this political aspect is not a mystic faith as if in some overruling providence that
cares for children, drunkards and others unable to help themselves. It marks a
well-attested conclusion from historical facts. We have every reason to think that
whatever changes may take place in existing democratic machinery, they will be
of a sort to make the interest of the public a more supreme guide and criterion of
governmental activity, and to enable the public to form and manifest its purposes
still more authoritatively. In this sense the cure for the ailments of democracy is
more democracy. The prime difficulty, as we have seen, is that of discovering the
means by which a scattered, mobile and manifold public may so recognize itself

as to define and express its interests. This discovery is necessarily precedent to any fundamental change in the machinery. We are not concerned therefore to set forth counsels as to advisable improvements in the political forms of democracy. Many have been suggested. It is no derogation of their relative worth to say that consideration of these changes is not at present an affair of primary importance. The problem lies deeper; it is in the first instance an intellectual problem: the search for conditions under which the Great Society may become the Great Community. When these conditions are brought into being they will make their own forms. Until they have come about, it is somewhat futile to consider what political machinery will suit them.

In a search for the conditions under which the inchoate public now extant may function democratically, we may proceed from a statement of the nature of the democratic idea in its generic social sense.[2] From the standpoint of the individual, it consists in having a responsible share according to capacity in forming and directing the activities of the groups to which one belongs and in participating according to need in the values which the groups sustain. From the standpoint of the groups, it demands liberation of the potentialities of members of a group in harmony with the interests and goods which are common. Since every individual is a member of many groups, this specification cannot be fulfilled except when different groups interact flexibly and fully in connection with other groups. A member of a robber band may express his powers in a way consonant with belonging to that group and be directed by the interest common to its members. But he does so only at the cost of repression of those of his potentialities which can be realized only through membership in other groups. The robber band cannot interact flexibly with other groups; it can act only through isolating itself. It must prevent the operation of all interests save those which circumscribe it in its separateness. But a good citizen finds his conduct as a member of a political group enriching and enriched by his participation in family life, industry, scientific and artistic associations. There is a free give-and-take: fullness of integrated personality is therefore possible of achievement, since the pulls and responses of different groups reenforce one another and their values accord.

Regarded as an idea, democracy is not an alternative to other principles of associated life. It is the idea of community life itself. It is an ideal in the only intelligible sense of an ideal: namely, the tendency and movement of some thing which exists carried to its final limit, viewed as completed, perfected. Since things do not attain such fulfillment but are in actuality distracted and interfered with, democracy in this sense is not a fact and never will be. But neither in this sense is there or has there ever been anything which is a community in its full measure, a community unalloyed by alien elements. The idea or ideal of a community presents, however, actual phases of associated life as they are freed from

2. The most adequate discussion of this ideal with which I am acquainted is T. V. Smith's *The Democratic Way of Life*.

restrictive and disturbing elements, and are contemplated as having attained their limit of development. Wherever there is conjoint activity whose consequences are appreciated as good by all singular persons who take part in it, and where the realization of the good is such as to effect an energetic desire and effort to sustain it in being just because it is a good shared by all, there is in so far a community. The clear consciousness of a communal life, in all its implications, constitutes the idea of democracy.

Only when we start from a community as a fact, grasp the fact in thought so as to clarify and enhance its constituent elements, can we reach an idea of democracy which is not utopian. The conceptions and shibboleths which are traditionally associated with the idea of democracy take on a veridical and directive meaning only when they are construed as marks and traits of an association which realizes the defining characteristics of a community. Fraternity, liberty and equality isolated from communal life are hopeless abstractions. Their separate assertion leads to mushy sentimentalism or else to extravagant and fanatical violence which in the end defeats its own aims. Equality then becomes a creed of mechanical identity which is false to facts and impossible of realization. Effort to attain it is divisive of the vital bonds which hold men together; as far as it puts forth issue, the outcome is a mediocrity in which good is common only in the sense of being average and vulgar. Liberty is then thought of as independence of social ties, and ends in dissolution and anarchy. It is more difficult to sever the idea of brotherhood from that of a community, and hence it is either practically ignored in the movements which identify democracy with Individualism, or else it is a sentimentally appended tag. In its just connection with communal experience, fraternity is another name for the consciously appreciated goods which accrue from an association in which all share, and which give direction to the conduct of each. Liberty is that secure release and fulfillment of personal potentialities which take place only in rich and manifold association with others: the power to be an individualized self making a distinctive contribution and enjoying in its own way the fruits of association. Equality denotes the unhampered share which each individual member of the community has in the consequences of associated action. It is equitable because it is measured only by need and capacity to utilize, not by extraneous factors which deprive one in order that another may take and have. A baby in the family is equal with others, not because of some antecedent and structural quality which is the same as that of others, but in so far as his needs for care and development are attended to without being sacrificed to the superior strength, possessions and matured abilities of others. Equality does not signify that kind of mathematical or physical equivalence in virtue of which any one element may be substituted for another. It denotes effective regard for whatever is distinctive and unique in each, irrespective of physical and psychological inequalities. It is not a natural possession but is a fruit of the community when its action is directed by its character as a community.

Associated or joint activity is a condition of the creation of a community. But association itself is physical and organic, while communal life is moral, that is emotionally, intellectually, consciously sustained. Human beings combine in behavior as directly and unconsciously as do atoms, stellar masses and cells; as directly and unknowingly as they divide and repel. They do so in virtue of their own structure, as man and woman unite, as the baby seeks the breast and the breast is there to supply its need. They do so from external circumstances, pressure from without, as atoms combine or separate in presence of an electric charge, or as sheep huddle together from the cold. Associated activity needs no explanation; things are made that way. But no amount of aggregated collective action of itself constitutes a community. For beings who observe and think, and whose ideas are absorbed by impulses and become sentiments and interests, "we" is as inevitable as "I." But "we" and "our" exist only when the consequences of combined action are perceived and become an object of desire and effort, just as "I" and "mine" appear on the scene only when a distinctive share in mutual action is consciously asserted or claimed. Human associations may be ever so organic in origin and firm in operation, but they develop into societies in a human sense only as their consequences, being known, are esteemed and sought for. Even if "society" were as much an organism as some writers have held, it would not on that account be society. Interactions, transactions, occur *de facto* and the results of interdependence follow. But participation in activities and sharing in results are additive concerns. They demand *communication* as a prerequisite.

Combined activity happens among human beings; but when nothing else happens it passes as inevitably into some other mode of interconnected activity as does the interplay of iron and the oxygen of water. What takes place is wholly describable in terms of energy, or, as we say in the case of human interactions, of force. Only when there exist *signs* or *symbols* of activities and of their outcome can the flux be viewed as from without, be arrested for consideration and esteem, and be regulated. Lightning strikes and rives a tree or rock, and the resulting fragments take up and continue the process of interaction, and so on and on. But when phases of the process are represented by signs, a new medium is interposed. As symbols are related to one another, the important relations of a course of events are recorded and are preserved as meanings. Recollection and foresight are possible; the new medium facilitates calculation, planning, and a new kind of action which intervenes in what happens to direct its course in the interest of what is foreseen and desired.

Symbols in turn depend upon and promote communication. The results of conjoint experience are considered and transmitted. Events cannot be passed from one to another, but meanings may be shared by means of signs. Wants and impulses are then attached to common meanings. They are thereby transformed into desires and purposes, which, since they implicate a common or mutually understood meaning, present new ties, converting a conjoint activity into a community of interest and endeavor. Thus there is generated what, metaphorically, may be termed a general will and social consciousness: desire and choice on the part of individuals in behalf of activities that, by means of symbols, are communicable and shared by all concerned. A community thus presents an order of energies transmuted into one of meanings which are appreciated and mutually referred by each to every other on the part of those engaged in combined action. "Force" is not eliminated but is transformed in use and direction by ideas and sentiments made possible by means of symbols.

The work of conversion of the physical and organic phase of associated behavior into a community of action saturated and regulated by mutual interest in shared meanings, consequences which are translated into ideas and desired objects by means of symbols, does not occur all at once nor completely. At any given time, it sets a problem rather than marks a settled achievement. We are born organic beings associated with others, but we are not born members of a community. The young have to be brought within the traditions, outlook and interests which characterize a community by means of education: by unremitting instruction and by learning in connection with the phenomena of overt association. Everything which is distinctively human is learned, not native, even though it could not be learned without native structures which mark man off from other animals. To learn in a human way and to human effect is not just to acquire added skill through refinement of original capacities.

To learn to be human is to develop through the give-and-take of communication an effective sense of being an individually distinctive member of a community; one who understands and appreciates its beliefs, desires and methods, and who contributes to a further conversion of organic powers into human resources and values. But this translation is never finished.

This is the meaning of the statement that the problem is a moral one dependent upon intelligence and education. We have in our prior account sufficiently emphasized the role of technological and industrial factors in creating the Great Society. What was said may even have seemed to imply acceptance of the deterministic version of an economic interpretation of history and institutions. It is silly and futile to ignore and deny economic facts. They do not cease to operate because we refuse to note them, or because we smear them over with sentimental idealizations. As we have also noted, they generate as their result overt and external conditions of action and these are known with various degrees of adequacy. What actually happens in consequence of industrial forces is dependent upon the presence or absence of perception and communication of consequences, upon foresight and its effect upon desire and endeavor. Economic agencies produce one result when they are left to work themselves out on the merely physical level, or on that level modified only as the knowledge, skill and technique which the community has accumulated are transmitted to its members unequally and by chance. They have a different outcome in the degree in which knowledge of consequences is equitably distributed, and action is animated by an informed and lively sense of a shared interest. The doctrine of economic interpretation as usually stated ignores the transformation which meanings may effect; it passes over the new medium which communication may interpose between industry and its eventual consequences. It is obsessed by the illusion which vitiated the "natural economy": an illusion due to failure to note the difference made in action by perception and publication of its consequences, actual and possible. It thinks in terms of antecedents, not of the eventual; of origins, not fruits.

We have returned, through this apparent excursion, to the question in which our earlier discussion culminated: What are the conditions under which it is possible for the Great Society to approach more closely and vitally the status of a Great Community, and thus take form in genuinely democratic societies and state? What are the conditions under which we may reasonably picture the Public emerging from its eclipse?

The study will be an intellectual or hypothetical one. There will be no attempt to state how the required conditions might come into existence, nor to prophesy that they will occur. The object of the analysis will be to show that *unless* ascertained specifications are realized, the Community cannot be organized as a democratically effective Public. It is not claimed that the conditions which will be noted will suffice, but only that at least they are indispensable. In other words, we shall endeavor to frame a hypothesis regarding the democratic state to stand in contrast with the earlier doctrine which has been nullified by the course of events.

Two essential constituents in that older theory, as will be recalled, were the notions that each individual is of himself equipped with the intelligence needed, under the operation of self-interest, to engage in political affairs; and that general suffrage, frequent elections of officials and majority rule are sufficient to ensure the responsibility of elected rulers to the desires and interests of the public. As we shall see, the second conception is logically bound up with the first and stands or falls with it. At the basis of the scheme lies what Lippmann has well called the idea of the "omnicompetent" individual: competent to frame policies, to judge their results; competent to know in all situations demanding political action what is for his own good, and competent to enforce his idea of good and the will to effect it against contrary forces. Subsequent history has proved that the assumption involved illusion.

Habit is the mainspring of human action, and habits are formed for the most part under the influence of the customs of a group. The organic structure of man entails the formation of habit, for, whether we wish it or not, whether we are aware of it or not, every act effects a modification of attitude and set which directs future behavior. The dependence of habit-forming upon those habits of a group which constitute customs and institutions is a natural consequence of the helplessness of infancy. The social consequences of habit have been stated once for all by [William] James: "Habit is the enormous fly-wheel of society, its most precious conservative influence. It alone is what keeps us within the bounds of ordinance, and saves the children of fortune from the uprisings of the poor. It alone prevents the hardest and most repulsive walks of life from being deserted by those brought up to tread therein. It keeps the fisherman and the deck-hand at sea through the winter; it holds the miner in his darkness, and nails the countryman to his log-cabin and his lonely farm through all the months of snow; it protects us from invasion by the natives of the desert and the frozen zone. It dooms us all to fight out the battle of life upon the lines of our nurture or our early choice, and to make the best of a pursuit that disagrees, because there is no other for which we are fitted and it is too late to begin again. It keeps different social strata from mixing."

The influence of habit is decisive because all distinctively human action has to be learned, and the very heart, blood and sinews of learning is creation of habitudes. Habits bind us to orderly and established ways of action because they generate ease, skill and interest in things to which we have grown used and because they instigate fear to walk in different ways, and because they leave us incapacitated for the trial of them. Habit does not preclude the use of thought, but it determines the channels within which it operates. . . . Hence the idea that men are moved by an intelligent and calculated regard for their own good is pure mythology. Even if the principle of self-love actuated behavior, it would still be true that the *objects* in which men find their love manifested, the objects which they take as constituting their peculiar interests, are set by habit reflecting social customs.

These facts explain why the social doctrinaires of the new industrial movement had so little prescience of what was to follow in consequence of it. These facts explain why the more things changed, the more they were the same; they account, that is, for the fact that instead of the sweeping revolution which was expected to result from democratic political machinery, there was in the main but a transfer of vested power from one class to another. A few men, whether or not they were good judges of their own true interest and good, were competent judges of the conduct of business for pecuniary profit, and of how the new governmental machinery could be made to serve their ends. It would have taken a new race of human beings to escape, in the use made of political forms, from the influence of deeply engrained habits, of old institutions and customary social status, with their inwrought limitations of expectation, desire and demand.

Nevertheless, changes take place and are cumulative in character. Observation of them in the light of their recognized consequences arouses reflection, discovery, invention, experimentation. When a certain state of accumulated knowledge, of techniques and instrumentalities is attained, the process of change is so accelerated, that, as today, it appears externally to be the dominant trait. But there is a marked lag in any corresponding change of ideas and desires.

What is more important, however, is that so much of knowledge is not knowledge in the ordinary sense of the word, but is "science." The quotation marks are not used disrespectfully, but to suggest the technical character of scientific material. The layman takes certain conclusions which get into circulation to be science. But the scientific inquirer knows that they constitute science only in connection with the methods by which they are reached. Even when true, they are not science in virtue of their correctness, but by reason of the apparatus which is employed in reaching them. This apparatus is so highly specialized that it requires more labor to acquire ability to use and understand it than to get skill in any other instrumentalities possessed by man.

For most men, save the scientific workers, science is a mystery in the hands of initiates, who have become adepts in virtue of following ritualistic ceremonies from which the profane herd is excluded. They are fortunate who get as far as a sympathetic appreciation of the methods which give pattern to the complicated apparatus: methods of analytic, experimental observation, mathematical formulation and deduction, constant and elaborate check and test. For most persons, the reality of the apparatus is found only in its embodiments in practical affairs, in mechanical devices and in techniques which touch life as it is lived.

Meanwhile the technological application of the complex apparatus which is science has revolutionized the conditions under which associated life goes on. This may be known as a fact which is stated in a proposition and assented to. But it is not known in the sense that men understand it. They do not know it as they know some machine which they operate, or as they know electric light and steam locomotives. They do not understand *how* the change has gone on nor *how* it affects their conduct. Not understanding its "how," they cannot use and control its manifestations. They undergo the consequences, they are affected by them. They cannot manage them, though some are fortunate enough—what is commonly called good fortune—to be able to exploit some phase of the process for their own personal profit.

The prime condition of a democratically organized public is a kind of knowledge and insight which does not yet exist. In its absence, it would be the height of absurdity to try to tell what it would be like if it existed. But some of the conditions which must be fulfilled if it is to exist can be indicated. We can borrow that much from the spirit and method of science even if we are ignorant of it as a specialized apparatus. An obvious requirement is freedom of social inquiry and of distribution of its conclusions. The notion that men may be free in their thought even when they are not in its expression and dissemination has been sedulously propagated. It had its origin in the idea of a mind complete in itself, apart from action and from objects. Such a consciousness presents in fact the spectacle of mind deprived of its normal functioning, because it is baffled by the actualities in connection with which alone it is truly mind, and is driven back into secluded and impotent revery.

There can be no public without full publicity in respect to all consequences which concern it. Whatever obstructs and restricts publicity, limits and distorts public opinion and checks and distorts thinking on social affairs. Without freedom of expression, not even methods of social inquiry can be developed.

It has been implied throughout that knowledge is communication as well as understanding. I well remember the saying of a man, uneducated from the standpoint of the schools, in speaking of certain matters: "Sometime they will be found out and not only found out, but they will be known." The schools may suppose that a thing is known when it is found out. My old friend was aware that a thing is fully known only when it is published, shared, socially accessible. Record and communication are indispensable to knowledge. Knowledge cooped up in a private consciousness is a myth, and knowledge of social phenomena is peculiarly dependent upon dissemination, for only by distribution can such knowledge be either obtained or tested. A fact of community life which is not spread abroad so as to be a common possession is a contradiction in terms. Dissemination is something other than scattering at large. Seeds are sown, not by virtue of being thrown out at random, but by being so distributed as to take root and have a chance of growth. Communication of the results of social inquiry is the same thing as the formation of public opinion. This marks one of the first ideas framed in the growth of political democracy as it will be one of the last to be fulfilled. For public opinion is judgment which is formed and entertained by those who constitute the public and is about public affairs. Each of the two phases imposes for its realization conditions hard to meet.

Opinions and beliefs concerning the public presuppose effective and organized inquiry. Unless there are methods for detecting the energies which are at work and tracing them through an intricate network of interactions to their consequences, what passes as public opinion will be "opinion" in its derogatory sense rather than truly public, no matter how widespread the opinion is. The number who share error as to fact and who partake of a false belief measures power for harm. Opinion casually formed and formed under the direction of those who have something at stake in having a lie believed can be *public* opinion only in name. Calling it by this name, acceptance of the name as a kind of warrant, magnifies its capacity to lead action estray. The more who share it, the more injurious its influence. Public opinion, even if it happens to be correct, is intermittent when it is not the product of methods of investigation and reporting constantly at work.

. . . Only continuous inquiry, continuous in the sense of being connected as well as persistent, can provide the material of enduring opinion about public matters.

There is a sense in which "opinion" rather than knowledge, even under the most favorable circumstances, is the proper term to use—namely, in the sense of judgment, estimate. For in its strict sense, knowledge can refer only to what *has* happened and been done. What is still *to be* done involves a forecast of a future still contingent, and cannot escape the liability to error in judgment involved in all anticipation of probabilities. There may well be honest divergence as to policies to be pursued, even when plans spring from knowledge of the same facts. But genuinely public policy cannot be generated unless it be informed by knowledge, and this knowledge does not exist except when there is systematic, thorough, and well-equipped search and record.

Moreover, inquiry must be as nearly contemporaneous as possible; otherwise it is only of antiquarian interest. Knowledge of history is evidently necessary for connectedness of knowledge. But history which is not brought down close to the actual scene of events leaves a gap and exercises influence upon the formation of judgment about the public interest only by guess-work about intervening events. Here, only too conspicuously, is a limitation of the existing social sciences. Their material comes too late, too far after the event, to enter effectively into the formation of public opinion about the immediate public concern and what is to be done about it.

A glance at the situation shows that the physical and external means of collecting information in regard to what is happening in the world have far outrun the intellectual phase of inquiry and organization of its results. Telegraph, telephone, and now the radio, cheap and quick mails, the printing press, capable of swift reduplication of material at low cost, have attained a remarkable development. But when we ask what sort of material is recorded and how it is organized, when we ask about the intellectual form in which the material is presented, the tale to be told is very different. "News" signifies something which has just happened, and which is new just because it deviates from the old and regular. But its *meaning* depends upon relation to what it imports, to what its social consequences are. This import cannot be determined unless the new is placed in relation to the old, to what has happened and been integrated into the course of events. Without coordination and consecutiveness, events are not events, but mere occurrences, intrusions; an event implied that out of which a happening proceeds. Hence even if we discount the influence of private interests in procuring suppression, secrecy and misrepresentation, we have here an explanation of the triviality and "sensational" quality of so much of what passes as news. The catastrophic, namely, crime, accident, family rows, personal clashes and conflicts, are the most obvious forms of breaches of continuity; they supply the element of shock which is the strictest meaning of sensation; they are the *new* par excellence, even though only the date of the newspaper could inform us whether they happened last year or this, so completely are they isolated from their connections.

So accustomed are we to this method of collecting, recording and presenting social changes, that it may well sound ridiculous to say that a genuine social science would manifest its reality in the daily press, while learned books and articles supply and polish tools of inquiry. But the inquiry which alone can furnish knowledge as a precondition of public judgments must be contemporary and quotidian. Even if social sciences as a specialized apparatus of inquiry were more advanced than they are, they would be comparatively impotent in the office of directing opinion on matters of concern to the public as long as they are remote from application in the daily and unremitting assembly and interpretation of "news." On the other hand, the tools of social inquiry will be clumsy as long as they are forged in places and under conditions remote from contemporary events.

We have but touched lightly and in passing upon the conditions which must be fulfilled if the Great Society is to become a Great Community; a society in which the ever-expanding and intricately ramifying consequences of associated activities shall be known in the full sense of that word, so that an organized, articulate Public comes into being. The highest and most difficult kind of inquiry and a subtle, delicate, vivid and responsive art of communication must take possession of the physical machinery of transmission and circulation and breathe life into it. When the machine age has thus perfected its machinery it will be a means of life and not its despotic master. Democracy will come into its own, for democracy is a name for a life of free and enriching communion. It had its seer in Walt Whitman. It will have its consummation when free social inquiry is indissolubly wedded to the art of full and moving communication.

[1927]

David B. Truman

from The Governmental Process

THE ALLEGED MISCHIEFS OF FACTION

Most accounts of American legislative sessions—national, state, or local—are full of references to the maneuverings and iniquities of various organized groups. Newspaper stories report that a legislative proposal is being promoted by groups of business men or school teachers or farmers or consumers or labor unions or other aggregations of citizens. Cartoonists picture the legislature as completely under the control of sinister, portly, cigar-smoking individuals labeled "special interests," while a diminutive John Q. Public is pushed aside to sulk in futile anger and pathetic frustration. A member of the legislature rises in righteous anger on the floor of the house or in a press conference to declare that the bill under discussion is being forced through by the "interests," by the most unscrupulous high-pressure "lobby" he has seen in all his years of public life. An investigating committee denounces the activities of a group as deceptive, immoral, and destructive of our constitutional methods and ideals. A chief executive attacks a "lobby" or "pressure group" as the agency responsible for obstructing or emasculating a piece of legislation that he has recommended "in the public interest."

From time to time a conscientious and observant reporter collects a series of such incidents and publishes them, exposing in the best muckraking tradition the machinations of these subversive "interests," and, if he is fortunate, breaking into the best-seller lists. Or a fictionalized treatment of them may be presented as the theme of a popular novel.

Such events are familiar even to the casual student of day-to-day politics, if only because they make diverting reading and appear to give the citizen the "low-down" on his government. He tends, along with many of his more sophisticated fellow citizens, to take these things more or less for granted, possibly because they merely confirm his conviction that "as everybody knows, politics is a dirty business." Yet at the same time he is likely to regard the activities of organized groups in political life as somehow outside the proper and normal processes of government, as the lapses of his weak contemporaries whose moral fiber is insufficient to prevent their defaulting on the great traditions of the Founding Fathers. These events appear to be a modern pathology.

Group Pressures and the Founding Fathers

Group pressures, whatever we may wish to call them, are not new in America. One of the earliest pieces of testimony to this effect is essay number 10 of *The Federalist,* which contains James Madison's classic statement of the impact of divergent groups upon government and the reasons for their development. He was arguing the virtues of the proposed Union as a means to "break and control the violence of faction," having in mind, no doubt, the groups involved in such actions of the debtor or propertyless segment of the population as Shay's Rebellion. He defined faction in broader terms, however, as "a number of citizens, whether amounting to a majority or minority of the whole, who are united and actuated by some common impulse of passion, or of interest. . . ." His observations on the source and character of such group differences merit quotation at length:

The latent causes of faction are . . . sown in the nature of man; and we see them everywhere brought into different degrees of activity, according to the different circumstances of civil society. A zeal for different opinions concerning religion, concerning government, and many other points, as well of speculation as of practice; an attachment to different leaders ambitiously contending for pre-eminence and power; or to persons of other descriptions whose fortunes have been interesting to the human passions, have, in turn, divided mankind into parties, inflamed them with mutual animosity, and rendered them much more disposed to vex and oppress each other than to co-operate for their common good. . . . But the most common and durable source of factions has been the various and unequal distribution of property. Those who hold and those who are without property have ever formed distinct interests in society. Those who are creditors, and those who are debtors, fall under a like discrimination. A landed interest, a manufacturing interest, a mercantile interest, a moneyed interest, with many lesser interests, grow up of necessity in civilized nations, and divide them into different classes, actuated by different sentiments and views. The regulation of these various and interfering interests forms the principal task of modern legislation, and involves the spirit of party and faction in the necessary and ordinary operations of the government.[1]

It should be noted that this analysis is not just the brilliant generalization of an armchair philosopher or pamphleteer; it represents as well the distillation from Madison's years of acquaintance with contemporary politics as a member of the Virginia Assembly and of Congress. Using the words "party" and "faction" almost

---

1. See Madison, *The Federalist,* No. 10. this volume.—ED.

interchangeably, since the political party as we know it had not yet developed, he saw the struggles of such groups as the essence of the political process. One need not concur in all his judgments to agree that the process he described had strong similarities to that of our own day.

The entire effort of which *The Federalist* was part was one of the most skillful and important examples of pressure group activity in American history. The state ratifying conventions were handled by the federalists with a skill that might well be the envy of a modern lobbyist. It is easy to overlook the fact that "unless the Federalists had been shrewd in manipulation as they were sound in theory, their arguments could not have prevailed."[2]

Since we have not yet come to the point of defining our terms, it may be asserted that the instances cited carry with them none of the overtones of corruption and selfishness associated with modern political groups. Such characteristics are not the distinguishing feature of group politics, but early cases of the sort are not hard to find. As early as 1720 a nearly successful effort was made to control the New Jersey Assembly, allegedly in the business interests of an outside manipulator.[3]

. . .

The Problem

It should be apparent from this brief discussion that the political interest group is neither a fleeting, transitory newcomer to the political arena nor a localized phenomenon peculiar to one member of the family of nations. The persistence and the dispersion of such organizations indicate rather that we are dealing with a characteristic aspect of our society. That such groups are receiving an increasing measure of popular and technical attention suggests the hypothesis that they are appreciably more significant in the complex and interdependent society of our own day than they were in the simpler, less highly developed community for which our constitutional arrangements were originally designed.

Many people are quite willing to acknowledge the accuracy of these propositions about political groups, but they are worried nevertheless. They are still concerned over the meaning of what they see and read of the activities of such organizations. They observe, for example, that certain farm groups apparently can induce the government to spend hundreds of millions of dollars to maintain the price of food and to take "surplus" agricultural produce off the market while many urban residents are encountering painful difficulty in stretching their food budgets to provide adequately for their families. They observe that various labor organizations seem to be able to prevent the introduction of cheaper methods into building

---

2. Samuel E. Morrison and Henry S. Commager, *The Growth of the American Republic* (New York: Oxford University Press, 1930), p. 163. See also Charles A. Beard, *An Economic Interpretation of the Constitution of the United States* (New York: The Macmillan Company, 1913), chaps. 6, 8, and 9.
   3. Cited in Robert Luce, *Legislative Assemblies* (Boston: Houghton Mifflin, 1924), p. 367.

codes, although the cost of new housing is already beyond the reach of many. Real estate and contractors' trade associations apparently have the power to obstruct various governmental projects for slum clearance and low-cost housing. Veterans' organizations seem able to secure and protect increases in pensions and other benefits almost at will. A church apparently can prevent the appropriation of federal funds to public schools unless such funds are also given to the schools it operates in competition with the public systems. The government has declared that stable and friendly European governments cannot be maintained unless Americans buy more goods and services abroad. Yet American shipowners and seamen's unions can secure a statutory requirement that a large proportion of the goods purchased by European countries under the Marshall Plan must be carried in American ships. Other industries and trade associations can prevent the revision of tariff rates and customs regulations that restrict imports from abroad.

In all these situations the fairly observant citizen sees various groups slugging it out with one another in pursuit of advantages from the government. Or he sees some of them cooperating with one another to their mutual benefit. He reads of "swarms" of lobbyists "putting pressure on" congressmen and administrators. He has the impression that any group can get what it wants in Washington by deluging officials with mail and telegrams. He may then begin to wonder whether a governmental system like this can survive, whether it can carry its responsibilities in the world and meet the challenges presented by a ruthless dictatorship. He wants to see these external threats effectively met. The sentimental nonsense of the commercial advertisements aside, he values free speech, free elections, representative government, and all that these imply. He fears and resents practices and privileges that seem to place these values in jeopardy.

A common reaction to revelations concerning the more lurid activities of political groups is one of righteous indignation. Such indignation is entirely natural. It is likely, however, to be more comforting than constructive. What we seek are correctives, protections, or controls that will strengthen the practices essential in what we call democracy and that will weaken or eliminate those that really threaten that system. Uncritical anger may do little to achieve that objective, largely because it is likely to be based upon a picture of the governmental process that is a composite of myth and fiction as well as of fact. We shall not begin to achieve control until we have arrived at a conception of politics that adequately accounts for the operations of political groups. We need to know what regular patterns are shown by group politics before we can predict its consequences and prescribe for its lapses. We need to re-examine our notions of how representative government operates in the United States before we can be confident of our statements about the effects of group activities upon it. Just as we should not know how to protect a farm house from lightning unless we knew something of the behavior of electricity, so we cannot hope to protect a governmental system from the results of group organization unless we have an adequate understanding of the political process of which these groups are a part.

GROUPS AND SOCIETY

Man is a social animal. Among other meanings involved in this Aristotelian statement is the observation that with rare exceptions man is always found in association with other men. John Dewey has observed: "Associated activity needs no explanation; things are made that way."[4] This association includes varying degrees of organization; that is, certain of the relationships among a collection of men regularly occur in certain consistent patterns and sequences. But there is another meaning in this classic proposition, closer to the one that Aristotle probably intended, namely, that men must exist in society in order to manifest those capacities and accomplishments that distinguish them from the other animals. These human accomplishments embrace not only the wondrous array of skills and creations that are thought of as civilization but also humbler and more fundamental developments such as primary intellectual growth and language.

We do not have to rely solely on Aristotle's confidence concerning the virtues of life in the city-state for support of the proposition that man is essentially social. The Robinson Crusoe hypothesis that men are best conceived of as isolated units is inadequate psychology as well as unfashionable economics. Accounts, at least partially authenticated, of children who by some chance of fate have been raised among animals, isolated from all contact with human beings, indicate not only that speech is not acquired under such circumstances but also that it is developed only very slowly after the child has been returned to human society. Cases of children who have been kept in solitary confinement during their early years illustrate the same point. An essentially human and social characteristic, speech, is not acquired, and, in fact, the very capacity to learn is apparently stunted or atrophied.[5] Man becomes characteristically human only in association with other men.

A more obvious sort of interdependence also requires man to live in society— purely physical dependence on others of his species. The family, the most primitive social unit, the only one that man shares generally with other mammals, exists in part to provide protection and training for the offspring during their long period of helplessness. Furthermore, the division of labor or specialization, which appears even in the simple family unit on the basis of age and sex differences and on which a high degree of skill and large productivity fundamentally depend, almost by definition involves the mutual dependence of men. A modern urban dweller who has experienced the consequences of an interruption in the milk supply, in the public transportation system, or in the distribution of electric power needs no introduction to the implications of specialization.

---

4. John Dewey, *The Public and Its Problems* (New York: Henry Holt & Company, Inc., 1927), p. 151.

5. See Arnold Gesell, *Wolf Child and Human Child* (New York: Harper and Brothers, 1939) and Kingsley Davis, "Extreme Social Isolation of a Child," *American Journal of Sociology,* Vol. 45, no. 4 (January 1940), pp. 554–65.

In this chapter, as the remarks above suggest, we shall not focus our attention primarily upon "political" behavior. We shall rather examine groups of all kinds and their significance in the social process generally. The point to bear in mind is that the dynamics of groups are not essentially different because the groups are labeled "political." Basically they show the same regularities as do other continuing social patterns. In this connection we shall discuss the meaning of the terms "group" and "interest group" and shall examine some of the characteristics of a peculiarly important type of group, the association.

· · ·

The Group Concept

If the uniformities consequent upon the behavior of men in groups are the key to an understanding of human, including political, behavior, it will be well to specify somewhat more sharply what is involved when the term "group" is used. An excessive preoccupation with matters of definition will only prove a handicap. "Who likes may snip verbal definitions in his old age, when his world has gone crackly and dry."[6] Nevertheless, a few distinctions may be useful.

We find the term "group" applied in two broad senses. Both popularly and in much technical literature it is used to describe any collection of individuals who have some characteristic in common. These are sometimes known as categoric groups. In this sense the word is applied to persons of a given age level, to those of similar income or social status, to people living in a particular area, as Westerners, and to assortments of individuals according to an almost endless variety of similarities—farmers, alcoholics, insurance men, blondes, illiterates, mothers, neurotics, and so on. Although this sense of the word may be useful, it omits one aspect of peculiar importance. The justification for emphasizing groups as basic social units, it will be recalled, is the uniformities of behavior produced through them. Such uniformities do not depend immediately upon such similarities as those mentioned above, but upon the relationships among the persons involved. The significance of a family group in producing similar attitudes and behaviors among its members lies, not in their physical resemblance or in their proximity, as such, to one another, but in the characteristic relationships among them. These interactions, or relationships, because they have a certain character and frequency, give the group its molding and guiding powers. In fact, they are the group, and it is in this sense that the term will be used.

A minimum frequency of interaction is, of course, necessary before a group in this sense can be said to exist. If a motorist stops along a highway to ask directions of a farmer, the two are interacting, but they can hardly be said to constitute a group except in the most casual sense. If, however, the motorist belongs to an

6. Arthur F. Bentley, *The Process of Government* (Chicago: University of Chicago Press, 1908), p. 199.

automobile club to the staff of which he and the other members more or less regularly resort for route information, then staff and members can be designated as a group. Similarly, groups in the first sense—collections of people with some common characteristic—may be groups in the proper sense if they interact with some frequency on the basis of their shared characteristics. If a number of mothers interact with one another as they tackle problems of child training, whether through a club or through subscription to a mothers' periodical, they have become a group, though the two forms differ in structure and frequency of interaction. If the members of any aggregation of blondes begin to interact as blondes, alcoholics as alcoholics (or former addicts), people over sixty as aged—they constitute groups. That is, under certain recurring conditions they behave differently with each other than with brunettes, teetotalers, or the young. In fact, the reason why the two senses of the term "group" are so close is that on the basis of experience it is expected that people who have certain attributes in common—neighborhood, consanguinity, occupation—will interact with some frequency. It is the interaction that is crucial, however, not the shared characteristic.[7]

. . .

Interest Groups

Various of these established designations will be useful from time to time, but one identifying term . . . may be discussed at some length, since it involves the central concern of these pages, the term "interest group." Like so many terms associated with the processes of government, it has been used for the purposes of polemics so freely that it has acquired certain emotional connotations which may render it ambiguous when used in analysis. *Political, partisan,* and even the word *politics* itself share with *interest, vested interest, special interest,* and *interest group,* among others, a connotation of impropriety and selfishness that almost denies them the neutral precision requisite to careful discussion.

As used here "interest group" refers to any group that, on the basis of one or more shared attitudes, makes certain claims upon other groups in the society for the establishment, maintenance, or enhancement of forms of behavior that are implied by the shared attitudes. . . . From interaction in groups arise certain common habits of response, which may be called norms, or shared attitudes. These afford the participants frames of reference for interpreting and evaluating events and behaviors. In this respect all groups are interest groups because they are shared-attitude groups. In some groups at various points in time, however, a second kind of common response emerges, in addition to the frames of reference. These are shared attitudes toward what is needed or wanted in a given society, observable as demands or claims upon other groups in the society. The term "interest group" will be reserved here for those groups that exhibit both aspects of the shared attitudes.

7. George A. Lundberg, *Foundations of Sociology* (New York: The Macmillan Company, 1939).

The shared attitudes, moreover, constitute the interests. It has been suggested that a distinction be made between the two terms, reserving the latter to designate "the objects toward which these . . . [attitudes] are directed."[8] Such a distinction may be highly misleading. If, for example, reference were made to oil interests, one would presumably be referring, among other things, to certain elements in the physical environment, petroleum and its by-products. These features, however, have no significance in society apart from the activities of men. There were no oil attitudes prior to the time when the productive behaviors of men led them to do something with petroleum.[9] As a consequence of the use of oil, an array of attitudes with respect to that use has developed—that it should not be wasted, that it should be marketed in a particular way, that it should be produced by many small groups or enterprises, that it should be controlled by an international organization, and so on. Some of these attitudes are represented by interest groups asserting that the behaviors implied by the attitudes should be encouraged, discouraged, or altered. The physical features of oil production have no significance for the student of society apart from the attitudes, or interests, and the behaviors that they suggest.

Definition of the interest group in this fashion has a number of distinct advantages in the task of political analysis. In the first place, it permits the identification of various potential as well as existing interest groups. That is, it invites examination of an interest whether or not it is found at the moment as one of the characteristics of a particular organized group. Although no group that makes claims upon other groups in the society will be found without an interest or interests, it is possible to examine interests that are not at a particular point in time the basis of interactions among individuals, but that may become such. Without the modern techniques for the measurement of attitude and opinion, this position would indeed be risky, since it would invite the error of ascribing an interest to individuals quite apart from any overt behavior that they might display.[10] In the scientific study of society only frustration and defeat are likely to follow an attempt to deal with data that are not directly observable. Even the most insistent defenders of the scientific position, however, admit that, although activity is the basic datum of social science, a "becoming" stage of activity must be recognized as a phase of activity if any segment of a moving social situation is to be understood. There are, in other words, potential activities, or "tendencies of activity."[11] These tendencies are the central feature of the most widely accepted social psychological definition of attitude. Gordon W. Allport, after examining a series of definitions, arrived at his own generally used statement: "An attitude is a mental and neural *state of readiness,* organized through experience, exerting a directive or dynamic influence upon the

8. Robert M. MacIver, "Interests," *Encyclopaedia of the Social Sciences.* And see Avery Leiserson, *Administrative Regulations: A Study in Representation of Interests* (Chicago: University of Chicago Press, 1942), pp. 1–10.

9. See Bentley, *The Process of Government,* pp. 193–94.

10. Ibid., p.213.

11. Ibid., pp. 184 ff.

individual's response to all objects and situations with which it is related."[12] On the basis of widely held attitudes that are not expressed in interaction, therefore, it is possible to talk of potential interest groups.

In the second place, as these statements suggest, this concept of interest group permits attention to what Lundberg calls the "degree of integrative interaction."[13] The frequency, or rate, of interaction will in part determine the primacy of a particular group affiliation in the behavior of an individual and, as will be indicated in more detail later, it will be of major importance in determining the relative effectiveness with which a group asserts its claims upon other groups. This approach affords all the advantages and none of the disadvantages that once accrued to the sociologists' concepts of "primary groups" and "secondary groups," meaning by the former face-to-face interaction as opposed to indirect contacts such as those made through the media of mass communication. Before the enormous expansion and development of the latter techniques, and still in societies where they have not penetrated, it was a verifiable fact that solidarity of group behavior depended largely upon physical proximity. Frequent face-to-face contact in no small measure accounted for the influence of such primary groups as the family, the neighborhood, and the like. As the social functions performed by the family institution in our society have declined, some of these secondary groups, such as labor unions, have achieved a rate of interaction that equals or surpasses that of certain of the primary groups. This shift in importance has been facilitated largely by the development of means of communication that permit frequent interaction among individuals not in face-to-face contact or not continuously so.

In this connection note the confidence that James Madison, in seeking restraints upon the "mischiefs of faction" (interest groups), placed in "the greater obstacles opposed to the concert" of such groups by the "extent of the Union."[14] Such faith in physical dispersion had some basis in a period when it took a week to travel a distance of three hundred miles. It would not be true to say that primary groups no longer achieve the integration once ascribed to them. A recent study has indicated, for example, that the prolonged resistance of the German army in the face of repeated defeats in 1944 and 1945 was a result of the solidarity and continued structural integrity of such primary groups as the squad.[15] It is primarily from the degree of interaction that the face-to-face group fosters, however, that its influence is derived. A high degree may also be achieved through secondary means.

In the third place, this concept of the interest group permits us to evaluate the significance of formal organization. The existence of neither the group nor the

12. Gordon W. Allport, "Attitudes," in Carl Murchison, ed.: *A Handbook of Social Psychology* (Worcester, Mass.: Clark University Press, 1935), chap. 17.

13. Lundberg, *Foundations of Sociology,* p. 310.

14. *The Federalist,* No. 10; see also No. 51 for similar arguments.

15. Edward A. Shils and Morris Janowitz, "Cohesion and Disintegration in the Wehrmacht in World War II," *Public Opinion Quarterly,* Vol. 12, no. 2 (Summer, 1948), pp. 280–315.

interest is dependent upon formal organization, although that feature has significance, particularly in the context of politics. Organization indicates merely a stage or degree of interaction. The fact that one interest group is highly organized whereas another is not or is merely a potential group—whether the interest involved is that of affording more protection to consumers, greater privileges for brunettes, or more vigorous enforcement of civil rights—is a matter of great significance at any particular moment. It does not mean, however, that the momentarily weaker group, or interest, will inevitably remain so. Events may easily produce an increased rate of interaction among the affected individuals to the point where formal organization or a significant interest group will emerge and greater influence will ensue. The point may be illustrated by noting that this increased rate of interaction is usually what is meant when the journalists speak of "an aroused public opinion."

Finally, this use of the concept also gives a proper perspective to the political activities of many interest groups that are the principal concern of this book. Although a characteristic feature of these groups is that they make claims upon other groups in the society, these claims may be asserted or enforced by means of a variety of techniques and through any of the institutions of the society, not merely the government. An interest group concentrating upon replacing the valuable shade trees in a village adjacent to a large gentleman's farm may achieve its objective by prevailing upon the baronial family to purchase the trees and pay for their planting. A group interested in the protection of certain moralities among the younger generation may secure the behaviors they desire in part through inducing motion picture producers to permit its officers to censor films before they are released. Whether a group operates in such fashions as these or attempts to work through governmental institutions, thereby becoming a political interest group, may be a function of circumstances; the government may have primary or exclusive responsibility in the area involved, as in the war-time allocation of scarce materials. Or the choice between political and other modes of operation may be a function of technique; it may be easier or more effective to achieve temperance objectives through the government than by prevailing upon people to sign pledges. The process is essentially the same whether the interest group operates through other institutions or becomes political.

To summarize briefly, an interest group is a shared-attitude group that makes certain claims upon other groups in the society. If and when it makes its claims through or upon any of the institutions of government, it becomes a political interest group. These are the meanings that we shall attach to these terms. . . . At times it will be convenient to omit the modifying term "political" in discussing interest group activity in the government. In such instances it will be clear from the context whether we are dealing with political interest groups or with groups that are making claims otherwise than through or upon the institutions of government.

It follows that any group in the society may function as an interest group and that any of them may function as political interest groups, that is, those that make their claims through or upon governmental institutions. An economic group, such as a corporation, that seeks a special tax ruling is in that respect functioning as a political interest group. Trade associations, labor unions, philatelic societies, world government societies, political parties, professional organizations, and a host of others can and do seek to achieve all or a portion of their objectives by operating through or upon the institutions of government. Even a family group, whose prestige or financial interests approach imperial proportions, may make such claims. It will be useful and significant to identify or classify such groups according to the regularity or the success with which such claims are advanced through these channels. Even the casual observer will give somewhat different places to the philatelic society that prevails upon the Postmaster General to provide special handling for letters bearing a new stamp issue and a trade association that seeks legislation to protect it against its competitors. These may sensibly be placed in separate subcategories, but they both display the fundamental characteristics of such groups.

Seen in these terms, is an interest group inherently "selfish"? In the first place, such judgments have no value for a scientific understanding of government or the operation of society. Schematically, they represent nothing more than the existence of a conflicting interest, possibly, but not necessarily, involving another group or groups. Judgments of this kind are and must be made by all citizens in their everyday life, but they are not properly a part of the systematic analysis of the social process. Secondly, many such political interest groups are from almost any point of view highly altruistic. One need only recall those groups that have consistently risen to defend the basic guarantees of the American constitution, to improve the lot of the underprivileged, or to diffuse the advantages stemming from scientific advance. Evaluations such as these may be made of particular groups, depending on the observer's own attitudes, but, as was indicated in the preceding chapter, they will not facilitate one's understanding of the social system of which the groups are a part.

Where does the term "pressure group" fit into this scheme? This expression, perhaps more than any other, has been absorbed into the language of political abuse. It carries a load of emotional connotations indicating selfish, irresponsible insistence upon special privileges. Any group that regards itself as disinterested and altruistic will usually repudiate with vigor any attempt to attach this label to it, a fact that suggests that the term has little use except to indicate a value judgment concerning those groups of which one disapproves. Some writers, however, in a courageous effort to reclaim for the term a core of neutral meaning, use it as a synonym for "political interest group."[16] This usage has certain disadvantages

---

16. See, e.g., V. O. Key, Jr., *Politics, Parties, and Pressure Groups,* 2d ed. (New York: Thomas Y. Crowell Co., 1947). Key, however, uses the terms somewhat more narrowly, confining them to "private associations formed to influence public policy" (p. 15).

aside from the obvious possibility that many readers will be unable to accept the suggestion that "the objectives of the pressure group may be good or bad; the group may be animated by the highest moral purpose or it may be driving for the narrowest kind of class gain."[17] If the word "pressure" has more than a simply figurative meaning, it suggests a method or a category of methods that may be used by an interest group to achieve its objectives.[18] Even if the methods implied can be described precisely, unless we can demonstrate that all political interest groups use them, the term "pressure group" will indicate merely a stage or phase of group activity and will not serve as a satisfactory equivalent for "interest group" or "political interest group," as these have been defined. In view of the improbability of satisfying the conditions specified, it will be avoided in these pages in favor of the more inclusive and more nearly neutral term.

· · ·

In all societies the association operates to relate and stabilize the interactions among persons in basic institutionalized groups. The association also has the attitude-forming, behavior-influencing group functions that we discussed earlier.

Because of their functions, moreover, associations are peculiarly likely to operate both as interest groups and as political interest groups. The political role constitutes their importance in the present context. In the process of affording a means of adjustment for the members of various institutionalized groups, they are likely to make claims upon other groups not part of the institutions of government—as the labor union upon management. They are equally likely to assert claims upon or through the government. So common is this tendency that some students choose to limit the concept of the political interest group to groups that qualify as associations.[19] Although a large proportion of the familiar political interest groups are of this type, it is not strictly accurate, for the reasons indicated in an earlier paragraph, to omit from the category other types of groups whose relations with governmental institutions are of the same general character. The Standard Oil Company of New Jersey is not an association. Nevertheless, it may operate as a significant political interest group. In addition, its officers may function through an association, such as the National Association of Manufacturers, that is also a political interest group. Any group in the society may at one time or another operate as a political interest group. The considerable political importance of associations, that is, the groups formed around tangent relations, lies not only in their strong tendency to operate through or upon the institutions of government but in their stabilizing functions, in the larger resources of various kinds that they can command as compared with any of the participant elements, and in their great numbers in our society.

17. Key, *Politics, Parties, and Pressure Groups,* pp. 16–17.

18. Robert M. MacIver, "Pressures, Social," in *Encyclopedia of the Social Sciences,* Vol. 12 (New York: Macmillan, 1953), pp. 344–48.

19. See Key, *Politics, Parties, and Pressure Groups.*

. . .

Group Diversity and Governmental Complexity

For all but those who see in the growth of new groups the evil ways of individual men, it is obvious that the trend toward an increasing diversity of groups functionally attached to the institutions of government is a reflection of the characteristics and needs, to use a somewhat ambiguous term, of a complex society. This conclusion stems necessarily from the functional concept of groups presented in the preceding [discussion]. Not all institutions of a society necessarily become complex simultaneously or at an even rate, of course. The religious institution may be highly complicated, for example, whereas economic institutions or the family may remain relatively simple. The political institutions of any culture are a peculiarly sensitive barometer of the complexity of the society, however, owing to their special function. Since they operate to order the relationships among various groups in the society, any considerable increase in the types of such groups, or any major change in the nature of their interrelationships, will be reflected subsequently in the operation of the political system. For example, as the Tanala of Madagascar shifted from a dry-land method of rice growing to a method based on irrigation, a series of consequent changes in the culture gradually took place. Village mobility disappeared in favor of settled communities, since the constant search for fertile soil was no longer necessary; individual ownership in land emerged, since the supply of appropriate soil was sharply limited; a system of slavery was developed; and the joint family was broken up into its constituent households. Finally, as a result of these changes in relationships and interests, and with the introduction of conflicts stemming from differences in wealth, the decentralized and almost undifferentiated political institution became a centralized tribal kingship.[20]

Alterations in response to technological or other changes are more rapid and more noticeable in a complex society in which a larger number of institutionalized groups are closely interdependent. Changes in one institution produce compensatory changes in tangent institutions and thus, inevitably, in government. A complex civilization necessarily develops complex political arrangements. Where the patterns of interaction in the society are intricate, the patterns of political behavior must be also. These may take several forms, depending upon the circumstances. In a society like ours, whose traditions sanction the almost unregulated development of a wide variety of associations, the new patterns are likely to involve the emergence of a wide variety of groups peripheral to the formal institutions of government, supplementing and complicating their operations.

This kind of complexity seems to stem in large measure . . . from the techniques employed in the culture and especially from the specialization that they involve. This situation is so familiar that it hardly needs explanation, yet its very familiarity

20. Ralph Linton, *The Study of Man* (New York: D. Appleton–Century Company, 1936), pp. 348–54.

easily leads to a neglect of its basic importance. The specialization necessary to supply a single commodity such as gasoline may provide a miniature illustration:

An oil operator brings oil to the surface of the ground; the local government prevents the theft of oil or destruction of equipment; a railroad corporation transports the oil; State and Federal Governments prevent interference with the transport of oil; a refining company maintains an organization of workers and chemical equipment to convert the oil into more useful forms; a retail distributor parcels out the resulting gasoline in small quantities to individuals requiring it; the Federal Government supplies a dependable medium of exchange which allows the oil operator, the railroad, the refining company, and the retailer to act easily in an organized fashion without being under a single administrative authority, and enforces contracts so that organizing arrangements on specific points can be more safely entered into; finally, government maintains a system of highways and byways which allow an ultimate consumer to combine the gasoline with other resources under his control in satisfying his desire for automobile travel.[21]

The intricacies of what are ordinarily thought of as economic behaviors by no means exhaust the picture, of course. One has only to think of the specialties appearing in various kinds of amusement and recreation to realize that these characteristics pervade the society. Professionalized sports such as baseball and an increasing number of others, the motion pictures with their wide range of "experts" of all sorts, not to mention the specialists necessary to the operations of the press—all illustrate the basic fact.

These specializations are created by the various techniques with which we meet the challenges and opportunities of the physical environment, and they are allocated to individuals . . . roughly on the basis of differences in skill. They produce a congeries of differentiated but highly interdependent groups of men whose time is spent using merely segments of the array of skills developed in the culture.[22] Men are preoccupied by their skills, and these preoccupations in large measure define what the members of such groups know and perceive about the world in which they live. As has been remarked in a slightly different connection: "Machines . . . make specifications, so to speak, about the character of the people who are to operate them."[23] Under favorable circumstances groups form among those who share this "knowledge" and the attitudes it fosters. Both the nature of the techniques utilized in the society and the interdependencies that they imply dictate the amount and kinds of interaction of this sort. Where the techniques are complex, the interactions must be also.[24]

21. U.S. National Resources Committee, *The Structure of the American Economy, Part I: Basic Characteristics* (Washington, D.C.: Government Printing Office, 1939), p. 96.

22. See Linton, *The Study of Man,* pp. 84, 272–73.

23. U.S. National Resources Committee, *The Problems of a Changing Population* (Washington, D.C.: Government Printing Office, 1938), p. 244.

24. Eliot D. Chapple and Carlton S. Coon, *Principles of Anthropology* (New York: Henry Holt and Co., 1942), pp. 140, 250–51, 365.

It is unnecessary here to attempt to trace historically the increasing diversity of groups. MacIver sees the "dawn of modern multi-group society" in the splitting of the single church in the sixteenth century, the consequent struggles over religious toleration, and the demands of the middle economic classes.[25] It is obvious that the process has been greatly accentuated by tremendous technological changes, well meriting the appellation "industrial revolution," which inevitably produced new contacts, new patterns of interaction, and new "foci of opposing interests."[26]

A precondition of the development of a vast multiplicity of groups, itself an instance of technological change of the most dramatic sort, is the revolution in means of communication. The mass newspaper, telephone, telegraph, radio, and motion pictures, not to mention the various drastic changes in the speed of transportation, have facilitated the interactions of men and the development of groups only slightly dependent, if at all, upon face-to-face contact. This factor in the formation of groups was noted by de Tocqueville when the first-named medium had scarcely appeared on the American scene:

In democratic countries . . . it often happens that a great number of men who wish or want to combine cannot accomplish it because they are very insignificant and lost amid the crowd, they cannot see and do not know where to find one another. . . . These wandering minds, which had long sought each other in darkness, at length meet and unite. The newspaper brought them together, and the newspaper is still necessary to keep them united.[27]

The revolution in communications has indeed largely rendered obsolete, as we have observed in another connection, Madison's confidence in the dispersion of the population as an obstacle to the formation of interest groups.

Among other influences greatly facilitating group formation are such major national efforts as a war mobilization or a collective attack upon the problems of an industrial depression. In recruiting the national resources for such an emergency, the government stimulates interaction throughout the nation. It is no accident, for example, that the periods of most rapid growth of trade associations in this country have included the years of World War I and the vigorous days of the ill-starred N.R.A. [National Reconstruction Administration].[28] Once the habit of associated activity was established under the stimulus of government encouragement, most such groups tended to persist and to invite imitation.

25. Robert M. MacIver, *The Web of Government* (New York: Macmillan, 1947), pp. 52, 71.

26. MacIver, *The Web of Government*, p. 52.

27. Alexis de Tocqueville, *Democracy in America*, J. P. Mayer, ed. (New York: Doubleday and Co., 1969), p. 518.

28. Herring, *Group Representation Before Congress*, pp. 51–52; U.S. Temporary National Economic Committee: *Trade Association Survey* (Monograph No. 18, Washington, D.C.: Government Printing Office, 1941), p. 368.

. . .

The Inevitable Gravitation toward Government

[As we have said], at various stages in their development, interest groups have become political. In each instance we have noted that they "inevitably" began to make claims through or upon the institutions of government. Why should this be so? We can observe in fact that such groups do operate in this fashion, but why is it justifiable to say that this was "inevitable"?

In the first place, it will be apparent that such a statement implies some special characteristic of interest groups, especially in their contemporary forms. We have seen that many of these groups, the associations, come into being or are activated as a consequence of disturbances—prolonged or intense or both—in the expected patterns of interaction. The associations function to restore a previous equilibrium or to facilitate the establishment of a new one. To a certain extent, depending upon the circumstances, groups can accomplish these goals without recourse to government action—that is, by the successful imposition of claims directly upon another group. An example can be seen in the operations of the early craft unions, which for many years were able to protect their members exclusively by direct claims upon employers. As we have seen, the situation grows somewhat complicated as the sources and effects of the disturbances giving birth to such associations are distributed over wider and wider areas. In response to this development have occurred the amalgamation and federation of local and regional groups into organizations of national and even international scope. In many instances, moreover, the new group still imposes its claims directly without important resort to a mediating institution such as the government.

As our society has become increasingly complex, however, these disturbances have affected not merely the relationships of widely distributed individuals; they have also created a new problem, by placing the means of adjustment beyond the resources of direct action by the groups involved. Thus, for example, disturbances growing out of the market cannot all be settled directly by trade associations or monopolistic economic groups. These groups must supplement direct action by making claims through or upon some mediating institutionalized group whose primary characteristic is its wider powers. In general, of course, the weaker the means of direct action available to an affected group, the more ready has it been to work through such mediating institutions. For example, farm groups have early resorted to political action, in some cases despite an announced intention to eschew political activity. The early years of the Grange are an illustration. The special characteristic of contemporary interest groups that has "inevitably" forced them to operate in the political sphere is this: unaided by the wider powers of some more inclusive institutionalized group, they cannot achieve their objectives; interest groups of the association type cannot, without such mediation, perform their basic function, namely, the establishment and maintenance of an equilibrium in the relationships of their members.

But why must this institution be government? Obviously, a second implication of the statement that the political action of interest groups is inevitable concerns some unique feature of modern government. Why should not interest groups seek the mediation of the church or some such institutionalized group other than governments? If we go back far enough, of course, we find that the church has generally performed just this function, though in simpler fashion than government does today. The clergy in the New England colonies of the seventeenth century functioned in much this fashion; an even better example is supplied by the medieval Church. It was the primary mediating device of the medieval period, because it comprehended within its jurisdiction all groups in the society, including the state itself. Moreover, interest groups still attempt to gain the aid of the churches, the press, and similar institutionalized groups. What labor union will not try to secure the support of both the church and the press in a dispute with employers? In some enclaves of our society, indeed, where a single church enjoys the support of all or a major portion of the population—for example, Quebec and certain metropolitan cities of the United States—it is still the principal mediator, exercising its control not only over interest groups but even over local governments.

Herein lies the clue to the universal tendency of interest groups to resort to government action in the present day. Such groups will supplement their own resources by operating upon or through that institutionalized group whose powers are most inclusive in that time and place. With such local exceptions as those just noted, that institution today is government. Governments, since the Renaissance, especially national governments, have become the most inclusive power concentrations in Western society, virtually unrivaled by any others. The reasons for this development are beyond the concern of these pages, but the fact is of pre-eminent importance.

The effects of such reliance upon government are cumulative. Just as the direct and indirect efforts of an interest group may disturb the equilibriums of related groups, so its operations through and upon government are likely to force the related groups also to assert their claims upon governmental institutions in order to achieve some measure of adjustment. For example, as we have noted above, the labor movement was drawn into politics in no small measure because of the use of governmental injunctive powers by employers. Both types of groups then attempted to assert their claims through the government.

Government is not simply a neutral force, however, moved this way and that solely by the relative vigor with which competing organized groups are able to assert themselves. Such an explanation is much too simple; the functions of government cannot be described in such narrow terms without ignoring significant aspects of its operations. Elucidation of this point must be delayed for later chapters. It must be mentioned here, however, in order to guard against the too literal reading of Madison's sage observation in essay number 10 of *The Federalist:* "The regulation of these various and interfering interests forms the principal task of modern legislation. . . ."

Summary

. . . We have noted that any groups, including institutionalized groups, may function as political interest groups. At the same time, the increasing complexity of our society and the rapidity with which changes have occurred—creating greater intensity as well as frequency of disturbances—have made the association the most characteristic and pervasive sort of political interest group.

These associations have sprung from disruption of the established patterns of behavior, but these disturbances show wide variety. For example, labor unions and their federations have been the product of the increasing division of labor within industry, the growing differentiation between employer and worker, and the consequent major changes in the status and rewards of both workers and managers. These disturbances have been aggravated by rapid developments in transportation and communication and by the shifts in economic organization that have removed policy makers in institutionalized economic groups from direct and intimate contact with workers. The disturbances resulting from these changes have produced the alterations in attitudes (interests) necessary for cohesive associations among workers. Finally, the tactics of opposing interest groups and the ineffectiveness of such traditional weapons as a monopoly of skill have led labor unions to make vigorous claims upon and through the institutions of government. Once made, such claims have been continued and expanded in order to strengthen and protect the measure of stability previously achieved.

Trade associations and their federations, on the other hand, have been formed to deal with the disturbances stemming from numerous technological changes and from the accompanying increased effects of market fluctuations. Supplementary causes have been the revolution in communications and the short-run need during war, depression, or other emergencies for organized groups that could supplement the work of government agencies in economic planning. The activities of competing groups and the ineffectiveness of the weapons available to the associations when working alone have led these groups, like the labor unions, to make increasing demands upon and through the government.

The growth of labor and trade associations, and of most others as well, exhibits a wavelike pattern; for the very success of one group in stabilizing its relationships creates new problems for others and makes necessary either new organizations or the extension and strengthening of existing ones.

The farmers' groups examined are in many ways similar to the trade associations (although there are differences in the specific character of the disturbances that stimulate their growth). The relative weakness of the farmer's bargaining position in the market and the relative strength resulting from the overrepresentation of rural areas in state and national legislatures combine to explain the readiness of these groups to resort to the government in order to achieve their objectives. The wide variety of groups that may be labeled agricultural illustrates how many are the segmental interests that may grow up around the activities of government.

Various professional and quasi-professional associations follow a pattern similar to that of other associations; they are founded in common attitudes (interests) that are created, in turn, by the special skills and preoccupations of their members, and they reach formal organization as the result of disturbances in the relationships of their members to one another or to other groups. The extent to which these associations are concerned with legislation or other government action in part reflects the extent to which disturbances have been produced by the political activity of competing groups and in part indicates the stake of these groups, especially lawyers and doctors, in the effective discharge of their professional functions. Such associations usually try to control (stabilize) their membership and their relationships with the rest of the society by seeking legislation defining standards of practice and requirements for admission to the profession.

These broad patterns can be seen equally clearly among a wide variety of non-occupational interest groups. For fundamental changes in society affect not only the stability of economic relationships but also the interests of almost infinitely many segments of society.

[1967]

from The Civic Culture

ORGANIZATIONAL MEMBERSHIP AND CIVIC COMPETENCE

A civic culture, we have argued, rests upon a set of nonpolitical attitudes and non-political affiliations. Many of these attitudes that we have discussed—general attitudes toward other people, sense of social trust—have little explicit political content, and many of the affiliations we have dealt with, primary group affiliations in particular, are quite distant from the political system. Our concentration on this level of social structure has not meant to imply that larger, secondary nonpolitical groups (voluntary associations are the main example) play an insignificant role in the democratic polity. Quite the contrary: though primary associations play an important role in the development of a citizen's sense of political competence and reflect an incipient capability to aggregate one's demands with others, they would, by themselves, represent a weak link between the individual and the polity. As [William] Kornhauser has pointed out, primary groups are still small and powerless compared with the mass institutions of politics. Larger institutions, close enough to the individual to allow him some participation and yet close enough to the state to provide access to power, are also a necessary part of the democratic infrastructure.[1]

Voluntary associations are the prime means by which the function of mediating between the individual and the state is performed. Through them the individual is able to relate himself effectively and meaningfully to the political system. These associations help him avoid the dilemma of being either a parochial, cut off from political influence, or an isolated and powerless individual, manipulated and mobilized by the mass institutions of politics and government. The availability of his primary groups as a political resource in times of threat gives him an intermittent political resource. Membership in voluntary associations gives him a more structured set of political resources, growing out of his varied interests.

If the citizen is a member of some voluntary organization, he is involved in the broader social world but is less dependent upon and less controlled by his political

1. William Kornhauser, *The Politics of Mass Society* (Glencoe, Ill.: Free Press, 1959).

system. The association of which he is a member can represent his needs and demands before the government. It can make the government more chary of engaging in activities that would harm the individual. Furthermore, communications from central governmental authorities are mediated by the associational memberships of the individual because individuals tend to interpret communications according to their memberships in social groupings—that is, they are likely to reject communications unfavorable to the association to which they belong—and because they may also receive communications from their associations and are thereby provided with alternate channels of political communication. Above all, from the point of view of the individual member, affiliation with some voluntary organization appears to have significant effects on his political attitudes. We shall try to specify these effects in this chapter.

In dealing with the data on associational membership, we must consider one further point. Associational membership may involve a low level of individual participation and competence: associations may be quite large; opportunities for participation limited. Thus the existence of a high frequency of membership may tell us more about the political institutions of a society than it does about the state of citizenship in that society. For the latter we shall have to know more about the nature of the membership—how active individuals are in their organizations and what effects their memberships have upon them.

The Distribution of Voluntary Association Membership

Voluntary association membership is more widespread in some countries than in others. This is apparent from Table 1. In the United States over half the respondents are members of some such organization.[2] In Britain and Germany somewhat less than half the respondents are members of some organization, whereas in Italy and Mexico the proportions are 29 percent and 25 percent, respectively.

To what sorts of organizations do individuals in the five countries belong? The range of specific organizations is wide. But Table 2 suggests some of the main types. In all countries organizations representing economic interests—unions, business organizations, farm organizations, and, perhaps, professional organiza-

2. These data are based on responses to this question: "Are you a member of any organization now—trade or labor unions, business organizations, social groups, professional or farm organizations, cooperatives, fraternal or veterans' groups, athletic clubs, political, charitable, civic or religious organizations, or any other organized group? Which ones?" The amount of voluntary association membership depends heavily upon the wording of the question and on the definition given the respondent of a voluntary association. The inclusion of trade unions, for instance, results in a somewhat higher figure than has been found in other studies. However, what is relevant here is not the absolute level of membership in any one nation, but the relative position of each of the five nations. What is significant, then, is that the same question was asked in all five nations.

TABLE I *Membership in voluntary associations; by nation*

Nation	(%)	(No.)*
United States	57	(970)
Great Britain	47	(963)
Germany	44	(955)
Italy	29	(995)
Mexico	25	(1,007)

*Numbers in parentheses refer to the bases upon which percentages are calculated.

tions—are frequently reported. Social organizations are mentioned by 10 percent or more of our sample in the United States, Britain, and Germany; and in the United states religious, civic-political, and fraternal organizations are also mentioned by 10 percent or more of the respondents. One point to note is that the extent of "politicization" of these organizations, that is, the extent to which they are overtly engaged in politics, probably varies greatly. Some of the economic organizations are obviously deeply politicized; some of the social ones may be completely nonpolitical. We shall return below to the implications of this for political attitudes.

The distribution of organizational membership is also interesting. If we look at the proportion of men and women who are members of some organizations, we see some striking results (see Table 3). The national differences in the number of individuals participating in associations can be largely explained by differences in the proportion of women who report such membership. Thus the high level of associational membership in the United States depends to a large extent on the high level of female participation. If only males are considered, associational participation in the United States is no more frequent than it is in Britain or Germany. It is, in fact, striking how similar the frequency of membership is among the three nations: about two-thirds of the male respondents in each of the three nations report such membership. Among females, on the other hand, participation in the United States is substantially more frequent than in Britain and about twice as frequent as in Germany. In Mexico and Italy the level of participation by both males and females is lower than in the other three countries. However, a similar relationship between frequency of male participation and frequency of female participation is found in all nations except the United States; that is, men participate in voluntary organizations about two to three times as frequently as do women. In the participatory role of women, then, the United States differs substantially from the other four countries, for American women, though they participate less frequently than American men in voluntary associations, do not differ from men in this respect as much as do women in other countries.

Just as men participate more frequently in voluntary associations, so do individuals with higher education. This is seen in Table 4. In all countries there is a

TABLE 2 *Membership in various types of organizations; by nation*

Organization	U.S.	U.K.	Germany	Italy	Mexico
Trade unions	14	22	15	6	11
Business	4	4	2	5	2
Professional	4	3	6	3	5
Farm	3	0	4	2	0
Social	13	14	10	3	4
Charitable	3	3	2	9	6
Religious[a]	19	4	3	6	5
Civic-political	11	3	3	8	3
Cooperative	6	3	2	2	0
Veterans'	6	5	1	4	0
Fraternal[b]	13				
Other	6	3	9	6	0
Total percentage of members	57	47	44	30	24
Total number of respondents	970	963	955	995	1,007

[a] This refers to church-related organizations, not to church affiliation itself.
[b] U.S. only.

sharp increase in organizational membership as one moves up the educational ladder. Among those with primary school education, memberships are much less frequent than among those with higher education, suggesting one of the reasons for the close relationship between education and political competence. Education has compound effects upon political competence. Not only does the more highly educated individual learn politically relevant skills within the school, but he is also more likely to enter into other nonpolitical relationships that have the effect of further heightening his political competence. Associational membership is one form of such nonpolitical participation. The individual with less education, and therefore less political competence, is also less likely to enter into relationships that would develop political competence in later years. The data, then, do suggest that the various functions performed by voluntary associations are performed more frequently for those with higher education.[3]

We are interested in the way in which voluntary association membership affects political attitudes. But the types of associations we are dealing with are many and varied, and one would expect different effects from membership in different types of organizations. One way in which the organizations vary is in the extent to which they are concerned with public affairs. Some of the associations are purely social, others are directly and overtly politically oriented. One can argue—and, indeed, this is one of the major hypotheses about voluntary association membership—that

3. Similar data could be presented for the distribution of organizational membership among the occupational strata. Higher occupational status generally involves more frequent voluntary association membership, though the relationship is not as close as that between education and affiliation.

TABLE 3 *Percentage of respondents who belong to some organization; by nation and sex*

Nation	Total		Male		Female	
	(%)	*(No.)**	*(%)*	*(No.)*	*(%)*	*(No.)*
United States	57	(970)	68	(455)	47	(515)
Great Britain	47	(963)	66	(460)	30	(515)
Germany	44	(955)	66	(449)	24	(506)
Italy	30	(995)	41	(471)	19	(524)
Mexico	24	(1,007)	43	(355)	15	(652)

*Numbers in parentheses refer to the bases upon which percentages are calculated.

membership in even a nonpolitical organization will affect political attitudes. The experience with social interaction within the organization, the opportunity to participate in the decisions of the organization (if there is such participation), and the general broadening of perspectives that occurs in any sort of social activity—all would be expected to increase an individual's potential for political involvement and activity. Nevertheless, one would also expect to find that those organizations more directly involved in politics would have greater effects on the political perspectives of their members.[4]

Unfortunately, our data do not allow us objectively to divide the voluntary organizations into different types, based on the degree to which they take an active political role. We do, however, know whether or not the individual member perceives of his organization as taking some part in politics. Respondents were asked if any organization they belonged to was "in any way concerned with governmental, political, or public affairs; for instance, do they take stands on or discuss public issues or try to influence governmental decisions?" It must be remembered that this question probes the perceptions of the respondents: it asks for their own definition of political affairs. Furthermore, many members may not be aware of the activities of their organizations. A member of a veterans' group that is actively lobbying for veterans' benefits or for certain foreign policies may perceive his group in essentially social terms. Thus these data do not necessarily reflect the actual state of political activity by voluntary associations. But we are interested in the impact of membership in political and nonpolitical organizations on political attitudes, and so these data on the individual's perception of the political role of his organization may be sufficient.

4. Similarly, such organizations would probably also have greater effects on the operation of the political system. Even those that take no active role in politics—do not press for legislation, are politically unconcerned—may have a significant role in political decisions. Their very existence as *potential* political organizations may affect the decisions of government officials in ways that would not happen if these particular groups were not organized. Yet all else being equal, one would expect an overtly political group to have more of an impact on political decisions.

TABLE 4 *Percentage of respondents who belong to some organization; by nation and education*

Nation	Total		Prim. Or less		Some sec.		Some univ.	
	(%)	*(No.)**	*(%)*	*(No.)*	*(%)*	*(No.)*	*(%)*	*(No.)*
United States	57	(970)	46	(339)	55	(443)	80	(188)
Great Britain	47	(963)	41	(593)	55	(322)	92	(24)
Germany	44	(955)	41	(792)	63	(124)	62	(26)
Italy	30	(995)	25	(692)	37	(245)	46	(54)
Mexico	24	(1,007)	21	(877)	39	(103)	68	(24)

*Numbers in parentheses refer to the bases upon which percentages are calculated.

Table 5 reports the frequency with which respondents in our five countries perceive that their organizations take some part in politics. In the United States about one in four respondents belongs to an organization that he perceives to be involved in politics.[5] The proportion falls off to 6 percent in Italy. Though the nations differ in the percentage of the *total population* who perceive that an organization of theirs is involved in political affairs (column 1), the proportion of *organizational members* who hold this perception is strikingly uniform among the nations (column 2). With the exception of Italy, approximately the same proportion of organizational members in each country—40 to 45 percent—perceives itself to be part of a politically active organization. For about one-fifth of the Italian members and about two-fifths of the members in each of the other nations, being part of an organization does involve (in terms of the individual's awareness) recruitment into the political system.

Organizational Membership and Political Competence

Political and Nonpolitical Organizations. What effect, if any, does organizational membership have on political attitudes? Do those individuals who are members of some organization differ in their political perspectives from those who are not members? And does membership in any sort of organization, political as well as nonpolitical, affect one's political views? Or is it only membership in a politically relevant organization that influences one's perspectives on politics? The political attitudes we are interested in are those associated with democratic citizenship, as

5. That the frequency with which an individual reports affiliation with a political organization varies with his definition of politics is suggested by a finding made by Woodward and Roper: 31 percent of their sample responded positively to the question, "Do you happen to belong to any organizations that sometimes take a stand on housing, better government, school problems, or other public issues?" In contrast, 24 percent in our sample answered our question positively. The difference may be due to the fact that many of our respondents would not consider "school problems" a political question. See Julian L. Woodward and Elmo Roper, "Political Activity of American Citizens," *American Political Science Review,* XLIV (1950), pp. 872–85.

TABLE 5 *Respondents who believe an organization of theirs is involved in political affairs; by nation*

Nation	% of Total population		% of Organizational members	
	(%)	(No.)*	(%)	(No.)
United States	24	(970)	41	(551)
Great Britain	19	(963)	40	(453)
Germany	18	(955)	40	(419)
Italy	6	(995)	20	(291)
Mexico	11	(1,007)	46	(242)

*Numbers in parentheses refer to the bases upon which percentages are calculated.

we have defined it. If organizational membership fosters the development of a democratic citizenry, one would expect the members, in comparison with those who are not members, to feel more confident of their ability to influence the government, to be more active in politics, more "open" in their political opinions, and, in general, more committed to democratic values.

Let us look first at the relationship between organizational membership and the individual's sense of ability to influence the government. This sense of competence, we have suggested earlier, is a major attitudinal variable in understanding the political perspectives of the individual, and it has significant implications for a wide range of other important political attitudes. Table 6 reports the proportion of respondents receiving high scores on the subjective competence scale among (1) those respondents who are members of organizations they consider to be involved in politics (2) those who are members of nonpolitical organizations, and (3) those who are members of no organizations. The results are striking, and quite uniform from nation to nation. In all nations those respondents who are members of no organization are generally lower in the scale than our organizational members. And among organizational members, those respondents who consider their organization to be involved in politics are most likely to receive high scores on the scale. In Great Britain, for instance, 80 percent of the members of a politically oriented organization are to be found in the highest three scores of the subjective competence scale; 69 percent of the members of a nonpolitical organization are in these top three categories; while only 56 percent of those who belong to no organization can be found in the highest categories of the scale. In Italy 77 percent of the members of politically oriented organizations score high on the scale, in contrast with 49 percent of those who belong to nonpolitical organizations, and 34 percent of those who belong to no organization.

Both subjective competence and the frequency of organizational membership are related to educational attainment. Thus it is important to note that this relationship between membership and sense of ability to influence the government persists when educational level is held constant. Only among British respondents

TABLE 6 *Percentage of respondents who scored highest in subjective competence[a] among members of political and nonpolitical organizations; by nation and education*

Nation	Member political organiz. (%)	(No.)[b]	Member nonpolitical organiz. (%)	(No.)	Non-member (%)	(No.)	Member political organiz. (%)	(No.)	Member nonpolitical organiz. (%)	(No.)	Non-member (%)	(No.)	Member political organiz. (%)	(No.)	Member nonpolitical organiz. (%)	(No.)	Non-member (%)	(No.)
United States	79	(228)	70	(322)	54	(418)	65	(91)	60	(163)	46	(263)	87	(137)	81	(160)	68	(156)
Great Britain	80	(193)	69	(157)	56	(510)	83	(97)	61	(144)	52	(352)	74	(86)	77	(112)	62	(148)
Germany	60	(172)	52	(246)	37	(534)	59	(137)	48	(184)	34	(471)	94	(32)	65	(63)	57	(55)
Italy	77	(56)	49	(234)	34	(701)	68	(25)	45	(148)	29	(519)	85	(31)	55	(85)	48	(183)
Mexico	57	(103)	45	(139)	33	(765)	54	(79)	40	(101)	33	(697)	64	(24)	58	(36)	46	(67)

[a] I.e., those who received three highest scores on the subjective competence scale.
[b] Numbers in parentheses refer to the bases upon which percentages are calculated.

with higher education is there a reversal of the trend: those respondents who are members of a nonpolitical organization score slightly better on the subjective competence scale than do the respondents who are members of a political organization. But the expected pattern is quite strong among British respondents in the lower educational groups and on both educational levels elsewhere.

Table 6 presents striking confirmation of the hypothesis about the impact of organizational membership on political attitudes. Such membership is indeed related to a citizen's self-confidence. The individual who belongs to an organization compared with one who does not, is more likely to feel competent to influence the government. The table shows that the kind of organization one belongs to also makes a difference. Those who are members of a politically related organization are more likely to feel competent in their relations with the government than are those who belong to a nonpolitical organization. But the most striking finding is the contrast between those who are members of organizations that they do not perceive as being political and those who are members of no organization. In all nations, on both levels of education, those who are members of a nonpolitical organization are more likely to feel subjectively competent than are those who belong to no organization. This, then, appears to confirm the fact that latent political functions are performed by voluntary associations, whether these organizations are explicitly political or not. Those who are members of some organization, even if they report that it has no political role, have more political competence than those who have no such membership.

A similar pattern appears if we consider political discussion. Members of politically oriented organizations report more often than the other respondents that they discuss politics. This is to be expected, and it appears in all five nations and on both levels of education (with the exception of the Mexican respondents with higher education, where there is a slight reversal). And, as with the data on subjective competence, the individual who is a member of a nonpolitical organization is more likely to report he discusses politics than is the individual who belongs to no organization. Thus in Germany: 88 percent of those who belong to a political organization discuss politics, in contrast with 70 percent of the members of a nonpolitical organization. And both these percentages contrast with the figure that represents the frequency of such discussion among nonmembers: 47 percent. Organizational membership, apparently, even if explicitly nonpolitical, makes it more likely that an individual will have a sense of ability to participate in politics and that he will actually participate in political discussion.

Organizational membership also seems to expand an individual's range of political opinion. If we compare members of politically oriented organizations, members of nonpolitical organizations, and nonmembers, according to their willingness to express opinions on a variety of political questions, we find that members of political organizations are most likely to express a wide range of political opinions; members of nonpolitical organizations and nonmembers followed in order. In Italy, for example, 68 percent of the members of some politically oriented organization answered all six questions used to measure range of opinion, in contrast with 36 percent of those who were members of a nonpolitical organization, and 20 percent of those who belonged to no organization at all.[6]

Membership in an organization, political or not, appears therefore to be related to an increase in the political competence and activity of the individual.[7] The member, in contrast with the nonmember, appears to approximate more closely what we have called the democratic citizen. He is competent, active, and open with his opinions.

Active and Passive Membership. One reason why organizational membership might be expected to effect political competence and activity is that the members of such organizations receive training for participation within the organization, and this training is then transferable to the political sphere. According to this argument, a member of an organization will have greater opportunity to participate actively within the organization than he would have within the larger political system. Organizations are, in a sense, small political systems, and both the skill in participation and the expectation that one can participate increase the individual's competence vis-à-vis the political system. Furthermore—and this is one of the most important effects imputed to organizational membership—training within these organizations means that there are alternate channels of recruitment into politics. If opportunities to participate in organizations did not exist, all such training for participation would have to take place within the political system itself, and would be dominated by the more general norms of that system. The existence of alternate channels means that the recruitment into political activity will not be as closely controlled by incumbent elites. In this way organizational participation leads to greater pluralism.

But we cannot assume that membership in a voluntary association necessarily involves active participation by the member. Many of these organizations are large and complex; to the individual member, perhaps they are as large and complex, with as distant centers of power, as his nation. Many of these organizations are centrally controlled, and allow little room for individual participation. Membership may offer very little training for political participation. A member of a large, centrally organized trade union, for example, may feel as passive a participant in his organization as does a subject in a large, authoritarian nation; and he may in fact have as little voice.

To trace the impact of organizational membership on political attitudes, therefore, it is important to consider the extent to which individuals take active roles in their organizations. The gross membership figures tell us nothing about this participation. In order to have some estimate of the extent to which membership

6. See chapter 11 for a description of the questions that are involved.

7. This relationship between group membership and political efficacy and activity is reported in some of the studies carried on by the Survey Research Center, and in other community studies. See Robert E. Lane, *Political Life,* p. 188.

TABLE 7 *Respondents who report having been officers in organizations; by nation*

Nation	Percentage of total population		Percentage of organization members	
	(%)	(No.)*	(%)	(No.)
United States	26	(970)	46	(551)
Great Britain	13	(963)	29	(453)
Germany	7	(955)	16	(419)
Italy	7	(995)	23	(291)
Mexico	8	(1,007)	34	(242)

* Numbers in parentheses refer to the bases upon which percentages are calculated.

involves active participation, those respondents who reported membership were asked if they took any active role within their organization: in particular, whether they had ever held any form of official position, high or low, in a local branch or in some central office.

The data (see Table 7) bring out more striking differences among countries than did the figures on gross membership. In the United States 26 percent of the respondents report that they have held some such position in an organization. In Britain the proportion, though lower (13 percent), is substantially above that in the other countries (7 to 8 percent). This suggests that the effect of voluntary associations upon the nature of citizenship may differ significantly from one country to another. In some countries there is a relatively large stratum of individuals who more or less actively participate in the decision making of voluntary associations; elsewhere, organizational membership may be relatively formal and lacking in participatory opportunities. Organizations in which there is some opportunity for the individual to take an active part may be as significant for the development of democratic citizenship as are voluntary organizations in general.

These considerations add another link to our discussion of the nature of participation in the five countries. In particular, they point to a sharp distinction between the nature of participation in Germany, on the one hand, and Great Britain and the United States, on the other. All three countries are relatively high on organizational

TABLE 8 *Organization members who ever been officers; by nation and sex*

Nation	Total		Male		Female	
	(%)	(No.)*	(%)	(No.)	(%)	(No.)
United States	46	(551)	41	(309)	52	(242)
Great Britain	29	(453)	32	(304)	22	(149)
Germany	16	(419)	18	(298)	9	(121)
Italy	23	(291)	24	(193)	19	(98)
Mexico	34	(242)	43	(146)	18	(96)

* Numbers in parentheses refer to the bases upon which percentages are calculated.

TABLE 9 *Organization members who have ever been officers; by nation and education*

Nation	Total (%)	(No.)*	Prim. Or less (%)	(No.)	Some sec. (%)	(No.)	Some univ. (%)	(No.)
United States	46	(551)	31	(156)	44	(245)	64	(150)
Great Britain	29	(453)	23	(241)	31	(176)	64	(22)
Germany	16	(419)	12	(321)	24	(79)	38	(16)
Italy	23	(291)	13	(173)	36	(91)	38	(26)
Mexico	33	(242)	30	(181)	39	(44)	52	(17)

* Numbers in parentheses refer to the bases upon which percentages are calculated.

membership, especially among males. Yet the differences in the proportions of members who are active participating members (as measured by whether or not they have ever held an official position) are sharp. If we look at the second column of Table 7 (the proportion of members who have held some official position), we see that 46 percent of American members and 29 percent of British members have held some official position in one of the organizations to which they belong, while only 16 percent of the German members have had experience in active participation. (In fact, the percentage of active group members is lower in Germany than in Mexico or Italy—although in the latter two countries we are dealing with a much smaller population of group members.) Here again is a reflection of the tendency for participation in Germany to be widespread but not intense. It tends to be formal and involves little direct individual commitment and activity. Formal organizations in Germany, like those in Britain and the United States, are widespread and important in policy determination. But they differ in the degree to which they afford opportunities for their members to participate in decisions. Once again we find that in Germany the structures of a democratic system are well developed, but they do not yet play significant roles in the perspectives and behavior of citizens. They are elements of a democratic political structure; they are not yet assimilated into a democratic political culture.

The differences in the frequency of participation within organizations are highlighted if we consider which members are likely to be active. In general, as the data in Tables 8 and 9 indicate, males and those with higher education are more likely to be active in their organizations than are female members and members with less education. An exception occurs in the United States, where female organizational members are more likely to be active participants than are men.[8]

It is of particular interest that the German pattern of frequent organizational membership, coupled with infrequent participation within the organization, is

8. A similar relationship was found in a study by John C. Scott ("Membership and Participation in Voluntary Associations," *American Sociological Review,* XXII [1957], pp. 315–26). He found that male respondents in a New England town were more likely than female respondents to belong to an organization. But among the organizational members, women were more likely to be officers than men. One reason for this may be the smaller size of the organizations to which women belong.

TABLE 10 *Percentage of respondents who scored highest in subjective competence^a by the extent of their activity in organizations; by nation and education*

Nation	Total						Primary or less						Secondary or more					
	Active member		Passive member		Non-member		Active member		Passive member		Non-member		Active member		Passive member		Non-member	
	(%)	(No.)b	(%)	(No.)	(%)	(No.)	(%)	(No.)	(%)	(No.)	(%)	(No.)	(%)	(No.)	(%)	(No.)	(%)	(No.)
United States	82	(253)	66	(298)	54	(418)	68	(98)	55	(166)	46	(263)	85	(165)	80	(132)	69	(156)
Great Britain	84	(130)	69	(320)	55	(510)	86	(56)	66	(184)	52	(352)	84	(69)	73	(127)	62	(148)
Germany	72	(65)	55	(353)	37	(534)	69	(39)	50	(282)	35	(471)	80	(25)	74	(69)	55	(55)
Italy	76	(66)	48	(224)	34	(701)	53	(32)	44	(150)	29	(519)	74	(43)	56	(73)	49	(183)
Mexico	68	(83)	42	(159)	33	(765)	63	(56)	39	(124)	32	(697)	76	(27)	49	(33)	46	(67)

[a] I.e., those who received three highest scores on the subjective competence scale.
[b] Numbers in parentheses refer to the bases upon which percentages are calculated.

relatively uniform among all the German subgroups. Though German males are members of organizations as frequently as are British or American males, and though Germans in particular educational groups are members as frequently as are their British or American counterparts, in no subgroup in Tables 8 or 9 do we find German respondents as frequently active within their organizations as are American and British respondents. Compare, for example, male respondents in the three countries. German males are as likely as British or American males to be members of voluntary associations: the proportions who report membership are 68 percent in the United States and 66 percent in Britain and Germany. On the other hand, 41 percent of American male members and 32 percent of the British male members report that they have been active in their organizations, whereas only 18 percent of the German male members report such participation. Similar contrasts can be found in Table 9 among the various educational groups, and can be observed as well within the various occupational groups.

The extent to which organizational membership involves some sort of active participation within that organization appears to vary significantly from nation to nation, and within nations among sex and educational groupings as well. Not all members take an active role in their organization. Furthermore, the extent to which an individual is active in the organization seems to be related to his political perspectives, as suggested clearly in Table 10. Again we use the subjective competence score to measure this relationship (though measures of political activity would give similar results). Organizational members who have held active positions in their organizations are more likely than rank-and-file members to receive high scores on this scale. In Italy, for instance, 76 percent of these respondents who report some active participation within their organization score in the top three categories of our scale of subjective competence, in contrast with 48 percent of the more passive organizational members. However, even passive membership, when compared with nonmembership, appears to be associated with an increased

TABLE 11 *Respondents who belong to one or more organizations; by nation*

Percentage who	U.S.	U.K.	Germany	Italy	Mexico
Belong to one organization	25	31	32	24	23
Belong to two organizations	14	10	9	5	2
Belong to three organizations	9	4	2	1	0
Belong to four or more organizations	9	2	1	–	–
Total percentage of multiple members	32	16	12	6	2
Total percentage of members	57 (970)[a]	47 (963)	44 (955)	30 (995)	25 (1007)

[a] Numbers in parentheses refer to the bases upon which percentages are calculated.

sense of political competence. Whereas 48 percent of the passive members score in the top three categories of the subjective competence scale, only 34 percent of the nonmembers are in the higher levels. And the pattern for Italy is apparent in all nations, for individuals on both educational levels and for men and women. Apparently both the type of organization one belongs to and the intensity of one's activity within it are related to one's political attitudes. Yet organizational membership per se appears to have a residual effect on political competence and activity. The passive member as well as the member of a nonpolitical organization still differ from the individual who reports no such membership.[9]

These findings strongly support the proposition associated with the theory of mass society that the existence of voluntary associations increases the democratic potential of a society. Democracy depends upon citizen participation, and it is clear that organizational membership is directly related to such participation. The organizational member is likely to be a self-confident citizen as well as an active one. We can also specify somewhat more precisely the impact on political competence of various types of organizational membership. Membership in a *politically oriented* organization appears to lead to greater political competence than does membership in a nonpolitical organization, and *active* membership in an organization has a greater impact on political competence than does passive membership. This fact is important because it helps explain the differential effect of organizational membership among the nations. Lipset, using data from a variety of surveys, points out that the frequency of voluntary association membership is about as great in such stable democracies as the United States, Britain, and Sweden as it is in the relatively less stable democracies of Germany and France—a finding that seems to challenge the idea of a connection between stable democracy and organizational membership.[10] Our data for the United States, Britain, and Germany confirm that the rates of membership are similar for the three nations. But our findings also indicate that organizational membership much more frequently involves active participation within the organization than it does in Germany, where relatively few members appear to take an active part. And, as our

9. In 1948 the American military government in Germany conducted a survey among German youth to evaluate how effective the newly formed youth organizations were in the inculcation of democratic attitudes. They found that there was relatively little difference between youth club members and nonmembers in their adherence to democratic attitudes. For instance, 58 percent of the youth club members and 55 percent of the nonmembers believed it was better for a club to have a leader elected by majority rule rather than appointed. In contrast, 72 percent of the club members whose own club leaders were elected favored election of leaders, in comparison with 48 percent of the club members whose own leaders were appointed. Apparently the nature of the authority structure in the youth club had a greater effect on youth attitudes than did the fact of membership per se. See Office of Military Government for Germany (U.S.), Opinion Survey Report No. 99, March 5, 1948, "A Report on German Youth." The survey of youth is based on 2,337 interviews with respondents between the ages of 10 and 25 years.

10. See Lipset, *Political Man,* p. 67.

data further show, the degree of activity within an organization has an effect upon political attitudes. The active member is more likely to be the competent democratic citizen.[11]

Multiple Membership. One other aspect of organizational participation must be considered to round out our picture of the differing patterns of participation and the impact of that participation on political attitudes among the nations. This is the number of organizations to which individuals belong. If one considers merely the frequency of membership and nonmembership among the nations, one finds some striking differences, yet this does not indicate the full extent of the differences in the amount of organizational participation. Nations differ, not only in the frequency with which respondents report membership, but also—and perhaps even more strikingly—in the frequency with which individuals report membership in more than one organization. This fact is illustrated in Table 11. In the United States about one-third of our total sample are members of more than one organization and, indeed, 9 percent of the sample are members of four or more organizations. In Britain 16 percent of the total sample are members of more than one organization. The figure falls off to 12 percent of the total in Germany, 6 percent in Italy, and 2 percent in Mexico. Though on many measures of participation Great Britain and the United States were quite similar, on the question of organizational membership the impressions of many observers prove correct. Organizational participation in the United States, both in the total number who are members and the number who are members of several organizations, is much higher than that of any other country. This is reflected in the proportion of the total sample who are multiple members, as well as in the proportion of organization members who are members of more than one organization. In the United States 55 percent of organizational members belong to more than one organization. The other figures are: Britain, 34 percent; Germany, 27 percent; Italy, 20 percent; and Mexico, 8 percent.

The number of organizations to which an individual belongs also affects his political competence. Organizational membership appears to have a cumulative effect; that is, membership in one organization increases an individual's sense of political competence, and membership in more than one organization leads to even greater competence. Those who belong to an organization show higher political competence than those who are members of no organization, but the members of more than one organization show even higher competence than those whose affiliation is limited to one.

What we have shown so far is that voluntary associations do play a major role in a democratic political culture. The organizational member, compared with the

11. We have no data that are comparable for Sweden or France, the other two nations cited by Lipset; but description of French voluntary associations strongly suggest that, like the German and unlike the American and British, they tend to be highly centralized and to allow little opportunity for active participation. See in particular Arnold Rose, *Theory and Method in the Social Sciences* (Minneapolis, 1954), p. 74, and M. Crozier, "La France, Terre du Commandement," *Esprit* XXV (1957), 779–98.

nonmember, is likely to consider himself more competent as a citizen, to be a more active participant in politics, and to know and care more about politics. He is, therefore, more likely to be close to the model of the democratic citizen. We have also shown that it makes a difference which type of organization an individual belongs to; political organizations yield a larger political "dividend" than do nonpolitical organizations. And it makes a difference how active an individual is within his own organization: the active member displays a greater sense of political competence than does the passive member. But perhaps the most striking finding is that any membership — passive membership or membership in a nonpolitical organization — has an impact on political competence. Membership in some association, even if the individual does not consider the membership politically relevant and even if it does not involve his active participation, does lead to a more competent citizenry. Pluralism, even if not explicitly political pluralism, may indeed be one of the most important foundations of political democracy.

[1963]

from *Selections from the Prison Notebooks*

The relationship between the intellectuals and the world of production is not as direct as it is with the fundamental social groups but is, in varying degrees, "mediated" by the whole fabric of society and by the complex of superstructures, of which the intellectuals are, precisely, the "functionaries." It should be possible both to measure the "organic quality" *[organicità]* of the various intellectual strata and their degree of connection with a fundamental social group, and to establish a gradation of their functions and of the superstructures from the bottom to the top (from the structural base upwards). What we can do, for the moment, is to fix two major superstructural "levels": the one that can be called "civil society," that is the ensemble of organisms commonly called "private," and that of "political society" or "the State." These two levels correspond on the one hand to the function of "hegemony" which the dominant group exercises throughout society and on the other hand to that of "direct domination" or command exercised through the State and "juridical" government. The functions in question are precisely organizational and connective. The intellectuals are the dominant group's "deputies" exercising the subaltern functions of social hegemony and political government. These comprise:

1. The "spontaneous" consent given by the great masses of the population to the general direction imposed on social life by the dominant fundamental group; this consent is "historically" caused by the prestige (and consequent confidence) which the dominant group enjoys because of its position and function in the world of production.
2. The apparatus of state coercive power which "legally" enforces discipline on those groups who do not "consent" either actively or passively. This apparatus is, however, constituted for the whole of society in anticipation of moments of crisis of command and direction when spontaneous consent has failed.

. . .

In the ancient and medieval State alike, centralization, whether political-territorial or social (and the one is merely a function of the other), was minimal. The State was, in a certain sense, a mechanical bloc of social groups, often of different race: within the circle of political-military compression, which was only exercised harshly at certain moments, the subaltern groups had a life of their own, institutions of their own, etc., and sometimes these institutions had State functions which made of the State a federation of social groups with disparate functions not subordinated in any way—a situation which in periods of crisis highlighted with extreme clarity the phenomenon of "dual power." The only group excluded from any organized collective life of its own was that of the slaves (and such proletarians as were not slaves) in the classical world, and is that of the proletarians, the serfs and the peasants in the medieval world. However, even though, from many points of view, the slaves of the ancient world and the medieval proletariat were in the same conditions, their situation was not identical: the attempted revolt by the Ciompi [in Florence in 1378] certainly did not have the impact that a similar attempt by the slaves of antiquity would have produced (Spartacus demanding to be taken into the government in collaboration with the plebs, etc.). While in the Middle Ages an alliance between proletarians and people, and even more so the support of the proletarians for the dictatorship of a prince, was possible, nothing similar was possible for the slaves of the classical world. The modern State substitutes for the mechanical bloc of social groups their subordination to the active hegemony of the directive and dominant group, hence abolishes certain autonomies, which nevertheless are reborn in other forms, as parties, trade unions, cultural associations. The contemporary dictatorships legally abolish these new forms of autonomy as well, and strive to incorporate them within State activity: the legal centralization of the entire national life in the hands of the dominant group becomes "totalitarian."

Guicciardini's assertion that two things are absolutely necessary for the life of a State: arms and religion. Guicciardini's formula can be translated by various other, less drastic formulae: force and consent; coercion and persuasion; State and Church; political society and civil society; politics and morality (Croce's ethical-political history); law and freedom; order and self-discipline; or (with an implicit judgement of somewhat libertarian flavor) violence and fraud. In any case, in the political conception of the Renaissance, religion was consent and the Church was civil society, the hegemonic apparatus of the ruling group. For the latter did not have its own apparatus, i.e. did not have its own cultural and intellectual organization, but regarded the universal ecclesiastical organization as being that. The only way in which this differed from the Middle Ages was the fact that religion was openly conceived of and analyzed as an *instrumentum regni*. It is from this point of view that the Jacobin attempt to institute a cult of the "Supreme Being" should be studied. This appears to be an attempt to create an identity between State and civil society; to unify in a dictatorial way the constitutive elements of the State (in the organic, wider sense of the State proper + civil society), in a desperate endeavor to keep a hold on all of popular and national life. But it appears too as the first root of the modern lay State, independent of the Church, which seeks and finds in itself, in its own complex life, all the elements of its historical personality.

History of the Subaltern Classes: Methodological Criteria

The historical unity of the ruling classes is realized in the State, and their history is essentially the history of States and of groups of States. But it would be wrong to think that this unity is simply juridical and political (though such forms of unity do have their importance too, and not in a purely formal sense); the fundamental historical unity, concretely, results from the organic relations between State or political society and "civil society."

The subaltern classes, by definition, are not unified and cannot unite until they are able to become a "State": their history, therefore, is intertwined with that of civil society, and thereby with the history of States and groups of States. Hence it is necessary to study: 1. the objective formation of the subaltern social groups, by the developments and transformations occurring in the sphere of economic production; their quantitative diffusion and their origins in pre-existing social groups, whose mentality, ideology and aims they conserve for a time; 2. their active or passive affiliation to the dominant political formations, their attempts to influence the programs of these formations in order to press claims of their own, and the consequences of these attempts in determining processes of decomposition, renovation or neo-formation; 3. the birth of new parties of the dominant groups, intended to conserve the assent of the subaltern groups and to maintain control over them; 4. the formations which the subaltern groups themselves produce, in order to press claims of a limited and partial character; 5. those new formations which assert the integral autonomy, . . . etc.

. . .

The history of subaltern social groups is necessarily fragmented and episodic. There undoubtedly does exist a tendency to (at least provisional stages of) unification in the historical activity of these groups, but this tendency is continually interrupted by the activity of the ruling groups; it therefore can only be demonstrated when an historical cycle is completed and this cycle culminates in a success. Subaltern groups are always subject to the activity of ruling groups, even when they rebel and rise up: only "permanent" victory breaks their subordination, and that not immediately. In reality, even when they appear triumphant, the subaltern groups are merely anxious to defend themselves (a truth which can be demonstrated by the history of the French Revolution at least up to 1830). Every trace of independent initiative on the part of subaltern groups should therefore be of incalculable value for the integral historian. Consequently, this kind of history can only be dealt with monographically, and each monograph requires an immense quantity of material which is often hard to collect.

[1934-35]

. . .

Hegemony (Civil Society) and Separation of Powers

The separation of powers, together with all the discussion provoked by its realization and the legal dogmas which its appearance brought into being, is a product of the struggle between civil society and political society in a specific historical period. This period is characterized by a certain unstable equilibrium between the classes, which is a result of the fact that certain categories of intellectuals (in the direct service of the State, especially the civil and military bureaucracy) are still too closely tied to the old dominant classes. In other words, there takes place within the society what Croce calls the "perpetual conflict between Church and State," in which the Church is taken as representing the totality of civil society (whereas in fact it is only an element of diminishing importance within it), and the State as representing every attempt to crystallize permanently a particular state of development, a particular situation. In this sense, the Church itself may become State, and the conflict may occur between on the one hand secular (and secularizing) civil society, and on the other State/Church (when the Church has become an integral part of the State, of political society monopolized by a specific privileged group, which absorbs the Church in order the better to preserve its monopoly with the support of that zone of "civil society" which the Church represents).

Essential importance of the separation of powers for political and economic liberalism; the entire liberal ideology, with its strengths and its weaknesses, can be encapsulated in the principle of the separation of powers, and the source of liberalism's weakness then becomes apparent: it is the bureaucracy—i.e. the crystallization of the leading personnel—which exercises coercive power, and at a certain point it becomes a caste. Hence the popular demand for making all posts elective—a demand which is extreme liberalism, and at the same time its dissolution (principle of the permanent Constituent Assembly, etc.; in Republics, the election at fixed intervals of the Head of State gives the illusion of satisfying this elementary popular demand).

Unity of the State in the differentiation of powers; Parliament more closely linked to civil society; the judiciary power, between government and Parliament, represents the continuity of the written law (even against the government). Naturally all three powers are also organs of political hegemony, but in different degrees: 1. Legislature; 2, Judiciary; 3. Executive. It is to be noted how lapses in the administration of justice make an especially disastrous impression on the public: the hegemonic apparatus is more sensitive in this sector, to which arbitrary actions on the part of the police and political administration may also be referred.

[1930-32]

The Conception of Law

A conception of the Law which must be an essentially innovatory one is not to be found, integrally, in any pre-existing doctrine (not even in the doctrine of the so-called positive school, and notably that of Ferri). If every State tends to create and maintain a certain type of civilization and of citizen (and hence of collective life and of individual relations), and to eliminate certain customs and attitudes and to disseminate others, then the Law will be its instrument for this purpose (together with the school system, and other institutions and activities). It must be developed so that it is suitable for such a purpose—so that it is maximally effective and productive of positive results.

The conception of law will have to be freed from every residue of transcendentalism and from every absolute; in practice, from every moralistic fanaticism. However, it seems to me that one cannot start from the point of view that the State does not "punish" (if this term is reduced to its human significance), but only struggles against social "dangerousness." In reality, the State must be conceived of as an "educator," in as much as it tends precisely to create a new type or level of civilization. Because one is acting essentially on economic forces, reorganizing and developing the apparatus of economic production, creating a new structure, the conclusion must not be drawn that superstructural factors should be left to themselves, to develop spontaneously, to a haphazard and sporadic germination. The State, in this field, too, is an instrument of "rationalization," of acceleration and of Taylorization. It operates according to a plan, urges, incites, solicits, and "punishes"; for, once the conditions are created in which a certain way of life is "possible," then "criminal action or omission" must have a punitive sanction, with moral implications, and not merely be judged generically as "dangerous." The Law is the repressive and negative aspect of the entire positive, civilizing activity undertaken by the State. The "prize-giving" activities of individuals and groups, etc., must also be incorporated in the conception of the Law; praiseworthy and meritorious activity is rewarded, just as criminal actions are punished (and punished in original ways, bringing in "public opinion" as a form of sanction).

[1933–34: 1st version 1931–32]

The State

In the new "juridical" tendencies represented by the *Nuovi Studi* of Volpicelli and Spirito, the confusion between the concept of class-State and the concept of regulated society[1] should be noted, as a critical point of departure. This confusion is especially noteworthy in the paper on *Economic Freedom* presented by Spirito at the

---

1. Spirito and Volpicelli were the principal theorists of the "corporate economy" in fascist Italy. They claimed that corporativism represented a "post-capital" economy, and that it had abolished the anarchy of liberal capitalism. Gramsci here refers to the confusion involved in the idea that a "regulated" society could co-exist with capitalism—the class-State. Elsewhere Gramsci uses "regulated society" to mean Communism.

Nineteenth Congress of the Society for Scientific Progress held in Bolzano in September 1930, and published in *Nuovi Studi* in the 1930 September–October issue.

As long as the class-State exists the regulated society cannot exist, other than metaphorically—i.e. only in the sense that the class-State too is a regulated society. The utopians, in as much as they expressed a critique of the society that existed in their day, very well understood that the class-State could not be the regulated society. So much is this true that in the types of society which the various utopias represented, economic equality was introduced as a necessary basis for the projected reform. Clearly in this the utopians were not utopians, but concrete political scientists and consistent critics. The utopian character of some of them was due to the fact that they believed that economic equality could be introduced by arbitrary laws, by an act of will, etc. But the idea that complete and perfect political equality cannot exist without economic equality (an idea to be found in other political writers, too, even right-wing ones—i.e. among the critics of democracy, in so far as the latter makes use of the Swiss or Danish model to claim that the system is a reasonable one for all countries) nevertheless remains correct. This idea can be found in the writers of the seventeenth century too, for example in Ludovico Zuccolo and in his book *Il Belluzzi,* and I think in Machiavelli as well. Maurras believes that in Switzerland that particular form of democracy is possible precisely because there is a certain common averageness of economic fortunes, etc.

The confusion of class-State and regulated society is peculiar to the middle classes and petty intellectuals, who would be glad of any regularization that would prevent sharp struggles and upheavals. It is a typically reactionary and regressive conception.

[1930–32]

In my opinion, the most reasonable and concrete thing that can be said about the ethical State, the cultural State, is this: every State is ethical in as much as one of its most important functions is to raise the great mass of the population to a particular cultural and moral level, a level (or type) which corresponds to the needs of the productive forces for development, and hence to the interests of the ruling classes. The school as a positive educative function, and the courts as a repressive and negative educative function, are the most important State activities in this sense: but, in reality, a multitude of other so-called private initiatives and activities tend to the same end—initiatives and activities which form the apparatus of the political and cultural hegemony of the ruling classes. Hegel's conception belongs to a period in which the spreading development of the bourgeoisie could seem limitless, so that its ethicity or universality could be asserted: all mankind will be bourgeois. But, in reality, only the social group that poses the end of the State and its own end as the target to be achieved can create an ethical State—i.e. one which tends to put an end to the internal divisions of the ruled, etc., and to create a technically and morally unitary social organism.

[1931–32]

Hegel's doctrine of parties and associations as the "private" woof of the State. This derived historically from the political experiences of the French Revolution, and was to serve to give a more concrete character to constitutionalism. Government with the consent of the governed—but with this consent organized and not generic and vague as it is expressed in the instant of elections. The State does have and request consent, but it also "educates" this consent, by means of the political and syndical associations; these, however, are private organisms, left to the private initiative of the ruling class. Hegel, in a certain sense, thus already transcended pure constitutionalism and theorized the parliamentary State with its party system. But his conception of association could not help still being vague and primitive, halfway between the political and the economic; it was in accordance with the historical experience of the time, which was very limited and offered only one perfected example of organization—the "corporative" (a politics grafted directly on to the economy). Marx was not able to have historical experiences superior (or at least much superior) to those of Hegel; but, as a result of his journalistic and agitational activities, he had a sense for the masses. Marx's concept of organization remains entangled amid the following elements: craft organization; Jacobin clubs; secret conspiracies by small groups; journalistic organization.

The French Revolution offered two prevalent types. There were the "clubs"—loose organizations of the "popular assembly" type, centralized around individual political figures. Each had its newspaper, by means of which it kept alive the attention and interest of a particular clientele that had no fixed boundaries. This clientele then upheld the theses of the paper in the club's meetings. Certainly, among those who frequented the clubs, there must have existed tight, select groupings of people who knew each other, who met separately and prepared the climate of the meetings, in order to support one tendency or another—depending on the circumstances and also on the concrete interests in play.

The secret conspiracies, which subsequently spread so widely in Italy prior to 1848, must have developed in France after Thermidor among the second-rank followers of Jacobinism: with great difficulty in the Napoleonic period on account of the vigilant control of the police; with greater facility from 1815 to 1830 under the Restoration, which was fairly liberal at the base and was free from certain preoccupations. In this period, from 1815 to 1830, the differentiation of the popular political camp was to occur. This already seemed considerable during the "glorious days" of 1830, when the formations which had been crystallizing during the preceding fifteen years now came to the surface. After 1830 and up to 1848, this process of differentiation became perfected, and produced some quite highly-developed specimens in Blanqui and Filippo Buonarroti.

It is unlikely that Hegel could have had first-hand knowledge of these historical experiences, which are, however, more vivid in Marx.

The revolution which the bourgeois class has brought into the conception of law, and hence into the function of the State, consists especially in the will to conform (hence ethicity of the law and of the State). The previous ruling classes were essentially conservative in the sense that they did not tend to construct an organic passage from the other classes into their own, i.e. to enlarge their class sphere "technically" and ideologically: their conception was that of a closed caste. The bourgeois class poses itself as an organism in continuous movement, capable of absorbing the entire society, assimilating it to its own cultural and economic level. The entire function of the State has been transformed; the State has become an "educator," etc.

That the everyday concept of State is unilateral and leads to grotesque errors can be demonstrated with reference to Danièl Halévy's recent book *Décadence de la liberté,* of which I have read a review in *Nouvelles Littéraires.* For Halévy, "State" is the representative apparatus; and he discovers that the most important events of French history from 1870 until the present day have not been due to initiatives by political organisms deriving from universal suffrage, but to those either of private organisms (capitalist firms, General Staffs, etc.) or of great civil servants unknown to the country at large, etc. But what does that signify if not that by "State" should be understood not only the apparatus of government, but also the "private" apparatus of "hegemony" or civil society? It should be noted how from this critique of the State which does not intervene, which trails behind events, etc., there is born the dictatorial ideological current of the Right, with its reinforcement of the executive, etc. However, Halévy's book should be read to see whether he too has taken this path: it is not unlikely in principle, given his antecedents (sympathies for Sorel, for Maurras, etc.).

[1930–32]

Curzio Malaparte, in the introduction to his little volume on the *Technique of the Coup d'Etat,* seems to assert the equivalence of the formula: "Everything within the State, nothing outside the State, nothing against the State" with the proposition: "Where there is freedom, there is no State." In the latter proposition, the term "freedom" cannot be taken in its ordinary meaning of "political freedom, freedom of the press, etc.," but as counterposed to "necessity"; it is related to Engels' proposition on the passage from the rule of necessity to the rule of freedom. Malaparte has not caught even the faintest whiff of the significance of the proposition.

[1931—32]

In the (anyway superficial) polemic over the functions of the State (which here means the State as a politico-juridical organization in the narrow sense), the expression "the State as *veilleur de nuit*" [night watchman] corresponds to the Italian expression "the State as policeman" and means a State whose functions are limited to the safeguarding of public order and of respect for the laws. The fact is glossed over that in this form of regime (which anyway has never existed except on paper, as a limiting hypothesis) hegemony over its historical development belongs to private forces, to civil society—which is "State" too, indeed is the State itself.

It seems that the expression *veilleur de nuit,* which should have a more sarcastic ring than "the State as policeman," comes from Lassalle. Its opposite should be "ethical State" or "interventionist State" in general, but there are differences between the two expressions. The concept of ethical State is of philosophical and intellectual origin (belonging to the intellectuals: Hegel), and in fact could be brought into conjunction with the concept of State-*veilleur de nuit;* for it refers rather to the autonomous, educative and moral activity of the secular State, by contrast with the cosmopolitanism and the interference of the religious-ecclesiastical organization as a medieval residue. The concept of interventionist State is of economic origin, and is connected on the one hand with tendencies supporting protection and economic nationalism, and on the other with the attempt to force a particular State personnel, of landowning and feudal origin, to take on the "protection" of the working classes against the excesses of capitalism (policy of Bismarck and of Disraeli).

These diverse tendencies may combine in various ways, and in fact have so combined. Naturally liberals ("economists") are for the "State as *veilleur de nuit,*" and would like the historical initiative to be left to civil society and to the various forces which spring up there—with the "State" as guardian of "fair play" and of the rules of the game. Intellectuals draw very significant distinctions as to when they are liberals and when they are interventionists (they may be liberals in the economic field and interventionists in the cultural field, etc.). The catholics would like the State to be interventionist one hundred percent in their favor; failing that, or where they are in a minority, they call for a "neutral" State, so that it should not support their adversaries.

[1935: 1st version 1930]

The following argument is worth reflecting upon: is the conception of the *gendarme*-nightwatchman State (leaving aside the polemical designation: *gendarme,* nightwatchman, etc.) not in fact the only conception of the State to transcend the purely "economic-corporate" stages?

We are still on the terrain of the identification of State and government—an identification which is precisely a representation of the economic-corporate form, in other words of the confusion between civil society and political society. For it should be remarked that the general notion of State includes elements which need to be referred back to the notion of civil society (in the sense that one might say that State = political society + civil society, in other words hegemony protected by the armor of coercion). In a doctrine of the State which conceives the latter as tendentially capable of withering away and of being subsumed into regulated society, the argument is a fundamental one. It is possible to imagine the coercive element of the State withering away by degrees, as ever-more conspicuous elements of regulated society (or ethical State or civil society) make their appearance.

The expressions "ethical State" or "civil society" would thus mean that this "image" of a State without a State was present to the greatest political and legal thinkers, in so far as they placed themselves on the terrain of pure science (pure utopia, since based on the premise that all men are really equal and hence equally rational and moral, i.e. capable of accepting the law spontaneously, freely, and not through coercion, as imposed by another class, as something external to consciousness).

It must be remembered that the expression "nightwatchman" for the liberal State comes from Lassalle, i.e. from a dogmatic and non-dialectical statalist (look closely at Lassalle's doctrines on this point and on the State in general, in contrast with Marxism). In the doctrine of the State as regulated society, one will have to pass from a phase in which "State" will be equal to "government," and "State" will be identified with "civil society," to a phase of the State as nightwatchman— i.e. of a coercive organization which will safeguard the development of the continually proliferating elements of regulated society, and which will therefore progressively reduce its own authoritarian and forcible interventions. Nor can this conjure up the idea of a new "liberalism," even though the beginning of an era of organic liberty be imminent.

[1930–32]

If it is true that no type of State can avoid passing through a phase of economic-corporate primitivism, it may be deduced that the content of the political hegemony of the new social group which has founded the new type of State must be predominantly of an economic order: what is involved is the reorganization of the structure and the real relations between men on the one hand and the world of the economy or of production on the other. The superstructural elements will inevitably be few in number, and have a character of foresight and of struggle, but as yet few "planned" elements. Cultural policy will above all be negative, a critique of the past; it will be aimed at erasing from the memory and at destroying. The lines of construction will as yet be "broad lines," sketches, which might (and should) be changed at all times, so as to be consistent with the new structure as it is formed. This precisely did not happen in the period of the medieval communes; for culture, which remained a function of the church, was precisely anti-economic in character (i.e. against the nascent capitalist economy); it was not directed towards giving hegemony to the new class, but rather to preventing the latter from acquiring it. Hence Humanism and the Renaissance were reactionary, because they signaled the defeat of the new class, the negation of the economic world which was proper to it, etc.

[1931–32]

. . .

Organization of National Societies

I have remarked elsewhere that in any given society nobody is disorganized and without party, provided that one takes organization and party in a broad and not a formal sense. In this multiplicity of private associations (which are of two kinds: natural, and contractual or voluntary) one or more predominates relatively or absolutely—constituting the hegemonic apparatus of one social group over the rest of the population (or civil society): the basis for the State in the narrow sense of the government-coercive apparatus.

It always happens that individuals belong to more than one private association, and often to associations which are objectively in contradiction to one another. A totalitarian policy is aimed precisely: 1. at ensuring that the members of a particular party find in that party all the satisfactions that they formerly found in a multiplicity of organizations, i.e. at breaking all the threads that bind these members to extraneous cultural organisms; 2. at destroying all other organizations or at incorporating them into a system of which the party is the sole regulator. This occurs: 1. when the given party is the bearer of a new culture—then one has a progressive phase; 2. when the given party wishes to prevent another force, bearer of a new culture, from becoming itself "totalitarian"—then one has an objectively regressive and reactionary phase, even if that reaction (as invariably happens) does not avow itself, and seeks itself to appear as the bearer of a new culture.

. . .

Who Is a Legislator?

The concept of "legislator" must inevitably be identified with the concept of "politician." Since all men are "political beings," all are also "legislators." But distinctions will have to be made. "Legislator" has a precise juridical and official meaning—i.e. it means those persons who are empowered by the law to enact laws. But it can have other meanings too.

Every man, in as much as he is active, i.e., living, contributes to modifying the social environment in which he develops (to modifying certain of its characteristics or to preserving others); in other words, he tends to establish "norms," rules of living and of behavior. One's circle of activity may be greater or smaller, one's awareness of one's own action and aims may be greater or smaller; furthermore, the representative power may be greater or smaller, and will be put into practice to a greater or lesser extent in its normative, systematic expression by the "represented." A father is a legislator for his children, but the paternal authority will be more or less conscious, more or less obeyed and so forth.

In general, it may be said that the distinction between ordinary men and others who are more specifically legislators is provided by the fact that this second group not only formulates directives which will become a norm of conduct for the others, but at the same time creates the instruments by means of which the directives themselves will be "imposed," and by means of which it will verify their execution. Of this second group, the greatest legislative power belongs to the State personnel (elected and career officials), who have at their disposal the legal coercive powers of the State. But this does not mean that the leaders of "private" organisms and organizations do not have coercive sanctions at their disposal too, ranging even up to the death penalty. The maximum of legislative capacity can be inferred when a perfect formulation of directives is matched by a perfect arrangement of the organisms of execution and verification, and by a perfect preparation of the "spontaneous" consent of the masses who must "live" those directives, modifying their own habits, their own will, their own convictions to conform with those directives and with the objectives which they propose to achieve. If everyone is a legislator in the broadest sense of the concept, he continues to be a legislator even if he accepts directives from others—if, as he carries them out, he makes certain that others are carrying them out too; if, having understood their spirit, he propagates them as though making them into rules specifically applicable to limited and definite zones of living.

[1933]

. . .

State and Parties

The function of hegemony or political leadership exercised by parties can be estimated from the evolution of the internal life of the parties themselves. If the State represents the coercive and punitive force of juridical regulation of a country, the parties—representing the spontaneous adhesion of an elite to such a regulation, considered as a type of collective society to which the entire mass must be educated—must show in their specific internal life that they have assimilated as principles of moral conduct those rules which in the State are legal obligations. In the parties necessity has already become freedom, and thence is born the immense political value (i.e. value for political leadership) of the internal discipline of a party, and hence the value as a criterion of such discipline in estimating the growth potential of the various parties. From this point of view the parties can be considered as schools of State life. Elements of party life: character (resistance to the pressures of surpassed cultures), honor (fearless will in maintaining the new type of culture and life), dignity (awareness of operating for a higher end), etc.

[1930–32]

. . .

Statolatry

Attitude of each particular group towards its own State. The analysis would not be accurate if no account were taken of the two forms in which the State presents itself in the language and culture of specific epochs, i.e., as civil society and as political society. The term "statolatry" is applied to a particular attitude towards the "government by functionaries" or political society, which in everyday language is the form of State life to which the term of State is applied and which is commonly understood as the entire State. The assertion that the State can be identified with individuals (the individuals of a social group), as an element of active culture (i.e. as a movement to create a new civilization, a new type of man and of citizen), must serve to determine the will to construct within the husk of political society a complex and well-articulated civil society, in which the individual can govern himself without his self-government thereby entering into conflict with political society—but rather becoming its normal continuation, its organic complement. For some social groups, which before their ascent to autonomous State life have not had a long independent period of cultural and moral development on their own (as was made possible in medieval society and under the absolute regimes by the juridical existence of the privileged Estates or orders), a period of statolatry is necessary and indeed opportune. This "statolatry" is nothing other than the normal form of "State life," or at least of initiation to autonomous State life and to the creation of a "civil society" which it was not historically possible to create before the ascent to independent State life. However, this kind of "statolatry" must not be abandoned to itself, must not, especially, become theoretical fanaticism or be conceived of as "perpetual." It must be criticized, precisely in order to develop and produce new forms of State life, in which the initiative of individuals and groups will have a "State" character, even if it is not due to the "government of the functionaries" (make State life become "spontaneous").

[1931–32]

"A New Evolutionism 1976"

The historic events that we call the Polish October [1956] were a source of hope that the communist system could evolve. This hope was grounded in two visions, two concepts of evolution. I will label them "revisionist" and "neopositivist."

The revisionist concept was based on a specific intraparty perspective. It was never formulated into a political program. It assumed that the system of power could be humanized and democratized and that the official Marxist doctrine was capable of assimilating contemporary arts and social sciences. The revisionists wanted to act within the framework of the Communist party and Marxist doctrine. They wanted to transform "from within" the doctrine and the party in the direction of democratic reform and common sense. In the long term, the actions of the revisionists seek to allow enlightened people with progressive ideas to take over the party. Władysław Bieńkowski, one of the most typical representatives of this group, defined these ideas as enlightened socialist despotism.

Stanisław Stomma, a leading exponent of the second type of evolutionist vision, called his orientation "neopositivist." In that vision, the strategy chosen by Roman Dmowski,[1] at the turn of the century, was to be applied to today's historical and political conditions. Stomma considered himself a Catholic and recognized Catholicism as a permanent component of Polish public life. As head of the Catholic Znak group, he wanted to repeat the maneuver of the leader and ideologue of the national democratic camp and, like Dmowski when he joined the tsarist Duma in 1906, Stomma and his colleagues entered the Sejm of the Polish People's Republic in January 1957. The group of Catholic activists around Stomma, who based his thinking on analysis of the geopolitical situation, aimed at creating a political movement that, at the right moment, could lead the Polish nation. For Dmowski, that moment came with the outbreak of World War I; for Stomma, it could possibly come with the decomposition of the Soviet bloc.

---

1. Roman Dmowski (1864–1939) was the spiritual father and political leader of the National Democratic party (SN-Endecja) and an antagonist of Józef Piłsudski.

From 1956 to 1959, Stomma's ideas had the partial support of the episcopate, owing to the concessions granted the Catholic Church by Władysław Gomułka's ruling group. Stomma's evolutionist concept differed fundamentally from the revisionist idea. First of all, neopositivism took for granted Poland's loyalty to the U.S.S.R. while at the same time rejecting Marxist doctrine and socialist ideology. Revisionists, by contrast, tended toward anti-Soviet rather than anti-Marxist sentiments, as was the case in Hungary. To use a metaphoric comparison, if one considers the state organization of the Soviet Union as the Church and the Marxist ideological doctrine as the Bible, then revisionism was faithful to the Bible while developing its own interpretations, whereas neopositivism adhered to the Church but with the hope that the Church would sooner or later disappear.

The two concepts shared the conviction that change would come from above. Both the revisionists and neopositivists counted on positive evolution in the party, to be caused by the rational policies of wise leaders, not by incessant public pressure. They both counted on the rational thinking of the communist prince, not on independent institutions that would gain control of the power apparatus. Most probably without making these assumptions, neither the neopositivists nor the revisionists would have been able to conduct their public activities, although, as it turned out, adoption of these assumptions inevitably led to political and intellectual defeat. Both the Church's revisionist critics and the neopositivist opponents of the Bible's principles were defeated.

The revisionist orientation definitely had some positive characteristics alongside its negative ones. We should remember both the intellectual fruits of the revisionism of that era and the political activity of important groups of the intelligentsia who were inspired by revisionism.

The former are obvious: it is enough to recall the outstanding books written by Leszek Kołakowski, Oskar Lange, Edward Lipiński, Maria Hirszowicz, Włodzimierz Brus, Krzysztof Pomian, Bronisław Baczko, and Witold Kula. Revisionism, in its broadest conception, was manifested on the literary front in the works of Kazimierz Brandys, Adam Ważyk, Wiktor Woroszylski, and Jacek Bocheński. All these books, whatever their scientific or artistic value, popularized the ideas of truth and humanism, which were under attack in the official propaganda. The publication of each of these books rapidly turned into a political event.

In addition to positively influencing Polish learning and culture, revisionism inspired political activity among the citizens. By opposing passivity and internal exile, revisionism laid the basis for independent participation in public life. Faith in one's ability to exert influence on the fate of society is an absolute prerequisite for political activity. In the case of the revisionists, this faith depended on a belief that the party could be reformed. We can see clearly today that their faith was based on delusions; still, civic activity and open demonstrations of opposition were its real and positive results in the years from 1956 to 1968. The majority of oppositionist initiatives during that period originated in these circles, not among steadfast and consistent anticommunists. It is important to remember this fact in weighing the responsibility for the Stalinist beliefs of Poland's leftist intelligentsia. It was the revisionist ex-Stalinists who originated and disseminated dissenting points of view among the intelligentsia—points of view which would later help to revive civil life in Poland in the midst of its difficult reality.

And yet revisionism had been tainted at its very source by the belief that the strivings and goals of the "liberal" wing in the party apparatus were identical to the demands of the revisionist intelligentsia. I think that the revisionists' greatest sin lay not in their defeat in the intraparty struggle for power (where they could not win) but in the character of that defeat. It was the defeat of individuals being eliminated from positions of power and influence, not a setback for a broadly based leftist and democratic political platform. The revisionists never created such a platform.

Revisionism was terminated by the events of March 1968. In that month the umbilical cord connecting the revisionist intelligentsia to the party was severed. After March 1968 the idea that a progressive and democratic wing existed in the party's leadership was never to regain wide currency. One of the few people who continued to cherish this political hope was Władysław Bieńkowski,[2] although his formulations were generally considered as protective coloring and not genuine reasoning. In fact, by popularizing his work, Bieńkowski created a completely new style of political activity. Previously, "staying inside the party"—that is, appealing for support only to party members—was an unwritten law of revisionism. Bieńkowski gave new substance to the old formulas; revisionism, conceived by him as a belief in the existence of a wise party leadership, was transformed into merciless and unceasing criticism of current leaders and their stupidity. On the one hand, he propagated ideas clearly hostile to the authorities and a program that was explicitly oppositional; but on the other hand, his program was addressed to the authorities and not to the public. Those of Bieńkowski's readers who were not party members could not learn from his writings how to live, how to act, and what to do to further democratic change.

Also in 1968, the year revisionism died, the demonstrating students chanted: "All Poland is waiting for its Dubček." For a while, the leader of Czech and Slovak communists became the symbol of hope. To this very day, the myth of Dubček and the Prague Spring has played an important role in Poland, and the meaning of this myth is far from simple. It serves to justify both radiant optimism and the darkest pessimism; it provides a defense for attitudes of conformism as well as for gestures of heroism. Why?

In October 1956 the threat of Soviet intervention in Poland made a national hero out of Władysław Gomułka—a man who would walk off the political stage

---

2. Władysław Bieńkowski wrote several books critical of the communist regime. Formerly he was an activist of the Polish Communist party and a close associate of Władysław Gomułka.

covered with infamy and contempt fourteen years later.[3] His example reveals the basic ambiguity in the whole myth of the heroic party leader. There are reasons to believe that even if there had been no armed intervention the extreme polarization and open conflict between the progressive wing of the party and the extraparty opposition KAN (club of the Non-party Engagés movement) were bound to surface in Czechoslovakia. It is difficult to predict the future, but I would venture that more than one "Dubčekite" would quickly have been transformed into a tamer of the turbulent opposition.

The myth of the "good" party leader is necessarily ambiguous. Many of those who joined the PUWP defended their decision in the following manner: "This way I will be able to serve the cause of Polish democracy, because in this way alone I will be able to lend effective support to the Polish Dubček when he appears." So far, this service to the cause of democracy has amounted to service to the totalitarian powers. Those who did not join the PUWP and who declared themselves to be totally anticommunist also use the example of Czechoslovakia to justify their decision to shun all oppositional behavior. These people call oppositionists "political troublemakers," and view the fate of Czechoslovakia and Dubček as proof that "there is no way anything is going to change here."

For me, the lesson of Czechoslovakia is that change is possible and that it has its limits. Czechoslovakia is an example of the fragility of totalitarian stability, and also of the desperation and ruthlessness of an empire under threat. The lesson of Czechoslovakia is that evolution has its limits and that it is possible.

The experiences of the neopositivists should also be closely examined. There is no doubt that their actions had the positive effect of helping to create an independent public opinion and of popularizing a way of thinking that differed completely from the obligatory official style of party propaganda.

As I have already mentioned, a starting point for the ideas of the Znak movement in 1956 was geopolitical realism and a rejection of the Poles' supposed predisposition to revolt—a lesson learned from the tragedy of the 1944 Warsaw Uprising. In return for backing Władysław Gomułka's new party leadership, the Znak movement received significant concessions from the authorities. Several Clubs of the Catholic Intelligentsia were formed, and *Tygodnik Powszechny,* the *Znak* [Sign] monthly, and the Znak publishing house were reactivated. The Znak movement gained the right to express its own opinions and to formulate its own model of national culture. One cannot overestimate the importance of the assimilation of contemporary Christian thought by Polish intellectual life. It would be equally difficult to overestimate the role of books written by Stefan Kisielewski, Hanna Malewska, Jerzy Turowicz, Jerzy Zawieyski, Stanisław Stomma, Antoni Gołubiew, or Jacek Woźniakowski. Because of the works by these authors, a broad base for a culture independent of official norms and

3. Władysław Gomułka is credited with winning in 1956 the trust of Nikita Khruschev and other Soviet leaders and thus preventing a Soviet invasion.

molds came into existence in Poland. Thanks to speeches made in the Sejm by Stefan Kisielewski, Jerzy Zawieyski, and Stanisław Stomma, young Poles were given an opportunity to become familiar with an ersatz political pluralism. By its very definition, the small group of Znak deputies was destined to fulfill the role of a realistic, pragmatic, and Catholic "opposition to Your Royal-socialist Majesty."

The *Więź* group of Polish Catholic left occupied a different niche, combining revisionist hopes with the political strategy of Znak's neopositivists. The innovative *ideas* of Tadeusz Mazowiecki, Anna Morawska, and other essayists published in *Więź* brought its editors into conflict with the episcopate; but these ideas also made possible an ideological dialogue with the lay intelligentsia. As paradoxical as this may sound, it was the *Więź* group which enabled the leftist intelligentsia to revise traditional stereotypes of Christianity and the Church.

The support lent to Gomułka by Znak and *Więź* was limited to a specific political objective—to expand the domain of civil liberties. An important component of this goal was normalization of relations between Church and State—for example, by freeing of the [then imprisoned] Primate of Poland, by relinquishing administrative harassment, by legalizing religious instruction, and so on. In these circumstances, the Znak movement confined its activities to loyal, albeit restrained and dignified, support of the authorities' policies. Much like the revisionists, the Catholic politicians believed in having concessions and rights "granted" from above rather than in organizing pressure from below. They sought harmony, not conflict; they cared for order, seeking agreement with the party, and sought to avoid imputations of oppositional attitudes.

Even though the leaders of Znak never committed the fundamental mistake of the revisionists—instead, they always stressed their ideological and political separateness—the history of their movement inspires critical thoughts about the line of action chosen by the Catholic neopositivists.

A policy of conciliation makes sense only if both sides take it seriously. In relation to communist power, whose political vocabulary lacks the word *conciliation*, such a policy has meaning only if it is conducted from a position of strength. Otherwise, conciliation turns into capitulation, and the policy of conciliation into a march toward political self-annihilation. This is how the Znak group of deputies evolved.

Agreement to a succession of personnel changes in the Znak group of deputies dictated by the authorities led to an increasing conformity of the movement's political line with the official line. Abandonment of its principles led the Znak deputies to lose their authority in the eyes of the people, who, even though they themselves were powerless, respected courage and consistency. The deputies followed a path that proceeded from compromise to loss of credibility. I am using strong language, yet it is difficult to find other words to describe the votes of the Znak deputies (except for those of Stanisław Stomma) in favor of the government amendments to the Constitution of the PPR [1976]—for amendments that were opposed by independent public opinion in Poland.[4] This was the last stage and the final product of their abandonment of principle in exchange for immediate but illusory gains. It is one of the many paradoxes of Polish history that Stanisław Stomma, a politician whose eyes were fixed on the example of Alexander the Great and his policy of realpolitik, ended his political career in the Polish People's Republic with a romantic gesture worthy of Rejtan.[5]

The ideas of the revisionists and the neopositivists contained two basic answers to the political dilemmas of the years 1957 to 1964—a period of social normalization and political thaw, increasing prosperity among the people, and relative expansion of civil liberties. Both groups reflected to a great degree the atmosphere of political peace and socio-psychological stability.

The fragility of both revisionism and neopositivism surfaced when social conflict became more acute, in the late sixties and seventies. The student and intellectual movement in March, 1968, the workers' explosion in June, 1976—both spontaneous public manifestations led to the downfall of the revisionists and neopositivists. The uselessness of both abstract formulas adopted from the history of philosophy and the tactical programs that resulted from these formulas was bared in the clash with real social processes. The conflicts between the public and the authorities showed the illusory character of the hopes held by both the revisionists and the neopositivists, and placed them in a situation in which they had to make a dramatic choice. When there is open conflict, one must clearly state a position and declare whose side one is on—that of those being beaten up or that of those doing the beating. Where the conflict is open, consistent revisionism as well as consistent neopositivism both inevitably lead to unity with the powers-that-be and assumption of their point of view. To offer solidarity with striking workers, with students holding a mass meeting, or with protesting intellectuals is to challenge the intraparty strategy of the revisionist and neopositivist policies of compromise. Social solidarity undermines the fundamental component of both strategies: acceptance of the government as the basic point of reference.

The dilemma of nineteenth-century leftist movements—"reform or revolution"—is not the dilemma of the Polish opposition. To believe in overthrowing the dictatorship of the party by revolution and to consciously organize actions in pursuit of this goal is both unrealistic and dangerous. As the political structure of the U.S.S.R. remains unchanged, it is unrealistic to count on subverting the party in Poland. It is dangerous to plan conspiratorial activities. Given the absence of an authentic political culture or any standards of democratic collective life, the existence of an underground would only worsen these illnesses and change little. Revolutionary theories and conspiratorial practices can only serve the police, making mass hysteria and police provocation more likely.

4. The protests against the changes in the constitution were the beginning of the self-organization of the opposition in Poland.

5. Tadeusz Rejtan (1746-1780), a deputy from Nowogródek to the 1773 Diet, tore his clothes and threw himself on the floor begging other envoys to reject the partition of Poland.

In my opinion, an unceasing struggle for reform and evolution that seeks an expansion of civil liberties and human rights is the only course East European dissidents can take. The Polish example demonstrates that real concessions can be won by applying steady public pressure on the government. To draw a parallel with events at the other end of our continent, one could say that the ideas of the Polish democratic opposition resemble the Spanish rather than the Portuguese model. This is based on gradual and piecemeal change, not violent upheaval and forceful destruction of the existing system.

The Soviet military and political presence in Poland is the factor that determines the limits of possible evolution, and this is unlikely to change for some time. The desire to resist has been paralyzed by the specter of Soviet military intervention and Soviet tanks in the streets of Warsaw. The memory of Budapest and Prague has led many people to believe that the Soviet leaders will not allow any changes whatsoever. But on closer examination, the matter seems much more complicated.

Let us recall: Władysław Gomułka owed his enormous popularity in 1956 to his skillful definition of the "Soviet question." Every competent party leader can win obedience and allegiance by cleverly juggling fear and the public's desire for security. Mieczysław Moczar tried to strike the right note, and Franciszek Szlachcic appealed to these popular sentiments with a phrase that made the rounds in Warsaw: "Polish-Soviet friendship should be like good tea: strong, hot, but not too sweet." These two politicians [and later security service officials] started their march to power by seeking greater popularity, and though they did not succeed, the Soviet question remains a showy stage for political exploitation.

When one analyzes the complexity of Polish-Soviet relations, it must be noted first of all that the interests of the Soviet political leadership, the Polish political leadership, and the Polish democratic opposition are basically concurrent. For all three parties, a Soviet military intervention in Poland would be a political disaster. For the Polish leadership, such an intervention would signify dethronement or the reduction of its position of leader of a nation of thirty-four million, with limited sovereignty, to that of policeman acting on behalf of the Soviet imperium. The Soviet leaders, however, certainly remember the international repercussions of their interventions in Hungary and Czechoslovakia, as well as the resolve of the Polish workers in December 1970 and June 1976. If we include also the traditional anti-Russian sentiments of the Poles, and their propensity to fight out of sheer desperation (as demonstrated, for instance, in the Warsaw Uprising of 1944), then we can conclude that a decision by Soviet leaders to intervene militarily in Poland would be equivalent to opting for war with Poland. It would be a war that Poland would lose on the battlefield but that the Soviet Union would lose politically. A victorious Soviet war with Poland would mean a national massacre for the Poles, but for the Soviets it would be a political catastrophe. This is why I believe the Soviet leaders, as well as the leadership of the PUWP, will go far to avoid such a conflict. This reluctance delineates the area of permissible political maneuver; this alignment of interests defines the sphere of possible compromise.

I am not contending that Soviet intervention in Poland is impossible. On the contrary, I believe that it may be unavoidable if the Moscow and Warsaw authorities on the one hand, and the Polish public on the other, lose their common sense and a sense of reality and moderation. The opposition must learn that in Poland change can only come—at least in its first stages—within the framework of the "Brezhnev doctrine."

The revisionists and neopositivists also believed that evolutionary change should be planned within the parameters of the "Brezhnev doctrine." I believe that what sets today's opposition apart from the proponents of those ideas is the belief that a program for evolution ought to be addressed to an independent public, not to totalitarian power. Such a program should give directives to the people on how to behave, not to the powers on how to reform themselves. Nothing instructs the authorities better than pressure from below.

"New evolutionism" is based on faith in the power of the working class, which, with a steady and unyielding stand, has on several occasions forced the government to make spectacular concessions. It is difficult to foresee developments in the working class, but there is no question that the power elite fears this social group most. Pressure from the working classes is a necessary condition for the evolution of public life toward democracy.

This evolution is not easy to chart; it requires that fear be constantly overcome and that a new political consciousness be developed. Factors that retard this process include the absence of authentic workers' institutions and of models and traditions for political resistance. The day the first independent organization for workers' self-defense was founded, when the strike committees in the shipyards of Szczecin and Gdańsk were formed, a new stage in worker consciousness began. It is hard to tell when and how other, more permanent institutions representing the interests of workers will be created and what form they will have. Will they be workers' committees following the Spanish model, or independent labor unions, or mutual aid societies? But when such institutions emerge, the vision of a new evolutionism will become more than just a creation of a mind in search of hope.

The role of the Catholic Church is a crucial element in Poland's situation. The majority of the Polish people feel close to the Church, and many Catholic priests have strong political influence. The evolution of the Polish episcopate's program of action should be carefully analyzed. This evolution can be observed easily in official Church documents. The Church hierarchy's consistently and specifically anticommunist position, in which all social and political changes that have taken place since 1945 were rejected, has been evolving into a more broadly antitotalitarian stance. Jeremiads against "godless ones" have given way to documents quoting the principles of the Declaration of Human Rights; in pastoral letters, Polish bishops have been defending the right to truth and standing up for human freedom and dignity. Most important, they have been defending the civil liberties of the working people, and particularly their right to strike and to form independent labor unions.

The Catholic Church, which consistently resists pressure from the government and defends Christian principles as well as the principles of the Declaration of Human rights, has necessarily become a place where attitudes of nonconformity and dignity among the people can mingle. It is therefore a key source of encouragement for those who seek to broaden civil liberties.

The new evolutionism aims at gradual and slow change. But this does not mean that the movement for change will always be peaceful—that it will not require sacrifices and casualties. In the past, this movement partially consisted of mass actions by workers and students—and this may continue into the future. Such actions are usually followed by disputes in the power elite. Therefore, we should ask whether forces within the party and its leadership exist which are capable of adopting a program of reform, and whether revisionism might reappear within the party. Can the democratic opposition find an ally in one of the party coteries?

Revisionism is a movement of intraparty renewal which came into being in the fifties and is now an outdated phenomenon. It is difficult to imagine a movement that would use Marxist-Leninist doctrine, or even any of its elements, to enforce reforms in Poland today, since this doctrine is a dead creature, an empty gesture, an official ritual. It no longer stimulates discussion or fires up emotions. It is incapable of causing internal tension and division.

I believe nevertheless that change within the party is inevitable. Among the hundreds of thousands of party members who have no interest whatsoever in dialectical materialism, there are many for whom membership in the PUWP is simply a necessary precondition for participation in public life. Among them are many believers in realpolitik, pragmatism and economic reform. Their political beliefs and decisions are shaped by the pressure of public opinion and by forces within the national economy. Pragmatism causes these people to let narrow ideological criteria be overridden by the need for the development of education, stronger scientific-technical cooperation with capitalist countries, and increased competition. This obviously does not mean that these individuals are striving for democracy. A party "pragmatist" has no reason to aim for democratic change— for pluralism and authentic self-government. But he does have reason to understand the effectiveness of compromising with forces favoring plurality instead of brutally suppressing them. For he knows very well that repression solves nothing and instead prepares the ground for the next explosion of social discontent, the consequences of which are impossible to foresee.

The party pragmatist will therefore do his best to avoid such situations. This is why he can be a partner of the democratic opposition, with whom it will be possible to reach a political compromise. But he will never be a political ally. I think that this distinction is important. If the people of the democratic opposition fail to distinguish the various trends that exist within the power apparatus, I believe they may ignore reality, become fanatical maximalists, and go astray into political adventurism. Identifying their own goals with those of the pragmatic wing of the party, however, could lead them to repeat the mistakes of the revisionists, to form false alliances and lose their ideological identity. The people of the democratic opposition should not place excessive hope in "reasonable" party leaders, or give in to arguments that "one should not make things more difficult for the current party leadership because the next one may be worse." The democratic opposition must formulate its own political goals and only then, with those goals in hand, reach political compromises. Take, for example, a situation in which the workers revolt and the government declares that it wants to "consult with the working class" instead of organizing a bloody massacre. The people of the democratic opposition should treat this reaction neither as a sufficient concession ("but they are not shooting") nor as a meaningless fiction. On the contrary, the democratic opposition must be constantly and incessantly visible in public life, must create political facts by organizing mass actions, must formulate alternative programs. Everything else is an illusion.

The intelligentsia's duty is to formulate alternative programs and defend the basic principles. More precisely, I refer to those small groups of intellectuals who believe in continuing the traditions of the "insubordinate" intelligentsia of the early 1900s—the traditions of writers such as Stanisław Brzozowski, Stanisław Wyspiański, Stefan Zeromski, and Zofia Nałkowska. I feel solidarity with those traditions and those people, although I am the last person to overestimate the importance of their actions. But those voices, albeit weak and sporadic, are nonetheless authentic: they form an independent public opinion, with nonconformist attitudes and oppositional thought. This course is being followed by people from various traditions and social strata: former revisionists (including the author of this article), former neopositivists, and those who become ideologically aware after the events of 1968.

The direction the ideological thinking of the young generation will take—as well as the drift of political change in Poland and in other countries of Eastern Europe—will depend on the convergence of these groups with the activities of the working class. When a free press and independent organizations do not exist, the moral and political responsibility of these groups is much greater than at any other time. The people of the opposition should renounce material profit and official esteem in order to fulfill this exceptional responsibility, so that we can expect the truth from them.

In searching for truth, or, to quote Leszek Kołakowski, "by living in dignity," opposition intellectuals are striving not so much for a better tomorrow as for a better today. Every act of defiance helps us build the framework of democratic socialism, which should not be merely or primarily a legal institutional structure but a real, day-to-day community of free people.

Paris, October 1976

from To Empower People

Mediating Structures and the Dilemmas of the Welfare State

Two seemingly contradictory tendencies are evident in current thinking about public policy in America. First, there is a continuing desire for the services provided by the modern welfare state. Partisan rhetoric aside, few people seriously envisage dismantling the welfare state. The serious debate is over how and to what extent it should be expanded. The second tendency is one of strong animus against government, bureaucracy, and bigness as such. This animus is directed not only toward Washington but toward government at all levels. Although this essay is addressed to the American situation, it should be noted that a similar ambiguity about the modern welfare state exists in other democratic societies, notably in Western Europe.

Perhaps this is just another case of people wanting to eat their cake and have it too. It would hardly be the first time in history that the people wanted benefits without paying the requisite costs. Nor are politicians above exploiting ambiguities by promising increased services while reducing expenditures. The extravagant rhetoric of the modern state and the surrealistic vastness of its taxation system encourage magical expectations that make contradictory measures seem possible. As long as some of the people can be fooled some of the time, some politicians will continue to ride into office on such magic.

But this is not the whole story. The contradiction between wanting more government services and less government may be only apparent. More precisely, we suggest that the modern welfare state is here to stay, indeed that it ought to expand the benefits it provides—but that *alternative mechanisms are possible to provide welfare-state services.*

The current anti-government, anti-bigness mood is not irrational. Complaints about impersonality, unresponsiveness, and excessive interference, as well as the perception of rising costs and deteriorating service—these are based upon empirical and widespread experience. The crisis of New York City, which is rightly seen as more than a fiscal crisis, signals a national state of unease with the policies followed in recent decades. At the same time there is widespread public support for publicly addressing major problems of our society in relieving poverty, in education, health care, and housing, and in a host of other human needs. What first appears as contradiction, then, is the sum of equally justified aspirations. The public policy goal is to address human needs without exacerbating the reasons for animus against the welfare state.

Of course there are no panaceas. The alternatives proposed here, we believe, can solve *some* problems. Taken seriously, they could become the basis of far-reaching innovations in public policy, perhaps of a new paradigm for at least sectors of the modern welfare state.

The basic concept is that of what we are calling mediating structures. The concept in various forms has been around for a long time. What is new is the systematic effort to translate it into specific public policies. For purposes of this study, mediating structures are defined as *those institutions standing between the individual in his private life and the large institutions of public life.*

Modernization brings about an historically unprecedented dichotomy between public and private life. The most important large institution in the ordering of modern society is the modern state itself. In addition, there are the large economic conglomerates of capitalist enterprise, big labor, and the growing bureaucracies that administer wide sectors of the society, such as in education and the organized professions. All these institutions we call the *megastructures.*

Then there is that modern phenomenon called private life. It is a curious kind of preserve left over by the large institutions and in which individuals carry on a bewildering variety of activities with only fragile institutional support.

For the individual in modern society, life is an ongoing migration between these two spheres, public and private. The megastructures are typically alienating, that is, they are not helpful in providing meaning and identity for individual existence. Meaning, fulfillment, and personal identity are to be realized in the private sphere. While the two spheres interact in many ways, in private life the individual is left very much to his own devices, and thus is uncertain and anxious. Where modern society is "hard," as in the megastructures, it is personally unsatisfactory; where it is "soft," as in private life, it cannot be relied upon. Compare, for example, the social realities of employment with those of marriage.

The dichotomy poses a double crisis. It is a crisis for the individual who must carry on a balancing act between the demands of the two spheres. It is a political crisis because the megastructures (notably the state) come to be devoid of personal meaning and are therefore viewed as unreal or even malignant. Not everyone experiences this crisis in the same way. Many who handle it more successfully than most have access to institutions that *mediate* between the two spheres. Such institutions have a private face, giving private life a measure of stability, and they have a public face, transferring meaning and value to the megastructures. Thus, mediating structures alleviate each facet of the double crisis of modern society. Their strategic position derives from their reducing both the anomic precariousness of individual existence in isolation from society and the threat of alienation to the public order.

Our focus is on four such mediating structures—neighborhood, family, church, and voluntary association. This is by no means an exhaustive list, but these institutions were selected for two reasons: first, they figure prominently in the lives of most Americans and, second, they are most relevant to the problems of the welfare state with which we are concerned. The proposal is that, if these institutions could be more imaginatively recognized in public policy, individuals would be more "at home" in society, and the political order would be more "meaningful."

Without institutionally reliable processes of mediation, the political order becomes detached from the values and realities of individual life. Deprived of its moral foundation, the political order is "delegitimated." When that happens, the political order must be secured by coercion rather than by consent. And when that happens, democracy disappears.

. . .

Democracy is "handicapped" by being more vulnerable to the erosion of meaning in its institutions. Cynicism threatens it; wholesale cynicism can destroy it. That is why mediation is so crucial to democracy. Such mediation cannot be sporadic and occasional; it must be institutionalized in *structures*. The structures we have chosen to study have demonstrated a great capacity for adapting and innovating under changing conditions. Most important, they exist where people are, and that is where sound public policy should always begin.

. . .

Also, on the practical political level, it might seem that mediating structures have universal endorsement. There is, for example, little political mileage in being anti-family or anti-church. But the reality is not so simple. Liberalism—which constitutes the broad center of American politics, whether or not it calls itself by that name—has tended to be blind to the political (as distinct from private) functions of mediating structures. The main feature of liberalism, as we intend the term, is a commitment to government action toward greater social justice within the existing system. (To revolutionaries, of course, this is "mere reformism," but the revolutionary option has not been especially relevant, to date, in the American context.)

Liberalism's blindness to mediating structures can be traced to its Enlightenment roots. Enlightenment thought is abstract, universalistic, addicted to what Burke called "geometry" in social policy. The concrete particularities of mediating structures find an inhospitable soil in the liberal garden. There the great concern is for the individual ("the rights of man") and for a just public order, but anything "in between" is viewed as irrelevant, or even an obstacle, to the rational ordering of society. What lies in between is dismissed, to the extent it can be, as superstition, bigotry, or (more recently) cultural lag.

American liberalism has been vigorous in the defense of the private rights of individuals, and has tended to dismiss the argument that private behavior can have public consequences. Private rights are frequently defended *against* mediating structures—children's rights against the family, the rights of sexual deviants against neighborhood or small-town sentiment, and so forth. Similarly, American liberals are virtually faultless in their commitment to the religious liberty of individuals. But the liberty to be defended is always that of privatized religion. Supported by a very narrow understanding of the separation of church and state, liberals are typically hostile to the claim that institutional religion might have public rights and public functions. As a consequence of this "geometrical" outlook, liberalism has a hard time coming to terms with the alienating effects of the abstract structures it has multiplied since the New Deal. This may be the Achilles heel of the liberal state today.

The left, understood as some version of the socialist vision, has been less blind to the problem of mediation. Indeed the term alienation derives from Marxism. The weakness of the left, however, is its exclusive or nearly exclusive focus on the capitalist economy as the source of this evil, when in fact the alienations of the socialist states, insofar as there are socialist states, are much more severe than those of the capitalist states. While some theorists of the New Left have addressed this problem by using elements from the anarcho-syndicalist tradition, most socialists see mediating structures as something that may be relevant to a post-revolutionary future, but that in the present only distracts attention from the struggle toward building socialism. Thus the left is not very helpful in the search for practical solutions to our problem.

On the right of the political broad center, we also find little that is helpful. To be sure, classical European conservatism had high regard for mediating structures, but, from the eighteenth century on, this tradition has been marred by a romantic urge to revoke modernity—a prospect that is, we think, neither likely nor desirable. On the other hand, what is now called conservatism in America is in fact old-style liberalism. It is the laissez-faire ideology of the period before the New Deal, which is roughly the time when liberalism shifted its faith from the market to government. *Both* the old faith in the market *and* the new faith in government share the abstract thought patterns of the Enlightenment. In addition, today's conservatism typically exhibits the weakness of the left in reverse: it is highly sensitive to the alienations of big government, but blind to the analogous effects of big business. Such one-sidedness, whether left or right, is not helpful.

As is now being widely recognized, we need new approaches free of the ideological baggage of the past. The mediating structures paradigm cuts across current ideological and political divides. This proposal has met with gratifying interest from most with whom we have shared it, and while it has been condemned as right-wing by some and as left-wing by others, this is in fact encouraging. Although the paradigm may play havoc with the conventional political labels, it is hoped that, after the initial confusion of what some social scientists call "cognitive shock," each implication of the proposal will be considered on its own merits.

The argument of this essay—and the focus of the research project it is designed to introduce—can be subsumed under three propositions. The first proposition is analytical: *mediating structures are essential for a vital democratic society.* The other two are broad programmatic recommendations: *public policy should protect and foster mediating structures,* and *wherever possible, public policy should utilize mediating structures for the realization of social purposes.* The research project will determine, it is hoped, whether these propositions stand up under rigorous examination and, if so, how they can be translated into specific recommendations.

The analytical proposition assumes that mediating structures are the value-generating and value-maintaining agencies in society. Without them, values become another function of the megastructures, notably of the state, and this is a hallmark of totalitarianism. In the totalitarian case, the individual becomes the object rather than the subject of the value-propagating processes of society.

The two programmatic propositions are, respectively, minimalist and maximalist. Minimally, public policy should cease and desist from damaging, mediating structures. Much of the damage has been unintentional in the past. We should be more cautious than we have been. As we have learned to ask about the effects of government action upon racial minorities or upon the environment, so we should learn to ask about the effects of public policies on mediating structures.

The maximalist proposition ("utilize mediating structures") is much the riskier. We emphasize, "wherever possible." The mediating structures paradigm is not applicable to all areas of policy. Also there is the real danger that such structures might be "co-opted" by the government in a too-eager embrace that would destroy the very distinctiveness of their function. The prospect of government control of the family, for example, is clearly the exact opposite of our intention. The goal in utilizing mediating structures is to expand government services without producing government oppressiveness. Indeed it might be argued that the achievement of that goal is one of the acid tests of democracy.

It should be noted that these propositions differ from superficially similar proposals aimed at decentralizing governmental functions. Decentralization is limited to what can be done *within* governmental structures; we are concerned with the structures that stand *between* government and the individual. Nor, again, are we calling for a devolution of governmental responsibilities that would be tantamount to dismantling the welfare state. We aim rather at rethinking the institutional means by which government exercises its responsibilities. The idea is not to revoke the New Deal but to pursue its vision in ways more compatible with democratic governance.

. . .

The theme is *empowerment.* One of the most debilitating results of modernization is a feeling of powerlessness in the face of institutions controlled by those whom we do not know and whose values we often do not share. Lest there be any doubt, our belief is that human beings, whoever they are, understand their own needs better than anyone else—in, say, 99 percent of all cases. The mediating structures under discussion here are the principal expressions of the real values and the real needs of people in our society. They are, for the most part, the people-sized institutions. Public policy should recognize, respect, and, where possible, empower these institutions.

Neighborhood

"The most sensible way to locate the neighborhood," writes Milton Kotler in *Neighborhood Government* (Bobbs-Merrill, 1959) "is to ask people where it is, for people spend much time fixing its boundaries. Gangs mark its turf. Old people watch for its new faces. Children figure out safe routes between home and school. People walk their dogs through their neighborhood, but rarely beyond it."

. . .

. . . [W]e contend—together with many others, both black and white, who have a strong record of commitment to racial justice—that strong neighborhoods can be a potent instrument in achieving greater justice for all Americans. It is not true, for example, that all-black neighborhoods are by definition weak neighborhoods. As we shall see, to argue the contrary is to relegate black America to perpetual frustration or to propose a most improbable program of social revolution. To put it simply, real community development must begin where people are. If our hopes for development assume an idealized society cleansed of ethnic pride and its accompanying bigotries, they are doomed to failure.

While social policy that can be morally approved must be attuned to the needs of the poor—and in America that means very particularly the black poor—the nonpoor also live in and cherish the values of neighborhood. The neighborhood in question may be as part-time and tenuous as the many bedroom communities surrounding our major cities; it may be the ethnic and economic crazy-quilt of New York's East village; it may be the tranquil homogeneity of the east side of Cisco, Texas. Again, a neighborhood is what the people who live there say is a neighborhood.

For public policy purposes, there is no useful definition of what makes a good neighborhood, though we can agree on what constitutes a bad neighborhood. Few people would choose to live where crime is rampant, housing deteriorated, and garbage uncollected. To describe these phenomena as bad is not an instance of imposing middle-class, bourgeois values upon the poor. No one, least of all the poor, is opposed to such "middle class" values as safety, sanitation, and the freedom of choice that comes with affluence. With respect to so-called bad neighborhoods, we have essentially three public policy choices: we can ignore them, we can attempt to dismantle them and spread their problems around more equitably, or we can try to transform the bad into the better on the way to becoming good. The first option, although common, should be intolerable. The second is massively threatening to the nonpoor, and therefore not feasible short of revolution. The third holds most promise for a public policy that can gain the support of the American people. And, if we care more about consequence than about confrontation, the third is also the most radical in long-range effect.

Because social scientists and planners have a penchant for unitary definitions that cover all contingencies, there is still much discussion of what makes for a good neighborhood. Our approach suggests that the penchant should be carefully restrained. It is not necessarily true, for example, that a vital neighborhood is one that supplies a strong sense of social cohesion or reinforces personal identity with the group. In fact many people want neighborhoods where free choice in association and even anonymity are cherished. That kind of neighborhood, usually urban, is no less a neighborhood for its lack of social cohesion. Cohesion exacts its price in loss of personal freedom; freedom may be paid for in the coin of alienation and loneliness. One pays the price for the neighborhood of one's choice. Making that choice possible is the function of the *idea* of neighborhood as it is embodied in many actual neighborhoods. It is not possible to create the benefits of each kind of neighborhood in every neighborhood. One cannot devise a compromise between the cohesion of a New England small town and the anonymity of the East Village without destroying both options.

Nor is it necessarily true that progress is marked by movement from the neighborhood of cohesion to the neighborhood of elective choice. Members of the cultural elite, who have strong influence on the metaphors by which public policy is designed, frequently feel they have escaped from the parochialisms of the former type of neighborhood. Such escapes are one source of the continuing vitality of great cities, but this idea of liberation should not be made normative. The Upper West Side of New York City, for example, the neighborhood of so many literary, academic, and political persons, has its own forms of parochialism, its taboos and restrictions, approved beliefs and behavior patterns. The urban sophisticate's conformity to the values of individual self-fulfillment and tolerance can be as intolerant of the beliefs and behavior nurtured in the community centered in the St. Stanislaus American Legion branch of Hamtramck, Michigan, as the people of Hamtramck are intolerant of what is called liberation on the Upper West Side.

. . .

The empowerment of people in neighborhoods is hardly the answer to all our social problems. Neighborhoods empowered to impose their values upon individual behavior and expression can be both coercive and cruel. Government that transcends neighborhoods must intervene to protect elementary human rights. Here again, however, the distinction between public and private spheres is critically important. In recent years an unbalanced emphasis upon individual rights has seriously eroded the community's power to sustain its democratically determined values in the public sphere. It is ironic, for example, to find people who support landmark commissions that exercise aesthetic censorship—for example, by forbidding owners of landmark properties to change so much as a step or a bay window without legal permission—and who, at the same time, oppose public control of pornography, prostitution, gambling, and other "victimless crimes" that violate neighborhood values more basic than mere aesthetics. In truth, a strong class factor is involved in this apparent contradiction. Houses in neighborhoods that are thought to be part of our architectural heritage are typically owned by people to whom values such as architectural heritage are important. These are usually not the people whose neighborhoods are assaulted by pornography, prostitution, and drug trafficking. In short, those who have power can call in the police to reinforce their values while the less powerful cannot.

. . .

One reason for the present confusion about individual and communal rights has been the unreflective extension of policies deriving from America's racial dilemma to other areas where they are neither practicable nor just. That is, as a nation, and after a long, tortuous, and continuing agony, we have solemnly covenanted to disallow any public regulation that discriminates on the basis of race. That national decision must in no way be compromised. At the same time, the singularity of America's racial history needs to be underscored. Public policy should be discriminating about discriminations. Discrimination is the essence of particularism and particularism is the essence of pluralism. The careless expansion of antidiscrimination rulings in order to appease every aggrieved minority or individual will have two certain consequences: first, it will further erode local communal authority and, second, it will trivialize the historic grievances and claims to justice of America's racial minorities.

In terms of communal standards and sanctions, deviance always exacts a price. Indeed, without such standards, there can be no such thing as deviance. Someone who engages in public and deviant behavior in, say, Paducah, Kentucky, can pay the social price of deviance, can persuade his fellow citizens to accept his behavior, or can move to New York City. He should not be able to call in the police to prevent the people of Paducah from enforcing their values against his behavior. (Obviously, we are not referring to the expression of unpopular political or religious views, which, like proscriptions against racial discrimination, is firmly protected by national law and consensus.) The city—variously viewed as the cesspool of wickedness or the zone of liberation—has historically been the place of refuge for the insistently deviant. It might be objected that our saying "he can move to the city" sounds like the "love it or leave it" argument of those who opposed anti-war protestors in the last decade. The whole point, however, is the dramatic difference between a nation and a neighborhood. One is a citizen of a nation and lays claim to the rights by which that nation is constituted. Within that nation there are numerous associations such as neighborhoods—more or less freely chosen—and membership in those associations is usually related to affinity. This nation is constituted as an exercise in pluralism, as the *unum* within which myriad *plures* are sustained. If it becomes national policy to make the public values of

Kokomo or Salt Lake City indistinguishable from those of San Francisco or New Orleans, we have as a nation abandoned the social experiment symbolized by the phrase "E Pluribus Unum."

Viewed in this light, the *national* purpose does not destroy but aims at strengthening particularity, including the particularity of the neighborhood. It would be naive, however, to deny that there are points at which the *unum* and the *plures* are in conflict. It is patently the case, for example, that one of the chief determinants in shaping neighborhoods, especially in urban areas, is the racism that marks American life. The problem, of course, is that racial discrimination is often inseparable from other discriminations based upon attitudes, behavior patterns, and economic disparities. One may sympathize with those who are so frustrated in their effort to overcome racial injustice that they advocate policies aimed at wiping out every vestige and consequence of past racial discrimination. In fact, however, such leveling policies are relentlessly resisted by almost all Americans, including the black and the poor who, rightly or wrongly, see their interests attached to a system of rewards roughly associated with "free enterprise." The more practicable and, finally, the more just course is advanced by those who advocate massive public policy support for neighborhood development as development is defined by the people in the neighborhoods. As people in poor neighborhoods realize more of the "middle class" goals to which they undoubtedly aspire, racial discrimination will be reduced or at least will be more readily isolated than now and thus more easily reachable by legal proscription. The achievement of the poor need not mean that achievers move out of poor neighborhoods, thus leaving behind a hard core of more "ghettoized" residents. It is often overlooked, for example, that many middle-class and wealthy blacks *choose* to live in Harlem, creating "good neighborhoods" within an area often dismissed as hopeless. The dynamics of such community maintenance deserve more careful study and wider appreciation.

. . .

If it is to make a real difference, neighborhood development should be distinguished from programs of decentralization. From Honolulu to Newton, Massachusetts, the last ten years have witnessed an explosion of neighborhood councils, "little city halls" dispersed through urban areas, and the like. Again, the decentralized operation of megastructures is not the same thing as the creation of vital mediating structures—indeed, it can be quite the opposite. Decentralization can give the people in the neighborhoods the feeling that they are being listened to, and even participating, but it has little to do with development and governance unless it means the reality as well as the sensations of power. Neighborhood governance exists when—in areas such as education, health services, law enforcement, and housing regulation—the people democratically determine what is in the interest of their own chosen life styles and values.

Many different streams flow into the current enthusiasms for neighborhood government. Sometimes the neighborhood government movement is dubbed "the

new Jeffersonianism." After two centuries of massive immigration and urbaniza-
tion, we cannot share Jefferson's bucolic vision of rural and small-town America,
just as we do not indulge the re-medievalizing fantasies associated in some quar-
ters with the acclaim for smallness. We believe the premise on which to devise
public policy is that the parameters of modern, industrial, technological society
are set for the foreseeable future. Our argument is not against modernity but in
favor of exploring the ways in which modernity can be made more humane. With
respect to neighborhood government, for example, it was widely assumed fifty
and more years ago that modernity required the "rationalization" of urban polity.
This was the premise of the "reform" and "good government" movements promoting the managerial, as distinct from partisan political, style of urban governance. The limitations of that approach are more widely recognized today.

. . .

One factor sparking enthusiasm for community control and neighborhood government is the growing realization that localities may not be receiving a fair break
when it comes to tax monies. That is, some studies suggest that even poor neighborhoods, after everything is taken into account, end up sending considerably
more out of the neighborhood in taxes than is returned. We do not suggest that the
income tax, for instance, should be administered locally. It is reasonable to inquire, however, whether the tax-collecting function of the federal and state
governments could not be maintained, while the spending function is changed to
allow tax monies to be returned in a noncategorical way to the places where they
were raised to begin with. Needless to say, this suggestion goes far beyond what is
currently called revenue sharing. Nor does it ignore the fact that sizable funds are
required for functions that transcend the purview of any neighborhood, such as
transportation or defense. But again—focusing on activities of the kind carried on
by the Department of Health, Education and Welfare (HEW)—it does imply that
the people in communities know best what is needed for the maintenance and development of those communities.

The Family

There are places, especially in urban areas, where life styles are largely detached
from family connections. This is, one hopes, good for those who choose it. Certainly such life styles add to the diversity, the creativity, even the magic, of the
city. But since a relatively small number of people inhabit these areas, it would be
both foolish and undemocratic to take such life styles as guidelines for the nation.
For most Americans, neighborhood and community are closely linked to the family as an institution.

The family may be in crisis in the sense that it is undergoing major changes of
definition, but there is little evidence that it is in decline. High divorce rates, for
example, may indicate not decline but rising expectations in what people look for

in marriage and family life. The point is underscored by high remarriage rates. It is noteworthy that the counterculture, which is so critical of the so-called bourgeois family, uses the terminology of family for its new social constructions, as do radical feminists pledged to "sisterhood." For most Americans, the evidence is that involvement in the bourgeois family, however modified, will endure.

Of course, modernization has already had a major impact on the family. It has largely stripped the family of earlier functions in the areas of education and economics, for example. But in other ways, modernization has made the family more important than ever before. It is the major institution within the private sphere, and thus for many people the most valuable thing in their lives. Here they make their moral commitments, invest their emotions, plan for the future, and perhaps even hope for immortality.

There is a paradox here. On the one hand, the megastructures of government, business, mass communications, and the rest have left room for the family to be the autonomous realm of individual aspiration and fulfillment. This room is by now well secured in the legal definitions of the family. At the same time, the megastructures persistently infringe upon the family. We cannot and should not eliminate these infringements entirely. After all, families exist in a common society. We can, however, take positive measures to protect and foster the family institution, so that it is not defenseless before the forces of modernity.

This means public recognition of the family *as an institution.* It is not enough to be concerned for individuals more or less incidentally related to the family as institution. Public recognition of the family as an institution is imperative because every society has an inescapable interest in how children are raised, how values are transmitted to the next generation. Totalitarian regimes have tried—unsuccessfully to date—to supplant the family in this function. Democratic societies dare not try if they wish to remain democratic. Indeed they must resist every step, however well intended, to displace or weaken the family institution.

Public concern for the family is not antagonistic to concern for individual rights. On the contrary, individuals need strong families if they are to grow up and remain rooted in a strong sense of identity and values. Weak families produce uprooted individuals, unsure of their direction and therefore searching for some authority. They are ideal recruits for authoritarian movements inimical to democratic society.

Commitment to the family institution can be combined, although not without difficulty, with an emphatically libertarian view that protects the private lives of adults against public interference of any kind. Public interest in the family is centered on children, not adults; it touches adults insofar as they are in charge of children. The public interest is institutional in character. That is, the state is to view children as members of a family. The sovereignty of the family over children has limits—as does any sovereignty in the modern world—and these limits are already defined in laws regarding abuse, criminal neglect, and so on. The onus of proof, however, must be placed on policies or laws that foster state interference rather than on those that protect family autonomy. In saying this we affirm what has been the major legal tradition in this country.

Conversely, we oppose policies that expose the child directly to state intervention, without the mediation of the family. We are skeptical about much current discussion of children's rights—especially when such rights are asserted *against* the family. Children do have rights, among which is the right to a functionally strong family. When the rhetoric of children's rights means transferring children from the charge of families to the charge of coteries of experts ("We know what is best for the children"), that rhetoric must be suspected of cloaking vested interests—ideological interests, to be sure, but, also and more crudely, interest in jobs, money, and power.

· · ·

Church

Religious institutions form by far the largest network of voluntary associations in American society. Yet, for reasons both ideological and historical, their role is frequently belittled or totally overlooked in discussions of social policy. Whatever may be one's attitude to organized religion, this blind spot must be reckoned a serious weakness in much thinking about public policy. The churches and synagogues of America can no more be omitted from responsible social analysis than can big labor, business corporations, or the communications media. Not only are religious institutions significant "players" in the public realm, but they are singularly important to the way people order their lives and values at the most local and concrete levels of their existence. Thus they are crucial to understanding family, neighborhood, and other mediating structures of empowerment.

· · ·

The evidence, at least in America, does not support the hypothesis of the inevitable decline of religion. Although the decline is perennially announced—its announcement being greeted with both cheers and lamentations—it is likely that religion is at least as institutionally intact as some other major institutions (such as, for example, higher education). It is worth noting that in recent years the alleged decline of religion has been measured by comparison with the so-called religious boom of the late 1950s. The comparison with that unprecedented period of institutional growth offers a very skewed perspective. But, even when the vitality of religion is measured by that misleading comparison, it is notable that in the past few years the indexes are again on the upswing. Church attendance, claimed affiliation, financial contributions, and other indicators all suggest that whatever decline there was from the apex of the late 1950s has now stopped or been reversed. It is perhaps relevant to understanding American society to note that on any given Sunday there are probably more people in churches than the total number of people who attend professional sports events in a whole year—or to note that there are close to 500,000 local churches and synagogues voluntarily supported by the American people.

. . .

The second assumption—that religion deals purely with the private sphere and is therefore irrelevant to public policy—must also be challenged. Although specifically religious activities have been largely privatized, the first part of the proposition overlooks the complex ways in which essentially religious values infiltrate and influence our public thought. But even to the extent that the first part of the proposition is true, it does not follow that religion is therefore irrelevant to public policy. The family, for example, is intimately involved in the institution of religions, and since the family is one of the prime mediating structures (perhaps the prime one), this makes the church urgently relevant to public policy. Without falling into the trap of politicizing all of life, our point is that structures such as family, church, and neighborhood are all public institutions in the sense that they must be taken seriously in the ordering of the polity.

The church (here meaning all institutions of religion) is important not only to the family but also to families and individuals in neighborhoods and other associations. For example, the black community, both historically and at present, cannot be understood apart from the black church. Similarly, the much discussed ethnic community is in large part religiously defined, as are significant parts of American Jewry (sometimes, but not always, subsumed under the phenomenon of ethnicity). And of course the role of religion in small towns or rural communities needs no elaboration. In none of these instances should the religious influence be viewed as residual. Few institutions have demonstrated and continue to demonstrate perduring power comparable to that of religion. It seems that influence is residual only to the extent that the bias of secularizing culture and politics is determined to act as though it is residual. Again, these observations seem to us to be true quite apart from what we may or may not *wish* the influence of religion to be in American society. We are convinced that there is a profoundly antidemocratic prejudice in public policy discourse that ignores the role of religious institutions in the lives of most Americans.

In the public policy areas most relevant to this discussion—health, social welfare, education, and so on—the historical development of programs, ideas, and institutions is inseparable from the church. In some parts of the country, notably in the older cities of the Northeast, the great bulk of social welfare services function under religious auspices. For reasons to be discussed further in the next section, the religious character of these service agencies is being fast eroded. Where government agencies are not directly taking over areas previously serviced by religious institutions, such institutions are being turned into quasi-governmental agencies through the powers of funding, certification, licensing, and the like. The loss of religious and cultural distinctiveness is abetted also by the dynamics of professionalization within the religious institutions and by the failure of the churches either to support their agencies or to insist that public policy respect their distinctiveness. The corollary to the proposition that government responsibilities must be governmentally implemented—a proposition we challenge—is that public is the opposite of sectarian. In public policy discourse sectarian is usually used as a term of opprobrium for anything religious. We contend that this usage and the biases that support it undermine the celebration of distinctiveness essential to social pluralism.

. . .

Obviously all these questions touch on the complex of issues associated with separation of church and state. We believe, together with many scholars of jurisprudence, that the legal situation of church/state questions is today bogged down in conceptual confusions and practical contradictions. "The wall of separation between church and state" (Jefferson's phrase, not the Constitution's) is a myth long overdue for thorough rethinking. We are deeply committed to the religion clauses of the First Amendment. They should not be understood, however, as requiring absolute separationism; such absolute separationism is theoretically inconceivable and practically contrary to the past and present interaction of church and state. It is yet another of those grand abstractions that have had such a debilitating effect upon the way society's institutions relate to one another and upon the way in which people actually order their own lives.

In brief, "no establishment of religion" should mean that no religious institution is favored by the state over other religious institutions. "Free exercise of religion" should mean that no one is forced to practice or profess any religion against his will. Where there is neither favoritism nor coercion by the state there is no violation of the separation of church and state. While the subject is more complicated than suggested here, and while the courts will no doubt take time to disentangle themselves from the confusions into which they have been led, it is to be hoped that public policy will, in general, more nearly approximate "the Kurland rule" (named after Philip Kurland of the University of Chicago), namely, that if a policy furthers a legitimate secular purpose it is a matter of legal indifference whether or not that policy employs religious institutions. Clearly, this has far-ranging implications in the areas of education, child care, and social services generally.

. . .

From the beginning, we have emphasized the importance of mediating structures in generating and maintaining values. We have already discussed the function of the family in this connection. Within the family, and between the family and the larger society, the church is a primary agent for bearing and transmitting the operative values of our society. This is true not only in the sense that most Americans identify their most important values as being religious in character, but also in the sense that the values that inform our public discourse are inseparably related to specific religious traditions. In the absence of the church and other mediating structures that articulate these values, the result is not that the society is left without operative values; the result is that the state has an unchallenged monopoly on the generation and maintenance of values. Needless to say, we would find this a very unhappy condition indeed.

· · ·

It might be objected that leaving such a wide range of social services to religious and other voluntary associations would mean that the many people who did not belong to such groups would go unserved. The objection is revealed as specious, however, when it is recalled that public funds would be made available to almost every conceivable kind of group so long as it were prepared to carry out the public policy purpose. Such agencies might espouse one religion, all religions, or none. Almost everyone belongs to some group that can, with public funds, facilitate public policy in the area of social services. In truth, if we are really concerned for those individuals who fall between the cracks, it is worth noting that the most anomic individuals in our society, the denizens of skid row for example, are cared for almost exclusively by voluntary associations, usually religious in character. Government bureaucracies—indeed by definition, all bureaucracies—demonstrate little talent for helping the truly marginal who defy generalized categories. The Salvation Army needs no lessons from the state on how to be nonsectarian in its compassion for people. The raison d'être of the Salvation Army is seriously undercut, however, if its workers cannot preach to those to whom they minister.

· · ·

Voluntary Association

The discussion of the church leads logically to the subject of the voluntary association. Of course the church is—in addition to whatever else it may be—a voluntary association. But the category of voluntary association includes many other structures that can play a crucial mediating role in society.

There is a history of debate over what is meant by a voluntary association. For our present purposes, a voluntary association is a body of people who have voluntarily organized themselves in pursuit of particular goals. (Following common usage, we exclude business corporations and other primarily economic associations.) Important to the present discussion is the subject of volunteer service. Many voluntary associations have both paid and volunteer staffing. For our purposes, the crucial point is the free association of people for some collective purpose, the fact that they may pay some individuals for doing work to this end not being decisive.

At least since de Tocqueville the importance of voluntary associations in American democracy has been widely recognized. Voluntarism has flourished in America more than in any other Western society and it is reasonable to believe this may have something to do with American political institutions. Associations create statutes, elect officers, debate, vote courses of action, and otherwise serve as schools for democracy. However trivial, wrongheaded, or bizarre we may think the purpose of some associations to be, they nonetheless perform this vital function.

Apart from this political role, voluntary associations are enormously important for what they have actually done. Before the advent of the modern welfare state, almost everything in the realm of social services was under the aegis of voluntary associations, usually religious in character. Still today there are about 1,900 private colleges and universities, 4,600 private secondary schools, 3,600 voluntary hospitals, 6,000 museums, 1,100 orchestras, 5,500 libraries and no less than 29,000 nongovernmental welfare agencies. Of course not all of these are equally important as mediating structures. Orchestras and groups promoting stamp-collecting or the preservation of antique automobiles are, however important in other connections, outside our focus here. We are interested in one type within the vast array of voluntary associations—namely, associations that render social services relevant to recognized public responsibilities.

Assaults on voluntary associations come from several directions, from both the right and left of the political spectrum. Some condemn them as inefficient, corrupt, divisive, and even subversive. Many subscribe to the axiom that public services should not be under private control. From the far left comes the challenge that such associations supply mere palliatives, perpetuate the notion of charity, and otherwise manipulate people into acceptance of the status quo.

Such assaults are not merely verbal. They reflect a trend to establish a state monopoly over all organized activities that have to do with more than strictly private purposes. This trend has borne fruit in outright prohibition, in repressive taxation, and in the imposition of licensing and operating standards that have a punitive effect on nongovernmental agencies.

Of course there are instances of corruption and inefficiency in voluntary agencies. A comparison of governmental and nongovernmental social services on these scores, however, hardly supports the case for governmental monopoly. It should be obvious that government bureaucrats have a vested interest in maintaining and expanding government monopolies. Similarly, politicians have an interest in setting up services for which they can claim credit and over which they can exercise a degree of power. In short, social services in the modern welfare state are inescapably part of the political pork barrel.

Pork barrels may be necessary to political democracy. The problem confronting us arises when the vested interests in question use coercive state power to repress individual freedom, initiative, and social diversity. We are not impressed by the argument that this is necessary because voluntary associations often overlap with the functions of government agencies. Overlap may in fact provide creative competition, incentives for performance, and increased choice. But our more basic contention is against the notion that anything public must *ipso facto* be governmental. That notion is profoundly contrary to the American political tradition and is, in its consequences, antidemocratic. It creates clients of the state instead of free citizens. It stifles the initiative and responsibility essential to the life of the polity.

Our present problem is also closely linked with the trend toward professionalization. Whether in government or nongovernment agencies, professionals attack allegedly substandard services, and substandard generally means nonprofessional. Through organizations and lobbies, professionals increasingly persuade the state to legislate standards and certifications that hit voluntary associations hard, especially those given to employing volunteers. The end result is that the trend toward government monopoly operates in tandem with the trend toward professional monopoly over social services. The connection between such monopoly control and the actual quality of services delivered is doubtful indeed.

Professional standards are of course important in some areas. But they must be viewed with robust skepticism when expertise claims jurisdiction, as it were, over the way people run their own lives. Again, ordinary people are the best experts on themselves. Tutelage by certified experts is bad enough when exercised by persuasion—as, for example, when parents are so demoralized that they feel themselves incapable of raising their children without ongoing reference to child-raising experts. It is much worse, however, when such tutelage is imposed coercively. And, of course, lower-income people are most effectively disfranchised by the successful establishment of expert monopolies.

. . .

In protesting the use of labor and feminist rhetoric to camouflage the establishment of coercive monopolies and the disfranchisement of people in the running of their own lives, our position is neither anti-union nor anti-feminist. Who defines exploitation? We trust people to know when they are being exploited, without the benefit of instruction by professionals, labor organizers, or feminist authors. So long as voluntary work is genuinely voluntary—is undertaken by free choice—it should be cherished and not maligned. It is of enormous value in terms of both the useful activity offered to volunteers and the actual services rendered. In addition, because of their relative freedom from bureaucratic controls, voluntary associations are important laboratories of innovation in social services; and, of course, they sustain the expression of the rich pluralism of American life.

Attacks on the volunteer principle also aid the expansion of the kind of capitalist mentality that would put a dollar sign on everything on the grounds that only that which has a price tag has worth. We believe it proper and humane (as well as "human") that there be areas of life, including public life, in which there is not a dollar sign on everything. It is debilitating to our sense of polity to assume that only private life is to be governed by humane, nonpecuniary motives, while the rest of life is a matter of dog-eat-dog.

. . .

With the immense growth of knowledge and skills in modern society, professions are necessary and it is inevitable that there be organizations and unions to defend their interests. This development cannot be, and should not be, reversed. It can, however, be redirected. The purpose of the professions is to serve society—not the other way around. Too often professionals regard those they serve as clients in the rather unfortunate sense the Latin word originally implied. The clients of a Roman patrician were one step above his slaves in the social hierarchy, not entirely unlike some of today's servile dependents upon professionals. Such a notion has no place in democratic society.

Professionals should be ancillary to the people they serve. Upper-income people refer to "our" doctor or "my" doctor, and whatever patterns of dependency they develop are largely of their own choosing. It should be possible for lower-income people to use the possessive pronoun in referring to professionals.

The policy implications of our approach touch also on the role of nonprofit foundations in our society. Technically, there are different kinds of foundations—strictly private, publicly supported, operating, and so on—but the current assault applies to all of them. The argument is summed up in the words of the late Wright Patman whose crusade against foundations led to Title I of the Tax Reform Act of 1969:

Today I shall introduce a bill to end a gross inequity which this country and its citizens can no longer afford: the tax-exempt status of the so-called privately controlled charitable foundations, and their propensity for domination of business and accumulation of wealth. . . . Put most bluntly, philanthropy—one of mankind's more noble instincts—has been perverted into a vehicle for institutionalized deliberate evasion of fiscal and moral responsibility to the nation. (*Congressional Record,* August 6, 1969)

Of course, foundations have engaged in abuses that need to be curbed, but the resentment and hostility manifested by the curbers also needs to be curbed if we are not to harm the society very severely. The curbers of foundations make up an odd coalition. Right-wing forces are hostile to foundations because of their social experimentation (such as the Ford Foundation's programs among inner-city blacks), while others are hostile because of the role of big business ("the establishment") in funding foundations. The most dangerous part of the 1969 legislation is the new power given to the Internal Revenue Service to police foundation activities. The power to revoke or threaten to revoke tax exemption is a most effective instrument of control. (In recent years such threats have been made against religious organizations that opposed the Vietnam War and advocated sundry unpopular causes.) More ominous than the prospect that a few millionaires will get away with paying less taxes is the prospect of government control over officially disapproved advocacy or programs.

. . .

Massive bureaucratization, the proliferation of legal procedures that generate both public resentment and business for lawyers, the atrophying of the humane impulse, the increase of alienation—these would be some of the costs. Minimally, it should be public policy to encourage the voluntarism that, in our society, has at least slowed down these costs of modernity.

As always, the maximalist side of our approach—that is, using voluntary associations as agents of public policies—is more problematic than the minimalist. One thinks, for example, of the use of foster homes and halfway houses in the treatment and prevention of drug addiction, juvenile delinquency, and mental illness. There is reason to believe such approaches are both less costly and more effective than using bureaucratized megastructures (and their local outlets).

. . .

We well know that proposals for community participation are not new. The most obvious example is the Community Action Program CAP), a part of the War Against Poverty of the 1960s. CAP led to much disillusionment. Some condemned it as a mask for co-opting those who did, or might, threaten local power elites. Thus, community organizations were deprived of real potency and turned into government dependents. From the other side of the political spectrum, CAP was condemned for funding agitators and subversives. Yet others charged that CAP pitted community organizations against the institutions of representative government. To some extent these criticisms are mutually exclusive—they cannot all be true simultaneously. Yet no doubt all these things happened in various places in the 1960s.

That experience in no way invalidates the idea of community participation. First, the peculiar developments of the 1960s made that decade the worst possible time to try out the idea (and the same might be said about experiments in the community control of schools during the same period). Second, and much more important, the institutions used to facilitate community participation were not the actual institutions of the community but were created by those in charge of the program. This was especially true in inner-city black areas—the chief focus of the program—where religious institutions were, for the most part, neglected or even deliberately undercut. So, to some extent, were the family structures of the black community. In short, the program's failures resulted precisely from its failure to utilize existing mediating structures.

That said, it remains true that mediating structures can be co-opted by government, that they can become instruments of those interested in destroying rather than reforming American society, and that they can undermine the institutions of the formal polity. These are real risks. On the other side are the benefits described earlier. Together they constitute a major challenge to the political imagination.

Empowerment Through Pluralism

The theme of pluralism has recurred many times in this essay. This final section aims simply to tie up a few loose ends, to anticipate some objections to a public policy designed to sustain pluralism through mediating structures, and to underscore some facts of *American* society that suggest both the potentials and limitations of the approach advanced here.

. . .

This approach assumes that the process symbolized by "E Pluribus Unum" is not a zero-sum game. That is, the *unum* is not to be achieved at the expense of the *plures.* To put it positively, the national purpose indicated by the *unum* is precisely to sustain the *plures.* Of course there are tensions, and accommodations are necessary if the structures necessary to national existence are to be maintained. But in the art of pluralistic politics, such tensions are not to be eliminated but are to be welcomed as the catalysts of more imaginative accommodations. Public policy in the areas discussed in this essay has in recent decades, we believe, been too negative in its approach to the tensions of diversity and therefore too ready to impose uniform solutions on what are perceived as national social problems. In this approach, pluralism is viewed as an enemy of social policy planning rather than as a source of more diversified solutions to problems that are, after all, diversely caused and diversely defined.

Throughout this paper, we have emphasized that our proposal contains no animus toward those charged with designing and implementing social policy nor any indictment of their good intentions. The reasons for present pluralism-eroding policies are to be discovered in part in the very processes implicit in the metaphors of modernization, rationalization, and bureaucratization. The management mindset of the megastructure—whether of HEW, Sears Roebuck, or the AFL-CIO—is biased toward the unitary solution. The neat and comprehensive answer is impatient of "irrational" particularities and can only be forced to yield to greater nuance when it encounters resistance, whether from the economic market of consumer wants or from the political market of organized special interest groups. The challenge of public policy is to anticipate such resistance and, beyond that, to cast aside its adversary posture toward particularism and embrace as its goal the advancement of the multitude of particular interests that in fact constitute the common weal. Thus, far from denigrating social planning, our proposal challenges the policy maker with a much more complicated and exciting task than today's approach. Similarly, the self-esteem of the professional in all areas of social service is elevated when he or she defines the professional task in terms of being helpful and ancillary to people rather than in terms of creating a power monopoly whereby people become dependent clients.

· · ·

Throughout this essay we have frequently referred to democratic values and warned against their authoritarian and totalitarian alternatives. We are keenly aware of the limitations in any notion of "the people" actually exercising the *kratein,* the effective authority, in public policy. And we are keenly aware of how far the American polity is from demonstrating what is possible in the democratic idea. The result of political manipulation, media distortion, and the sheer weight of indifference is that the great majority of Americans have little or no political will, in the sense that term is used in democratic theory, on the great questions of domestic and international policy. Within the formal framework of democratic polity, these questions will perforce be answered by a more politicized elite. But it is precisely with respect to mediating structures that most people do have, in the most exact sense, a political will. On matters of family, church, neighborhood, hobbies, working place, and recreation, most people have a very clear idea of what is in their interest. If we are truly committed to the democratic process, it is *their* political will that public policy should be designed to empower. It may be lamentable that most Americans have no political will with respect to U.S. relations with Brazil, but that is hardly reason to undercut their very clear political will about how their children should be educated. Indeed policies that disable political will where it does exist preclude the development of political will where it does not now exist, thus further enfeebling the democratic process and opening the doors to its alternatives.

. . .

The subculture that envisages its values as universal and its style as cosmopolitan is no less a subculture for all that. The tribal patterns evident at an Upper West Side cocktail party are no less tribal than those evident at a Polish dance in Greenpoint, Brooklyn. That the former is produced by the interaction of people trying to transcend many particularisms simply results in a new, and not necessarily more interesting, particularism. People at the cocktail party may think of themselves as liberated, and indeed they may have elected to leave behind certain particularisms into which they were born. They have, in effect, elected a new particularism. *Liberation is not escape from particularity but discovery of the particularity that fits.* Elected particularities may include life style, ideology, friendships, place of residence, and so forth. Inherited particularities may include race, economic circumstance, region, religion, and in most cases, politics. Pluralism means the lively interaction among inherited particularities and, through election, the evolution of new particularities. The goal of public policy in a pluralistic society is to sustain as many particularities as possible, in the hope that most people will accept, discover, or devise one that fits.

. . .

But of *this* we are convinced: America has a singular opportunity to contest the predictions of the inevitability of mass society with its anomic individuals, alienated and impotent, excluded from the ordering of a polity that is no longer theirs. And we are convinced that mediating structures might be the agencies for a new empowerment of people in America's renewed experiment in democratic pluralism.

[1977]

from Strong Democracy: Participatory Politics for a New Age

CITIZENSHIP AND COMMUNITY: POLITICS AS SOCIAL BEING

> *There can be no patriotism without liberty; no liberty without virtue; no virtue without citizens; create citizens and you will have everything you need; without them, you will have nothing but debased slaves, from the rulers of the state downwards.* —Jean-Jacques Rousseau

> *But what is government itself but the greatest of all reflections on human nature?* —James Madison

> *The State of Civil Society is a state of nature. . . . Man's nature is Art.* —Edmund Burke

If government is but the greatest of all reflections on human nature and if, in Rousseau's inversion of Madison's claim, a people can be "no other than the nature of its government," then there is no better way to elucidate the difference between strong democracy and liberal democracy than by comparing how they portray human nature.[1] . . . We [have] examined the liberal portrait of human nature, which construed the human essence as radically individual and solitary, as hedonistic and prudential, and as social only to the extent required by the quest for preservation and liberty in an adversary world of scarcity.

This conception presented human behavior as necessarily self-seeking, albeit

---

1. Jean-Jacques Rousseau, *Confessions,* book 9. The full quotation reads: "I had come to see that everything was radically connected with politics, and that however one proceeded, no people would be other than the nature of its government."

in a premoral way. People entered into social relations only in order to exploit them for their own individual ends. Because modern liberal democracy is an accretion of democracy on a liberal philosophical base, American democratic theory has from its beginnings been weighted down by radical individualism. This association has created tensions within liberal democracy that, because they are rooted in conflicting notions of the human essence, cannot easily be resolved by politics. Marx took note of these tensions in the aftermath of the French Revolution. Rather than resurrecting freedom, he remarked, it produced a profound cleavage between man conceived as an individual member of civil society pursuing his private aims in conflict with others and man conceived as a citizen cooperating in "illusory" universals—namely, the "political state."[2]

In the *Grundrisse,* Marx offered an alternative construction of human nature as socially determined, a construction that links Aristotle to the modern sociological conception. "The human being," Marx wrote, "is in the most liberal sense a *zoön politikon,* not merely a gregarious *[geselliges]* animal, but an animal that can individuate itself only in the midst of society."[3]

The social construction of man is not, however, simply the antithesis of the individual construction formed in social-contract theory. It is dialectical, for it perceives an ongoing interaction by which world and man together shape each other.[4] Peter Berger and Thomas Luckmann capture the dialectic perfectly in this post-Marxist depiction of man's social nature: "Man is biologically predestined to construct and inhabit a world with others. This world becomes for him the dominant and definitive reality. Its limits are set by nature, but once constructed, this world acts back upon nature. In the dialectic between nature and the socially constructed

---

2. In *On the Jewish Question,* Marx writes:

> Where the political state has attained to its full development, man leads . . . a double existence—celestial and terrestrial. He lives in the *political community,* where he regards himself as a *communal being,* and in *civil society* where he acts simply as a *private individual,* treats other men as means, degrades himself to the role of a mere means, and becomes the plaything of alien powers. . . . Man . . . in civil society, is a profane being. . . . In the state, on the contrary, where he is regarded as a species-being, man is the imaginary member of an imaginary sovereignty, divested of his real, individual life, and infused with an unreal universality. (In Robert C. Tucker, ed., The Marx-Engels Reader [New York: Norton, 1972], p. 32.)

3. Karl Marx, *Grundrisse: Foundations of the Critique of Political Economy,* trans. M. Nicolaus (New York: Vintage Books, 1973), p. 84. In the better-known *Sixth Thesis on Feuerbach,* Marx and Engels wrote that "the human essence is no abstraction inherent in each single individual. In its reality it is the ensemble of social relations" (in Tucker, ed., *Reader, Theses on Feuerbach,* p. 109).

4. Continental existentialists typically commence the confrontation with human existence by presenting man as a "being-in-the world," which makes a much more useful starting point for political reflection. Heidegger's *Being at Time* thus explicitly associates the hyphenated man-in-the-world with the inescapable dialectic that links particular human nature to the character of being in general.

world the human organism itself is transformed. In this same dialectic, man produces reality and thereby produces himself."[5]

Strong democratic theory posits the social nature of human beings in the world and the dialectical interdependence of man and his government. As a consequence, it places human self-realization through mutual transformation at the center of the democratic process. Like the social reality it refracts, human nature is compound; it is potentially both benign and malevolent, both cooperative and antagonistic. Certain qualities enjoin a "degree of circumspection and distrust," as Madison prudently notes in *The Federalist Papers;* others may "justify a certain portion of esteem and confidence."[6] But all these qualities may be transformed by legitimate and illegitimate social and political forces. For man is a developmental animal—a creature with a compound and evolving telos whose ultimate destiny depends on how he interacts with those who share the same destiny. Such creatures possess neither fixed natures nor absolutely, independently grounded notions of reality and right. They seem rather to follow what Alexander Bickel has called the Whig model of political life. This model posits that human nature is "flexible, pragmatic, slow-moving, and highly political" and therefore that politics will be a process of "untidy accommodation."[7]

Political animals interact socially in ways that abstract morals and metaphysics cannot account for. Their virtue is of another order, although the theorists who have defended this claim have been called everything from realists to immoralists for their trouble. Yet Montaigne caught the very spirit of social man when he wrote, "the virtue assigned to the affairs of the world is a virtue with many bends, angles, and elbows, so as to join and adapt itself to human weakness; mixed and artificial, not straight, clean, constant or purely innocent."[8]

5. Peter L. Berger and Thomas Luckmann, *The Social Construction of Reality* (New York: Doubleday, 1966), p. 183. In his classic study *Community,* Robert MacIver makes the simple assertion: "Every individual is born into community and owes its life to community, . . . community is always there" ([London: Macmillan, 1917], p. 204).

6. James Madison et al., *Federalist Papers,* no. 55 (New York: Random House, 1937), p. 365. Hanna Pitkin offers a characterization of man that is completely in the spirit of the following discussion.

> Man is neither a species of organic being whose behavior is causally determined, like that of a river, nor an angel who always does what is right because it is right, independently of any needs, fears, or feelings. Politics is neither the greedy machinations of selfish power seekers nor the selfless pursuit of a higher good unrelated to purposes. Nor does the truth lie "somewhere in between." We are creatures who can be seen in . . . both of these seemingly incompatible ways; we are engaged in the continual, endless transformation of organic into moral, of instinct into authority . . . a continual translating of partial interest and private need into public decisions and authoritative structures. ("Inhuman Conduct and Unpolitical Theory," *Political Theory* 4, 3 [August 1976]: p. 136.)

7. Alexander Bickel, *The Morality of Consent* (New Haven: Yale University Press, 1975), p. 4.

8. Montaigne, "Of Vanity," in Donald M. Frame, ed., *The Complete Essays of Montaigne* (Stanford: Stanford University Press, 1965), p. 758.

If the human essence is social, then men and women have to choose not between independence or dependence but between citizenship or slavery. Without citizens, Rousseau warns, there will be neither free natural men nor satisfied solitaries—there will be "nothing but debased slaves, from the rulers of the state downwards."

To a strong democrat, Rousseau's assertion at the opening of his *Social Contract* that man is born free yet is everywhere in chains does not mean that man is free by nature but society enchains him.[9] It means rather that natural freedom is an abstraction, whereas dependency is the concrete human reality, and that the aim of politics must therefore be not to rescue natural freedom from politics but to invent and pursue artificial freedom within and through politics. Strong democracy aims not to disenthrall men but to legitimate their dependency by means of citizenship and to establish their political freedom by means of the democratic community.

In *Emile,* Rousseau wrote: "We are born weak, we need strength; we are born totally unprovided, we need aid; we are born stupid, we need judgment. Everything we do not have at our birth and which we need when we are grown is given us by education."[10] The corresponding political assertion would be: "We are born insufficient, we need cooperation; we are born with potential natures, we require society to realize them; we are born unequal, we need politics to make us equal; we are born part slave, part free, we can secure full liberty only through democratic community."

Citizenship and community are two aspects of a single political reality: men can only overcome their insufficiency and legitimize their dependency by forging a common consciousness. The road to autonomy leads through not around commonality. As George Bernard Shaw wrote: "When a man is at last brought face to face with himself by a brave individualism, he finds himself face to face, not with an individual, but with a species, and knows that to save himself he must save the race. He can have no life except a share in the life of the community."[11]

In this chapter we will examine both aspects of the civic relationship: (1) the democratic community, defined by the participation of free, active, self-governing citizens in the creation of their common future in the absence of independent grounds and (2) the democratic citizen as the participant in a self-governing democratic community. Then we will look at both the conditions that facilitate strong democratic citizenship and the limits that constrain it. The facilitating conditions include civic education, leadership, religion, and patriotism; the limits include the problem of scale, structural inequality, rights, and the ultimate uncertainty of all human vision—and of public vision in particular—in a

9. Jean-Jacques Rousseau, *The Social Contract,* book 1, chap. 1.

10. Jean-Jacques Rousseau, *Emile, or Education,* trans. Allan Bloom (New York: Basic Books, 1979), p. 38.

11. George Bernard Shaw, "Commentary on Ibsen's *Little Eyolf,*" in Shaw, *The Quintessence of Ibsenism* (New York: Hill and Wang, 1957), p. 130.

world where no knowledge is certain, no grounds absolute, and no political decision irrevocable.

Citizenship

If we accept the postulate that humans are social by nature, then we cannot regard citizenship as merely one among many artificial social roles that can be grafted onto man's natural solitariness. It is rather the only legitimate form that man's natural dependency can take. The civic bond is the sole legitimator of the indissoluble natural bond: it makes *voluntary* those ties that cannot in any case be undone, and it makes *common* and susceptible to mutuality the fate that is in any case shared by all men. As Aristotle noticed long ago, the civic bond is in fact the one bond that orders and governs all others—the bond that creates the public structure within which other more personal and private social relationships can flourish.

We can expand on these rather general considerations, first by relating them to the several distinct types of citizenship and then by seeing how the various forms of democracy answer the three questions that can be put to any theory of citizenship: what is the basis or grounds of citizenship? What are the character and the quality of the civic bond? And where does one place the boundaries of citizenship? The answers to these three questions will reveal how representative, unitary, and strong democracy view the origin, the nature, and the extent of the civic tie and will permit us to elucidate in full the strong democratic theory of citizenship.

The Grounds of Citizenship. In modern states, territory is generally regarded as the primary ground of citizenship. Nonetheless, a number of alternative grounds can also be extrapolated from the history of civic identity in the West. Among these are blood (as in the clan or tribe); personal fealty (as in early feudalism); proprietary jurisdiction (as in the feudalism of the High Middle Ages); common belief (as in early Christian communities or Augustine's City of God); economic contract (as in the Renaissance economic association *[Genossenschaft]* or Robert Nozick's "protective association"); political contract (as in the Mayflower Compact); and a commitment to common processes and common ends (as in such traditional face-to-face communes as the Alpine *Gemeinde* or the New England town).

The three kinds of modern democracy (representative, unitary, and strong) are all territorial in the fundamental legal sense, but each one is also inclined to accept a secondary and distinctive ground for civic identity (see Figure 1). Thus representative or thin democracy conceives the civic bond as an original contract that authorizes the sovereign to govern individuals, on their behalf and in their name. This citizenship is a function of an original and abstract authorship of the regime and consequently has a watchdog quality: it is passive rather than active, and it implies potentiality (abstract legal status) rather than actuality (concrete political status). To be a citizen is to be a party to the social contract and thus to be a legal person.

FIGURE I *Forms of Citizenship*

	Representative Democracy	Unitary Democracy	Strong Democracy
Citizens Conceived	legal persons	brothers	neighbors
Bound Together by	contract	blood	common participatory activity
Related to Government as	sovereign but also subject	corporate body	active participants
By Ties That Are	vertical (citizen to government)	horizontal (citizen to citizen)	dialectical ("levels" vanish)
Political Style	distrustful, passive	self-abnegating, submissive	cooperative, active
Civic Virtue	accountability (reciprocal control)	fraternity (reciprocal love and fear)	civility (reciprocal empathy and respect)
Status of Citizenship (vis-à-vis other social identities)	discretionary (one among many)	omnicompetent (the only permissible one)	sovereign (the first among equals)
Idea Ground (actual ground is territory)	common contract (generic consensus)	common beliefs, values, ends, identity (substantive consensus)	common talk, decision, work (creative consensus)

Unitary democracy scoffs at legal personhood as a lifeless fiction. It prefers to root citizenship in the much more vivid idea of blood: citizens are blood brothers united by a genetic (rather than a generic) consensus and bound together almost preternaturally—certainly not by choice or will. Pan-Slavism or Aryan nationalism or even Zionism may be taken as an example of such civic ideologies rooted in blood, where territory follows rather than precedes civic identity. (Modern Israel faces a civic quandary precisely because Zionist tendencies are at odds with its secular, territorial tendencies, so that the Israeli citizen is torn between the competing claims of Jewish birth and mission and the Israeli constitution and laws.)

Strong democracy places the democratic process itself at the center of its definition of citizenship. In this perspective, voluntary will is an active and continuing function of politics that becomes critical to the civic tie. Citizens are neighbors bound together neither by blood nor by contract but by their common concerns and common participation in the search for common solutions to common conflicts.

In actual democratic states, as one might expect, a compound notion of citizenship is at work: territory and birth are the condition of citizenship, whereas contract (the basis of governmental legitimacy), blood (the sense of a national culture), and common activity (practical politics as a process) give it its concrete character. Nevertheless, each form of democracy emphasizes a particular ideal ground and thereby endows its view of citizenship with a particular character. This point becomes increasingly convincing when we look more closely at the nature (as opposed to the grounds) of the civic tie.

The Character and Quality of the Civic Bond. As Figure I suggests, the three forms of democracy differ most sharply in their evaluations of the quality of the civic bond. From these differences emerge others that account for the forms' varying interpretations of ties to government, political style, civic virtue, and citizen relations.

In representative democracies such as the United States, citizens define themselves as legal persons and as autonomous parties to a sovereign compact. Their civic identities tie them not to one another but to the government, first as sovereign contracting parties, second as subjects or beneficiaries. The citizen is a citizen exclusively by virtue of his relationship to the government, of which he is both author and subject. His relations with his fellow citizens are entirely private and have nothing of the civic about them. This privatization helps to explain the fearsome civic anomie that has bereaved the Western democracies of almost all civility and has made representative democracy so hostile to the idea of communitarian ties among citizens.

It may also explain the civic climate—the political style—of passive distrust that has made America at once a bastion of private rights and a graveyard of public action. When the citizenry is a watchdog that waits with millennial patience for its government to make a false move but that submits passively to all other legitimate governmental activity, citizenship very quickly deteriorates into a latent function. Civic virtue remains, but it is a civic virtue that is defined by reciprocal control or *accountability.* Government is responsible to and for the body of citizens but is in no way comprised of that body. The chief device of accountability is representation itself, an institution that permits public watchdogs to spend most of their time pursuing their private business while functionaries and hirelings (delegates and representatives) minister to the public business.

Understood in this fashion, citizenship is only one of many roles available to individuals who live in a pluralistic society that assumes that all roles are roughly equal. "Citizen" becomes an identity on a par with "worker," "parent," "Catholic," or "commuter." It loses its ordering function (its "sovereignty") and its association with commonality and becomes synonymous with particularistic and mostly client-style roles, such as taxpayer, welfare recipient, special-interest advocate, or constituent. The very term *constituent* has been transmogrified from a noble word signifying constitutional author into a term for voter and thence into an almost derisive synonym for *client*—for the individual whom representatives must please and pacify in order to retain their offices.

Constituents of thin democracies are normally stirred into action only by constitutional crises and governmental defalcations; otherwise, they are content to leave the governing to others and to reserve their energies for the boundless private sphere. Aside from the occasional election, the infrequent letter to a congressperson, or the biennial media event of a political scandal, citizenship reduces to either an exercise in client relations or a political insurance policy—a powerful fire extinguisher that reads, "To be used only in cases of constitutional conflagration."

Unitary democracy has a quite different character. It manages to remedy (or to avoid) many of the weaknesses and defects of thin democracy, but its version of democratic citizenship introduces new and more alarming problems. Because citizens in a unitary state are bound together by powerful "personal" ties that, at least metaphorically, are "blood ties," they understand their citizenship as a function of their relations with their fellow citizens. The government embodies the unitary community created by these strong lateral ties—the citizen is the community, which is the state—and thus functions directly in the name of the citizenry. "I am Germany," Hitler might have said, "and Germany is the community of pure-blooded Aryans, so that when I act, Germany acts, which is to say each and every Aryan acts." The point is not that Hitler *represents* Germany or the Aryan community, but that he *is* Germany; for it is precisely the aim of unitary communities to bridge the chasm between individuals and to forge out of single persons one organic whole—the people or the nation or the Collective Will.

Where thin democracy makes accountability its primary virtue, unitary democracy celebrates the more active and inspirational ideal of fraternity as its primary virtue. This is perfectly in keeping with the lateral ties that characterize unitary civic relations. Under the best of conditions, fraternity enjoins mutual love and respect; under conditions of mass or totalistic society, however, it may motivate only through fear. Fraternity is certainly associated with a submissive political style, with a form of civic obligation that demands self-abnegation. The sociologist Durkheim thus cannot avoid concluding that in order for society to establish the rule of morals, the individual must "yield" to an authority higher than himself.[12] Goebbels, pursuing a

12. Emile Durkheim, *Moral Education* (Glencoe, Ill.: Free Press, 1961), p. 34.

much purer form of unitary community, proclaimed: "To be socialist is to submit the I to the thou; socialism is sacrificing the individual to the whole."[13] There is no Rousseauian dialectic here, in which by obeying others we obey only ourselves. Autonomy is sublimated; the political mode that results is sacrificial.

Associated with the political style of self-abnegation is the omnicompetence of the civic role. Whereas in thin democracy, citizenship is only one among many coequal social roles, in unitary democracy it is the only legitimate role. Other identities are not merely subordinate to it but utterly inconsequential compared to it. Thus can parents turn in their children as "traitors" in a unitary regime (that has democratic pretensions) such as Khomeini's Iran; thus are religion and art made to serve higher community goals in a revolutionary monolith such as the France of 1792; thus can money-making and childbearing be declared impious by a unitary sect such as the Shakers, where the religious-civic role is omnicompetent. In primitive unitary communities there is little need for actual force, because consensus is natural and the fraternal tie uncontested. But in larger, modern societies that have had some experience with multiple social identities and cleavages of interest, force becomes a necessary concomitant of civic omnicompetence.

Citizens in a unitary democracy need not fear the civic languor typical of thin democracy; but they face the still greater danger of an activist totalism. Where politics means too little to the privatized denizens of the representative system, it means far too much to the blood brothers of the organic community. On these latter, politics exerts a relentless pressure, and it leaves little of them behind as individuals. Such forms of politics are rightly feared by those who cherish liberty no less than community and who seek a form of public being that can preserve and enhance the autonomy of the participants.

Somewhere between the wan residualism of instrumentalist democracy and the omnicompetent totalism of unitary democracy lies the public realm of strong democratic politics. In this realm, citizenship is a dynamic relationship among strangers who are transformed into neighbors, whose commonality derives from expanding consciousness rather than geographical proximity. Because the sharp distinction that separates government and citizenry in representative systems is missing, the civic bond under strong democracy is neither vertical nor lateral but circular and dialectical. Individuals become involved in government by participating in the common institutions of self-government and become involved with one another by virtue of their common engagement in politics. They are united by the ties of common activity and common consciousness—ties that are willed rather than given by blood or heritage or prior consensus on beliefs and that thus depend for their preservation and growth on constant commitment and ongoing political activity. Such latent virtues as accountability permit common ties to wither,

13. Joseph Goebbels, cited in Erich Fromm, *Escape from Freedom* (New York: Rinehart, 1941), p. 223.

whereas virtues as powerful and unitary as fraternity make ties rigid and immutable and place them beyond the pale of individual volition.

The political style that emerges from this dialectic of common association is one of activity and cooperation, and the civic virtue that distinguishes that style from other styles is civility itself. Strong democracy promotes reciprocal empathy and mutual respect, whereas unitary democracy promotes reciprocal love and fear and thin democracy promotes reciprocal control. Civility is rooted in the idea that consciousness is a socially conditioned intelligence that takes into account the reality of other consciousnesses operating in a shared world. As Michael Oakeshott has suggested, civility assumes free agents who are roughly equal, not necessarily by nature or right but by virtue of their shared consciousness. Oakeshott writes of citizens: "*Cives* are not neurophysiological organisms, genetic characters, psychological egos or components of a 'social process,' but 'free' agents whose responses to one another's actions and utterances is one of understanding; and civil association is not an organic, evolutionary, teleological, functional, or syndromic relationship but an understood relationship of intelligent agents."[14]

It is neither in time nor in space but in the imagination that strong democratic citizens become "neighbors." Theirs is the neighborhood of creative consciousness struggling with material conflicts, in which the necessity that outcomes be commonly conceived disciplines the adversary competition of the divided and plural present.

The civic role here is not omnicompetent or exclusionary, but neither is it merely one among many roles. It is primus inter pares. Citizenship is not necessarily the highest or the best identity that an individual may assume, but it is the moral identity par excellence. For it is as citizen that the individual confronts the Other and adjusts his own life plans to the dictates of a shared world. *I* am a creature of need and want; *we* are a moral body whose existence depends on the common ordering of individual needs and wants into a single vision of the future in which all can share. The citizen does not define civic wants and needs; he develops common measures by which private wants and needs can be transformed into public goods and ends.

To return to the point from which we started: the ideal ground of thin democracy is *generic consensus*—a common contract that authorizes a sovereign, who is accountable to the contractees, to provide for their interests. James Buchanan thus describes democratic government as an efficient means of achieving our individual objectives.[15] The ideal ground of unitary democracy is *substantive consensus*—common beliefs, values, and ends that precede government and predefine the

---

14. Michael Oakeshott, *On Human Conduct* (Oxford: Clarendon Press, 1975), p. 112. It is ironic that conservative thinkers such as Oakeshott have developed the idea of civility with considerably more conviction than have democrats—who one might think would benefit from this line of thinking.

15. A democratic approach, Buchanan writes, "is merely a variant on the definitional norm for individualism. Each man counts for one, and that is that. . . . A situation is judged 'good' to the extent that it

community in and through which individuals can realize themselves (these selves being defined by the community). And the ideal ground of strong democracy is *creative consensus* — an agreement that arises out of common talk, common decision, and common work but that is premised on citizens' active and perennial participation in the transformation of conflict through the creation of common consciousness and political judgment.

Evidently, the fact that all modern democratic regimes base their definition of citizenship on territory is of little consequence when set against these remarkable differences in their conceptions of civic relations, ideal grounds, civic virtue, and political style. These differences, of course, do little more than reflect and enhance the sharp fundamental differences between the three types of democracy.

The Boundaries of Citizenship. If territoriality seems the obvious common ground of all modern forms of democratic citizenship, then universality appears to be the obvious common response to the question of the extent or boundaries of citizenship in modern democracies. It is indeed true that every modern form of democracy claims to extend the civic franchise to "all" or to "all human beings" or to "all members of the community." Yet that "all" is always conditional, and "universal" always refers to some particular universe with its own presumptive boundaries. There was a sense in which Aristotle endorsed universal citizenship for the entire human community — for each and every *zoön politikon* resident in the polis. But of course Aristotle did not count women, or slaves, or barbarians as fully human. Because they were incomplete, something less than *zoön politikon,* Aristotle could bar these individuals from the polis without compromising the ideal of "universal citizenship." Few tyrannies that have wanted to march under the banner of democracy have been unable to reconcile theoretical universality with the most arbitrarily restrictive civic practices — simply by ruling women or blacks or Jews or even the poor (Locke's "quarrelsome and contentious") out of the human race.[16]

Moreover, even those who most zealously honor the principle of universality find themselves bending the abstract boundaries of the biological species when dealing with the civic role of children, criminals, the insane, and "foreigners." Boundaries also tend to give way when one tries to sort out competing levels of citizenship (federal versus state versus local, or example) or overlapping civic responsibilities (national versus international obligations, for example).

The principle of universality conceals more than it reveals about the boundaries

---

allows individuals to get what they want to get, whatsoever this might be, limited only by the principle of mutual agreement. Individual freedom becomes the overriding objective for social policy" (*The Limits of Liberty: Between Anarchy and Leviathan* [Chicago: University of Chicago Press, 1975], p. 2).

16. Commentators from Rousseau to C. B. Macpherson have pointed to the inegalitarian implications of Locke's distinction between the "Industrious and the Rational," for whose use God gave the world, and the "Quarrelsome and Contentious" who — it would seem to follow — are entitled neither to property nor to citizenship (in chap. 5 ["On Property"] of the *Second Treatise of Civil Government*).

of citizenship. Apparently, a more precise and pertinent test must be found, one that will determine *how* boundaries are drawn rather than *where* they are drawn; for how boundaries are drawn affects not only where they are drawn but also how flexible or rigid, how reasonable or arbitrary, and how self-governing or independently grounded they are.

When one begins to ask how boundaries are determined instead of what those boundaries are, important distinctions become apparent. Representative democracy seems to posit a generic standard embodied in a fixed constitution; unitary democracy seems to posit a substantive standard embodied in a fixed identity; and strong democracy seems to posit a procedural standard embodied in a notion of dynamic activity. In other words, in representative systems the extent of citizenship is a function of *what we agree to* and thus a matter of contract; in unitary systems it is a function of *what or who we are* and thus a matter of identity; and in strong democratic systems it is a function of *what we do* and thus a matter of activity. In the third case the point is not that those who are citizens participate in self-governance but that those who participate in self-governance are citizens of a polity in which participation is open, access to self-governance is unobstructed, and participatory institutions are generally available. Of the three, this alternative would seem to be the least exclusionary, although it is also the most prone to ambiguity and thus to perversion and abuse.

Constitutional definitions of citizenship that are based on generic consensus can exclude from participation as many kinds of people (women or slaves or non-property owners, for example) as the consensus chooses to proscribe, but those who do count as parties to the contract receive firm guarantees of a permanent and inviolable citizenship, regardless of performance, as it were. The standard is inflexible and may in its origin be discriminatory, but it is unimpeachable. Unitary democracy is also capable of generic exclusion—of excluding those who do not fit into the substantive community or *volk* or tribe identity that is the basis of citizenship. ("All Aryans are members of the German Nation and thus citizens of the National Socialist State, therefore Jews cannot be German citizens.") But unitary democracy also guarantees a certain irrevocable citizenship to those with the correct identity. In both representative and unitary democracy, the independent ground that allegedly gives politics an incorrigible, nonpolitical base also legitimates the drawing of civic boundaries.

Eschewing all independent grounds, strong democracy cannot develop arguments that exclude particular sets or classes of human beings from potential membership in the polity because they do not conform to a prior standard (such as a contract rooted in right and the binding character of all promises). The scope of citizenship itself becomes a subject for ongoing democratic discussion and review, and one's participation in such discussion becomes a brief for inclusion. This procedural conception has a welcome openness and dynamism, but it introduces dangers of a kind to which both representative and unitary democracy are immune. For instance, if activity is a measure of citizenship, will the lethargic, the apathetic, and the alienated be excluded, as Hannah Arendt seems to believe? Or do they exclude themselves and suffer defacto servitude even where their civic identity is constitutionally certified or unconditionally attested to by the blood that runs in their veins?

If citizenship is not a constant but instead a function of changing attitudes and historical activity, would not transient majorities, made powerful and intolerant precisely by the aggressive activity that signifies their civic legitimacy, have limitless opportunities to exclude the weak and disadvantaged? Because activity is power, the powerful will always have a special claim on activity. If the idea of open citizenship is not to become a one-way door through which undesirables are continuously ejected, it must be conditioned by the premise of biological universality. This concept maintains that every biological human being is potentially a citizen and that, consequently, the burden of proof must always be on the would-be excluders rather than on those who favor inclusion. Moreover, an excluded individual or class must automatically be reincluded in the absence of a conscious and determinate renewal of the exclusion (i.e., a "sunset" provision that limits every temporary exclusion).

Given the importance of active participation to the definition of citizenship itself, the autonomous individual would seem to enjoy a "right" of citizenship that he can forfeit only by his own action—which is to say, by his own inaction—and then only temporarily. This "right" is political rather than natural; it is created by the polity rather than prior to it. Children may be incapable of political action and so disqualified from citizenship, but they remain potential citizens and need only await the awakening of their political senses to claim their "rights." Criminals, as criminals, forfeit their citizenship not because they revert to the "state of nature" where any man may kill them (Hobbes), or because they shed their tribal identity by contravening the mores of the tribe (the true Aryan will not steal from the Fatherland), but because they have ceased to engage in talk, deliberation, and common action and have substituted private force for public thinking. If this definition enlarges the pale of criminality, it nonetheless displays a beneficence toward the criminal, who may reclaim his civic identity (if not necessarily his freedom from incarceration) merely by forswearing force and reengaging in dialogue. By the same token, immigrants in a strong democratic regime acquire the right to vote as they acquire the ability and will to participate.

This discussion should make it evident that the American idea of citizenship incorporates elements of each of the three civic formulas. A contractual element informs the legal conception of citizenship (the American as a person at law); a communal element lies behind the national conception of citizenship (the American as a native-born Yankee); and an activist element supports the civic conception of citizenship used in devising standards for "new" citizens (the American as a literate, participating actor). Consequently, the argument for strong democracy suggests not that we substitute civic participation for the traditional legal and national definitions of citizenship but that we give greater prominence to the role of civic activity. Measured by national identity and by the standard of the constitution, there are more than a hundred million American citizens. Of these, however, most are passive, apathetic, inactive, and generally uninterested in things public. As Robert Lane has pointed out, a great majority of Americans count government (and the civic identity it entails) as a very small part of their "life satisfaction"—Lane's figure is 5 percent. Indeed, according to Lane, "Most people are unable to state how government affects their lives at all."[17] In the language of this book, this finding means that most people have no sense of themselves as citizens.

Definitions of citizenship that do not include a measure of political activity may seem wan and unconvincing; the citizen who does not engage in civic activity is at best a citizen *in posse*—the watchdog we have learned to know so well from thin democracy's prudent obsession with accountability and control. Unfortunately, the legal and communal definitions of citizenship have let sovereignty fall way from the American idea of civic identity and have replaced it with a sociological pluralism that makes every identity—the civic one included—the competitive equal of every other. But civic activity, though omnicompetent only in unitary democracy, stands in lexical priority to all social activities in strong democracy. Because it is public it orders and guides all forms of private activity. These private forms may be more valuable and precious than civic activity, but they are nonetheless only possible in a framework of public seeing and within a workable public order.

If to make the civic role sovereign over other forms of identity resolves the problem of the relationship of public to private, it leaves open—indeed, it complicates—the problem of the relationship among the various levels of "public" activity. How do we rank neighborhood and national citizenship? Aristotle's principle of "the higher, the more sovereign" would suggest that national takes priority over municipal. But the fact that concrete local participation is greater and more intense than abstract national participation might suggest an inversion of those priorities. Certainly in practice the two levels seem to be in competition—at least as to how each would handle many particular political issues such as taxation, economic redistribution, educational opportunity, and so forth. The ideal solution is to bring the intimacy and intensity of local political engagement to the highest level of association while bringing some of the power of central government down to the neighborhood level. Some of the institutions portrayed in the next chapter aspire to do just this. In practice, however, the tension will remain and the commitment to intense engagement and vigorous participation will yield a more local and restricted measure for ideal citizenship than the commitment to sovereignty and to the all-seeing character of true public vision. As with telescopes, the higher the level of magnification, the dimmer the vision; as the compass of the public enlarges, our capacity to see publicly is diminished. The ideal of the

17. Robert Lane, "Government and Self-Esteem," *Political Theory* 10, 1 (February 1982), pp. 7–8.

world citizen is a splendid one, but the world citizen reaches the limits of public vision and seems to vanish beyond the pale into darkness. Finally, this is the problem of scale, which we shall review shortly as one of the several limits on strong democracy.

Strong Democratic Community

If we were trying here only to construct a typology, we might advance the discussion of strong democratic community by proceeding analytically (enumerating key conceptual distinctions) or by listing ideal types (identifying clusters of concepts around logical or historical archetypes). We could use the analytic category of hierarchy to distinguish hegemonic from egalitarian communities; of ascriptive identity to distinguish status-ordered from voluntaristic communities; of mutability over time to distinguish static from dynamic communities; of scale to distinguish small-scale or face-to-face communities from large or impersonal communities; of jurisdiction to distinguish personal from territorial communities; and of grounding values or beliefs to distinguish spiritual from secular communities. Each of these contrasts suggests the dimensions along which the communal character of particular societies might be measured. Thus, the Swiss town of Glarus in the fourteenth century would appear as predominantly egalitarian, voluntaristic, dynamic, small-scale, territorial, and secular. The Holy Roman Empire of the German nation would look hegemonic, ascriptive, static, large-scale, personal, and ecclesiastic.

Historians and political anthropologists more often approach a subject by seeking clusters of characteristics that define types or ideal types because such types correspond more readily with historical experience and its organizing categories. The "feudal corporation," the "tribal society," the "Renaissance city," the "community of true believers," the "modern bureaucratic state," or Ferdinand Tonnies's *Gemeinschaft* and *Gesellschaft* are not simply examples of clusters of communal traits; they are recurring archetypes in the history of man's social organization and of his theories about that organization.

But typology is not the aim here. Rather, we are attempting to clarify the notion of community as an aspect of the representative, the unitary, and the strong theories of democracy and of the forms of citizenship we have associated with these theories. It quickly becomes apparent that as when they discuss democracy itself, democratic theorists too often see community in terms of neat antitheses. On the one hand, the liberal democrat's purely voluntaristic community is an aggregate of interest-seeking individuals. These make up at best (in de Tocqueville's phrase) "a motley multitude" that pays for equality with conformity and mediocrity and that is free only because it is anomic and tied together by no significant social bonds whatsoever. On the other hand, the traditionalist's consensual community is bound together, in Robert Nisbet's words, by "affection, friendship, prestige and recognition" and nourished by "work, love, prayer, devotion to freedom and order."[18] This conservative notion of community, favored by sociologists who wear the Burkean mantle, makes the radically antidemocratic claim that "inequality is the essence of the social bond.[19] This claim not only polarizes egalitarianism and communitarianism but also explodes the integral notion of democracy itself as a theory of citizenship.

Thus the radically individualistic community is populated by competitors whose commonality is understood as nothing more than an "efficient means of achieving individual objectives,"[20] whereas in the organic community of status and hierarchy the individual is altogether sublimated. These two rough caricatures in fact can serve nicely as models of the archetypical thin democratic community and of the archetypical unitary democratic community. The middle ground (strong democracy) is omitted. In the first case, the community of citizens results wholly from a social contract and owes its existence and its legitimacy to the voluntary consent of a self-constituted aggregation of individuals seeking the preservation of their lives, liberties, properties, and happiness. In the second case, the community is bound together by existential ties that define and limit the individual members no less than the community to which they belong. These ties, because they are primarily affective, historical, and unchosen, create a structure that can be hegemonic and inegalitarian. Although it does guarantee a place to every member, such a community often subverts equality.

Neither of these two alternatives offers a satisfactory picture of democratic community. The first commits the fallacy of aggregation, presupposing that a community represents *only* the characteristics of its constituent parts. The second commits the fallacy of organicism, presupposing that a community represents *none* of the characteristics of its constituent parts. Thus, the thin liberal community lacks any semblance of public character and might better be called a multilateral bargaining association, a buyer-seller cooperative, or a life-insurance society. It eschews every advantage of affect, historical continuity, and common vision; it is, in typical reductionist fashion, a collection rather than a collectivity. By contrast, the traditional hegemonic community achieves the integral and public character missing in thin democratic communities—but only by bartering away autonomy and equality. The vision of self-government by a community of equals is not well served by either of these versions of community.

In a strong democratic community, our third alternative, the individual members are transformed, through their participation in common seeing and common work, into citizens. Citizens are autonomous persons whom participation endows with a capacity for common vision. A community of citizens owes the character

---

18. Robert A. Nisbet, *The Quest for Community* (Oxford: Oxford University Press, 1953), p. 50.

19. Robert A. Nisbet, *The Twilight of Authority* (New York: Oxford University Press, 1975), p. 217.

20. Buchanan, *Limits*, p. 2.

of its existence to what its constituent members have in common and therefore cannot be treated as a mere aggregation of individuals. The strong democratic community is not (at least initially) an association of friends, because the civic tie is a product of conflict and inadequacy rather than of consensus. But that community cannot remain an association of strangers because its activities transform men and their interests.

What is crucial about democratic community is that, as Rousseau understood, it "produces a remarkable change in man"; that is to say, through participation in it, man's "faculties are exercised and developed, his ideas broadened, his feelings ennobled, and his whole soul elevated."[21] Thin democratic community leaves men as it finds them, because it demands of men only the self-interested bargain and of community only that it provide and protect market mechanisms. Unitary community creates a common force, but it does so by destroying autonomy and individuality altogether. In the first instance, individuals are left alone; in the second, they are extirpated. Only in strong democratic community are individuals transformed. Their autonomy is preserved because their vision of their own freedom and interest has been enlarged to include others; and their obedience to the common force is rendered legitimate because their enlarged vision enables them to perceive in the common force the working of their own wills.

The perspective of the citizen and of the community, joined in Rousseau's account, are nonetheless distinct. Each serves the other, but conditions independent of the individual have a great effect on citizenship. Traditional democratic theorists have devoted much attention to these conditions, and with good reason. Some of the conditions support democracy, or are even prerequisites to it; these can be called *facilitating* conditions. Others are obstructive or *limiting* conditions. Among the former are civic education, leadership, and *moeurs,* which lend institutional support to integrative and affective values that issue naturally from patriotism, public culture, philosophy, and religion and that are indispensable to the creation and survival of cohesive communities. Among the limiting conditions are the problem of scale, the persistence of structural socioeconomic inequality, and the ultimate uncertainty of public vision.

The Facilitating Conditions of Citizenship

Given the intractability of dissensus and the problematic character of even the strongest democratic institutions, most theorists have sought support for democracy in second-order facilitating institutions. The challenge they have faced is how to contrive institutions that facilitate democracy without supplanting it and that

21. Jean-Jacques Rousseau, *The Social Contract,* book 1, chap. 8.

enhance participation without making it unnecessary.[22] The danger is that the nurturing of affective ties will impede genuine cognitive debate and that the enhancement of empathetic imagination will corrupt the capacity for moral autonomy. Thus a civil religion that is too powerful will impose consensus on individuals before they have time to perceive and assess their individuality and to identify the legitimate claims that arise out of it. Or a binding set of values encapsulated as patriotism can forge a people so uniform in their interests that conflict or dissent of any kind becomes tantamount to treason. Leadership that arouses popular feelings but preempts civic activity suffocates participation. The challenge facing strong democratic theory is to elaborate institutions that can catalyze community without undermining citizenship. With this goal in mind, we will survey typical supporting institutions, starting with civic education.

Civic Education. Civic education for democracy can take at least three pertinent forms: formal pedagogy (institutional schooling in civics, history, and citizenship); private-sphere social activity; and participatory politics itself.[23]

Formal pedagogy, understood as formal socialization into the political community, is probably most useful as a training device for unitary democracy and least useful for strong democracy. A basic knowledge of the nation's constitution and legal system, of its political history and institutions, and of its culture and political practice is obviously indispensable to democracy in any form. But there is no necessary correlation between educational training and political or moral judgment, although there is a connection between knowledge and civic aptitude. The American system takes some responsibility for the procedural aspects of civic education through its election laws, equal-time provisions for the media, and enforcement of the Bill of Rights; but it seems little concerned to provide education on substantive issues. Like most other public responsibilities, this crucial function is left largely in private hands.

Strong democracy, in any case, relies less on formal civic education: knowing your rights and knowing the law are concomitants first of all of minimalist or weak democratic politics. In the strong democratic perspective, knowledge and the quest for knowledge tend to follow rather than to precede political engagement: give people some significant power and they will quickly appreciate the need for knowledge, but foist knowledge on them without giving them responsibility and they will display only indifference.

Local public or small-scale private activity seems to be vital to civic education

22. This is the problem Rousseau faces in books 3 and 4 of *The Social Contract*. He tries to give the procedural devices of the General Will the support of customs and mores, but these customs and mores suggest a form of unitary consensus that is inimical to genuine democratic politics.

23. I am concerned here with conscious forms of learning and of political experience rather than with "political socialization"—a phrase preferred by many political scientists but that I find both too general and too biased in favor of environmentalist answers to crucial questions of will.

in all three forms of modern democracy. It promotes affective links that support unitary democracy, measures of judgment useful to representative institutions, and forms of public thinking essential to strong democracy. De Tocqueville saw in local institutions and voluntary associations a key to national democracy in America: "Municipal institutions constitute the strength of free nations. Town meetings are to liberty what primary schools are to science; they bring it within the people's reach, they teach men how to use and enjoy it. A nation may establish a free government, but without municipal institutions it cannot have the spirit of liberty."[24]

Like de Tocqueville, many modern advocates of "mediating structures" and intermediate associations argue that voluntary associations, church groups, and the family have an important democratic effect in guiding the elephantine nation-state and in giving a palpable local expression to the idea of national citizenship. Peter Berger and Richard Neuhaus see in such mediating institutions the only instruments of "empowerment" that can oppose the pervasive alienating effect of modern centrist politics.[25]

Local institutions can indeed be a crucial training ground for democracy. But to the extent that they are privatistic, or parochial, or particularistic, they will also undermine democracy. Parochialism enhances the immediate tie between neighbors by separating them from alien "others," but it thereby subverts the wider ties required by democracy—ties that can be nurtured only by an expanding imagination bound to no particular sect or fraternity.

Strong democracy creates a continuum of activity that stretches from the neighborhood to the nation—from private to public—and along which the consciousness of participating citizens can expand. "As soon as you are obliged to see with another's eyes," wrote Rousseau in *Emile,* "you must will what he wills."[26] The circle of common volition is only as wide as the circle of common perception; if perception and imagination can be made to grow progressively as the result of common activities, parochialism can be overcome. Participants who are active simultaneously in a local church, a municipal community board, a national service corps, a grass-roots political organization, and a national referendum campaign

24. Alexis de Tocqueville, *Democracy in America* (New York: Vintage Books, 1960), vol. 1, p. 63. Elsewhere in his classic study, he argues: "Civil associations, therefore, facilitate political association. . . . [A] political association draws a number of individuals at the same time out of their own circle; however they may be naturally kept asunder by age, mind, and fortune, it places them nearer together and brings them into contact" (vol. 2, pp. 123–24).

25. "One of the most debilitating results of modernization is a feeling of powerlessness in the face of institutions controlled by those whom we do not know and whose values we often do not share. . . . [T]he mediating structures under discussion here are the principal expressions of the real values and the real needs of people in our society. . . . [P]ublic policy should recognize, respect, and, where possible, empower these institutions" (Peter L. Berger and Richard John Neuhaus, *To Empower People: The Role of Mediating Structures in Public Policy* [Washington, D.C.: American Enterprise Institute, 1977], p. 7).

26. Rousseau, *Emile,* book 2.

are more likely than a church deacon or a senator to perceive their activities as overlapping and mutually reinforcing.

Finally, however, only direct political participation—activity that is explicitly public—is a completely successful form of civic education for democracy. The politically edifying influence of participation has been noted a thousand times since first Rousseau and then Mill and de Tocqueville suggested that democracy was best taught by practicing it. De Tocqueville argued that participation could at a single stroke solve two problems. It could interest people in citizenship even though liberty demanded such an "arduous" apprenticeship, and it could educate them to prudent self-government even when they comprised an "unfit multitude." Of the first problem—made famous by Oscar Wilde's complaint about the number of free evenings that could be taken up in the quest to become a good socialist—de Tocqueville wrote: "I maintain that the most powerful and perhaps the only means that we still possess of interesting men in the welfare of their country is to make them partakers in the government. . . . civic zeal seems to me to be inseparable from the exercise of political right."[27] Too often liberals have had it both ways: life is supposed to be a "ceaseless search for power after power unto death," yet men for the most part supposedly have little interest in civic participation. Of course when participation is neutered by being separated from power, then civic action will be only a game and its rewards will seem childish to women and men of the world; they will prefer to spend their time in the "real" pursuit of private interests. But, as the Hobbesian phrase suggests, most citizens will care for participation because it alone gives them power over their lives.

In addressing the problem of motivation, de Tocqueville also responds to the question of motive. The most frequent complaint lodged against democracy has been the unfitness of the masses to rule. De Tocqueville acknowledges the point: "It is incontestable," he begins, "that the people frequently conduct public business very badly." Yet he continues: "It is impossible that the lower orders should take a part in public business without extending the circles of their ideas and quitting the ordinary routines of their thoughts. The humblest individual who cooperates in the government of society acquires a certain degree of self-respect . . . he is canvassed by a multitude of applicants and in seeking to deceive him in a thousand ways, they really enlighten him."[28]

False consciousness appears here as the road to political consciousness, because those who attempt to manipulate the popular will in fact help to inform it. As the Age of Populism proved, the rhetoric of self-government is hard to contain. And once implanted, self-respect is difficult to "use," because self-respect entails a new way of seeing oneself and the world. Lawrence Goodwyn, in his brilliant portrait of American populism, writes: "Populism is the story of how a large number of

27. De Tocqueville, *Democracy*, vol. 1, p. 252.
28. Ibid., pp. 260–61.

people, through a gradual process of self-education that grew out of their cooper-ative efforts, developed a new interpretation of their society and new political in-stitutions to give expression to these interpretations. Their new ideas grew out of their new self-respect."[29]

It has generally been recognized that the political wisdom of representative statesmen and politicians is determined in large part by the extent of their political experience. Why should it be different with citizens? To rule well they need first to rule. To exercise responsibility prudently they must be given responsibility. Faith in democracy requires a belief neither in the benevolence of abstract human character nor in the historical altruism of democratic man. Altruists do not need government. What is required is nothing more than a faith in the democratizing effects that political participation has on men, a faith not in what men are but in what democracy makes them. Strong democrats need be no more sanguine about man's *natural* capacity for self-government than was the skeptical Madison. Un-like Madison, however, they suspect that empowerment renders men artificially responsible, just as the art of politics means confrontation with the myriad others with whom a common world must be shared.

Liberal democracy makes government accountable, but it does not make women and men powerful. It thrusts latent responsibilities on them while at the same time insisting that they keep a wholly passive watch over their treasured rights. For this self-contradictory form of popular government there can be no ad-equate preparation and no fit education. Strong democracy alone seems capable of educating by practice and thus of preserving and enhancing democracy.

[1998]

29. Lawrence Goodwyn, *Democratic Promise: The Populist Movement in America* (New York: Oxford University Press, 1976), p. 88. Peter Dennis Bathory draws out the implications that Goodwyn's and de Tocqueville's arguments have for leadership in his *Leadership in America* (New York: Longman, 1978), pp. 39–59.

from Free Spaces: The Sources of Democratic Change in America

In 1849, one of Herman Melville's characters in his novel *Mardi* presented to the people of Vivenza—the United States—a document that reminded them "freedom is more social than political," meant to suggest that democracy depended upon the virtue and intelligence of the citizens themselves. In outrage, the Vivenzans shredded the document. The book's dismal sales in the mid-nineteenth century seemed to Melville a disgusting confirmation of his warning. Today, the same idea sounds to some a distant echo from the past.[1]

"Democracy" is a term used frequently and with little content. American Presidents like Ronald Reagan, who, shortly after his election, declared to the British Parliament his intention to launch a program to spread "democracy throughout the world," invoke it to separate the "free world" from "communist totalitarianism." The idea of citizenship, however, was entirely missing from the President's discussion of democracy. Yet, as Sheldon Wolin has observed, "the silence on the subject is not peculiar to conservatives or reactionaries. . . . Most Marxists are interested in the 'masses' or the workers, but they dismiss citizenship as a bourgeois conceit, formal and empty." The problem has a simple source. Notions of active citizenship and the common good have all but disappeared from our modern vocabulary because we have come to define the arenas in which active citizenship is nourished and given meaning as entirely outside of "politics" and "public life."[2]

More than thirty years ago, Baker Brownell, a philosophy professor at Northwestern University who had been involved in a number of community development projects, wrote a book entitled *The Human Community*. It polemicized

---

1. The story of Melville is from Larzer Ziff, "Landlessness: Melville and the Democratic Hero," *democracy* 1 (July 1981): 130–31.

2. Sheldon Wolin, "What Revolutionary Action Means Today," *democracy* 2 (Fall 1982): 18.

angrily against the academic world from which he came. "Truth is more than a report," said Brownell. "It is an organization of values. Efficiency is more than a machine; it is a human consequence." Captivated by technique, procedure, method, and specialization, Brownell argued, the educated middle class had lost sight of actual face-to-face relations—the actual life of communities themselves—which create the most important criteria for judging any innovation or change. "It is the persistent assumption of those who are influential . . . that large-scale organization and contemporary urban culture can somehow provide suitable substitutes for the values of the human communities that they destroy," he declared. "For want of a better word I call these persons 'the educated' professionals, professors, businessmen, generals, scientists, bureaucrats, publicists, politicians, etc. They may be capitalist or they may be Communist in their affiliations, Christian or Jew, American, English, German, Russian or French. But below these relatively superficial variations among the 'educated' there is a deeper affiliation. They are affiliated in the abstract, anonymous, vastly expensive culture of the modern city."[3]

Brownell stated the case starkly. He largely neglected motivations other than a narrowly individualist search for power and achievement that leads people away from settled communities.[4] And he paid little attention to the enormous complexity of community life. Ties of place, gender, memory, kinship, work, ethnicity, value and religious belief, and many other bonds may in different contexts be sources of communal solidarity or of fragmentation. Communities can be open, evolving, and changing—or static, parochial, defensive, and rigid. They can

---

3. Baker Brownell, *The Human Community* (New York: Harper, 1953), pp. 135, 19–20.

4. In particular, Brownell neglected what Robert Bellah and others have termed the "expressive individualist" strain in American culture that is embodied in much therapeutic language—notions that the basic commitments and purposes of one's life come through the search for *self-realization* and self expression. The focus on expressive individualism in American culture, especially as it has melded with consumerism and high rates of mobility and the like, may have contributed to the weakening of what Bellah and his associates call "communities of memory and hope," more stable, continuous sets of relationships characteristic of working-class (and, interestingly, in different terms, upper-class) life. But at times it is also the source of creative intellectual and artistic energy—much of the protean American spirit that is so attractive to other peoples in the world. And the fusion of expressive individualist and communal themes in free spaces gives public life a remarkable dynamism and vitality. The effort to balance communal commitments and individual expression has informed some of the richest explorations of the meaning of democracy. Thus, for instance, for D. H. Lawrence, "the first great purpose of Democracy" was for each to be "spontaneously" themselves; "each man himself, each women herself. . . . None shall try to determine the being of any other." But Lawrence defined "freedom" in terms sharply different from contemporary cultural radicals who marginalize communal ties. Humans are free, he argued, "only when they belong to a living, organic, believing community." Simple individualism for Lawrence led to commercialism, sex without relationship, and death of the spirit. Lawrence quoted in Raymond Williams, *Culture and Society* (New York: Harper Torchbooks, 1972), pp. 208–10, 212.

Robert Bellah et al., *Habits of the Heart: Individualism and Commitment in American Life* (Berkeley: University of California Press, 1985), especially chap. 11.

encourage new roles for those traditionally marginalized or powerless within their midst, or they can reinforce patterns of exclusivity and parochialism. Without attention to the specific features and processes that democratize community life, any invocation of communal values is prey to telling criticisms of sentimentality and naïveté.

Despite the complexity of communities, however, Brownell accurately identified an intellectual stance that has characterized thought across the political and social spectrum. Close-knit communities where people live in multidimensional relations with one another—what is called *Gemeinschaft* in social theory—are thought to give way with "progress" to relations based on reason, functional identities like work and profession, and voluntarily conceived association. As a result, conventional approaches marginalize or ignore particular identities of all sorts. As Arthur Schlesinger put it in 1949, "Modern technology created free society, but created it at the expense of the protective tissues which had bound together feudal society. . . . New social structures must succeed where the ancient jurisdictions of the family, the clan and the guild and nation-state have failed." Marshal Berman's celebration of the modernist sensibility in 1982, *All That Is Solid Melts into Air,* conveys the same message. "He [modern man, personified in figures like Goethe's *Faust*] won't be able to create anything unless he's prepared to let everything go, to accept the fact that all that has been created up to now—and, indeed, all that he may create in the future—must be destroyed to pave the way for more creation. This is the dialectic that modern man must embrace in order to move and live."[5]

From a democratic perspective, more is lost through the eclipse of community than a sense of belonging and secure identity. Citizenship itself disappears from view. And the very arenas where it is nourished and given meaning—communally grounded voluntary associations of the sort we have called, throughout this work, free spaces—are defined simply as bulwarks of order and the status quo. Such a perspective, for instance, characterizes much of contemporary conservatism.

Neoconservative thought has as its central theme a reassertion of the importance of voluntary associations and communally based groupings like family, religious congregations, and neighborhoods. These are said to stand between, or "mediate," the private world of the individual and the "public" world of large institutions like bureaucracy, profession, trade union, and corporation.

The intellectual roots of neoconservatism lie in the 1950s, when social critics like Robert Nisbet argued that totalitarianism depends upon the elimination of voluntary and autonomous communal ties of all sorts. Even the most innocuous, like musical clubs, were outlawed by the Nazi government, for example, because they were organized "for purposes, however innocent, that did not reflect those of the central government." Current theorists like Peter Berger, drawing on such

---

5. Arthur Schlesinger, *The Vital Center* (Cambridge, Mass.: Houghton Mifflin, 1949), pp. 4, 51; Marshall Berman, *All That Is Solid Melts into Air: The Experience of Modernity* (New York: Simon & Schuster, 1982), p. 48.

work, have maintained that communal groups create a bulwark against the discontents and dangers of modern life. "The best defenses against the threat are those institutions, however weakened, which still give a measure of stability to private life. These are, precisely, the mediating institutions, notably those of family, church, voluntary association, neighborhood and subculture."[6]

But in Berger's perspective, like that of other neoconservatives, such smaller-scale settings are seen entirely in static, narrow, and defensive ways. For order and stability, one must have a generally accepted pattern of "morality," and such morality can only be taught effectively through experiences close to home. "Without mediating structures, the political order is [unsettled] by being deprived of the moral foundation upon which it rests." Thus, Berger sees change and social upheaval as a function of the weakness or disappearance of community institutions. Such a solely defensive perspective, ironically, produces a political and social vision which contributes to the erosion of the very community institutions neoconservatives purport to support. In a view like Berger's, every community is ultimately left on its own. Government become simply "the problem." And the marketplace and acquisitive individualism become the measure of "public" life. Such a perspective offers no model of collective action to regain control over massive economic dislocations, from plant closings to toxic waste dumps, nor any notion of how different communities might join together to pursue a common good.[7]

In mainstream liberal and left-wing thought, as well as neoconservative approaches, the emphasis has been on the ways voluntary associations and communal ties undergird and stabilize the status quo. Douglas Kellner summarized the usual argument: "[Dominant] ideology is transmitted through an ideological apparatus consisting of the family, school, church, media, workplace and social group." Thus, the left tends to see the delegitimization of such associations as the necessary prerequisite for progressive action. The notion of the collectivity is a solidarity based upon rational association by "masses": individuals whose ties to their communal roots of place, religion, ethnicity, and so forth have become sundered. The good social order is imagined, as John Rawls recently put it, as "a voluntary scheme [whose] members are autonomous and the obligations they recognize self-imposed." Such a vision of abstractly conceived individuals, in turn, is easily absorbed into an abstract "public" realm, defined as the state.[8]

Thus, a fascinating convergence of views, left and right, about such voluntary groups exists. Conservatives believed in defending voluntary, autonomous groups

6. Robert A. Nisbet, "The Total Community," in Marvin E. Olsen, ed., *Power in Societies* (New York: Macmillan, 1970), p. 423; Peter Berger, *Facing Up to Modernity: Excursions in Society, Politics and Religion* (New York: Basic Books, 1977), p. 134.

7. Berger, p. 135.

8. Douglas Kellner, "Ideology, Marxism and Advanced Capitalism," *Socialist Review* 42 (1978): 53; John Rawls, *A Theory of Justice* (New York: Oxford University Press, 1972), p. 13.

against the force of the modern state (though they slighted capitalism's impact on such structures). Radicals have tended to see their disruption as necessary for the creation of cosmopolitan consciousness. But both traditions have defined such institutions as bulwarks of the existing order.

Thinkers on both sides overlook the dynamic character of communal spaces. Under certain conditions, communal associations become free spaces, breeding grounds for democratic change. Indeed, the historical evidence now suggests that popular movements with enduring power and depth always find their strength in community-based associations. As sociologist Craig Calhoun has put it, "communities give people the 'interests' for which they will risk their lives—family, friends, customary crafts, and ways of life."[9]

Thus, for instance, the new labor history demonstrates clearly that people draw upon a range of ethnic, kinship, religious, and other traditional relations in fighting back and in developing a collective consciousness: even within the factory, people are never merely "workers," and other aspects of their identities prove centrally important. In turn, capitalist development has, indeed, fragmented such identities, distancing workplace from community life. Such fragmentation has reinforced and facilitated the growth of large-scale, bureaucratized unions and political parties, which normally work carefully within the framework of the system and see their members largely as clients, not active participants. One strong theme in democratic movements, as we approach the present day, in fact, has thus been the repair and revitalization of memories, communal ties, and voluntary associations weakened by modern corporate and bureaucratic institutions. The labor protests of the 1930s, the civil rights movement of the 1960s, and the farm workers' movements of recent years all have had, as an essential component, "bringing our country back to the wells of democracy," as Martin Luther King described the purpose of the sit-in demonstrators.

Our concern in *Free Spaces* has been to understand the ways in which the defensive and limited impulses which spark most social protests, especially in their early stages, can be transformed into democratic initiatives. What are the features of the environments in which people discover their capacities to overcome deferential

9. Craig Calhoun, "The Radicalism of Tradition: Community Strength or Venerable Disguise and Borrowed Language?," *The American Journal of Sociology* 88 (March 1983): 898. Throughout *Free Spaces* "community" is intended as a concept suggesting density and texture of a relationship. Thus, though community in this sense most often has a spatial dimension—a "neighborhood" implication— such a dimension is not part of the definition; rather, communal ties depend on a complex set of social relationships that overlap and reinforce each other. Craig Calhoun has characterized community in these terms as meaning a "greater 'closeness' of relations" than is true for society as a whole. "This closeness seems to imply, though not rigidly, face-to-face contact, commonality of purpose, familiarity and dependability," Craig Calhoun, "Community: Toward a Variable Conceptualization for Comparative Research," *Social History* 5 (January 1980): 111.

patterns of behavior, outgrow parochialisms of class, race, or sex, and form a broader conception of the common good? How do people develop new visions in which elements of tradition become resources for democratic activity?

In the course of *democratic* movements, as a people move into action, they change. They discover in themselves and in their ways of life new democratic potentials. They find out new political facts about the world. They build networks and seek contacts with other groups of the powerless to forge a broader group identity. In turn, for such processes to occur requires more than local, communal roots. Such spaces must also be relatively autonomous, free from elite control.

Thus, the *voluntary* aspect of such community environments is an important element. Unstructured by the imperatives of large and bureaucratic organizations, communal groups that people own themselves allow them to rework ideas and themes from the dominant culture in ways which bring forth hidden and potentially subversive dimensions. Thus, black churches have served as the organizational and visionary heart of the movement from slavery to civil rights. There, black ministers were able to draw on insurgent, populist themes within the very Christian tradition that had been taught to slaves as a method of pacification.

Some social spaces have a long history of autonomy. Within them, collective action seems almost as natural as breathing. Groups which have had little experience of collective strength and self-confidence, however, remain vulnerable to manipulation by demagogic appeals. Their democratic self-consciousness—not only of themselves but of themselves in egalitarian relation to other powerless groups—is weak. Among lower-class southern whites, for example, where voluntary associations and communal life remained largely under elite control, movement culture in the Knights of Labor or the populist cooperatives depended upon newly created free spaces. The defeat of these movements, in large part because of successful elite manipulation of racist traditions in the South, cut off a historical process of self-discovery that had only begun. By contrast, where free social spaces were deeply embedded in community life—as in the Richmond black community—the Knights of Labor served as a catalyst to bring the mobilized power of the community onto a stage of broader action.

With the emergence of enormous institutions of government and economic life in the twentieth century, the difficulties in maintaining autonomy have taken new form. Government programs, the lure of subsidies, commercialized packaging of candidates, corporate grants, the mass media—all such pressures can severely erode the freedom of action and initiative possessed by voluntary associations, and can obscure the broader civic and democratic implications of civic involvement. Yet in the very different environment of 1960s activism, young organizers at times also gained an understanding of the need for free space that recalled the insights of activists a century or more earlier. Casey Hayden, a young white southerner who spent years working in the civil rights movement, argued in 1965:

I think we've learned a few things about building and sustaining a radical movement: People need institutions that belong to them, that they can experiment with and shape. In that process it's possible to develop new forms for activity which can provide new models for how people can work together so participants can think radically about how society could operate. People stay involved and working when they can see the actual results of their thought and work in the organization. . . . [10]

Finally, movements also require means for developing a broader public vision and sense of the common good. While certain forms of older divisions, like ethnic cleavages, may no longer be as sharply etched, new problems stand in the way of any broader sense of community. Many traditional public meeting places, from village town square to neighborhood grocer, have largely disappeared. Citizens have few ways to talk about public values and purposes across their immediate lines of friendship and private life. On the one hand, in "normal" times mass culture imposes a chilling silence on public discussion. Politics resembles a "marketplace" where citizens become consumers and are encouraged to think of themselves in the most narrowly self-interested of terms. On the other hand, in time of widespread social unrest like the 1960s, the weakening of deep communities and communal discourse can lead to a rapid commercialization and trivialization of protest, where "media stars" and rapidly shifting political fashion replace deliberation and responsible democratic politics.[11]

Communal roots and independence are insufficient to generate Walt Whitman's large-spirited and generous citizenry. Indeed, authoritarian and parochial protests—the Ku Klux Klan, book burnings, religiously bigoted movements and the like—also emerge from communal settings where people have capacities for independent action. Thus, democratic action today, as in the past, also depends upon an open and participatory public life that can bring together diverse communities and nourish the values of citizenship. The richness and vitality of public life in free spaces stands in marked contrast to the static and thin quality of "public" in reactionary protests.

"The reabsorption of government by the citizens of a democratic community," Lewis Mumford once wrote, "is the only safeguard against those bureaucratic

---

10. Quoted in Sara M. Evans, *Personal Politics: The Roots of Women's Liberation in the Civil Rights Movement and the New Left* (New York: Knopf, 1978), p. 125.

11. Todd Gitlin examines this phenomenon in detail in his work on the student movement, *The Whole World Is Watching: Mass Media in the Making and Unmaking of the New Left* (Berkeley: University of California Press, 1980). "The media brings a manufactured public world into private space," Gitlin argues. "From within their private crevices, people find themselves relying on the media for concepts, for images . . . for guiding information, for emotional charges, for a recognition of public values, for symbols in general, even for language" (pp. 1–2). Gitlin, however, neglects the role of free spaces as an intermediate place between private identities and large-scale institutions. When free space has deep roots in ongoing "communities of memory and hope"—as in the black church base of the civil rights movement, for example—movements are much more resistant to media fads and rapidly changing fashions, and the possibilities for serious alternative media are far greater.

interventions that tend to arise in every state." Democratic movements have always expressed this sensibility—in contrast to the conventional assumptions that "public" and "government" are virtually identical. They have seen government as properly the agency and instrument of the self-organized community, neither itself the problem (as conservative ideology tends to view it) nor the solution (the typical perspective of modern liberalism). Thus, for instance, as the nineteenth-century Knights of Labor engaged in electoral activity, they understood such involvement to be an *expression* of values and community life, not as an end in itself.[12]

For a well-developed consciousness of broader community and generalized, active citizenship to emerge requires ways for people to build direct, face-to-face and egalitarian relationships, beyond their immediate circles of friends and smaller communities. Thus, a prelude to democratic movement, visible in different times and settings, has been the emergence of avenues for wider sociability. From the Hicksite Quakers and female abolition networks to benevolent societies in Richmond's black community or the large-scale ethnic associations in Steelton which laid the groundwork for the steelworkers' unionization, such associations create a consciousness that many people can act together. Moreover, when public arenas that allow active participation become politicized in the context of changing conditions, they offer broad opportunities for the acquisition and development of basic skills of public life. People learn to speak in public, run meetings, analyze problems and their sources, write leaflets, and so forth—the sorts of skills that are essential to sustaining democracy.

As democratic movements develop, they create movement institutions and networks that generate still more inclusive understandings of "the people." The Women's Christian Temperance Union, the Knights of Labor, and the Farmers' Alliances in the nineteenth century found counterparts in the twentieth-century movement institutions such as the CIO in the 1930s, the Southern Christian Leadership Conference, and the Students for a Democratic Society in the 1960s. The public life that emerges out of such networks constitutes an alternative movement culture, an identifying feature of democratic movements. Movement cultures have been visible in the lecture circuits, newspapers, and mass encampments of the 1890s Populists, the celebrations, labor press, and labor education schools of the 1930s, the Freedom schools of civil rights, and the alternative institutions of the women's movement, alike. In movement cultures, a newly open and vital intellectual life takes hold. Alternative media, like newspapers, magazines, and movement schools, offer forums for new ideas and an ongoing process of movement education. Diversity and difference may help people simultaneously to experiment with novel and unorthodox ideas and to think differently about their histories and traditions. They unearth buried insurgent elements in their own traditions, find out new facts about the world, debate alternatives, develop a vision of the common good that transcends limited and particular interests.

12. Lewis Mumford, *The Condition of Man* (New York: Harcourt, 1951), p. 282.

The nature of free social space also shapes specific leadership styles, with powerful consequences for social movements. From the time of slavery, the black church served as the training ground for black leaders, creating a unique, powerful, and largely male rhetorical style. The charismatic tones of the preacher, from Andrew Bryan to Jesse Jackson, have led hundreds of diverse struggles. Yet the dispersed nature of black churches and religious associations also guaranteed the constant production of new leaders, curbing in some ways the antidemocratic dimensions of charisma. By way of contrast, populist movements, whose underlying culture had little opportunity to develop such strengths, proved vulnerable to the manipulation of a long line of southern demagogues, from Ben Tillman to George Wallace.

Leaders have played crucial roles in articulating the democratic and empowering threads within the American ideological heritage. Republicanism and the biblical themes of justice, community, and equality have provided democratic resources for an extraordinary range of movements. At the same time, such traditions also provide the ideological underpinning of antidemocratic impulse. For example, the right-wing version of republicanism justifies unbridled economic individualism and greed, just as biblical themes can be used by those who advocate racial and sexual subordination. The appropriation of democratic possibility depends on the collective experience we have identified with free social spaces. Simply, democratic ideas only make sense in the context of democratic experience. When people begin to see in themselves the capacity to end their own hurts, to take control of their lives, they gain the capacity to tap the democratic resources in their heritage. Thus, workers drew on biblical, artisanal, and republican traditions throughout the nineteenth century and on ethnic cultures shaped to the new environments of urban, industrial America. The separation of home and work spaces made the existence of community institutions such as taverns, churches, reading rooms, clubs, and other groups all the more essential in order to create a vocabulary in opposition to the emerging industrial order, with its focus on individual achievement and consumption. That women were excluded from most of these spaces, that few environments permitted much cross-cultural sharing, that republican traditions themselves were filled with contradictions—all represented limitations on democracy.

The richness and complexity of these processes has become apparent to a new generation of social historians, exploring the lives and experiences of those whom traditional historical approaches largely overlooked. As Gerda Lerner noted some time ago, "The very term 'Women's History' calls attention to the fact that something is missing from historical scholarship, and it aims to document and reinterpret that which is missing."[13]

But the broader implications have yet to be explored in detail. Conventional

13. Gerda Lerner, *The Majority Finds Its Past: Placing Women in History* (New York: Oxford University Press, 1979), pp. xiv.

social-science approaches to the study of social movements normally assume that there is no analytical difference between democratic and nondemocratic movements and thus manage to obliterate the issue. Even when the question of democratic participation is posed, themes of citizenship, "citizenship education," and the common good are rarely explored. Conservatives and leftists, convinced that the communal associations of daily life represent bulwarks of the status quo, fail to see the sources of democratic change. None of these perspectives can comprehend the tragedy built into the logic of many social movements throughout modern history. As social movement leaders over time became distanced from the communal foundations of democratic revolt, and adopted dominant categories and vocabularies of change that rendered the experiences in such foundations largely invisible, they often forgot or dismissed the very histories that had shaped them, thus hastening the process of bureaucratization and incorporation of protest into the language and terms of modern, centralized authority.

Yet the processes of communal transformation that generate democratic change continue to grow in modern America, sometimes despite great difficulties. These "experiments in democracy" regenerate community and create a space linking public activity and private identities that also has an integrity and specific existence of its own. They maintain some measure of autonomy, and revive notions of citizenship and civic virtue. Most free spaces remain embedded in the institutions of daily life: voluntary groups, religious congregations, union locals, schools, neighborhoods. Others represent new experiments, redefining communities and asking new questions about the past. Whether their insurgent and visionary possibilities will be realized remains impossible to predict, but it is important to recognize the existence of these free spaces, and to develop an understanding of democracy that appreciates their crucial role in reviving active citizenship and conceptions of the common good.

A public housing project in St. Louis provides one dramatic example of community renewal leading to broadened forms of civic involvement. This area in St. Louis is perhaps most famous for Pruitt Iago, a housing project so violent, filthy, and damaged that the city decided to blow up the buildings, erasing its existence. Cochran Gardens was an older project in the same area of the city, also a high-rise, with many of the same problems. By the 1960s, its tenants were all black and the city housing authority had virtually abandoned its maintenance responsibilities. Terrorism by youthful gangs, alcoholics, and drug addicts shaped tenants' lives. Killings were common. Graffiti covered the walls, and elevators reeked of urine. Social workers, service companies, even the police feared to go there. Cochran Gardens was a prime candidate for demolition.

Yet today Cochran Gardens is meticulously clean. Its twelve-story high-rise buildings have been renovated according to plans developed by committees of residents working with architects and planners. Playgrounds were moved, for example, to locations that could be observed from within the apartments. A senior-citizens' building has its own small enclosed play area for visiting grandchildren. Green grass and flowerbeds have replaced dirt, mud, and broken glass. Hallways are always freshly swept, each family taking their allotted turn.

Behind these surface evidences of order and mutual respect lies the story of a community that reclaimed itself. Today Cochran Gardens is tenant-run. A tenant manager lives in each building. Tenant councils decide and enforce policies for admission, standards of behavior, and plans for the future. Tenants run several day-care centers, programs to bring together the elderly and the young, food service companies to provide meals for seniors and day-care, a security service, and a new community center. It all started when Bertha Gilkey, herself a young mother on welfare who had grown up in Cochran Gardens, began to organize in a single building. Their first victory was the installation of a laundry washer in an abandoned first-floor apartment. They celebrated with a ribbon cutting and party. Then she organized tenants, floor by floor, to paint their hallways. Gilkey remembered the days when Cochran was a safe and clean and friendly place to live. She was determined to convey that memory, and to see tenants gain control over those forces which had rendered them helpless and dependent. As people began to win specific victories, looking to each other for strength and support, they came to share the vision. And their participation led to active involvement with other poor communities around the country.

Bertha Gilkey now serves as national co-chair of the National Congress of Neighborhood Women, a different kind of experiment. An organization of women in an ethnic, blue-collar area of Brooklyn with affiliates in several cities, the National Congress has consistently avoided taking stands on issues which many see as basic to feminism as conventionally conceived, such as the Equal Rights Amendment and abortion. It began in 1974 when Jan Peterson and other feminists sought to extend the women's movement to working-class and poor women in a manner that would respect their high commitment to neighborhood and family.[14]

As the organization became ethnically more diverse and began to place a positive value on that diversity, organizers developed a sharing process which extends in new directions the notion that "the personal is political." At NCNW meetings and conferences, "identity groups"—defined as participants choose to do so—meet to discuss the meaning of their shared heritage, both the hard parts and the positive dimensions. Each group then presents to the whole what they would like others to know about themselves and their culture. The result is a series of histories: the spiritual values of traditional Lakota culture and their long history of resistance against the loss of their land, their hunting economy, and their sacred places; the racial diversity of Puerto Rico and the importance of Spanish as a mother tongue; the experiences of Italian immigrants on Ellis Island; the historic strength of black women in their communities. And in each case there is also an

14. Gilkey story taken from Harry C. Boyte, *Community Is Possible: Repairing America's Roots* (New York: Harper, 1984), pp. 95–113.

explanation of the pain caused by stereotyping: the Mafia jokes, the blame heaped on "black matriarchs," the combination of romanticism and disrespect for Native Americans in our popular culture. The impact for many participants is a rediscovery of the bonds among women in a context which does not require the shedding of other identities. For Bertha Gilkey, involvement in the National Congress revealed the feminist dimension of her work. Most of the residents in Cockran Gardens are women. The movement they organized was led by women, and today women occupy most positions of leadership. This recognition also broadened their sense of who could be their allies.[15]

The growth of numerous neighborhood and citizen efforts in recent years that transcend barriers of parochialism, defensiveness, and powerlessness are other instances of free space. The reclaiming and redefinition of citizen participation in public life is evident, for instance, in what has come to be called "value-based community organizing." This method adapts participatory understandings of democracy to the dilemmas of modern culture and the era of large-scale institutions like government and corporations, recognizing as problematic such terms as "community," "tradition," and "public life." In recent years, such groups as the Communities Organized for Public Service in San Antonio, East Brooklyn Churches, the San Francisco Organizing Project, and others have linked particular issues of concern to their members with extensive processes of community renewal, value discussion, and "citizenship education."

Ernesto Cortes, the first organizer of Communities Organized for Public Service (COPS), distinguished between "self-interest" and "narrow self-interest," or "selfishness." He argued that people's basic concerns are not only financial or narrowly for themselves but also include communal ties such as the happiness of their families, the well-being of their neighbors and friends, the vitality of their faith and their traditions, and their own feelings of dignity and worth. Workshops that Cortes and others in COPS have conducted reflect on the communal and civic values people learn from American democratic traditions, their churches and neighborhoods—participation, pluralism, civic involvement, the dignity of the individual, equality, community, love of neighbor, concern for poor. People talk about the ways in which such values are constantly undermined by the dominant principles of corporations, large bureaucracies, and the mass culture. And COPS combines such value and ideological discussion with a tremendously detailed process of what they call "citizenship education," teaching tens of thousands of people the basics of running meetings, analyzing problems, dealing with the press, conducting research, and planning campaigns around the issues.

15. Sara Evans interviews with leaders and participants in National Congress of Neighborhood Women: Marie Bueno, Brooklyn, N.Y., Apr. 4, 1983; Jan Peterson, Brooklyn, N.Y., Apr. 19, 1983, Jan Kowalsky, Brooklyn, N.Y., Apr. 20, 1983; Alice Quinn, Brooklyn, N.Y., Apr. 20, 1983; Sally Martino Fisher, Brooklyn, N.Y., Apr. 21, 1983; Francine Moccio, Brooklyn, N.Y., Apr. 21, 1983.

COPS defines itself as a new sort of "public arena" that in many ways is self-conscious of the dimensions of "free space." COPS sees itself reflecting the values of the democratic tradition and the Judeo-Christian heritage, and it advances the concrete needs of families, neighborhoods, congregations, and individuals. But it also takes on an independent life of its own, different from private life, on the one hand, or large "public" institutions, on the other hand. Though it intervenes with remarkable effectiveness in the political process—COPS has won more than $400 million in community development projects in the Mexican communities, mounting an extraordinary challenge to traditional political and economic elites in the process—it makes a clear distinction between its notion of political involvement and "politics as usual." COPS, according to Cortes, "is like a university where people come to learn about public policy, public discourse, and public life."[16]

The result has been not only material changes in the barrios but also changes in mood and spirit. Leaders speak about the "cultural changes" they have seen, as people have come to value the broader community good and ask what areas of town are most in need of aid. Young people increasingly remain, rather than fleeing for the northern areas of town. Women have taken on unprecedented leadership roles, including the last several presidencies of the organization. Individual congregations have seen a democratization of their internal life, with lay leaders emerging in every aspect. This sort of activity, making affirmation of democratic values integral to its definition, begins to repair bonds that have been gravely weakened by mass culture and economic pressure.[17]

The COPS model of community renewal, citizenship, and cultural revitalization has begun to have significant impact elsewhere in the organizing world. For example, the San Francisco Organizing Project (SFOP) has applied such techniques to the heterogeneous communities of the Bay Area. The organizing effort began with in-depth community renewal and work on issues in specific congregations, community groups, and labor union locals. In parishes like St. Elizabeth's, for example, a largely white ethnic area in the southeast section of the city, congregation members were trained to interview residents in the neighborhood about their concerns and problems, whether or not they were Catholic. Through such interviews they developed a detailed sense of community issues and created ties to people who were all but invisible. Workshops on values gave people a unique chance to talk to others, often for the first time in any public setting, about what had been troubling them. "One day, we had fifty people show up for a brainstorming session that lasted five hours," related one woman. "We talked about what we believe in—our families, neighborhoods, love, respect for each other, being tolerant. And we talked about what threatened those values. Large corporations. How much of society today is being run by media hype. How can you bombard children with all of this and not have them buy into it?" For some months people held such

16. Harry C. Boyte interview with Ernesto Cortes, San Antonio, Texas, July 3, 1983.
17. COPS impact described in Boyte, *Community*, chap. 5.

discussions and others on concrete organizational skills, and combined them with work on particular issues like the uses of an abandoned school building. Then the parish held a large convention. It recognized and celebrated different groups in the community, and made decisions about priority areas for action.[18]

This kind of organizing process not only involved traditional community "activists," but as in the case of COPS and similar groups, it built directly upon the core leaders involved in sustaining and renewing community life. These are the people—often women—who work, frequently behind the scenes, to keep the PTAs going, to organize block parties, to run children's sports activities, and so forth. Value-based organizing gives such community leaders new skills, support, and public recognition, changing the very definitions of "leadership" and "public" in the process. Moreover, in the context of a pluralist and diversified organizing effort like SFOP's, such organizing introduces people to other communities in ways that allow serious dialogue.

Nationally, citizen initiatives have now resulted in efforts like Citizen Action, a diverse coalition of community, labor union, senior citizen, rural, environmental, and other groups which defines itself as a "new democratic populism." Since its formation in late 1979, Citizen Action has developed a presence in twenty-five states, and has played a key organizing role in campaigns from toxic waste and farm foreclosure to energy prices and plant shutdowns. Indeed, the changing economic and political environment of the 1980s has tended to generate this sort of larger-scale coalition, in ways that may presage the formation of new citizen movements. "It's a very different time than when I started out organizing ten years ago," recounted Robert Hudak, Citizen Action's field director, in 1985. "In the 1970s, if your community group had a problem you'd go to the county board. They made a decision and it made a difference in people's lives." But Hudak had seen a rapidly growing recognition that coalitions are the only possible way to win against intransigent opposition. "You take a local dump site activist who's been concerned about kids being poisoned by toxic waste. They go to the bureaucracy and get a runaround. It's very easy for them to understand that the only way this sort of problem is really going to be solved is if the government clamps down on corporations and establishes a cleanup fund."[19]

In sum, the historical and contemporary record calls for a new attentiveness to the life of rooted communities themselves, whose institutions are the foundation and wellspring for any sustained challenge to autocratic power. It is through the structures of community life, which sustain and reproduce a group's shared bonds of historical memory and culture, that an oppressed people begin to come to self-consciousness. Through their activity in new contexts, groups may acquire public skills, reinforce democratic values, and form new links between subcommunities

---

18. SFOP described in ibid., chap. 6.
19. Harry C. Boyte interview with Robert Hudak, Des Plaines, Ill., Apr. 27, 1985.

into larger networks and organizations. And it is through such processes that a powerless people constitutes itself as a force for democratic transformation of the broader social structure and as a school for its own education in a democratic sensibility. Loss of organic connection to the communal sources of social movement can lead to the amorphous and rootless stridency of the late new left on the one hand, or to the bureaucratic stagnation apparent in many contemporary trade unions on the other.

Yet the evidence also draws attention to the *complexity* of community life, and the relative powerlessness of communities by themselves, from a democratic perspective. If democratic movements necessarily draw their strength, vision, and power from communitarian settings, these also limit the nature of such movements. Leaders, organizational forms, and broader strategies may help movements overcome parochialism and ethnocentrism, may expand the democratic processes within the group life, may make the decisive difference in how effectively the movement influences the broader society. But the requirement for such developments is a willingness to admit and address communities' limitations, as well as a respect for communities' importance.

In present-day America, recognition of both the centrality and the limitations of communities assumes no small urgency. Where are the places in our culture through which people sustain bonds and history? What are the processes through which they may broaden their sense of the possible, make alliances with others, develop the practical skills and knowledge to maintain democratic organization? What are the languages of protest, dissent, and change that express moral and communal themes in inclusive ways that reach beyond particular boundaries of race, ethnicity, gender, and class? Such questions confer the dignity of historical authorship upon ordinary people.

Finally, democratic movements, drawing their spirit from voluntary associations of all sorts, have not only sought structural changes to realize a wider, more inclusive and participatory "democracy." From the commonwealth vision of the WCTU, the Knights of Labor, and the nineteenth-century Populists, to the Citizenship Schools of the Southern Christian Leadership Conference in the 1960s and the citizenship education programs in community groups today, such movements have also illustrated the inextricable links between participation and citizenship. Thus, such movements, and the free spaces at their heart, suggest the need for a basic reworking of conventional ideas about "public life" and "democracy." They call attention to that vast middle ground of communal activity, between private life and large-scale institutions, as the arenas in which notions of civic virtue and a sense of responsibility for the common good are nourished, and democracy is given living meaning. And they remind us, repeatedly, how ordinary people can discover who they are and take democratic initiative, on their own terms.

[1986]

from Civil Society and Political Theory

We are on the threshold of yet another great transformation of the self-understanding of modern societies. There have been many attempts from various points of view to label this process: the ambiguous terms "postindustrial" and "postmodern" society reflect the vantage points of economic and cultural concerns. Our interest is in politics. But from this standpoint, the changes occurring in political culture and social conflicts are poorly characterized by terms whose prefix implies "after" or "beyond." To be sure, for a variety of empirical and theoretical reasons the old hegemonic paradigms have disintegrated, as have the certainties and guarantees that went with them. Indeed we are in the midst of a remarkable revival of political and social thought that has been going on for the last two decades.

One response to the collapse of the two dominant paradigms of the previous period—pluralism and neo-Marxism—has been the attempt to revive political theory by "bringing the state back in." While this approach has led to interesting theoretical and empirical analyses, its state-centered perspective has obscured an important dimension of what is new in the political debates and in the stakes of social contestation.[1] The focus on the state is a useful antidote to the reductionist functionalism of many neo-Marxian and pluralist paradigms that would make the political system an extension, reflex, or functional organ of economic (class) or social (group) structures of selectivity and domination. In this respect the theoretical move served the cause of a more differentiated analysis. But with respect to all that is nonstate, the new paradigm continues the reductionist tendency of Marxism and neo-Marxism by identifying class relations and interests as the key to contemporary forms of collective action. Moreover, the legal, associational,

---

1. Of course, Karl Polànyi's *Great Transformation* [1944] (Boston: Beacon Press, 1957), which has been a major touchstone for our work, brought the state "back in" in the mid–1940s. But see Peter Evans et al., eds., *Bringing the State Back In* (Cambridge, England: Cambridge University Press, 1985).

cultural, and public spheres of society have no theoretical place in this analysis. It thereby loses sight of a great deal of interesting and normatively instructive forms of social conflict today.

The current "discourse of civil society," on the other hand, focuses precisely on new, generally non–class-based forms of collective action oriented and linked to the legal, associational, and public institutions of society. These are differentiated not only from the state but also from the capitalist market economy. Although we cannot leave the state and the economy out of consideration if we are to understand the dramatic changes occurring in Latin America and Eastern Europe in particular, the concept of civil society is indispensable if we are to understand the stakes of these "transitions to democracy" as well as the self-understanding of the relevant actors. It is also indispensable to any analysis that seeks to grasp the import of such changes for the West, as well as indigenous contemporary forms and stakes of conflict. In order to discover, after the demise of Marxism, if not a common normative project between the "transitions" and radical social initiatives under established liberal democracies, then at least the conditions of possibility of fruitful dialogue between them, we must inquire into the meaning and possible shapes of the concept of civil society.

Admittedly, our inclination is to posit a common normative project, and in this sense we are post-Marxist. In other words, we locate the pluralist core of our project within the universalistic horizon of critical theory rather than within the relativistic one of deconstruction. At issue is not only an arbitrary theoretical choice. We are truly impressed by the importance in East Europe and Latin America, as well as in the advanced capitalist democracies, of the struggle for rights and their expansion, of the establishment of grass roots associations and initiatives and the ever renewed construction of institutions and forums of critical publics. No interpretation can do these aspirations justice without recognizing both common orientations that transcend geography and even social-political systems and a common normative fabric linking rights, associations, and publics together. We believe that civil society, in fact the major category of many of the relevant actors and their advocates from Russia to Chile, and from France to Poland, is the best hermeneutic key to these two complexes of commonality.

Thus we are convinced that the recent reemergence of the "discourse of civil society" is at the heart of a sea change in contemporary political culture. Despite the proliferation of this "discourse" and of the concept itself, however, no one has developed a systematic *theory* of civil society. This book is an effort to begin doing just that. Nevertheless, systematic theory cannot be built directly out of the self-understanding of actors, who may very much need the results of a more distanced and critical examination of the possibilities and constraints of action. Such theory must be internally related to the development of relevant theoretical debates. At first sight the building of a theory of civil society seems to be hampered by the fact that the stakes of contemporary debates in political theory seem to be located around different axes than the nineteenth-century couplet of society and state. It is our belief, however, that the problem of civil society and its democratization is latently present in these discussions and that it constitutes the theoretical terrain on which their internal antinomies might be resolved.

Three debates of the last fifteen to twenty years seem to tower above all the rest. The first continues an older controversy within the field of democratic theory between defenders of elite vs. participatory models of democracy.[2] The second, for the most part restricted to the Anglo-American world, is between what has come to be called "rights-oriented liberalism" and "communitarianism." While it covers some of the same ground as the first controversy, the terms of the second discussion are quite distinct for, unlike the first, it occurs within the field of normative political philosophy rather than between empiricists and normativists.[3] The third debate, pitting neoconservative advocates of the free market against defenders of the welfare state, has animated discussion on both sides of the Atlantic.[4] Its context is, of course, the notorious crisis of the welfare state that intruded on political consciousness in the mid-1970s. These debates are interrelated, and, as already indicated, there are overlaps. Nevertheless, each of them has culminated in a distinct set of antinomies leading to a kind of standoff and increasing sterility. What no one seems to have realized, however, is that the relatively unsystematic and heterogeneous discourse of the revival of civil society can be brought to bear on these debates and indeed can provide a way out of the antinomies that plague them. Accordingly, we shall briefly summarize these debates in the introduction and show how our book provides a new paradigm for thinking about the issues they raise.

2. This debate began in the mid-1950s and reemerged in the aftermath of the New Left. For a chronology, see John F. Manley, "Neo-Pluralism: A Class Analysis of Pluralism I and Pluralism II," *American Political Science Review* 77, no. 2 (June 1983): 368–383. The list of participants in this debate is long. Let us mention just a few key figures and representative works on each side. Elite theorists include Joseph Schumpeter, *Capitalism, Socialism and Democracy* (New York: Harper & Row, 1942); S. M. Lipset, *Political Man* (New York: Doubleday, 1963); Robert Dahl, *Polyarchy* (New Haven: Yale University Press, 1971); William Kornhauser, *The Politics of Mass Society* (New York: Free Press, 1959); G. Almond and S. Verba, *The Civic Culture* (Boston: Little Brown, 1963). Participatory democrats include Peter Bachrach, *The Theory of Democratic Elitism: A Critique* (Boston: Little Brown, 1967); Carole Pateman, *Participation and Democratic Theory* (Cambridge, England: Cambridge University Press, 1970); Sheldon Wolin, *Politics and Vision* (Boston: Little Brown, 1960). For an overview of the debate, see Quentin Skinner, "The Empirical Theorists of Democracy and Their Critics: A Plague on Both Their Houses," *Political Theory* 1 (1973): 287–306.

3. A volume that brings together both sides of the debate is Michael Sandel, ed., *Liberalism and its Critics* (New York: New York University Press, 1984).

4. See Michel Crozier et al., eds., *The Crisis of Democracy* (New York: New York University Press, 1975), and Claus Offe, *Contradictions of the Welfare State* (Cambridge: MIT Press, 1984).

Debates in Contemporary Political Theory

Elite vs. Participatory Democracy

It would not be an exaggeration to say that the debate between elite and participatory models of democracy has been going around in circles ever since [Joseph] Schumpeter threw down the gauntlet to the normativists in 1942.[5] Schumpeter's claim that "the democratic method is that institutional arrangement for arriving at political decisions in which individuals acquire the power to decide via a competitive struggle for the people's vote"[6] has formed the core of the elite model of democracy ever since. Democracy is defined not as a kind of society or as a set of moral ends or even as a principle of legitimacy but rather as a method for choosing political leaders and organizing governments. The elite model of democracy claims to be realistic, descriptive, empirically accurate, and the only model that is appropriate to modern social conditions.

Far from indulging in utopian illusions about the possibility of either conjuring away the phenomenon of power or the gap between rulers and ruled, this approach assumes that no society, and certainly no modern one, could function without both. A "realistic" appraisal of democratic societies must grant that the motor of the political system is power just as the motor of the economy is profit. The struggle to acquire and use power is at the heart of the political. What distinguishes democratic from nondemocratic societies is thus the way in which power is acquired and decisions are arrived at: so long as some core set of civil rights is respected and regularly contested elections are held on the basis of a universal franchise, so long as alternation in power is accepted by elites and occurs smoothly without violence or institutional discontinuity, so long as decision making involves compromises among elites and (passive) acceptance by the population, a polity can be considered democratic. The main concern here is obviously with the ability of a government to produce decisions, to have them accepted, and to ensure orderly transitions, i.e., stability.

The elite model of democracy prides itself on providing an operationalizable and empirically descriptive account of the practices of politics considered to be democratic. There is no pretense here that voters either set the political agenda or make political decisions; they neither generate issues nor choose policies. Rather, leaders (political parties) aggregate interests and decide which are to become politically salient.[7] Moreover, they select issues and structure public opinion. The

---

5. Joseph Schumpeter, *Capitalism, Socialism, and Democracy* (New York: Harper & Row, 1942), 232–302.

6. Ibid., 269.

7. The model of the political party is the catch-all party. For the concept, see Otto Kirchheimer, "The Transformation of the Western European Party System," in Frederic S. Burin and Kurt L. Shell, eds., *Politics, Law, and Social Change: Selected Essays of Otto Kirchheimer* (New York: Columbia University Press, 1969), 346–371. Some elite theorists who are also pluralists include interest groups

true function of the vote is simply to choose among the bids for power by political elites and to accept leadership. The voters are consumers, the parties are entrepreneurs offering alternative packages or personnel; it is they who create demand, bowing to consumer sovereignty only with regard to the yes/no decision by the voters about who among the preselected candidates will be their "representatives" (using the latter term very loosely indeed).[8] In short, the empirical theories of democracy (elite, pluralist, corporatist, and rational choice models) tend quite openly to reduce the normative meaning of the term to a set of minimums modeled on a conception of bargaining, competition, access and accountability derived more from the market than from earlier models of citizenship.

Competitiveness in acquiring political power and in making policy decisions is, of course, the core of this model of democracy. The competitive element is deemed to be the source of creativity, productivity, responsibility, and responsiveness. The ultimate sanction of the vote, together with the necessity on the part of elites to compete for it, will supposedly keep things fair, encourage authorities to be responsive to a multiplicity of demands and accountable to the citizenry, and foster their willingness to compromise with one another. To be sure, this model of democracy rests on certain preconditions that it supposedly should be able to reproduce: high-quality leadership with a tolerance for differences of opinion, a restricted range of political decision,[9] and an elite political culture based on democratic self-control.[10] These preconditions are predicated in turn on the fact of social pluralism or cleavage, which the democratic method institutionalizes into nonviolent competition for office and influence. A final precondition, deemed indispensable for a stable political system to be able to make decisions, is that it must be shielded from too much participation by the population: citizens must, as it were, accept the division of labor between themselves and the politicians they elect.[11] Accordingly, this model of democracy argues that the secret ballot, civil

as actors in the political system (see Dahl, *Polyarchy*). However, the idea that interests emerge spontaneously and autonomously in civil society and are then aggregated by political parties has been criticized not only by Marxists but also by theorists of neocorporatism. For an excellent overview of these criticisms, see Suzanne Berger, *Organizing Interests in Western Europe* (Cambridge, England: Cambridge University Press, 1981), 1–23.

8. On this model, societal interests cannot be represented. Neither public opinion nor raw individual interests find representation in the political system; instead, interests are aggregated and given their political salience by elites.

9. According to Schumpeter, *Capitalism, Socialism, and Democracy,* 292–293, not everything in a democracy is subject to the democratic method. For example, judges, federal agencies, and bureaucracies are beyond the reach of this method but are not thereby antidemocratic.

10. Ibid., 289–295.

11. Just what counts as too much participation is a matter of debate. While the elite-democracy school partially buys into this idea and extols a mixture of activism and apathy (see Almond and Verba, *The Civic Culture,* and Lipset, *Political Man*), along with civil privatism, Schumpeter went the furthest in this direction. In arguing against the imperative mandate, Schumpeter insists that people should accept the division of labor between leaders and followers, give up on the idea of instructing delegates, and even cease from bombarding their representatives with letters and telegrams!

rights, alternation, regular elections, and party competition are central to every modern conception of democracy if democracy is to have any place at all in complex modern societies.

We find this last statement to be quite convincing, so far as it goes. But the normativist critique of the elite model of democracy is also convincing. It is especially compelling against the elite model's tendency to extol apathy, civil privatism, and the necessity to shield the political system from "excess" demands of the population as *democratic* principles, the meaning of this excess to be determined by the elites alone.[12] The normativists correctly point out that what makes for stability and continuity in a polity is not identical with what makes it democratic. From the standpoint of participation theory, the elite model of democracy is both too broad and too narrow. To define a polity as democratic if it periodically holds contested elections and guarantees civil rights, regardless of what sorts of public institutions or private arrangements exist, is to extend democratic legitimacy to an enormously wide range of societies while simultaneously shielding them from critical scrutiny. At the same time the concept of democracy at play here is too narrow, for it is defined by procedures that have little to do with the procedures and presuppositions of free agreement and discursive will formation.[13] Indeed the participation theorists argue that the "realistic" model has denuded the concept of democracy of so many of its elements that it has lost any connection with its past meaning.[14] What is left if one drops the ideas of self-determination, participation, political equality, discursive processes of political will formation among peers, and the influence of autonomous public opinion on decision making? In short, the price of the elite model's realism is the loss of what has always been taken to be the core of the concept of democracy, namely, the citizenship principle. Moreover, by restricting the concept of democracy to a method of leader selection and to procedures regulating the competition and policy making of elites, this model sacrifices the very principles of democratic legitimacy on which it is nevertheless parasitic. It loses all criteria for distinguishing between formalistic ritual, systematic distortion, choreographed consent, manipulated public opinion, and the real thing.[15]

The participatory model of democracy maintains that what makes for good leaders also makes for good citizens—active participation in ruling and being ruled (i.e., in the exercise of power) and also in public will and public opinion formation. Democracy in this sense would allow all citizens, and not only elites, to acquire a democratic political culture. For it is through political experience that

12. See Bachrach, *Theory of Democratic Elitism.*

13. Jürgen Habermas, "Legitimation Problems in the Modern State," in *Communication and the Evolution of Society* (Boston: Beacon Press, 1979), 186–187.

14. Bachrach, *Theory of Democratic Elitism.*

15. That is, it loses a standard with which to judge whether consent, procedures, and so on are what they claim to be. See Phillippe C. Schmitter, "Democratic Theory and Neocorporatist Practice," *Social Research* 50, no. 4 (Winter 1983): 885–891.

one develops a conception of civic virtue, learns to tolerate diversity, to temper fundamentalism and egoism, and to become able and willing to compromise.[16] Hence the insistence that without public spaces for the active participation of the citizenry in ruling and being ruled, without a decisive narrowing of the gap between rulers and ruled, to the point of its abolition, polities are democratic in name only.[17]

For the most part, however, when it comes to conceptualizing alternatives, participation theorists offer institutional models that are meant to substitute for rather than complement the allegedly undemocratic (and/or bourgeois) forms of representative government that exist today.[18] Whether the theorist harkens back to an idealized model of the Greek *polis,* to the republican tradition of the late medieval city-state, or to the new forms of democracy generated within the milieus of the workers' movement (council communism, revolutionary syndicalism), in each case the alternative is presented as the single organizational principle for society as a whole. Accordingly, the underlying thrust of these models is the dedifferentiation of society, the state, and the economy. Small wonder that participationists in turn are accused by their opponents of utopianism and/or antimodernism.

To sum up, this debate leaves us with the following antinomy: contemporary democratic theory involves either some rather undemocratic adjustments to the "exigencies of complex industrial societies" coupled with an abandonment of the normative core of the very concept of democracy, or it proffers somewhat hollow normative visions that cannot be reconciled with the institutional requirements of modern society.

Rights-Oriented Liberalism vs. Communitarianism

The debate between political liberals and communitarians reproduces some of the arguments described above but on a different terrain. In one respect, both sides in this debate challenge the elite/pluralist model of democracy. Both reject the anti-normative, empiricist, utilitarian strain in this model and both seek to develop a convincing normative theory of democratic legitimacy or justice. The dispute is over how to formulate such a theory. Despite this shift in emphasis, however, this debate also culminates in a set of antinomic positions from which it seems unable to extricate itself.

At the center of the controversy are two interrelated issues, one epistemological, the other political. The first revolves around the question of whether it is possible to articulate a formal, universalistic (deontological) conception of justice without presupposing a substantive (historically and culturally specific) concept

16. See Hannah Arendt, *On Revolution* (New York: Penguin, 1963), and Wolin, *Politics and Vision.* See also Benjamin Barber, *Strong Democracy* (Berkeley: University of California Press, 1984).

17. Barber, *Strong Democracy.*

18. This is not true of Pateman, *Participation and Democratic Theory.*

of the good. The second revolves around the question of how freedom can be realized in the modern world. At issue here is whether the idea of freedom should be explicated primarily from the standpoint of individual rights or of the community's shared norms.[19] Each side comes up with a different, indeed opposed, set of responses as to what constitutes the legitimating principles of a constitutional democracy. In the process, however, the very conception of liberal democracy disintegrates into its components parts.

Liberal theorists see the respect for individual rights and the principle of political neutrality as the standard for legitimacy in constitutional democracies. The core premise of rights-oriented liberalism is that individuals qua individuals have moral rights that serve as constraints on government and on others—constraints that are under the control of the rights holder. They have these rights not on the grounds of some social convention, aggregate common utility, tradition, or dispensation from God, but by virtue of their having some "property" (moral autonomy, human dignity) that constitutes them as bearers of rights. The liberal sees individual autonomy, moral egalitarianism, and universalism as inherent in the idea of moral rights.[20] As such, rights constitute the heart of a conception of justice that makes plausible the claim to legitimacy of any modern polity. Law and political decisions are binding to the degree to which they respect individual rights.[21]

The communitarian critique of the rights thesis focuses on its individualist presuppositions and universalist claims. With respect to the first, communitarians argue that the liberal ideals of moral autonomy and individual self-development are based on an atomistic, abstract, and ultimately incoherent concept of the self as the subject of rights.[22] This allegedly leads to a focus on nonpolitical forms of freedom (negative liberty) and an impoverished conception of political identity, agency, and ethical life. Accordingly, the communitarians invoke a set of empirical and normative arguments against these assumptions. First, they argue that individuals are situated within an

19. Sandel, *Liberalism and Its Critics*.

20. The rights thesis is predicated on the following assumptions: (1) there is no authority other than human reason for judging moral claims; (2) all individuals must be seen as equal partners in the moral dialogue when it comes to asserting and defending rights claims—moral reasons have to be given; (3) any tradition, prerogative, or claim is open to critique; (4) the values that individuals defend, including rights, are valid because they can be argued for vis-à-vis other moral systems. All values are values for individuals. If something is valuable for a community, it must be shown to be a value for the individual as well. See Janos Kis, *L'Ègale dignité. Essai sur les fondements des droits de l'homme* (Paris: Seuil, 1989).

21. Hence the priority of the right or justice over the good.

22. See Michael Sandel (*Liberalism and the Limits of Justice* [Cambridge, England: Cambridge University Press, 1982]), Charles Taylor (*Hegel* [Cambridge, England: Cambridge University Press, 1975]), and Michael Walzer (*Spheres of Justice* [New York: Basic Books, 1983]). Sandel, Taylor, and Walzer all criticize these epistemological assumptions allegedly underlying rights-oriented liberalism. Amy Gutman, "Communitarian Critics of Liberalism," *Philosophy and Public Affairs* 14, no. 4 (1985); 308–322, rejects the thesis as fallacious.

historical and social context; they are socialized into communities through which they derive their individual and collective identity, language, world concepts, moral categories, and so forth. Hence the empirical primacy of the social over the individual is asserted against the alleged priority of the asocial individual to society. Second, on the normative level, communitarians charge that liberals fail to see that communities are independent sources of value and that there are communal duties and virtues (loyalty, civic virtue) distinct from duties to others qua their abstract humanity. Indeed, duties of loyalty and membership are and must be primary.

As far as universalism goes, communitarians claim that what the liberal sees as universal norms grounded in the universal character of humanity (dignity or moral autonomy) are in fact particular norms embedded in shared understandings of specific communities. The individual cannot have a firm basis for moral judgment without getting it from a community to which one is committed. The strongest claim is that there are no duties pertaining to abstract man but only to members: The proper basis of moral theory is the community and its good, not the individual and her rights. Indeed, individuals have rights to the degree to which these flow from the common good. According, the idea of moral rights is an empty universalism that mistakenly abstracts from the only real basis of moral claims, the community. Only on the basis of a shared conception of the good life, only within the framework of a substantive ethical political community (with a specific political culture) can we lead meaningful moral lives and enjoy true freedom.

For those communitarians who see themselves as democrats,[23] the concept of freedom thus has to do not with the idea of moral rights but with the specific way in which agents come to decide what they want and ought to do. Taken together, the empirical and normative criticisms of the rights thesis imply that freedom must have its original locus not in the isolated individual but in the society that is the medium of individuation: in the structures, institutions, practices of the larger social whole. Civic virtue rather than negative liberty, the public good as distinct from the right, democratic participation unlike individual rights (and the concomitant adversarial political culture), involve a communal practice of citizenship that should pervade the institutions of society on all levels and become habitualized in the character, customs, moral sentiments of each citizen. By implication, and on the strongest version of these claims, a society in which claims of individual rights proliferate cannot be a solidary community but must be alienated, anomic, privatized, competitive and lacking in moral substance.

This debate also leads to an apparently unresolvable antinomy. On the one side, the liberal tradition itself, with its focus on individual rights and its illusions about the possibility of political neutrality, appears as the source of egoistic, disintegrative tendencies in modern society and hence as the main impediment to achieving a democratic society predicated on civic virtue. The other side counters with the contention that modern societies are precisely *not* communities integrated around

---

23. That is, Charles Taylor, Michael Walzer, and Benjamin Barber.

a single conception of the good life. Modern civil societies are characterized by a plurality of forms of life; they are structurally differentiated and socially heterogeneous. Thus, to be able to lead a moral life, individual autonomy and individual rights must be secured. On this view, it is democracy, with its emphasis on consensus, or at least on majority rule, that is dangerous to liberty, unless suitably restricted by constitutionally guaranteed basic rights that alone can render them legitimate in the eyes of minorities.

The Defense of Welfare State vs. Neoconservative Antistatism

The debate between defenders of the welfare state and its neo laissez-faire critics has also been going around in circles, albeit for a shorter time than the controversy plaguing democratic theory.[24] Arguments for the welfare state have been made on both economic and political grounds.[25] According to Keynesian economic doctrine, welfare state policies serve to stimulate the forces of economic growth and to prevent deep recessions by encouraging investment and stabilizing demand. Fiscal and monetary incentives for investors coupled with social insurance, transfer payments, and public services for workers compensate for the dysfunctions, uncertainties and risks of the market mechanism and contribute to overall stability. High growth rates, full employment, and low inflation should be the result of this policy.

The political aspects of the welfare state would also increase stability and productivity. On the one side, legal entitlements to state services and transfer payments simultaneously aid those who feel the negative effects of the market system while removing potentially explosive needs or issues from the arena of industrial conflict. On the other side, the recognition of the formal role of labor unions in collective bargaining and in the formation of public policy "balances" the asymmetrical power relations between labor and capital and mitigates class conflict.[26] The overall increase in social justice would lead to fewer strikes, greater productivity, and an overall consensus of capital and labor that they have a mutual interest in the success of the political economic system: Growth and productivity serve everyone. The welfare state would finally deliver on the claim of liberal capitalist societies to be egalitarian and just, by supporting the worst off and by creating the preconditions of a true equality of opportunity, which in the eyes of defenders of the welfare state is the only context in which civil and political rights can function in a universalistic manner. Instead of being concerned by the anomalous status of the so-called social rights, for a theorist such as T. H. Marshall these represent the highest and most fundamental type of citizen rights.[27]

24. Since the 1970s. For the left critique of the welfare state, see Offe, *Contradictions,* chapters 1 and 6.

25. For a discussion of various defenses and criticisms of the welfare state, see Offe, *Contradictions,* 35–206, 252–302. He gives a definition on page 194.

26. Ibid., 147.

27. T. H. Marshall, *Class Citizenship and Social Development* (New York: Doubleday, 1964).

Certainly the remarkable growth rates, relative stability, and increase in the standard of living in postwar Western capitalist economies have, until recently, made the arguments for state intervention convincing to all but a very few. In a new context of more limited possibilities for growth, neoconservative defenders of a return to "laissez-faire" criticize both the economic and political claims of the welfare state model. Unfortunately for the latter, their arguments also carry weight. Indeed, it was not difficult for these critics to point to the high rates of unemployment and inflation and low growth rates that have plagued Western capitalist economies since the 1970s as proof that state-bureaucratic regulation of the economy is counterproductive. They can also point to successes in these domains where their own policies have been applied.

On the economic front, three claims are made against the policies of welfare states: that they lead to a disincentive to invest and a disincentive to work, and that they constitute a serious threat to the viability of the independent middle class.[28] The burden imposed by the regulatory and fiscal policies on capital together with the power of unions to extract high wages allegedly contribute to declining growth rates and, in a context of severe competition, lead to the perception that investment in home markets will be unprofitable. The disincentive to work is attributed to extensive social security and unemployment provisions that allow workers to avoid undesirable jobs and to escape the normal pressure of market forces. The quantity of available workers shrinks as whole sectors of the working class are turned into welfare state clients, while the work ethic declines as workers become simultaneously more demanding and less willing to spend effort on their work. Finally, the independent middle class finds itself squeezed by high rates of taxation and inflation. The emergence of the "new middle class" of civil service professionals and higher-level bureaucrats only exacerbates these problems because these strata have an interest in reproducing and expanding the client population on which their jobs depend. Welfare state economic policies are thus antinomic in more than one respect: Policies meant to stimulate demand undermine investment, policies meant to provide economic security for workers undermine the willingness to work, the policy of tempering the undesirable side effects deriving from unregulated market forces creates even greater economic problems in the form of a vastly expanded, expensive, unproductive state sector.

On the political front, neoconservatives argue that the very mechanisms introduced by welfare states to resolve conflicts and create greater equality of opportunity, namely legal entitlements and the expanded state sector, have led to new conflicts and have violated the rights and liberty of some for the sake of others. By impinging upon the core right of liberal market systems, namely, private property, state intervention and regulation undermine both the liberty of entrepreneurs and the incentive to achieve on the part of the working population. Far from increasing

28. Offe, *Contradictions*, 149–154.

social justice or equality of opportunity, welfare undermines the preconditions for both of these. In short, it rewards failure rather than success. In the name of equality, moreover, state intervention in the everyday lives of its clients poses a severe threat to liberty, privacy, and autonomy.

In addition, these mechanisms have allegedly generated a set of rising expectations and increasing demands that lead to an overall situation of ungovernability.[29] Indeed, the very institutions of welfare state mass democracy that promised to channel political conflict into acceptable and harmless forms (the end of ideology) and to integrate workers especially into the political and economic system of late capitalism (deradicalization)—i.e., the competitive (catchall) party system based on universal suffrage, interest group politics, collective bargaining, and extensive social rights—lead to a dangerous overload of the political system and a crisis of authority.[30] In short, the rights explosion that so irritates democratic communitarians is even more alarming to neoconservative critics of "statism." By placing obligations upon itself that it cannot possibly fulfill,[31] the state creates rising yet unsatisfiable expectations, becomes overexpanded and weak at the same time, and suffers from a dangerous loss of authority. Indeed, on this view, there is a central political contradiction inherent in the welfare state: In order for the performance capacity of the state to be enhanced vis-à-vis the number of demands, the very freedoms, modes of participation, and sets of rights associated with it would have to be curtailed.[32]

The neo-laissez-faire economic and political alternatives, however, do not escape the fate of becoming merely one of the untenable sides of an antinomic structure. "Supply-side" economists seek to dismantle the welfare state in order to eliminate the "disincentive" to invest, but to do so would be to abolish precisely those "buffers" that stabilize demand.[33] If the socioeconomic supports for workers and the poor are terminated in the name of refurbishing the work ethic, the compulsion of the market will certainly return, but so will the gross injustices, dissatisfaction, instability, and class confrontations that characterized the capitalist economies prior to welfare state policies.

Of course, the attack on the welfare state is predicated on the idea that there is an unlimited growth potential for marketable goods and services that would be unleashed once the state is pushed back into its proper, minimal terrain. Privatization and deregulation would allegedly restore competition and end the inflation of political demands. However, the political presuppositions for such a policy conflict with its goals of social peace and social justice. Necessarily repressive policies regarding the right to associate and efforts to abolish social

29. See especially Crozier et al., eds., *The Crisis of Democracy*.

30. Huntington, "The United States," in Crozier et al., eds., *The Crisis of Democracy*, 73.

31. See James O'Connor, *The Fiscal Crisis of the State* (New York: St. Martin's Press, 1973); Habermas, *Legitimation Crisis*, Part II; and Offe, *Contradictions*, 35–64.

32. For the reasons for this claim, see Offe, *Contradictions*, 67–76.

33. Claus Offe, *Disorganized Capitalism* (Cambridge: MIT Press, 1985), 84.

rights ranging from social security to unemployment compensation, not to mention welfare, are scarcely conducive to consensus. While the "freedom-threatening" dimensions of state intervention, namely the regulation of proprietors, the supervision and control of clients, and the spiraling cycle of dependency, would end, so would all of the gains in social justice, equality, and rights. Moreover, efforts to restore state authority by limiting its scope and by shielding it from popular demands would not reduce state activism but would simply shift it from the political to the administrative terrain. For, if one reduces the ability of democratic institutions such as the party system, elections, and parliaments to provide for the articulation of political conflict, alternative channels, such as the neocorporatist arrangements proliferating in Western Europe, will develop. While these arrangements successfully shield the state from excess demands, they hardly indicate a shift from state to market regulation. Thus the neo-laissez-faire alternative to the "crisis" of the welfare state is as internally contradictory as the illness it purports to cure.

We are accordingly left with following antinomy: either we choose more social engineering, more paternalism and leveling, in short, more statism, in the name of egalitarianism and social rights, or we opt for the free market and/or the refurbishing of authoritarian social and political forms of organization and relinquish the democratic, egalitarian components of our political culture in order to block further bureaucratization of everyday life. It seems that liberal democratic market societies cannot coexist with, nor can they exist without, the welfare state.

Revival of the Concept of Civil Society

The early modern concept of civil society was revived first and foremost in the struggles of the democratic oppositions in Eastern Europe against authoritarian socialist party-states. Despite different economic and geopolitical contexts, it does not seem terribly problematic to apply the concept also to the "transitions from authoritarian rule" in southern Europe and Latin America, above all because of the common task shared with the oppositions of the East to constitute new and stable democracies. But why should such a concept be particularly relevant to the West? Is not the revival of the discourse of civil society in the East and the South simply part of a project to attain what the advanced capitalist democracies already have: civil society guaranteed by the rule of law, civil rights, parliamentary democracy, and a market economy? Could one not argue that struggles in the name of creating civil and political society especially in the East are a kind of repeat of the great democratic movements of the eighteenth and nineteenth centuries that created a type of duality between state and civil society which remains the basis for Western democratic and liberal institutions? And isn't this an admission that the elite theorists, the neoconservatives, or at best the liberals are right after all? Put this way, the revival of the discourse of civil society appears to be just that, a revival, with little political or theoretical import for Western liberal democracies. And if this is so, why would a civil-society-oriented perspective provide a way out of the antinomies plaguing *Western* political and social thought?

Several interrelated issues that have emerged in the current revival go beyond the model of the historical origins of civil society in the West and therefore have important lessons to offer established liberal democracies. These include the conception of self-limitation, the idea of civil society as comprised of social movements as well as a set of institutions, the orientation to civil society as a new terrain of democratization,[34] the influence of civil on political and economic society, and finally an understanding that the liberation of civil society is not necessarily identical with the creation of bourgeois society but rather involves a choice between a plurality of types of civil society. All these notions point beyond a restriction of the theory of civil society merely to the constituent phase of new democracies.

The idea of self-limitation, all too often confused with the strategic constraints on emancipatory movements, is actually based on learning in the service of democratic principle. The post-revolutionary or self-limiting "revolutions" of the East are no longer motivated by fundamentalist projects of suppressing bureaucracy, economic rationality, or social division. Movements rooted in civil society have learned from the revolutionary tradition that these fundamentalist projects lead to the breakdown of societal steering and productivity and the suppression of social plurality, all of which are then reconstituted by the forces of order only by dramatically authoritarian means. Such an outcome leads to the collapse of the forms of self-organization that in many cases were the major carriers of the revolutionary process: revolutionary societies, councils, movements. Paradoxically, the self-limitation of just such actors allows the continuation of their social role and influence beyond the constituent and into the constituted phase.

This continuation of a role of civil society beyond the phase of transition can be coupled with domestication, demobilization, and relative atomization. That would mean convergence with society as the Western elite pluralists see it. But in the post-authoritarian settings actors who have rejected fundamentalism and raised civil society to a normative principle show that we do have a choice. While the total democratization of state and economy cannot be their goal, civil society itself, as de Tocqueville was the first to realize, is a important terrain of democratization, of democratic institution building. And if East European oppositionals were driven to this alternative at first only by blockages in the sphere of state organization, there is certainly a good chance that the idea of the further democratization of civil society will gain emphasis in the face of the inevitable disappointments, visible above all in Hungary (East) Germany, and Czechoslovakia, with the emergence of the typical practices of Western democracies. Thus, the actors of the new political societies would do well, if they value their long-term legitimacy, to

---

34. This includes the family with civil society. See our discussion of Hegel in chapter 2 [of *Civil Society and Political Theory*].

promote democratic institution building in civil society, even if this seems to increase the number of social demands on them.

The idea of the democratization of civil society, unlike that of its mere revival, is extremely pertinent to existing Western societies. Indeed, the tendency to see extrainstitutional movements and initiatives in addition to settled institutions as integral parts of civil society is found earlier in Western than in Eastern experience, to which it is rapidly being extended primarily by new and old movements and initiatives. It is quite possible that some of the emerging Eastern constitutions will embody new sensitivity to an active civil society, a sensitivity that should in turn influence Western constitutional developments. These potential normative gains will confirm, in the East as well as the West, the idea that there can be very different types of civil society: more or less institutionalized, more or less democratic, more or less active. Discussions in the milieu of Solidarity in Poland raised these choices explicitly as early as 1980, along with the choice of political vs. antipolitical models of civil society. In the current wave of economic liberalism in Poland, Czechoslovakia, and Hungary, another question inevitably arises concerning the connection between economy and civil society and the choice between an economic, individualistic society and a civil society based on solidarity, protected not only against the bureaucratic state but also against the self-regulating market economy. This debate, too, will be directly relevant in Western contexts, as it already has been in Latin America, and conversely Western controversies around the welfare state and the "new social movements" should have much intellectual material to offer Eastern radical democrats hoping to protect the resource of solidarity without paternalism.

The aim of our book is to further develop and systematically justify the idea of civil society, reconceived in part around a notion of self-limiting democratizing movements seeking to expand and protect spaces for both negative liberty and positive freedom and to recreate egalitarian forms of solidarity without impairing economic self-regulation. Before turning to this task, we would like to conclude this introduction by illustrating the important, and perhaps decisive, contribution of our theory of civil society to the three theoretical antinomies mentioned above.[35]

Civil Society and Contemporary Political Theory

It might seem that our position is already anticipated by one of the six theoretical traditions involved in the debates depicted above, namely the pluralist version of the elite democratic tradition of political theory.[36] Indeed, the pluralists' addition to the elite model of democracy is precisely a conception of a "third

---

35. These discussions have, in turn, been highly instructive for the development of our conception.
36. See note 7.

realm" differentiated from the economy and the state (what we call "civil society").[37] On the pluralist analysis, a highly articulated civil society with cross-cutting cleavages, overlapping memberships of groups, and social mobility is the presupposition for a stable democratic polity, a guarantee against permanent domination by any one group and against the emergence of fundamentalist mass movements and antidemocratic ideologies.[38] Moreover, a civil society so constituted is considered to be capable of acquiring influence over the political system through the articulation of interests that are "aggregated" by political parties and legislatures and brought to bear on political decision making, itself understood along the lines of the elite model of democracy.

Although we use many of the terms of this analysis in our work on civil society, our approach differs in several key respects from that of the pluralists. First, we do not accept the view that the "civic culture" most appropriate to a modern civil society is one based on civil privatism and political apathy. As is well known, the pluralists value involvement in one's family, private clubs, voluntary associations, and the like as activities that deflect from political participation or activism on the part of citizens.[39] It is this which allegedly makes for a stable democratic polity. Moreover, it makes no difference to this model what the internal structure of the institutions and organizations of civil society is.[40] Indeed, in their haste to replace "utopian (participatory democratic) principles" with realism, the pluralists tend to consider attempts to apply the egalitarian norms of civil society to social institutions as naive.

We do not share this view. Instead, we build upon the thesis of one of the most important predecessors of the pluralist approach, Alexis de Tocqueville, who argued that without *active* participation on the part of citizens in *egalitarian* institutions and civil associations, as well as in politically relevant organizations, there will be no way to maintain the democratic character of the political culture or of social and political institutions. Precisely because modern civil society is based on egalitarian principles and universal inclusion, experience in articulating the political will and in collective decision making is crucial to the reproduction of democracy.

This, of course, is the point that is always made by participation theorists. Our approach differs from theirs in arguing for more, not less, structural differentiation. We take seriously the normative principles defended by radical democrats, but we locate the genesis of democratic legitimacy and the chances for direct participation

37. Although they do not use the term, pluralists include voluntary associations, interest groups, a free press, and basic rights within the societal realm that is distinct from the economy. The most sophisticated three-part model to be found in pluralist theory is that of Talcott Parsons.

38. See Kornhauser, *The Politics of Mass Society.*

39. This is very much contrary to the spirit of Alexis de Tocqueville, whom the pluralists frequently cite as one of their most important forerunners.

40. It is not a matter of concern whether the nuclear family is patriarchal or whether interest groups are in fact highly bureaucratized or hierarchically organized.

not in some idealized, dedifferentiated polity but within a highly differentiated model of civil society itself. This shifts the core problematic of democratic theory away from descriptive and/or speculative models to the issue of the relation and channels of influence between civil and political society and between both and the state, on the one side, and to the institutional makeup and internal articulation of civil society itself, on the other. Moreover, we believe that the democratization of civil society—the family, associational life, and the public sphere—necessarily helps open up the framework of political parties and representative institutions.[41]

Indeed, these concerns open the way to a dynamic conception of civil society, one that avoids the apologetic thrust of most pluralist analyses. Far from viewing social movements as antithetical to either the democratic political system or to a properly organized social sphere (the pluralists' view), we consider them to be a key feature of a vital, modern, civil society and an important form of citizen participation in public life. Yet we do not see social movements as prefiguring a form of citizen participation that will or even ought to substitute for the institutional arrangements of representative democracy (the radical democratic position). In our view, social movements for the expansion of rights, for the defense of the autonomy of civil society, and for its further democratization are what keep a democratic political culture alive. Among other things, movements bring new issues and values into the public sphere and contribute to reproducing the consensus that the elite/pluralist model of democracy presupposes but never bothers to account for. Movements can and should supplement and should not aim to replace competitive party systems. Our conception of civil society thus retains the normative core of democratic theory while remaining compatible with the structural presuppositions of modernity. Finally, while we also differentiate the economy from civil society, we differ from the pluralists in that we do not seal off the borders between them on the basis of an allegedly sacrosanct freedom of contract or property right. Nor do we seek to "re-embed" the economy in society. Instead, on our analysis, the principles of civil society can be brought to bear on economic institutions within what we call economic society. The question here, as in the case of the polity, is what channels and receptors of influence do, can, and ought to exist. Indeed, we are able to pose such questions on the basis of our model without risking the charges of utopianism or antimodernism so frequently and deservedly leveled against worker-based versions of radical democracy.

It is also our thesis that the tensions between rights-oriented liberalism and, at least, democratically oriented communitarianism can be considerably diminished if not entirely overcome on the basis of a new theory of civil society. While the idea of rights and of a democratic political community derive from distinct traditions in political philosophy, today they belong to the same political culture. They

41. In this sense, we do not agree with Norberto Bobbio, who seeks to add the democratization of civil society to elite democratic structures that he takes to be given and unchangeable. See Norberto Bobbio, *The Future of Democracy* (Minneapolis: University of Minnesota Press, 1987).

need not be construed as antithetical, although on an empirical level the rights of an individual may conflict with majority rule and "the public interest," necessitating a balancing between the two sides. Nor is it necessary to view these as based on two conflicting sets of principles or presuppositions, such that one could accommodate the first set only insofar as it is instrumental to the achievement or preservation of the other. On the contrary, we contend that what is best in rights-oriented liberalism and democratically oriented communitarianism constitutes two mutually reinforcing and partly overlapping sets of principles. Two steps are necessary to argue this thesis and to transcend the relevant antinomies. First, one must show that there is a philosophical framework that can provide a political ethic able to redeem the normative claims of both rights-oriented liberalism and radical democracy. Second, one must revise the conception of civil society as the private sphere, shared by both theoretical paradigms, in order to grasp the institutional implications of such an ethic.

We also defend the principles of universality and autonomy to which the rights these is wed, but we deny that this commits us either to the liberal notion of neutrality or to an individualist ontology. The communitarians are right: much of liberal theory, especially the contract tradition from Hobbes to Rawls, has relied on either one or both of these principles. However, the Habermasian theory of discourse ethics, on which we rely, provides a way to develop conceptions of universality and autonomy that are free of such presuppositions. On this theory, universality does not mean neutrality with respect to a plurality of values or forms of life but rather refers, in the first instance, to the metanorms of symmetric reciprocity that are to act as regulative principles guiding discursive processes of conflict resolution and, in the second instance, to those norms or principles to which all those who are potentially affected can agree. The procedure of universalization defended here involves an actual rather than a hypothetical dialogue. It does not require that one abstract from one's concrete situation, need interpretations, or interests in order to engage in an unbiased moral testing of principles. Instead, it requires that these be freely articulated. It also requires that all those potentially affected by institutionalized norms (laws or policies) be open to a multiplicity of perspectives. Accordingly, universality is a regulative principle of a discursive process in and through which participants reason together about which values, principles, need-interpretations merit being institutionalized as common norms.[42] Thus, the atomistic disembodied individual allegedly presupposed by procedural (deontological) ethics is most emphatically not the basis of this approach. Assuming that individual and collective identities are acquired through complex processes of socialization that involve both internalizing social norms or traditions, and developing reflective and critical capacities vis-à-vis norms, principles, and

---

42. It excludes only those need-interpretations and forms of life that are incompatible with the metanorms of symmetric reciprocity—that is, forms of life that deny equal concern and respect to others, that silence, dominate, denigrate, or otherwise treat people as mere means.

traditions, this theory has at its core an intersubjective, interactive conception of both individuality and autonomy. It is thus able to accommodate the communitarian insights into the social core of human nature without abandoning the ideas of either universality or moral rights. Indeed, discourse ethics provides a philosophical basis for democratic legitimacy that presupposes valid rights, even if not all of these rights are derivable from it.

While it is of course individuals who have rights, the concept of rights does not have to rest on philosophical or methodological individualism, nor, for that matter, on the idea of negative liberty alone. Although most liberal and communitarian theorists have assumed that such a conception of freedom and of individualism is presupposed by the very concept of rights, we believe that only some rights involve primarily negative liberty while none requires a philosophically atomistic conception of individuality. It is here that a revised conception of civil society, together with a new theory of rights, must enter into the analysis. For every theory of rights, every theory of democracy, implies a model of society. Unfortunately, communitarians and liberals also agree that the *societal* analogue of the rights thesis is a civil society construed as the private sphere, composed of an agglomeration of autonomous but egotistic, exclusively self-regarding, competitive, possessive individuals whose negative liberty it is the polity's task to protect. It is their assessments and not their analysis of this form of society that diverge.

But this is only one possible version of civil society and certainly not the only one that can be "derived' from the rights thesis. Only if one construes property to be not simply a key right but the core of the conception of rights—only, that is, if one places the philosophy of possessive individualism at the heart of one's conception of civil society and then reduces civil to bourgeois society—does the rights thesis come to be defined in this way.[43] If, however, one develops a more complex model of civil society, recognizing that it has public and associational components as well as individual, private ones, and if, in addition, one sees that the idea of moral autonomy does not presuppose possessive individualism, then the rights thesis begins to look a bit different. In short, rights do not only secure negative liberty, the autonomy of private, disconnected individuals. They also secure the autonomous (freed from state control) *communicative interaction* of individuals with one another in the public and private spheres of civil society, as well as a new relation of individuals to the public and the political spheres of society and state (including, of course, citizenship rights). Moral rights are thus not by definition apolitical or antipolitical, nor do they constitute an exclusively private domain with respect to which the state must limit itself. On the contrary, the rights to communication, assembly, and association, among others, constitute the public and associational spheres of civil society as spheres of *positive freedom* within which agents can collectively debate issues of common concern, act in

43. This is really an extreme libertarian rather than a liberal view. See Robert Nozick, *Anarchy, State and Utopia* (New York: Basic Books, 1974).

concert, assert new rights, and exercise influence on political (and potentially economic) society. Democratic as well as liberal principles have their locus here. Accordingly, some form of differentiation of civil society, the state, and the economy is the basis for both modern democratic and liberal institutions. The latter presuppose neither atomistic nor communal but rather associated selves. Moreover, on this conception the radical opposition between the philosophical foundations and societal presuppositions of rights-oriented liberalism and democratically oriented communitarianism dissolves. This conception of civil society does not, of course, solve the question of the relation between negative and positive liberty, but it does place this issue within a common societal and philosophical terrain. It is on this terrain that we learn how to compromise, take reflective distance from our own perspective so as to entertain others, learn to value difference, recognize or create anew what we have in common, and come to see which dimensions of our traditions are worth preserving and which ought to be abandoned or changed.

This brings us to the heart of our differences with the neoconservative model of civil society. The neoconservative slogan, "society against the state," is often based on a model in which civil society is equivalent to market or bourgeois society. Another version of this approach does, however, recognize the importance of the cultural dimension of civil society. We have serious objections even to this second version, whose strategies for unburdening the state are aimed in part at the institutions involved in the formation and transmission of cultural values (art, religion, science) and in socialization (families, schools). An important component of the neoconservative thesis of "ungovernability" is the argument that the excessive material demands placed by citizens on the state are due not only to welfare institutions themselves but also to our modernist political, moral, and aesthetic culture. The latter allegedly weakens both traditional values and the agencies of social control (such as the family) that tempered hedonism in the past.[44] In this view, we need to resacralize our political culture, revive faltering traditional values such as self-restraint, discipline, and respect for authority and achievement, and shore up "nonpolitical" principles of order (family, property, religion, schools), so that a culture of self-reliance and self-restraint replaces the culture of dependency and critique.[45] The cultural politics of neoconservatism that accompanies the policies

44. See Daniel Bell, *The Cultural Contradictions of Capitalism* (New York: Basic Books, 1976). Bell is not, strictly speaking, a neoconservative, since he defends liberal democracy as well as socialism in the realm of the economy. For an overview of neoconservative cultural assumptions, see Peter Steinfels, *The Neo-Conservatives* (New York: Simon and Schuster, 1979).

45. For an argument in favor of resacralizing the political, see Edward Shils, *Tradition* (Chicago: University of Chicago Press, 1981). For arguments bewailing our hedonist culture and advocating a revived family life, see Christopher Lasch, *The Culture of Narcissism* (New York: Norton, 1979) and *Haven in a Heartless World* (New York: Basic Books, 1977). For criticisms of the modernist culture of critique, see Bell, *Cultural Contradictions of Capitalism,* and Alvin Gouldner, *The Future of Intellectuals and the Rise of the New Class* (New York: Seabury, 1979).

of deregulation and privatization are thus based on the defense or re-creation of a traditionalist and authoritarian lifeworld.[46]

Our conception of civil society points to a different assessment. First, we try to show that the resources for meaning, authority, and social integration are undermined not by cultural or political modernity (based on the principles of critical reflection, discursive conflict resolution, equality, autonomy, participation, and justice) but, rather, by the expansion of an increasingly illiberal corporate economy as well as by the overextension of the administrative apparatus of the interventionist state into the social realm. The use of economic and political power to shore up (or worse, re-create) the "traditional" hierarchical, patriarchal, or exclusionary character of many of the institutions of civil society is, on our view, what fosters dependency. We agree that certain features of the welfare state[47] fragment collectivities, destroy horizontal solidarities, isolate and render private individuals dependent on state apparatuses. Unrestrained capitalist expansion, however, has the same destructive consequences. But appeals to family, tradition, religion, or community could foster the destructive fundamentalism of false communities so easily manipulated from above, unless the achievements of liberalism (the principle of rights), democracy (the principles of participation and discourse), and justice (a precondition for solidarity) are first defended and then supplemented with new democratic and egalitarian forms of association within civil society.

Moreover, to opt for the preservation of traditions, if accompanied by a denial of the universalist tradition of cultural and political modernity, implies fundamentalism. Accordingly, the question that flows from our model becomes: which traditions, which family form, which community, which solidarities are to be defended against disruptive intervention? Even if cultural modernity itself is just one tradition among many, its universal thrust is the reflexive, nonauthoritarian relation toward tradition—an orientation that can be applied to itself and that implies autonomy (allegedly cherished by the neoconservative) rather than heteronomy. Indeed, traditions that have become problematic can be preserved only on the terrain of cultural modernity, i.e., through arguments that invoke principles. Such discussion does not mean the abolition of tradition, solidarity, or meaning; rather, it is the only acceptable procedure for adjudicating between competing traditions, needs, or interests that are in conflict. Accordingly, our model points toward the

---

46. A series of books on "mediating structures" sponsored by the American Enterprise Institute offers a case in point. See John Neuhaus and Peter Berger, *To Empower People: The Role of Mediating Structures in Public Policy* (Washington: American Enterprise Institute, 1978), Michael Novak, ed., *Democracy and Mediating Structures* (Washington: American Enterprise Institute, 1990), and Nathan Glazer, *The Limits of Social Policy* (Cambridge: Harvard University Press, 1988).

47. Surely not all of them. We fail to see how social security, health insurance, job training programs for the unemployed, unemployment insurance, and family supports such as day care or parental leave create dependency rather than autonomy, even if the particular administrative requirements for such programs as AFDC (such as the man-in-the-house rule) do create dependency and are humiliating. But these are empirical questions.

further modernization of the culture and institutions of civil society as the only way to arrive at autonomy, self-reliance, and solidarity among peers allegedly desired by the neoconservative critics of the welfare state.

Our conception of civil society seeks to demystify the other strain within neoconservatism, namely, that the only alternative to the paternalism, social engineering, and the bureaucratization of our lives typical of welfare state systems is to shift steering back to the magic of the marketplace (and of course to renounce distributive justice and egalitarianism). This "solution" is not only politically untenable and normatively undesirable; it is also based on the fallacious assumption that no other options exist. Our framework, however, allows in principle for a third approach, one that does not seek to correct the economic or state penetration of society by shifting back and forth between these two steering mechanisms. Instead, the task is to guarantee the autonomy of the modern state and economy while simultaneously protecting civil society from destructive penetration and functionalization by the imperatives of these two spheres. For now, of course, we have only some of the elements of a theory that can thematize both the differentiation of civil society from state and economy and its reflexive influence over them through the institutions of political and economic society. But we believe that our conception has the best prospects for future theoretical progress and for integrating the diverse conceptual strategies that are currently available. The project it implies would avoid correcting the results of state paternalism by another form of colonization of society, this time by an unregulated market economy. It would seek to accomplish the work of social policy by more decentralized and autonomous civil-society-based programs than in traditional welfare states and the work of economic regulation by nonbureaucratic, less intrusive forms of legislation, "reflexive law," focusing on procedures and not results. In our view this synthetic project should be described not only by Habermas's term, "the reflexive continuation of the welfare state," but also by the complementary idea of the "reflexive continuation of the democratic revolution." The former arises in the context of Western welfare states, the latter in that of the democratization of authoritarian regimes. The two ideas can and should be combined. Thus far, the recent revival and development of the concept of civil society has involved learning from the experience of the "transitions to democracy." The idea of the reflexive continuation of the welfare state and of liberal democracy should, however, open the way for enriching the intellectual resources of democrats in the East by what has been learned in a double critique of already established welfare states and of their neoconservative discontents. A theory of civil society informed by such ideas should also inform the projects of all those in the West who seek the further democratization of liberal democracies.

[1992]

"The Virtue of Civil Society"

Since Montesquieu, writers on politics have been aware that there might be an association of particular moral qualities and beliefs with particular political regimes. The association between virtue and republican governments, although duly recorded by students of Montesquieu's thought, has however been passed over. The disposition to participate in politics, the sense of political potency or impotence, certain traits of personality such as could be summarized in the term "authoritarian personality," et cetera, have all been studied by theorists of democracy. Virtue, or public spirit or civility, has been neglected.

I would like to take up Montesquieu's theme once more. I wish to enquire into the place of virtue or what I call civility in the liberal democratic order, which Montesquieu referred to as the republican type of government. Latterly the term "civil society" has come to be used very loosely as equivalent to "liberal democratic society." They are not entirely the same and the difference between them is significant. In civility lies the difference between a well-ordered and a disordered liberal democracy.

Civil Society

The idea of civil society is the idea of a part of society which has a life of its own, which is distinctly different from the state, and which is largely in autonomy from it. Civil society lies beyond the boundaries of the family and the clan and beyond the locality; it lies short of the state.

This idea of civil society has three main components. The first is a part of society comprising a complex of autonomous institutions—economic, religious, intellectual and political—distinguishable from the family, the clan, the locality and the state. The second is a part of society possessing a particular complex of relationships between itself and the state and a distinctive set of institutions which safeguard the separation of state and civil society and maintain effective ties between them. The third is a widespread pattern of refined or civil manners. The first has been called civil society; sometimes the entire inclusive society which has those specific properties is called civil society.

Regarding the separation of state from civil society, that part of society with which we are concerned here consists of individual and collective activities which are not guided primarily by the rules of primordial collectivities and which are also not directed by the state. These activities have rules of their own, both formal and informal. The state lays down laws which set limits to the actions of individuals and collectivities but within those limits, which in a civil society are ordinarily wide, the actions of individuals and collectivities are freely chosen or are performed in accordance with explicit agreement among the participants or are based on calculations of individual or collective interest or on the rules of the constituent collectivity. It is in this sense that civil society is separate from the state.

Civil society is not totally separate form the state. It would not be part of the society as a whole if it were totally separated, just as the family, different and distinctive though it is, is not totally separated from civil society and the state. The state lays down laws which set the outermost boundaries or the autonomy of the diverse spheres and sectors of civil society; so, civil society from its side lays down limits on the actions of the state. Civil society and the state are bound together by the constitution and by traditions which stress the obligations of each to the other as well as their rights vis-à-vis each other. The rights of individuals and collectivities with respect to each other are provided by the constitutions and the laws and traditions.

A civil society is a society of civility in the conduct of the members of the society towards each other. Civility enters into conduct between individuals and between individuals towards society. It likewise regulates the relations of collectivities towards each other, the relations between collectivities and the state and the relations of individuals with the state.

Revival of the Concept

In recent years, the term "civil society" has appeared relatively suddenly upon the intellectual scene. It has nevertheless hovered in numerous variants on the edge of discussions of society every since antiquity; sometimes it entered more centrally. It was a term of ancient jurisprudence. It was a fluctuating presence in medieval political philosophy where it was distinguished from ecclesiastical institutions. In the seventeenth century it was contrasted with the state of nature; it was a condition in which men lived under government. In the eighteenth century it came into something like its present usage, as a type of society which was larger than and different from a tribe. Adam Ferguson, when he wrote *The History of Civil Society,* meant a society of less barbarous manners, a society which practiced the cultivation of the mind by arts and letters. Civil society was seen as one in which urban life and commercial activities flourished. Adam Ferguson regarded associations for commercial ends, associations which were not primordial, as characteristic of civil society. In the views which prevailed in the eighteenth century, civil society was pluralistic; minimally it was a society with numerous private activities, outside the family and not assimilated into the state. Without referring to it by name, the pattern of the civil society was most fully delineated by Adam Smith. The outlines of the civil society were sharpened by the German romantic precipitation of the idea of the "folk," which was thought to be a complete antithesis of the market. The "folk society" was a small local society, dominated by tradition and history; it was a society in a condition where "status" governed action; the individual had no standing on the basis of his individual qualities and achievements. It was a society of agriculturists and craftsmen in small communities largely self-contained. These views were elaborated to contrast with the individualism, rational thinking and commercial activities of territorially extensive societies. In 1887, Ferdinand Tönnies summarized the contrast in the terms *Gemeinschaft* and *Gesellschaft*.

In the nineteenth century the notion of civil society was most elaborately considered by Hegel in his *Philosophy of Right (Philosophie des Rechts);* Hegel drew much from Adam Ferguson and Adam Smith. For Hegel the civil society, or rather the civil part of society, was distinguished from the family and the state. It was the market, the commercial sector of society and the institutions which were necessary to the functioning of the market and the protection of its members. It was conducive to the realization of the interests of individuals but it also, through corporations, formed individuals into super-individual collectivities with their own collective self-consciousnesses and integrated them into a single larger collective self-consciousness which was fully realized in the state. Like all other usages of "civil society" in modern times, Hegel's usage enunciated the right to the private ownership of property as the central and indispensable feature of civil society. Hegel used the term *bügerliche Gesellschaft,* which has been translated as "bourgeois society" and as "civil society."

From Hegel, the idea of civil society came into the thought of Marx. For Marx, it came to mean something different from what Adam Ferguson thought of when he wrote *The History of Civil Society*. Commerce was only one feature of civil society according to Adam Ferguson. Marx's conception of civil society, developed more than a half century after Adam Smith's analysis of the market, was an extension of Smith's views, and of the successors of Smith, to the "factory system." The division of labor, exchange, and private ownership of the instruments of production, already crucial in Hegel's thought, and the society divided into the property-owners and the propertyless—which Marx added from earlier writers of the eighteenth and nineteenth centuries—were the heart of the civil society envisaged by Marx. Marx disregarded Adam Smith's views about moral sentiments, just as he rejected Hegel's views about the unification of individual minds in the *Geist*. He gave his attention to the commercial or economic aspect of civil society. Marx followed Hegel in his use of the designation *bügerliche Gesellschaft,* but he also used the term to refer to all of society and not solely to refer to a part of it. Marx made "civil society," in the narrower Hegelian sense, the determinant of the whole society. Marx equated "civil society" with bourgeois "capitalistic society." For Marx, civil society was certainly not a society of more polished manners; it was not even a society held in coherence by the mutual dependence of partners in a relationship of exchange. It was rather a society in which the propertyless mass of the population was coercively held in subjugation by the owners of the instruments of production. The relationships of production, and the division of society into the propertied classes and the propertyless classes were the defining features of civil society. All else was derivative from that.

In all these variations and shifts in meaning, from the eighteenth century onward, the term "civil society" retained certain central features. First, it was a part of a society distinct from and independent of the state. Where it had not yet reached the point of independence from the state, it was argued that it should become so. Secondly, it provided for the rights of individuals and particularly for the rights of property. Thirdly, civil society was a constellation of many autonomous economic units or business firms, acting independently of the state and competing with each other.

An additional feature, not much emphasized in the nineteenth century—perhaps it was no more than an overtone—was the idea of a political community. This carried with it the idea of citizenship. This is an aspect which was not stressed by the Scottish writers or their Germanic continuators. Nevertheless, it was there, carrying forward the image of a *polis,* of a municipality, of citizens with rights to public office and to participation in discussions of and decisions about public issues. This was an inheritance received from the jurisprudential and political philosophies of classical antiquity to early modern times. "Civil" was contrasted with "natural." It was the condition of men living in society, living in accordance with rules.

One component of civil society which was neglected in practically all discussions in the nineteenth century was the nation or nationality. Nation and nationality were thought to be characteristic of the type of society which was being superseded by civil society. Nevertheless, as civil societies came to be increasingly realized in the course of the nineteenth century, the nation or nationality provided the cohesion which would otherwise have been lacking in those civil societies.

Since the nineteenth century, the term "civil society" has been used to refer to a part of society and to refer to the entire society which possesses such a part. That part has not been found in all societies and so not all societies have been civil societies.

Civil Society and Marxism-Leninism

Despite the coerced ascendancy of Marxism in the communist countries of Eastern and Central Europe, for nearly three-quarters of a century in the Russian Empire

and for nearly a half century in Poland, Hungary, the Balkans and Czechoslovakia, and the distortion of the idea, the two central features of the idea of civil society—private property and independence from the state—with the overtone of citizenship, have never been extinguished from memory. "Civil society," meaning a
market economy running separately from the state, and citizenship meaning the
exercise of civil capacities, i. e., participation in the affairs of the collectivity, i. e.,
pronouncing judgment on them and sharing in decisions about them, did not entirely fade from memory.

Polished or refined manners meant respect for the dignity of the members of
society. A society of refined manners was one in which the members acted with
consideration towards each other, with an acknowledgment, institutionally embodied and assured, of the dignity of the individual, derived from his humanity
and from his membership in the political community. Refined or polished manners are the antithesis of rudeness of bureaucrats and the gross brutality of the police. The communist, like the Nazi and fascist, treatment of political opponents
and the communist and Nazi rhetoric in addressing or speaking about their opponents, were the polar opposite of civil manners. The invocation of the idea seems
to have flared up and expanded in the communist countries. From there, its echo
has spread into the countries of the West which have been more or less civil societies for several centuries, although with only rare use of the term in common discourse or by academic political scientists. Its greatest popularity in the West over
the past two decades seems to have occurred among dissident or disillusioned
Marxists.

This is not an accident. Marxist-Leninists declared themselves to be enemies
of civil society. Although they sought to extinguish civil society and its idea, they
did in fact preserve the idea of civil society while suppressing civil society itself.
The polemical rhetoric of Marxism-Leninism preserved the idea, just as the idea
of the devil was preserved in the theology which attempted to circumscribe and
render him powerless.

Capitalistic or bourgeois society replaced "civil society"; the term *bürgerlich*
survived the changed interpretation. The Marxist-Leninist interpretation of
Hegel's idea rejected his notion of the pluralism of civil society; it changed his notion of reciprocal autonomy and interdependence of the state and society by making the state entirely dependent on the ruling stratum of society and placing society completely under the control of the state. Marxist-Leninists retained enough
of the fundamental categories of its intellectual inheritance to permit that inheritance to be discerned and retrieved.

Civil and Market Societies

A market economy is the appropriate pattern of the economic life of a civil society. (Hegel saw this quite clearly; indeed, he made the market the decisive, if not

the sole, feature of civil society.) There is, however, much more to civil society than the market. The hallmark of a civil society is the autonomy of private associations and isntitutions, as well as that of private business firms.

The pluralism of civil society is two-fold. Its pluralism comprises the partially autonomous spheres of economy, religion, culture, intellectual activity, political activity, and so on, vis-à-vis each other. These spheres are never wholly autonomous in their relations with each other; their boundaries are not impermeable. Nevertheless, the spheres are different from each other and, in the objects they pursue in a pluralistic society, they are also largely autonomous. The pluralism of civil society also comprises, within each sphere, a multiplicity of many partially autonomous corporations and institutions; the economic sphere comprises many industries and many business firms; the religious sphere comprises many churches and sects; the intellectual sphere comprises many universities, independent newspapers, periodicals and broadcasting corporations; the political sphere includes many independent political parties. There are many independent voluntary philanthropic and civic associations, and the like.

The Hegelian tendency to define civil society as coterminous with the market, and the Marxian *Umstülpung* of the relations between "*Geist*" and "material conditions" have contributed to the deformation of the idea of civil society. They have led to the diminution of the significance of the other spheres, making the other spheres appear to be derivative from or dependent on the market.

Civil society does not include the state but it presupposed its existence. It presupposes a particular kind of state, namely, a state of limited powers. Among these powers are the powers to enact laws which protect the market. A civil society must provide for private contracts which assert binding obligations and the judicial enforcement of such arrangements; it should provide for collective bargaining and wage-contracts. Civil society requires that the state (or government) be limited in the scope of its activities and that it be bound by law but that it be effective in executing the laws which protect the pluralism of civil society and its necessary liberties. Civil society consists, among other things, of institutions which hedge about the state, which sustain it and delimit the scope of its activities and powers. Civil society requires a distinctive set of political institutions.

The civil society must be more than a set of markets and market-like institutions. What else does it need to be a civil society? It must possess the institutions which protect it from the encroachment of the state and which keep it as a civil society. A civil society must have a system of competing political parties. It required the competition of political parties, seeking the support of universal suffrage with periodic elections for the election of representative legislative bodies which once elected must have a modicum of autonomy vis-à-vis the electorate. It must possess an independent judiciary which upholds the rule of law and protects the liberty of individuals and institutions. It must possess a set of institutions for making known the activities of government; it includes a free press reporting freely on the activities of government. (The press includes here the printed press, radio and television broadcasting, published learned investigation, critical discussion and assessment of the activities of politicians and bureaucrats and of the forms of political and governmental institutions.) These are the primary institutions of civil society because they are the safeguards of the separation of civil society from the state.

Essential to the functioning of the primary institutions are the supporting institutions: voluntary associations and their exercise of the freedoms of association, assembly and representation of petition. Individuals must enjoy the corresponding freedom to associate, assemble and petition. Naturally, freedom of religious belief and worship, association and education are part of civil society. Freedom of academic teaching and study, of investigation and publication are also part of the complex pattern of civil society.

These are the institutions by which the state is kept within substantive and procedural confinement. The confinement, which might be thought to be negative, is sustained on behalf of a positive ideal, the ideal of individual and collective freedom.

Civil society postulates and accentuates the pluralism of autonomous spheres and autonomous institutions acting with and between such spheres. Civil society accepts the diversity of interests and ideal which will arise in any numerous society. It allows diversity of the objectives pursued by individuals and institutions—but not by all and any means whatsoever.

Liberal Democracy and Civility

Liberal democracy is the most general class of society, variants of which, among others, are mass democracy, "retrospective" democracy and civil society. Mass or populistic democracy is a variant of liberal democracy. It is at another pole from civil society insofar as it considers one stratum of society, albeit the majority of the population, as the properly sole beneficiary of policies regarding the distribution of goods, services and honors. Mass democracy would disregard representative institutions, replacing them by demonstrations and plebiscites. Mass democracy is conducive to demagogy and to the extension of governmental powers for the provision of substantive justice. Still another alternative is the "retrospective" democracy formulated by Max Weber[1] in his conversation with Ludendorff in 1919 and by Joseph Schumpeter[2] in which the electorate confirms or dismisses its rulers in accordance with whether it is satisfied with their accomplishments during the most recent electoral period. Civil society differs from mass democracy in its concern for the interests and ideals of all sections of the population and not just for one. It

1. Max Weber, *Zur Neuordnung Deutschlands: Schriften und Reden 1918–1920. Gesamtausgabe* (Tübingen: J. C. B. Mohr, 1988), Abt I, Band 16, p. 553.

2. Joseph Schumpeter, *Capitalism, Socialism and Democracy* (London: Allen & Unwin, 1943), pp. 269–83.

differs from retrospective democracy in its constant scrutiny and assessment of government and its refusal to allow it to extend its range or depth of activities.

Insofar as they work, more or less effectively, to maintain liberal democracy, it may be said that the institutions of liberal democracy "embody" civility; they could not work without a certain minimum of civility.

Civility is an attitude and a pattern of conduct. It is approximately the same as what Montesquieu called virtue. Montesquieu said, "Virtue, in a republic, is a very simple thing; it is love of the republic.' It is 'love of one's country.' 'Love of the republic in a democracy is love of democracy. . . ."[3]

Civility is an appreciation of or attachment to the institutions which constitute civil society. It is an attitude of attachment to the whole society, to all its strata and sections. It is an attitude of concern for the good of the entire society. Civility is simultaneously individualistic, parochial and "holistic." It is solicitous of the well-being of the whole, or the larger interest.

More fundamentally, civility is the conduct of a person whose individual self-consciousness has been partly superseded by his collective self-consciousness, the society as a whole and the institutions of civil society being the referents of his collective self-consciousness.

In 1973, Mr. Ferdinand Mount published an excellent essay, entitled "The Recovery of Civility."[4] It was mainly about civility in the sense of good manners and courtesy towards political opponents as well as towards political allies. He said that "civility . . . implied . . . inclusion in the same moral universe."

The term "civility" has usually, both in the past and in its recent revival, been interpreted to mean courtesy, well-spokenness, moderation, respect for others, self-restraint, gentlemanliness, urbanity, refinement, good manners, politeness. All those terms have generally been reserved for the description of the conduct of individuals in the immediate presence of each other. In all of these usages, there are intimations of consideration for the sensibilities of other persons and particularly for their desire to be esteemed. Thus, it would be antithetical to civility to refuse esteem or deference to another person. Civility treats others as, at least, equal in dignity, never as inferior in dignity.

Civility and Good Manners

What does civility have to do with civil society? What place do good manners, courtesy, et cetera, have in a civil society of partially autonomous spheres and many, partially autonomous and competing individuals and associations? What does the civility of good manners have in common with the civility of civil society? Let me begin by saying that both postulate a minimal dignity of all citizens. The

3. Montesquieu, *de L'Esprit des lois (Oeuvres)* (Paris: Dalibon, 1822, II), pp. 213–14.
4. *Encounter* XLI, 1 July 1973, pp. 31–43.

dignity which is accorded to a person who is the object of civil conduct or good manners is dignity of moral worth. Good manners postulate the moral dignity of the other person who is seen face-to-face, and in public discourse about individuals and groups who are not immediately present. It makes no reference to his merit or dignity in general, in all other situations. Civility as a feature of civil society considers others as fellow-citizens of equal dignity in their rights and obligations as members of civil society; it means regarding other persons, including one's adversaries, as members of the same inclusive collectivity, i.e., as members of the same society, even though they belong to different parties or to different religious communities or to different ethnic groups. Civility in the former sense is included in civility in the latter sense. But in the latter sense, it includes concern for the good of adversaries as well as for the good of allies. Therein lies the difference between civility understood as good manners or courtesy and civility as the virtue of civil society.

The two kinds of civility are different from each other; they are also similar to each other. They are interdependent; one contributes to the other. Civility in the sense of courtesy mollifies or ameliorates the strain which accompanies the risks, the dangers of prospective loss and the injuries of the real losses of an economically, politically and intellectually competitive society in which some persons are bound to lose. Courtesy makes life a bit more pleasant; it is easier to bear than harshness. Softly spoken, respectful speech is more pleasing to listen to than harsh, contemptuous speech. Civility in manners holds anger and resentment in check; it has a calming, pacifying effect on the sentiment. It might make for less excitability. Civil manners are aesthetically pleasing and morally right. Civil manners redound to the benefit of political activity.

Civil manners reach into politics in legislative assemblies, in public political meetings, in committees of legislative bodies—in all situations in which individuals can see each other and hear each other and in which individuals are addressed directly by other individuals, each of whom is present as the representative of a political group or as the exponent of a political view. They make relationships among the members of such institutions more agreeable. They make opposition less rancorous; they make opponents less irreconcilable.

Civil manners are beneficial to the working of civil society. Civil manners contribute in many situations to the peaceful working of the institutions of civil society and to the relations between them. The absence of civil manners introduces an unsettling effect on institutions.

Civility as a Mode of Political Action

There is more to civility than good manners and conciliatory tones. Civility is also a mode of political action. It is a mode of political action which postulates that antagonists are also members of the same society, that they participate in the same collective self-consciousness. The individual who acts with civility regards the individuals who are its objects as being one with himself and each other, as being parts of a single entity. Civility rests, at bottom, on the collective self-consciousness of civil society. Of course, individuals participate in many collectivities and they are also individuals. They participate in many collective self-consciousnesses and they also have their own individual self-consciousness, but in a civil society they participate in, they are parts of the collective self-consciousness of society.

The image of the common good is inherent in the nature of collective self-consciousness. Collective self-consciousness does not obliterate individual self-consciousness; collective self-consciousness has influence on conduct only through the activity of individual self-consciousness. In the other direction, no individual can live without a modicum of collective self-consciousness. No society could exist without it. Collective self-consciousness is generated wherever there are enduring relationships among human beings.

Collective self-consciousness which is a cognitive state of seeing one's self as part of a collectivity, has inherently within it a norm which gives precedence to the interest of the collectivity over the individual or parochial interest. All societies engender some degree of collective self-consciousness. This does not mean that the collective self-consciousness always prevails over the individual's self-consciousness. On the contrary, the opposite is very frequently the case. Nor does it by any means imply that the more inclusive collective self-consciousness always takes precedence over the less inclusive collective self-consciousness. Nevertheless, the existence of the inclusive collective self-consciousness has a restraining effect. It is never obliterated, even in a society in a state of civil war. It is the inclusive collective self-consciousness which prevents society from degenerating completely into the state of nature.

The late Carl Schmitt said that political activity of a society is organized around the poles of friends and enemies. This is true of societies which are on the verge of or are already engaged in civil war. This is the antithesis of civil society. Civility is a mode of conduct which protects liberal democratic society from the danger of extremes of the partisanship which it, itself, generate; civility limits the potential sources or compensates some of the real losses which are bound to be inflicted on a society in which conflicts are both inherent in—they are inherent in all societies— and provided for by the competitive pluralism of its liberal democratic constitution. Without such civility, a pluralistic society can degenerate into a war of each against all. Civility works like a governor of civil society. It limits the intensity of conflict. It reduces the distance between conflicting demands: it is a curb on centrifugal tendencies. Civility, by the attachment of its individual bearers to the society as a whole, places a limit on the irreconcilability of the parochial ends pursued. Attachment to the whole reduces the rigidity of attachment to the parts, whether it be a social class or an occupational or ethnic group or a political party or a religious community.

All societies, the highly differentiated as well as the relatively homogeneous, are sites of conflicting interests in the sense that, at any given moment, when one part obtains more of anything, there is less for the other part. These conflicts and contentions do not occur or are not severe as long as total demands do not greatly exceed total supply of the valued things which will satisfy them.

Ideals and beliefs too have limited opportunities for their realization; the realization of the ideals of one group would usually preclude the realization of the ideals and beliefs of other groups within the same society. Where contention among the advocates of the diverse ideals and beliefs is free, there will naturally be more public contention than in an unfree society.

Contention is unsettling not only because it raises desire for gains and fears of losses, but also because it causes its participants and others in the same society to regard contention as inevitable and necessary. It supports the view that life is exclusively a matter of "dog eat dog." It makes for a hardening of contention and an irreconcilability of differences in interests and ideals. The tendency of contention to be expressed in a hyperbolic rhetoric aggravates fear of the other parties to the conflict. It makes for distrust.

Civil Society and the State

Although autonomy vis-à-vis the state is one of the features of a civil society, the autonomy is far from complete. Civil society operates within the framework set by laws. The laws of such a society are, among other things, intended to hold conflict in check by compelling adherence to agreements, and by inflicting sanctions on actions which criminally damage other persons. Laws require that rights within the civil society be respected that duties be performed.

A civil society is a society where law binds the state as well as the citizens. It protects the citizens from arbitrary and unjust decisions of high political authorities, bureaucrats, the police, the military, and the rich and the powerful. A civil society is one where the law prevails equally against the impulses of citizens to seek their own immediate advantage. The effectiveness of the laws both in the state and in civil society—and the family—depends in part on the civility of individuals. Of course, the effectiveness of the laws depends upon the executive organs of the state but it cannot be effective through the actions of those organs alone. The executive organs of society cannot cope with all the situations and actions to which they refer; even the best police force cannot detect, trace and capture all criminals, to say nothing of juvenile delinquents. It is true of course that if the investigative parts of officialdom and the police are very successful in tracking and finding most of those who have infringed the law and if they succeed to have them found guilty on the basis of sound evidence and punished accordingly, the high degree of probability of detection and punishment might have a deterrent effect. This alone would be insufficient. The tendency towards law-abidingness must be reinforced by belief in the legitimacy of the laws or the regulations. Legitimacy in a pluralistic, civil society depends on the civil attachments of the bulk of the citizenry to the central institutions of society.

Substantive Civility

Substantive civility is the virtue of civil society. It is the readiness to moderate particular, individual or parochial interests and to give precedence to the common good. The common good is not susceptible to an unambiguous definition; consensus about it is probably not attainable. It is however certainly meaningful to speak about it. Wherever two antagonistic advocates arrive at a compromise through the recognition of a common interest, they redefine themselves as members of a collectivity, the good of which has precedence over their own particular objectives. The good which is accorded precedence by that decision might be no more than the continued existence of the collectivity in which they both participate. The common good is acknowledged wherever a more inclusive collectivity is acknowledged.

Every action in which thinking of and attempting to reduce the prospective loss inflicted on one section of a society when another section would benefit from a particular event or policy is an act of substantive civility. It is always possible to consider the consequences of any particular action in the light of its effect on the wider circle within which a decision is made. Every action which bears in mind the well-being of a more inclusive collectivity is an action on behalf of the common good.

The Civil Politician

Max Weber in his lecture on "Politik als Beruf" spoke very eloquently about conflicts of values. Such conflicts cannot, according to Max Weber, be reconciled into a logically harmonious pattern; what can be done is to act in the light of what the attainment of each value costs in terms of each other value. The adherent of the ethos and politics of responsibility[5]—he called it *Veranwortungsethik* and implied the category of *Verwantwortungspolitik*—has however to arrive at a decision. He has to make the best decision possible, arrived at by the weighing of each of the values and its costs. There is no formula for making benefits and costs homogeneous so that an arithmetic sum of a maximal realization can be arrived at.

In another essay, written by Max Weber as an occasional political pamphlet during the First Word War *(Parlament und Regierung im neugeordneten Deutschland)*,[6] he argued for parliamentary government as a school for the selection of political leaders with sufficient force of character and sufficiently great persuasive powers to be able to maintain their parliamentary majorities or to keep their parties coherent and positive when in opposition. The task of such leaders is to fuse

5. Max Weber, *Politik als Beruf* (Munich: Leipzig, Dunker & Humblot 1919), pp. 48ff.
6. Max Weber, *Zur Politik im Weltkrieg* (Schriften und Reden, 1914-1918). *Gesamlausgabe* (Tübingen: J. C. B. Mohr, 1984), Abt I, Band 5, pp. 421-596.

into a single coherent collectivity the diverse circles of adherents such as are drawn into association with a political party.

These two works of Max Weber, when brought together, define the task of a civil politician. Speaking on behalf of the whole is the task of the politician of a civil, i. e., liberal democratic society. They also define the task of the civil citizen; the citizen has the task of promulgating an objective which is broader than that of a leader of a political party. It is to seek consensus about an objective which will benefit the entire society and which will be sought by the entire society. Of course, the word "entire" is excessive; the support of the entire society is impossible and unnecessary. What is needed is sufficient consensus to permit government to work effectively towards the common good. (The effectiveness of government is also dependent on its practical knowledge and its capacity for realistic judgment, not just on the consensus of its supporters and its critics.)

A society possessing the institutions of civil society needs a significant component of ordinary citizens and politicians who exercise the virtue of civility. How large must that component of civil citizens be? How much civility does a liberal democratic society need to be a civil society? Where in the society must civility be located?

Of no society can it be expected that all its citizens will have a very high degree of civility. The capacity of civility—the capacity for imagination and cognition of the properties of one's fellow men and the capacity to entertain and give precedence to the inclusive collective self-consciousness within one self over one's individual self-consciousness—is probably rather unevenly distributed within any society. There are some persons in whom civil preponderates; there are others in whom it is usually at a low ebb. For a civil society to benefit from the former, it is important that many of them should be in authoritative positions. There are certain roles in society in which civility is particularly important for that society. The higher judiciary, senior civil servants, leading legislators, eminent academics, prominent businessmen, influential journalists, and others like them, nationally and locally, must have relatively high degrees of civility. At least some of the leading members of each of these professions should have it; their civility should furthermore be visible. There must also be a scatter of persons of moderate degrees of civility throughout the society. There must be at least small degrees of civility in most citizens. There must be areas of concentration and larger areas of dispersion of civility.

Civility not only has immediate effectiveness in the actions of those who possess it; it also has a radiative or reinforcing effect. Those who have a larger degree of civility animate the civility of those who have less, and so on downward in a pyramid of civility towards those with least civility and least responsiveness. A spark of civility exists in the breast of most individuals even though it is not strong. It is certainly strengthened by the scatter of civil persons throughout any modern society and in particular by the presence and visibility of civil persons in the institutions of civil society.

What we ought to hope for is enough civility in the participants in those institutions to maintain them effectively as civil institutions—and not as sites of intense conflicts between irreconcilable interests and ideas espoused by uncompromising parochial groups and inflexibly egoistic individuals. Civility can only be an ingredient of a civil society; it can serve to offset the perpetual drives towards the preponderance of individual self-consciousness and parochial collective self-consciousness.

Even those persons who are highly civil are not likely to manifest their civility with equal intensity on all occasions. Most human beings have some parochial attachment to their immediate and extended families, to their locality, to their social class, to their profession, their religious community, their generation, ethnic group, and so on. These attachments, like civility, are unequally distributed among occasions and among individuals. They cannot be entirely abrogated or suppressed; nor is it desirable that they should be. Even persons with a large measure of civility will possess attachments to their other parochial or less inclusive collectivities. Civility does not require their complete renunciation but it does require that they yield precedence on many occasions.

To summarize: the center and the main sub-centers of society need to be civil to a greater extent than the peripheries. But in the peripheries to these, some civility is necessary to offset the partisanship of persons at the centers and sub-centers.

The idea of the common good and its other variants like the idea of the happiness of the greatest number are frequently invoked. They are frequently invoked with the intention to deceive. But even where they are honestly invoked, they are ambiguous. It is very difficult to define them precisely. For this and for more important reasons, there are bound to be in any civil society, diverse conceptions of the common good, conflicting with each other in varying degrees. The proponent of one conception of the common good might denounce the proponents of the other conceptions.

This does not invalidate the conception of the common good. In disagreement though they might be, they also recognize that there is a difference between parochial interests and the interests of more inclusive collectivities. What they disagree about is the weight to be assigned to different valued conditions, which they evaluate somewhat differently. Difference of opinion are aggravated by disagreements about facts.

Thus the ideal of the common good is a practicable ideal, even though there is like at any given moment to be disagreement about its substance, and even though it can never be completely realized.

[1997]

"A Better Vision: The Idea of Civil Society"

My aim in this essay is to defend a complex, imprecise, and, at crucial points, uncertain account of society and politics. I have no hope of theoretical simplicity, not at this historical moment when so many stable oppositions of political and intellectual life have collapsed; but I also have no desire for simplicity, since a world that theory could fully grasp and neatly explain would not, I suspect, be a pleasant place. In the nature of things, then, my argument won't be elegant, and though I believe that arguments should march, the sentences following one another like soldiers on parade, the route of my march today will be twisting and roundabout. I shall begin with the idea of civil society, recently revived by Central and East European intellectuals, and go on to talk about the state, the economy, and the nation, and then about civil society and the state again. These are the crucial social formations that we inhabit, but we don't at this moment live comfortably in any of them. Nor is it possible to imagine, in accordance with one or another of the great simplifying theories, a way to choose among them—as if we were destined to find, one day, the best social formation. I mean to argue against choosing, but I shall also claim that it is from within civil society that this argument is best understood.

The words "civil society" name the space of uncoerced human association and also the set of relational networks—formed for the sake of family, faith, interest, and ideology—that fill this space. Central and East European dissidence flourished within a highly restricted version of civil society, and the first task of the new democracies created by the dissidents, so we are told, is to rebuild the networks: unions, churches, political parties and movements, cooperatives, neighborhoods, schools of thought, societies for promoting or preventing this and that. In the West, by contrast, we have lived in civil society for many years without knowing it. Or, better, since the Scottish Enlightenment, or since Hegel, the words have been known to the knowers of such things but they have rarely served to focus anyone else's attention. Now writers in Hungary, Czechoslovakia, and Poland invite us to think about how this social formation is secured and invigorated.

We have reasons of our own for accepting the invitation. Increasingly, associational life in the "advanced" capitalist and social democratic countries seems at risk. Publicists and preachers warn us of a steady attenuation of everyday cooperation and civic friendship. And this time it's possible that they are not, as they usually are, foolishly alarmist. Our cities really are noisier and nastier than they once were. Familial solidarity, mutual assistance, political likemindedness—all these are less certain and less substantial than they once were. Other people, strangers on the street, seem less trustworthy than they once did. The Hobbesian account of society is more persuasive than it once was.

Perhaps this worrisome picture follows—in part, no more, but what else can a political theorist say?—from the fact that we have not thought enough about solidarity and trust or planned for their future. We have been thinking too much about social formations different from, in competition with, civil society. And so we have neglected the networks through which civility is produced and reproduced. Imagine that the following questions were posed one or two centuries ago to political theorists and moral philosophers: what is the preferred setting, the most supportive environment, for the good life? What sorts of institutions should we work for? Nineteenth- and twentieth-century social thought provides four different, by now familiar, answers to these questions. Think of them as four rival ideologies, each with its own claim to completeness and correctness. Each is importantly wrong. Each neglects the necessary pluralism of any civil society. Each is predicated on an assumption I mean to attack: that such questions must receive a singular answer.

Definitions from the Left

I shall begin, since this is for me the best-known ground, with two leftist answers. The first of the two holds that the preferred setting for the good life is the political community, the democratic state, within which we can be citizens: freely engaged, fully committed, decision-making members. And a citizen, on this view, is much the best thing to be. To live well is to be politically active, working with our fellow citizens, collectively determining our common destiny—not for the sake of this or that determination but for the work itself, in which our highest capacities as rational and moral agents find expression. We know ourselves best as persons who propose, debate and decide.

This argument goes back to the Greeks, but we are most likely to recognize its neoclassical versions. It is Rousseau's argument or the standard leftist interpretation of Rousseau's argument. His understanding of citizenship as moral agency is one of the key sources of democratic idealism. We can see it at work in a liberal such as John Stuart Mill, in whose writing is produced an unexpected defense of syndicalism (what is today called "workers' control") and, more generally, of social democracy. It appeared among nineteenth- and twentieth-century democratic radicals, often with a hard populist edge. It played a part in the reiterated demand for social inclusion by women, workers, blacks, and new immigrants, all of whom based their claims on their capacity as agents. And this same neoclassical idea of citizenship resurfaced in the 1960s in New Left theories of participation, where it was, however, like latter-day revivals of many ideas, highly theoretical and without much local resonance.

Today, perhaps in response to the political disasters of the late sixties, "communitarians" in the United States struggle to give Rousseauian idealism a historical reference, looking back to the early American republic and calling for a renewal of civic virtue. They prescribe citizenship as an antidote to the fragmentation of contemporary society—for these theorists, like Rousseau, are disinclined to value the fragments. In their hands, republicanism is still a simplifying creed. If politics is our highest calling, then we are called away from every other activity (or, every other activity is redefined in political terms); our energies are directed toward policy formation and decision making in the democratic state.

I don't doubt that the active and engaged citizen is an attractive fixture—even if some of the activists that we actually meet carrying placards and shouting slogans aren't all that attractive. The most penetrating criticism of this first answer to the question about the good life is not that the life isn't good but that it isn't the "real life" of very many people in the modern world. This is so in two senses. First, though the power of the democratic state has grown enormously, partly (and rightly) in response to the demands of engaged citizens, it can't be said that the state is fully in the hands of its citizens. And the larger it gets, the more it takes over those smaller associations still subject to hands-on control. The rule of the demos is in significant ways illusory: the participation of ordinary men and women in the activities of the state (unless they are state employees) is largely vicarious; even party militants are more likely to argue and complain than actually to decide.

Second, despite the singlemindedness of republican ideology, politic rarely engages the full attention of the citizens who are supposed to be its chief protagonists. They have too many other things to worry about. Above all, they have to earn a living. They are more deeply engaged in the economy than in the political community. Republican theorists (like Hannah Arendt) recognize this engagement only as a threat to civic virtue. Economic activity belongs to the realm of necessity, they argue, politics to the realm of freedom. Ideally, citizens should not have to work; they should be served by machines, if not by slaves, so that they can flock to the assemblies and argue with their fellows about affairs of state. In practice, however, work, though it begins in necessity, takes on a value of its own—expressed in commitment to a career, pride in a job well done, a sense of camaraderie in the workplace. All of these are competitive with the values of citizenship.

The second leftist position on the preferred setting for the good life involves a turning away from republican politics and a focus instead on economic activity. We can think of this as the socialist answer to the questions I began with; it can be found in Marx and also, though the arguments are somewhat different, among the utopians he hoped to supersede. For Marx, the preferred setting is the cooperative economy, where we can all be producers—artists (Marx was a romantic), inventors, and artisans. (Assembly-line workers don't quite seem to fit.) This again is much the best thing to be. The picture Marx paints is of creative men and women making useful and beautiful objects, not for the sake of this or that object but for the sake of creativity itself, the highest expression of our "species-being" as *homo faber,* man-the-maker.

The state, in this view, ought to be managed in such a way as to set productivity free. It doesn't matter who the managers are so long as they are committed to this goal and rational in its pursuit. Their work is technically important but not substantively interesting. Once productivity is free, politics simply ceases to engage anyone's attention. Before that time, in the Marxist here and now, political conflict is taken to be the superstructural enactment of economic conflict, and democracy is valued mainly because it enables socialist movements and parties to organize for victory. The value is instrumental and historically specific. A democratic state is the preferred setting not for the good life but for the class struggle; the purpose of the struggle is to win, and victory brings an end to democratic instrumentality. There is no intrinsic value in democracy, no reason to think that politics has, for creatures like us, a permanent attractiveness. When we are all engaged in productive activity, social division and the conflicts it engenders will disappear, and the state, in the once-famous phrase, will "wither away."

In fact, if this vision were ever realized, it is politics that would wither away. Some kind of administrative agency would still be necessary for economic coordination, and it is only a Marxist conceit to refuse to call this agency a state. "Society regulates the general production," Marx wrote in *The German Ideology,* "and thus makes it possible for me to do one thing today and another tomorrow . . . just as I have a mind." Because this regulation is nonpolitical, the individual producers are freed from the burdens of citizenship. They attend instead to the things they make and to the cooperative relationships they establish. Exactly how one can work with other people and still do whatever one pleases is unclear to me and probably to most other readers of Marx. The texts suggest an extraordinary faith in the virtuosity of the regulators. No one, I think, quite shares this faith today, but something like it helps to explain the tendency of some leftists to see even the liberal and democratic state as an obstacle that has to be, in the worst of recent jargons, "smashed."

The seriousness of Marxist antipolitics is nicely illustrated by Marx's own dislike of syndicalism. What the syndicalists proposed was a neat amalgam of the first and second answers to the question about the good life: for them, the preferred setting was the worker-controlled factory, where men and women were simultaneously citizens and producers, making decisions and making things. Marx seems to have regarded the combination as impossible; factories could not be both democratic and productive. This is the point of Engel's little essay on authority, which I take to express Marx's view also. More generally, self-government on the job called into question the legitimacy of "social regulation" or state planning, which alone, Marx thought, could enable individual workers to devote themselves, without distraction, to their work.

But this vision of the cooperative economy is set against an unbelievable background—a nonpolitical state, regulation without conflict, "the administration of things." In every actual experience of socialist politics, the state has moved rapidly into the foreground, and most socialists, in the West at least, have been driven to make their own amalgam of the first and second answers. They call themselves *democratic* socialists, focusing on the state as well as (in fact, much more than) on the economy and doubling the preferred settings for the good life. Because I believe that two are better than one, I take this to be progress. But before I try to suggest what further progress might look like, I need to describe two more ideological answers to the question about the good life, one of them capitalist, the other nationalist. For there is no reason to think that only leftists love singularity.

A Capitalist Definition

The third answer holds that the preferred setting for the good life is the marketplace, where individual men and women, consumers rather than producers, choose among a maximum number of options. The autonomous individual confronting his, and now her, possibilities—this is much the best thing to be. To live well is not to make political decisions or beautiful objects; it is to make personal choices. Not any particular choices, for no choice is substantively the best: it is the activity of choosing that makes for autonomy. And the market within which choices are made, like the socialist economy, largely dispenses with politics; it requires at most a minimal state—not "social regulation," only the police.

Production, too, is free even if it isn't, as in the Marxist vision, freely creative. More important than the producers, however, are the entrepreneurs—heroes of autonomy, consumers of opportunity—who compete to supply whatever all the other consumers want or might be persuaded to want. Entrepreneurial activity tracks consumer preference. Though not without its own excitements, it is mostly instrumental: the aim of all entrepreneurs (and all producers) is to increase their market power, maximize their options. Competing with one another, they maximize everyone else's options too, filling the marketplace with desirable objects. The market is preferred (over the political community and the cooperative economy) because of its fullness. Freedom, in the capitalist view, is a function of plenitude. We can only choose when we have many choices.

It is also true, unhappily, that we can only make effective (rather than merely speculative or wistful) choices when we have resources to dispose of. But people come to the marketplace with radically unequal resources—some with virtually nothing at all. Not everyone can compete successfully in commodity production, and therefore not everyone has access to commodities. Autonomy turns out to be a high-risk value, which many men and women can only realize with help from their friends. The market, however, is not a good setting for mutual assistance, for I cannot help someone else without reducing (for the short term, at least) my own options. And I have no reason, as an autonomous individual, to accept any reductions of any sort for someone else's sake. My argument here is not that autonomy collapses into egotism, only that autonomy in the marketplace provides no support for social solidarity. Despite the successes of capitalist production, the good life of consumer choice is not universally available. Large numbers of people drop out of the market economy or live precariously on its margins.

Partly for this reason, capitalism, like socialism, is highly dependent on state action—not only to prevent theft and enforce contracts but also to regulate the economy and guarantee the minimal welfare of its participants. But these participants, insofar as they are market activists, are not active in the state: capitalism in its ideal form, like socialism again, does not make for citizenship. Or, its protagonists conceive of citizenship in economic terms, so that citizens are transformed into autonomous consumers, looking for the party or program that most persuasively promises to strengthen their market positions. They need the state but have no moral relation to it, and they control its officials only as consumers control the producers of commodities, by buying or not buying what they make.

Because the market has no political boundaries, capitalist entrepreneurs also evade official control. They need the state but have no loyalty to it; the profit motive brings them into conflict with democratic regulation. So arms merchants sell the latest military technology to foreign powers, and manufacturers move their factories overseas to escape safety codes or minimum-wage laws. Multinational corporations stand outside (and to some extent against) every political community. They are known only by their brand names, which, unlike family names and country names, evoke preferences but not affections or solidarities.

A Nationalist Response

The fourth answer to the question about the good life can be read as a response to market amorality and disloyalty, though it has, historically, other sources as well. According to the fourth answer, the preferred setting is the nation, within which we are loyal members, bound to one another by ties of blood and history. And a member, secure in membership, literally part of an organic whole—this is much the best thing to be. To live well is to participate with other men and women in remembering, cultivating, and passing on a national heritage. This is so, on the nationalist view, without reference to the specific content of the heritage, so long as it is one's own, a matter of birth, not choice. Every nationalist will, of course, find value in his or her own heritage, but the highest value is not in the finding but in the willing: the firm identification of the individual with a people and a history.

Nationalism has often been a leftist ideology, historically linked to democracy and even to socialism. But it is most characteristically an ideology of the right, for its understanding of membership is ascriptive; it requires no political choices and no activity beyond ritual affirmation. When nations find themselves ruled by foreigners, however, ritual affirmation isn't enough. Then nationalism requires a more heroic loyalty: self-sacrifice in the struggle for national liberation. The capacity of the nation to elicit such sacrifices from its members is proof of the importance of this fourth answer. Individual members seek the good life by seeking autonomy not for themselves but for their people. Ideally, this attitude ought to survive the liberation struggle and provide a foundation for social solidarity and mutual assistance. Perhaps, to some extent, it does; certainly the welfare state has had its greatest successes in ethnically homogeneous countries. It is also true, however, that once liberation has been secured, nationalist men and women are commonly content with a vicarious rather than a practical participation in the community. There is nothing wrong with vicarious participation, on the nationalist view, since the good life is more a matter of identity than activity—faith, not works, so to speak, though both of these are understood in secular terms.

In the modern world, nations commonly seek statehood, for their autonomy will always be at risk if they lack sovereign power. But they don't seek states of any particular kind. No more do they seek economic arrangements of any particular kind. Unlike religious believers who are their close kin and (often) bitter rivals, nationalists are not bound by a body of authoritative law or a set of sacred texts. Beyond liberation, they have no program, only a vague commitment to continue a history, to sustain a "way of life." Their own lives, I suppose, are emotionally intense, but in relation to society and economy this is a dangerously free-floating intensity. In time of trouble, it can readily be turned against other nations, particularly against the internal others: minorities, aliens, strangers. Democratic citizenship, worker solidarity, free enterprise, and consumer autonomy—all these are less exclusive than nationalism but not always resistant to its power. The ease with which citizens, workers, and consumers become fervent nationalists is a sign of the inadequacy of the first three answers to the question about the good life. The nature of nationalist fervor signals the inadequacy of the fourth.

Can We Find a Synthesis?

All these answers are wrongheaded because of their singularity. They miss the complexity of human society, the inevitable conflicts of commitment and loyalty. Hence I am uneasy with the idea that there might be a fifth and finally correct answer to the question about the good life. Still, there is a fifth answer, the newest one (it draws upon less central themes of nineteenth- and twentieth-century social thought), which holds that the good life can only be lived in civil society, the realm of fragmentation and struggle but also of concrete and authentic solidarities, where we fulfill E. M. Forster's injunction, "only connect," and become sociable or communal men and women. And this is, of course, much the best thing to be. The picture here is of people freely associating and communicating with one another, forming and reforming groups of all sorts, not for the sake of any particular formation—family, tribe, nation, religion, commune, brotherhood or sisterhood, interest group or ideological movement—but for the sake of sociability itself. For we are by nature social, before we are political or economic beings.

I would rather say that the civil society argument is a corrective to the four ideological accounts of the good life—part denial, part incorporation—rather than a fifth to stand alongside them. It challenges their singularity but it has no singularity of its own. The phrase "social being" describes men and women who are citizens, producers, consumers, members of the nation, and much else besides—and none of these by nature or because it is the best thing to be. The associational life of civil society is the actual ground where all versions of the good are worked out and tested . . . and proved to be partial, incomplete, ultimately unsatisfying. It can't be the case that living on this ground is good in itself; there isn't any other place to live. What is true is that the quality of our political and economic activity and of our national culture is intimately connected to the strength and vitality of our associations.

Ideally, civil society is a setting of settings: all are included, none is preferred. The argument is a liberal version of the four answers, accepting them all, insisting that each leave room for the others, therefore not finally accepting any of them. Liberalism appears here as an anti–ideology, and this is an attractive position in the contemporary world. I shall stress this attractiveness as I try to explain how civil society might actually incorporate and deny the four answers. Later on, however, I shall have to argue that this position too, so genial and benign, has its problems.

Let's begin with the political community and the cooperative economy, taken together. These two leftist versions of the good life systematically undervalued all associations except the demos and the working class. Their protagonists could imagine conflicts between political communities and between classes but not within either; they aimed at the abolition or transcendence of particularism and all its divisions. Theorists of civil society, by contrast, have a more realistic view of communities and economies. They are more accommodating to conflict—that is, to political opposition and economic competition. Associational freedom serves for them to legitimate a set of market relations, though not necessarily the capitalist set. The market, when it is entangled in the network of associations, when the forms of ownership are pluralized, is without doubt the economic formation most consistent with the civil society argument. This same argument also serves to legitimate a kind of state that is liberal and pluralist more than republican (not so radically dependent upon the virtue of its citizens). Indeed, a state of this sort, as we shall see, is necessary if associations are to flourish.

Once incorporated into civil society, neither citizenship nor production can ever again be all-absorbing. They will have their votaries, but these people will not be models for the rest of us—or, they will be partial models only, for some people at some time of their lives, not for other people, not at other times. This pluralist perspective follows in part, perhaps, from the lost romance of work, from our experience with the new productive technologies and the growth of the service economy. Service is more easily reconciled with a vision of human beings as social animals than with *homo faber*. What can a hospital attendant or a school teacher or a marriage counselor or a social worker or a television repairperson or a government official be said to *make*? The contemporary economy does not offer many people a chance for creativity in the Marxist sense. Nor does Marx (or any socialist thinker of the central tradition) have much to say about those men and women whose economic activity consists entirely in helping other people. The helpmate, like the housewife, was never assimilated to the class of workers.

In similar fashion, politics in the contemporary democratic state does not offer many people a chance for Rousseauian self-determination. Citizenship, taken by itself, is today mostly a passive role: citizens are spectators who vote. Between elections they are served, well or badly, by the civil service. They are not at all like those heroes of republican mythology, the citizens of ancient Athens meeting in assembly and (foolishly, as it turned out) deciding to invade Sicily. But in the associational networks of civil society—in unions, parties, movements, interest groups, and so on—these same people make many smaller decisions and shape to some degree the more distant determinations of state and economy. And in a more densely organized, more egalitarian civil society, they might do both these things to greater effect.

These socially engaged men and women—part-time union officers, movement activists, party regulars, consumer advocates, welfare volunteers, church members, family heads—stand outside the republic of citizens as it is commonly conceived. They are only intermittently virtuous; they are too caught up in particularity. They look, most of them, for many partial fulfillments, no longer for the one clinching fulfillment. On the ground of actuality (unless the state usurps the ground), citizenship shades off into a great diversity of (sometimes divisive) decision-making roles; and, similarly, production shades off into a multitude of (sometimes competitive) socially useful activities. It is, then, a mistake to set politics and work in opposition to one another. There is no ideal fulfillment and no essential human capacity. We require many settings so that we can live different kinds of good lives.

All this is not to say, however, that we need to accept the capitalist version of competition and division. Theorists who regard the market as the preferred setting for the good life aim to make it the actual setting for as many aspects of life as possible. Their singlemindedness takes the form of market imperialism; confronting the democratic state, they are advocates of privatization and laissez-faire. Their ideal is a society in which all goods and services are provided by entrepreneurs to consumers. That some entrepreneurs would fail and many consumers find themselves helpless in the marketplace—this is the price of individual autonomy. It is, obviously, a price we already pay: in all capitalist societies, the market makes for inequality. The more successful its imperialism, the greater the inequality. But were the market to be set firmly within civil society, politically constrained, open to communal as well as private initiatives, limits might be fixed on its unequal outcomes. The exact nature of the limits would depend on the strength and density of the associational networks (including, now, the political community).

The problem with inequality is not merely that some individuals are more capable, others less capable, of making their consumer preference effective. It's not that some individuals live in fancier apartments than others, or drive better-made cars, or take vacations in more exotic places. These are conceivably the just rewards of market success. The problem is that inequality commonly translates into domination and radical deprivation. But the verb "translates" here describes a socially mediated process, which is fostered or inhibited by the structure of its mediations. Dominated and deprived individuals are likely to be disorganized as well as impoverished, whereas poor people with strong families, churches, unions, political parties, and ethnic alliances are not likely to be dominated or deprived for long. Nor need these people stand alone even in the marketplace. The capitalist answer assumes that the good life of entrepreneurial initiative and consumer choice is a life led most importantly by individuals. But civil society encompasses or can encompass a variety of market agents: family businesses, publicly owned or municipal companies, worker communes, consumer cooperatives, nonprofit organizations of many different sorts. All these function in the market even though they have their origins outside. And just as the experience of democracy is expanded and enhanced by groups that are in but not of the state, so consumer choice is expanded and enhanced by groups that are in but not of the market.

It is only necessary to add that among the groups in but not of the state are market organizations, and among the groups in but not of the market are state organizations. All social forms are relativized by the civil society argument—and on the actual ground too. This also means that all social forms are contestable; moreover, contests can't be won by invoking one or another account of the preferred setting—as if it were enough to say that market organizations, insofar as they are efficient, don't have to be democratic or that state firms, insofar as they are democratically controlled, don't have to operate within the constraints of the market. The exact character of our associational life is something that has to be argued about, and it is in the course of these arguments that we also decide about the forms of democracy, the nature of work, the extent and effects of market inequalities, and much else.

The quality of nationalism is also determined within civil society, where national groups coexist and overlap with families and religious communities (two social formations largely neglected in modernist answers to the question about the good life) and where nationalism is expressed in schools and movements, organizations for mutual aid, cultural and historical societies. It is because groups like these are entangled with other groups, similar in kind but different in aim, that civil society holds out the hope of a domesticated nationalism. In states dominated by a single nation, the multiplicity of the groups pluralizes nationalist politics and culture; in states with more than one nation, the density of the networks prevents radical polarization.

Civil society as we know it has its origin in the struggle for religious freedom. Though often violent, the struggle held open the possibility of peace. "The establishment of this one thing," John Locke wrote about toleration, "would take away all ground of complaints and tumults upon account of conscience." One can easily imagine groundless complaints and tumults, but Locke believed (and he was largely right) that tolerance would dull the edge of religious conflict. People would be less ready to take risks once the stakes were lowered. Civil society simply is that place where the stakes are lower, where, in principle at least, coercion is used only to keep the peace and all associations are equal under the law. In the market, this formal equality often has no substance, but in the world of faith and identity, it is real enough. Though nations don't compete for members in the same way as religions (sometimes) do; the argument for granting them the associational freedom of civil society is similar. When they are free to celebrate their histories, remember their dead, and shape (in part) the education of their children, they are more likely to be harmless than when they are unfree. Locke may have put the claim too strongly when he wrote, "There is only one thing which gathers people into seditious commotions, and that is oppression," but he was close enough to the truth to warrant the experiment of radical tolerance.

But if oppression is the cause of seditious commotion, what is the cause of oppression? I don't doubt that there is a materialist story to tell here, but I want to stress the central role played by ideological singlemindedness: the intolerant universalism of (most) religions, the exclusivity of (most) nations. The actual experience of civil society, when it can be had, seems to work against these two. Indeed, it works so well, some observers think, that neither religious faith nor national identity is likely to survive for long in the network of free associations. But we really don't know to what extent faith and identity depend upon coercion or whether they can reproduce themselves under conditions of freedom. I suspect that they both respond to such deep human needs that they will outlast their current organizational forms. It seems, in any case, worthwhile to wait and see.

Still a Need for State Power

But there is no escape from power and coercion, no possibility of choosing, like the old anarchists, civil society alone. A few years ago, in a book called *Anti-Politics,* the Hungarian dissident George Konrad described a way of living alongside the totalitarian state but, so to speak, with one's back turned toward it. He urged his fellow dissidents to reject the very idea of seizing or sharing power and to devote their energies to religious, cultural, economic, and professional associations. Civil society appears in his book as an alternative to the state, which he assumes to be unchangeable and irredeemably hostile. His argument seemed right to me when I first read his book. Looking back, after the collapse of the communist regimes in Hungary and elsewhere, I can easily see how much it was a product of its time—and how short that time was! No state can survive for long if it is wholly alienated from civil society. It cannot outlast its own coercive machinery; it is lost, literally, without its firepower. The production and reproduction of loyalty, civility, political competence, and trust in authority are never the work of the state alone, and the effort to go it alone—one meaning of totalitarianism—is doomed to failure.

The failure, however, has carried with it terrible costs, and so one can understand the appeal of contemporary antipolitics. Even as Central and East European dissidents take power, they remain, and should remain, cautious and apprehensive about its uses. The totalitarian project has left behind an abiding sense of bureaucratic brutality. Here was the ultimate form of political singlemindedness, and though the "democratic" (and, for that matter, the "communist") ideology that they appropriated was false, the intrusions even of a more genuine democracy are rendered suspect by the memory. Post-totalitarian politicians and writers have, in addition, learned the older antipolitics of free enterprise—so that the laissez-faire market is defended in the East today as one of the necessary institutions of civil society, or, more strongly, as the dominant social formation. This second view takes on plausibility from the extraordinary havoc wrought by totalitarian economic "planning." But it rests, exactly like political singlemindedness, on a failure to recognize the pluralism of associational life. The first view leads, often, to a more interesting and more genuinely liberal mistake: it suggests that pluralism is self-sufficient and self-sustaining.

This is, indeed, the experience of the dissidents: the state could not destroy their unions, churches, free universities, illegal markets, *samizdat* publications. Nonetheless, I want to warn against the antipolitical tendencies that commonly accompany the celebration of civil society. The network of associations incorporates, but it cannot dispense with, the agencies of state power; neither can socialist cooperation or capitalist competition dispense with the state. That's why so many dissidents are ministers now. It is indeed true that the new social movements in the East and the West—concerned with ecology, feminism, the rights of immigrants and national minorities, workplace and product safety, and so on—do not aim, as the democratic and labor movements once aimed, at taking power. This represents an important change, in sensibility as much as in ideology, reflecting a new valuation of parts over wholes and a new willingness to settle for something less than total victory. But there can be no victory at all that doesn't involve some control over, or use of, the state apparatus. The collapse of totalitarianism is empowering for the members of civil society precisely because it renders the state accessible.

Here, then, is the paradox of the civil society argument. Citizenship is one of many roles that members play, but the state itself is unlike all the other associations. It both frames civil society and occupies space within it. It fixes the boundary conditions and the basic rules of all associational activity (including political activity). It compels association members to think about a common good, beyond their own conceptions of the good life. Even the failed totalitarianism of, say, the Polish communist state had this much impact upon the Solidarity union: it determined that Solidarity was a Polish union, focused on economic arrangements and labor policy within the borders of Poland. A democratic state, which is continuous with the other associations, has at the same time a greater say about their quality and vitality. It serves, or it doesn't serve, the needs of the associational networks as these are worked out by men and women who are simultaneously members and citizens. I shall give only a few obvious examples, drawn from American experience.

Families with working parents need state help in the form of publicly funded day care and effective public schools. National minorities need help in organizing and sustaining their own educational programs. Worker-owned companies and consumer cooperatives need state loans or loan guarantees; so do (even more often) capitalist entrepreneurs and firms. Philanthropy and mutual aid, churches and private universities, depend upon tax exemptions. Labor unions need legal recognition and guarantees against "unfair labor practices." Professional associations need state support for their licensing procedures. And across the entire range of association, individual men and women need to be protected against the power of officials, employers, experts, party bosses, factory foremen, directors, priests, parents, patrons; and small and weak groups need to be protected against large and powerful ones. For civil society, left to itself, generates radically unequal power relationships, which only state power can challenge.

Civil society also challenges state power, most importantly when associations have resources or supporters abroad; world religions, pan-national movements, the new environmental groups, multinational corporations. We are likely to feel differently about these challenges, especially after we recognize the real but relative importance of the state. Multinational corporations, for example, need to be constrained, much like states with imperial ambitions; and the best constraint probably lies in collective security, that is, in alliances with other states that give economic regulation some international effect. The same mechanism may turn out to be useful to the new environmental groups. In the first case, the state pressures the corporation; in the second it responds to environmentalist pressure. The two cases suggest, again, that civil society requires political agency. And the state is an indispensable agent—even if the associational networks also, always, resist the organizing impulses of state bureaucrats.

Only a democratic state can create a democratic civil society: only a democratic civil society can sustain a democratic state. The civility that makes democratic politics possible can only be learned in the associational networks; the roughly equal and widely dispersed capabilities that sustain the networks have to be fostered by the democratic state. Confronted with an overbearing state, citizens, who are also members, will struggle to make room for autonomous associations and market relationships (and also for local governments and decentralized bureaucracies). But the state can never be what it appears to be in liberal theory, a mere framework for civil society. It is also the instrument of the struggle, used to give a particular shape to the common life. Hence citizenship has a certain practical pre-eminence among all our actual and possible memberships. That's not to say that we must be citizens all the time, finding in politics, as Rousseau urged, the greater part of our happiness. Most of us will be happier elsewhere, involved only sometimes in affairs of state. But we must have a state open to our sometime involvement.

Nor need we be involved all the time in our associations. A democratic civil society is one controlled by its members, not through a single process of self-determination but through a large number of different and uncoordinated processes. These needn't all be democratic, for we are likely to be members of many associations, and we will want some of them to be managed in our interests, but also in our absence. Civil society is sufficiently democratic when in some, at least, of its parts we are able to recognize ourselves as authoritative and responsible participants. States are tested by their capacity to sustain this kind of participation—which is very different from the heroic intensity of Rousseauian citizenship. And civil society is tested by its capacity to produce citizens whose interests, at least sometimes, reach farther than themselves and their comrades, who look after the political community that fosters and protects the associational networks.

In Favor of Inclusiveness

I mean to defend a perspective that might be called, awkwardly, "critical associationalism." I want to join, but I am somewhat uneasy with, the civil society argument. It can't be said that nothing is lost when we give up the single-mindedness of democratic citizenship or socialist cooperation or individual autonomy or national identity. There was a kind of heroism in those projects—a concentration of energy, a clear sense of direction, an unblinking recognition of friends and enemies. To make one of these one's own was a serious commitment. The defense of civil society doesn't seem quite comparable. Associational engagement is conceivably as important a project as any of the others, but its greatest virtue lies in its inclusiveness, and inclusiveness does not make for heroism. "Join the associations of your choice" is not a slogan to rally political militants. And yet that is what civil society requires: men and women actively engaged—in state, economy, and nation, and also in churches, neighborhoods, and families, and in many other settings too. To reach this goal is not as easy as it sounds: many people, perhaps most people, live very loosely within the networks; a growing number of people seem to be radically disengaged—passive clients of the state, market dropouts, resentful and posturing nationalists. And the civil society project doesn't confront an energizing hostility, as all the others do; its protagonists are more likely to meet sullen indifference, fear, despair, apathy, and withdrawal.

In Central and Eastern Europe, civil society is still a battle cry, for it requires a dismantling of the totalitarian state and it brings with it the exhilarating experience of associational independence. Among ourselves what is required is nothing so grand; nor does it lend itself to a singular description (but this is what lies ahead in the East too). The civil society project can only be described in terms of all the other projects, against their singularity. Hence my account in these pages, which suggests the need (1) to decentralize the state so that there are more opportunities for citizens to take responsibility for (some of) its activities; (2) to socialize the economy so that there is a greater diversity of market agents, communal as well as private; and (3) to pluralize and domesticate nationalism, on the religious model, so that there are different ways to realize and sustain historical identities.

None of this can be accomplished without using political power to redistribute resources and to underwrite and subsidize the most desirable associational activities. But political power alone cannot accomplish any of it. The kinds of "action" discussed by theorists of the state need to be supplemented (not, however, replaced) by something radically different: more like union organizing than political mobilization, more like teaching in a school than arguing in the assembly, more like volunteering in a hospital than joining a political party, more like working in an ethnic alliance or a feminist support group than canvassing in an election, more like shaping a co-op budget than deciding on national fiscal policy. But can any of these local and small-scale activities ever carry with them the honor of citizenship? Sometimes, certainly, they are narrowly conceived, partial and particularist; they need political correction. The greater problem, however, is that they seem so ordinary. Living in civil society, one might think, is like speaking in prose.

But just as speaking in prose implies an understanding of syntax, so these forms of action (when they are pluralized) imply an understanding about which we can be entirely confident these days. There is something to be said for the neoconservative argument that in the modern world we need to recapture the density of associational life and relearn the activities and understandings that go with it. And if this is the case, then a more strenuous argument is called for from the left: we have to reconstruct that same density under new conditions of freedom and equality. It would appear to be an elementary requirement of social democracy that there exist a *society* of lively, engaged, and effective men and women—where the honor of "action" belongs to the many and not to the few.

Against a background of growing disorganization—violence, homelessness, divorce, abandonment, alienation, and addiction—a society of this sort looks more like a necessary achievement than a comfortable reality. In truth, however, it was never a comfortable reality, except for the few. Most men and women have been trapped in one or another subordinate relationship, where the "civility" they learned was deferential rather than independent and active. That is why democratic citizenship, socialist production, free enterprise, and nationalism were all of them liberating projects. But none of them has yet produced a general, coherent, or sustainable liberation. And their more single-minded adherents, who have exaggerated the effectiveness of the state or the market or the nation and neglected the networks, have probably contributed to the disorder of contemporary life. The projects have to be relativized and brought together, and the place to do that is in civil society, the setting of settings, where each can find the partial fulfillment that is all it deserves.

Civil society itself is sustained by groups much smaller than the demos or the working class or the mass of consumers or the nation. All these are necessarily fragmented and localized as they are incorporated. They become part of the world of family, friends, comrades, and colleagues, where people are connected to one another and made responsible for one another. Connected and responsible: without that, "free and equal" is less attractive than we once thought it would be. I have no magic formula for making connections or strengthening the sense of responsibility. These aren't aims that can be underwritten with historical guarantees or achieved through a single unified struggle. Civil society is a project of projects; it requires many organizing strategies and new forms of state action. It requires a new sensitivity for what is local, specific, contingent—and, above all, a new recognition (to paraphrase a famous sentence) that the good life is in the details.

[1990]

from Making Democracy Work

The Civic Community: Some Theoretical Speculations

In sixteenth-century Florence, reflecting on the unstable history of republican institutions in ancient times as well as in Renaissance Italy, Nicolò Machiavelli and several of his contemporaries concluded that whether free institutions succeeded or failed depended on the character of the citizens, or their "civic virtue."[1] According to a long-standing interpretation of Anglo-American political thought, this "republican" school of civic humanists was subsequently vanquished by Hobbes, Locke, and their liberal successors. Whereas the republicans had emphasized community and the obligations of citizenship, liberals stressed individualism and individual rights.[2] Far from presupposing a virtuous, public-spirited citizenry, it was said, the U.S. Constitution, with its checks and balances, was designed by Madison and his liberal colleagues precisely to make democracy safe for the unvirtuous. As a guide to understanding modern democracy, civic republicans were passé.

In recent years, however, a revisionist wave has swept across Anglo-American political philosophy "The most dramatic revision [of the history of political thought] of the last 25 years or so," reports a not-uncritical Don Herzog, is the "the discovery—and celebration—of civic humanism."[3] The revisionists argue that an important republican or communitarian tradition descended from the Greeks and Machiavelli through seventeenth-century England to the American Founders.[4] Far from exalting individualism, the new republicans recall John

1. See J. G. A. Pocock, *The Machiavellian Moment: Florentine Political Thought and the Atlantic Republican Tradition* (Princeton: Princeton University Press, 1975).

2. Of course, neither "republican" nor "liberal" has the same meaning in this historical dialogue as in contemporary American partisan politics. For the classic liberal interpretation of Anglo-American political thought, see Louis Hartz, *The Liberal Tradition in America* (New York: Harcourt, Brace, 1955).

3. Don Herzog, "Some Questions for Republicans," *Political Theory* 14 (1986): 473.

4. In this wide-ranging debate, see (among many others) Robert N. Bellah, Richard Madsen, William M. Sullivan, Ann Swidler, and Steven M. Tipton, *Habits of the Heart: Individualism and*

Winthrop's eloquent, communitarian admonition to the citizens of his "city set upon a hill": "We must delight in each other, make others' conditions our own, rejoice together, mourn together, labor and suffer together, always having before our eyes our community as members of the same body."[5]

The new republican theorists have not gone unchallenged. The defenders of classical liberal individualism argue that the notion of community lauded by the new republicans is a "dangerous and anachronistic ideal."[6] Remarkably, this wide-ranging philosophical debate has so far taken place almost entirely without reference to systematic empirical research, whether within the Anglo-American world or elsewhere. Nevertheless, it contains the seeds for a theory of effective democratic governance: "As the proportion of nonvirtuous citizens increases significantly, the ability of liberal societies to function successfully will progressively diminish."[7] We want to explore empirically whether the success of a democratic government depends on the degree to which its surroundings approximate the ideal of a "civic community."[8]

But what might this "civic community" mean in practical terms? Reflecting upon the work of republican theorists, we can begin by sorting out some of the central themes in the philosophical debate.

Civic Engagement

Citizenship in a civic community is marked, first of all, by active participation in public affairs. "Interest in public issues and devotion to public causes are the key signs of civic virtue," suggests Michael Walzer.[9] To be sure, not all political activity

---

Commitment in American Life (New York: Harper and Row, 1986); Isaac Kramnick, "Republican Revisionism Revisited," *American Historical Review* 87, no. 3 (June 1982): 629–664; Alasdair MacIntyre, *After Virtue* (Notre Dame: Notre Dame University Press, 1981); Pocock, *The Machiavellian Moment;* Dorothy Ross, "The Liberal Tradition Revisited and the Republican Tradition Addressed," in John Higham and Paul Conkin, eds., *New Directions in American Intellectual History* (Baltimore: Johns Hopkins University Press, 1979); Michael Sandel, "The Procedural Republic and the Unencumbered Self," *Political Theory* 12 (1984): 81–96; Quentin Skinner, "The Idea of Negative Liberty: Philosophical and Historical Perspectives," in *Philosophy in History,* eds. Richard Rorty, J. B. Schneewind, and Quentin Skinner (New York: Cambridge University Press, 1984); Michael Walzer, "Civility and Civic Virtue in Contemporary America," in his *Radical Principles* (New York: Basic Books, 1980); and Gordon Wood, *The Creation of the American Republic: 1776–1787* (Chapel Hill: University of North Carolina Press, 1969).

5. Cited in Bellah et al., *Habits of the Heart,* p. 28.

6. Harry N. Hirsch, "The Threnody of Liberalism: Constitutional Liberty and the Renewal of Community," *Political Theory* 14 (1986): 441.

7. William A. Galston, "Liberal Virtues," *American Political Science Review* 82 (1988): 1281.

8. Within empirical political science, much of the inspiration for this approach to understanding differences in democratic performance is traceable to the landmark study by Gabriel A. Almond and Sidney Verba, *The Civic Culture: Political Attitudes and Democracy in Five Nations* (Princeton: Princeton University Press, 1963).

9. Walzer, "Civility and Civic Virtue," p. 64.

deserves the label "virtuous" or contribute to the commonweal. "A steady recognition and pursuit of the public good at the expense of all purely individual and private ends" seems close to the core meaning of civic virtue.[10]

The dichotomy between self-interest and altruism can easily be overdrawn, for no mortal, and no successful society, can renounce the powerful motivation of self-interest. Citizens in the civic community are not required to be altruists. In the civic community, however, citizens pursue what de Tocqueville termed "self-interest properly understood," that is, self-interest defined in the context of broader public needs, self-interest that is "enlightened" rather than "myopic," self-interest that is alive to the interests of others.[11]

The absence of civic virtue is exemplified in the "amoral familism" that Edward Banfield reported as the dominant ethos in Montegrano, a small town not far from our Pietrapertosa: "Maximize the material, short-run advantage of the nuclear family; assume that all others will do likewise."[12] Participation in a civic community is more public-spirited than that, more oriented to shared benefits. Citizens in a civic community, though not selfless saints, regard the public domain as more than a battleground for pursuing personal interest.

Political Equality

Citizenship in the civic community entails equal rights and obligations for all. Such a community is bound together by horizontal relations of reciprocity and cooperation, not by vertical relations of authority and dependency. Citizens interact as equals, not as patrons and clients nor as governors and petitioners. To be sure, not all classical republican theorists were democrats. Nor can a contemporary civic community forego the advantages of a division of labor and the need for political leadership. Leaders in such a community, however, must be, and must conceive themselves to be, responsible to their fellow citizens. Both absolute power and the absence of power can be corrupting, for both instill a sense of irresponsibility.[13] The more that politics approximates the ideal of political equality among citizens following norms of reciprocity and engaged in self-government, the more civic that community may be said to be.

Solidarity, Trust, and Tolerance

Citizens in a civic community, on most accounts, are more than merely active, public-spirited, and equal. Virtuous citizens are helpful, respectful, and trustful

10. Skinner, "The Idea of Negative Liberty," p. 218.

11. Alexis de Tocqueville, *Democracy in America,* ed. J. P. Mayer, trans. George Lawrence (Garden City, N.Y.: Anchor Books, 1969), pp. 525–528.

12. Edward C. Banfield, *The Moral Basis of a Backward Society* (Chicago: The Free Press, 1958), p. 85.

13. Here, and throughout our discussion of civic virtue, we draw on the insights of Jeff W. Wein-

toward one another, even when they differ on matters of substance. The civic community is not likely to be blandly conflict-free, for its citizens have strong views on public issues, but they are tolerant of their opponents. "This is probably as close as we can come to the 'friendship' which Aristotle thought should characterize relations among members of the same political community," argues Michael Walzer.[14] As Gianfranco Poggi has noted of de Tocqueville's theory of democratic governance, "Interpersonal trust is probably the moral orientation that most needs to be diffused among the people if republican society is to be maintained."[15]

Even seemingly "self-interested" transactions take on a different character when they are embedded in social networks that foster mutual trust. Fabrics of trust enable the civic community more easily to surmount what economists call "opportunism," in which shared interests are unrealized because each individual, acting in wary isolation, has an incentive to defect from collective action.[16] A review of community development in Latin America highlights the social importance of grass-roots cooperative enterprises and of episodes of political mobilization—even if they are unsuccessful in immediate, instrumental terms—precisely because of their indirect effects of "dispelling isolation and mutual distrust."[17]

Associations: Social Structures of Cooperation

The norms and values of the civic community are embodied in, and reinforced by, distinctive social structures and practices. The most relevant social theorist here remains Alexis de Tocqueville. Reflecting on the social conditions that sustained "Democracy in America," de Tocqueville attributed great importance to the Americans' propensity to form civil and political organizations:

Americans of all ages, all stations in life, and all types of disposition are forever forming associations. There are not only commercial and industrial associations in which all take part, but others of a thousand different types—religious, moral, serious, futile, very general and very limited, immensely large and very minute. . . . Thus the most democratic country in the world now is that in which men have in our time carried to the highest perfection the art of pursuing in common the objects of common desires and have applied this new technique to the greatest number of purposes.[18]

---

traub, *Freedom and Community: The Republican Virtue Tradition and the Sociology of Liberty* (Berkeley: University of California Press, 1992).

14. Walzer, "Civility and Civic Virtue," p. 62.

15. Gianfranco Poggi, *Images of Society: Essays on the Sociological Theories of Tocqueville, Marx, and Durkheim* (Stanford: Stanford University Press. 1972), p. 59.

16. Mark Granovetter, "Economic Action and Social Structure: the Problem of Embeddedness," *American Journal of Sociology* 91 (November 1985): 481–510.

17. Albert O. Hirschman, *Getting Ahead Collectively: Grassroots Experiences in Latin America* (New York: Pergamon Press, 1984), p. 57 *et passim*.

18. De Tocqueville, *Democracy in America*, pp. 513–514. [See chapter 9 of this volume.]

Civil associations contribute to the effectiveness and stability of democratic government, it is argued, both because of their "internal" effects on individual members and because of their "external" effects on the wider polity.

Internally, associations instill in their members habits of cooperation, solidarity, and public-spiritedness. De Tocqueville observed that "feelings and ideas are renewed, the heart enlarged, and the understanding developed only by the reciprocal action of men one upon another."[19] This suggestion is supported by evidence from the *Civic Culture* surveys of citizens in five countries, including Italy, showing that members of associations displayed more political sophistication, social trust, political participation, and "subjective civic competence."[20] Participation in civic organizations inculcates skills of cooperation as well as a sense of shared responsibility for collective endeavors. Moreover, when individuals belong to "cross-cutting" groups with diverse goals and members, their attitudes will tend to moderate as a result of group interaction and cross-pressures.[21] These effects, it is worth noting, do not require that the manifest purpose of the association be political. Taking part in a choral society or a bird-watching club can teach self-discipline and an appreciation for the joys of successful collaboration.

Externally, what twentieth-century political scientists have called "interest articulation" and "interest aggregation" are enhanced by a dense network of secondary associations. In de Tocqueville's words:

When some view is represented by an association, it must take clearer and more precise shape. It counts its supporters and involves them in its cause; these supporters get to know one another, and numbers increase zeal. An association unites the energies of divergent minds and vigorously directs them toward a clearly indicated goal.[22]

According to this thesis, a dense network of secondary associations both embodies and contributes to effective social collaboration. Thus, contrary to the fear of faction expressed by thinkers like Jean-Jacques Rousseau, in a civic community associations of like-minded equals contribute to effective democratic governance.[23]

More recently, an independent line of research has reinforced the view that associationism is a necessary precondition for effective self-government. Summarizing scores of case studies of Third World development, Milton Esman and Norman

19. Ibid., p. 515.

20. Almond and Verba, *The Civic Culture,* chapter 11.

21. Arend Lijphart, *Democracy in Plural Societies* (New Haven: Yale University Press, 1977), pp. 10–11; Lipset, *Political Man;* David Truman, *The Governmental Process: Political Interests and Public Opinion* (New York: Knopf, 1951).

22. De Tocqueville, *Democracy in America,* p. 190.

23. Not all associations of the like-minded are committed to democratic goals nor organized in an egalitarian fashion; consider, for example, the Ku Klux Klan or the Nazi party. In weighing the consequences of any particular organization for democratic governance, one must also consider other civic virtues, such as tolerance and equality.

Uphoff conclude that local associations are a crucial ingredient in successful strategies of rural development:

A vigorous network of membership organizations is essential to any serious effort to overcome mass poverty under the conditions that are likely to prevail in most developing countries for the predictable future. . . . While other components—infrastructure investments, supportive public policies, appropriate technologies, and bureaucratic and market institutions—are necessary, we cannot visualize any strategy of rural development combining growth in productivity with broad distribution of benefits in which participatory local organizations are not prominent.[24]

Unhappily from the point of view of social engineering, Esman and Uphoff find that local organizations "implanted" from the outside have a high failure rate. The most successful local organizations represent indigenous, participatory initiatives in relatively cohesive local communities.[25]

Although Esman and Uphoff do not say so explicitly, their conclusions are quite consistent with Banfield's interpretation of life in Montegrano, "the extreme poverty and backwardness of which is to be explained largely (but not entirely) by the inability of the villagers to act together for their common good or, indeed, for any end transcending the immediate material interest of the nuclear family."[26] Banfield's critics have disagreed with his attribution of this behavior to an "ethos," but they have not dissented from his description of the absence of collaboration in Montegrano, the striking lack of "deliberate concerted action" to improve community conditions.[27]

24. Milton J. Esman and Norman T. Uphoff, *Local Organizations: Intermediaries in Rural Development* (Ithaca: Cornell University Press, 1984), p. 40.

25. Esman and Uphoff, *Local Organizations,* pp. 99–180, and David C. Korten, "Community Organization and Rural Development: A Learning Process Approach," *Public Administration Review* 40 (September–October 1980): 480–511.

26. Banfield, *Moral Basis of a Backward Society,* p. 10.

27. See Alessandro Pizzorno, "Amoral Familism and Historical Marginality," *International Review of Community Development* 15 (1966): 55–66, and Sydel F. Silverman, "Agricultural Organization, Social Structure, and Values in Italy: Amoral Familism Reconsidered," *American Anthropologist* 70, no. 1 (February 1968): 1–19.

Robert N. Bellah, Richard Madsen,
William M. Sullivan, Ann Swidler,
and Stephen M. Tipton

from Habits of the Heart

Introduction to the Updated Edition

"How ought we to live? . . . Who are we, as Americans?" Since we wrote those questions at the beginning of *Habits of the Heart,* over a decade ago, they have taken on a critical urgency. Their meaning has been contested since the beginning of the republic, but never more than at present, when we hear calls to "renew America" or to overcome "moral crisis."

We Americans have always wanted to make something of ourselves. We have aspired to be self-confident and energetic, trusting that, by dint of hard work and good character, we could achieve self-respect and integrity in an open society. Looking around at what is happening to us as a nation, however, everywhere we find uneasiness about the soundness of our society and concern about its future. More and more of us doubt whether we can trust our institutions, our elected officials, our neighbors, or even our ability to live up to our own expectations for our lives. And anxiety is always close to the surface, a haunting fear that things have somehow gone wrong. For many Americans, these fears come to a head in worries about crime, moral decline, and the deepening divides of income and opportunity. There is a gnawing uncertainty about the future of our jobs, of adequate income, and of our family life, especially our children's welfare.

Underlying many of these fears is the realization that, for most Americans, growth of the global economy no longer means opportunity but, rather, "downsizing," "re-engineered" jobs, and the pink slip of dismissal. Yet through all these wrenching throats to prosperity there has been curiously little public protest about the changing rules of the economic game. We are divided, we are told, by race, by culture, by creed, by differing views of the national identity. But we are united, as it turns out, in at least one core belief, even across lines of color, religion, region, and occupation: the belief that economic success or misfortune is the individual's responsibility, and his or hers alone.

How can we account for this overwhelming value consensus which seems to fly in the face of our usual picture of America as a contentious, deeply divided society? The fact becomes even more puzzling once we notice that this common American belief is shared by the population of no other industrial nation, either in Europe or in East Asia. Those nations too are experiencing the disorienting shocks of the new global economy. Yet the gap in income between the best-off and the worst-off is vastly greater in the United State than in any of them, and we continue to tolerate significantly higher rates of economic deprivation than they do. Why are we paying a higher cost, as a society, for economic change? Is this high cost related to the decline of trust and confidence? Could these developments share a common source in some of our unquestioned beliefs about individuals and their responsibilities? In other words, is this conundrum rooted in cultural values which are so taken for granted as to be nearly invisible to Americans?

Individualism Again

In *Habits of the Heart* we attempted to understand this cultural orientation. Following Alexis de Tocqueville, we called it individualism. Individualism, the first language in which Americans tend to think about their lives, values independence and self-reliance above all else. These qualities are expected to win the rewards of success in a competitive society, but they are also valued as virtues good in themselves. For this reason, individualism places high demands upon every person even as the open nature of American society entices with chances of big rewards.

American individualism, then demands personal effort and stimulates great energy to achieve, yet it provides little encouragement for nurturance, taking a sink-or-swim approach to moral development as well as to economic success. It admires toughness and strength and fears softness and weakness. It adulates winners while showing contempt for losers, a contempt that can descend with crushing weight on those considered either by others or by themselves, to be moral or social failures.

In *Habits* we explored this American individualism. We asked where it came from and sought to describe its anatomy. We found that it took both a "hard" utilitarian shape and a "soft" expressive form. One focused on the bottom line, the other on feelings, which often were viewed therapeutically. Most critically, we questioned whether individualism in either form serves us well as a society, whether it serves even the most successful among us, that educated upper middle class which has historically been most devoted to many of the values of individualism. Our answer then was a qualified no. We argued, again inspired by Tocqueville, that individualism has been sustainable over time in the United States only because it has been supported and checked by other, more generous moral understandings.

In times of economic prosperity, Americans have imagined individualism as a self-sufficient moral and political guide. In times of social adversity such as the present, they are tempted to say that it is up to individuals to look after their own interests. Yet many of us have felt, in times both of prosperity and of adversity, that there is something missing in the individualist set of values, that individualism alone does not allow persons to understand certain basic realities of their lives, especially their interdependence with others. These realities become more salient as individual effort alone proves inadequate to meet the demands of living. At such times in the past Americans have turned to other cultural traditions, particularly those we termed the biblical and civic republican understandings of life. These two traditions have served the nation well when united action to address common problems has been called for.

The biblical tradition, a second language familiar to most Americans through a variety of communities of faith, teaches concern for the intrinsic value of individuals because of their relationship to the transcendent. It asserts the obligation to respect and acknowledge the dignity of all. This tradition has played a crucial political role since the beginning of the republic, especially at moments of national crisis and renewal such as the Civil War, by insisting that the nation rests on a moral foundation. At such times currents in biblical religion have made common cause with the civic republicanism which guided the nation's founders, to insist that the American experiment is a project of common moral purpose, one which places upon citizens a responsibility for the welfare of their fellows and for the common good.

The key point of connection between these traditions, one which sets them off from radical individualism, is their appreciation for the social dimensions of the human person. These voices have contested individualism's mistaken identification of individuality with the typical virtues of adolescence, initiative and independence, along with their less savory concomitants of adulation of success and contempt for weakness. Civic republicanism and biblical religion remind us that being an individual—being one's own person—does not entail escaping our ties to others, and that real freedom lies not in rejecting our social nature but in fulfilling it in a critical and adult loyalty, as we acknowledge our common responsibility to contribute to the wider fellowship of life. It was these voices above all which we sought to amplify in the public conversation even as we feared that our national discourse was being impoverished by the monotones of a strident and ultimately destructive individualism.

Strongly though we emphasized the importance of individualism when we published *Habits,* we perhaps understated the ambiguity of its relationship to the biblical and republican traditions, which in some ways mitigate individualism but in other ways significantly contribute to it. As Ernst Troeltsch pointed out, ascetic Protestantism, the form of biblical religion most pervasive in our formative period and still widely influential, has a strongly anti-political, even anti-civic, side.[1] The state and the larger society are considered unnecessary because the saved take care of themselves. Even more problematic is the tendency in this same strand of Protestantism to exclude those who are considered morally unworthy—unworthiness often being determined by their lack of economic success (the undeserving poor)—from the social body altogether. This attitude is countered by other Protestants and particularly by the Catholic tradition, in which an emphasis on the common good precludes the exclusion of anyone from society's care and concern. As opposed to that strand in Protestantism which looks at work as a way individuals prove themselves, this other view sees work as a contribution to a common endeavor in which all do what they can but none is rejected because of inability. Still, we cannot forget that one influential strand of biblical religion in America encourages secession from public life rather than civic engagement, and is even tempted to condemn the most vulnerable as morally unworthy.

Further, one influential type of republicanism that we inherited from the eighteenth century, our version of the English Whig tradition, best known in its early form as anti-federalism, was anti-state and anti-urban, idealizing the yeoman farmer in all his independence. Jefferson's insistence on putting the nation's capital in a swamp was not accidental. Jefferson-Madison republicanism viewed with hostility not only cities but also taxation and virtually any functions for the state. A paranoid fear of the state is not something new, but can be seen from the earliest days of the republic.[2]

We also underestimated the *moral* meaning of the individualism we called utilitarian. In at least one version of utilitarian individualism the real focus is on moral self-discipline and self-help, not primarily on extrinsic rewards. Worldly rewards are simply signs of good moral character—an idea that developed gradually in the Calvinist tradition. The individualist focus on adolescent independence, which we certainly emphasized, involves enduring fears of a meddling, powerful father who might push one back to childish dependence, fears easily transferred to a paternalistic state seen as threatening to reduce free citizens to helpless subjects.[3] This moral utilitarianism works out in class terms: the rich are independent adults and the poor are dependent children, and both have only themselves to thank or blame. American individualism resists more adult virtues, such as care and generativity, let alone wisdom, because the struggle for independence is all-consuming.

---

1. On page 810 of Volume II of *The Social Teaching of the Christian Churches* (London: Allen and Unwin, 1931 [1911]), Ernst Troeltsch writes that ascetic Protestantism "regards the State from a purely utilitarian standpoint" and denies that "the State [is] an ethical end in itself, which was self-evident to the Ancient World, and has reappeared within the modern world." This is "the natural result of the transference of all true life-values into the religious sphere, which means that even in the most favorable light the rest of the life-values are only regarded as means to an end." Although this is a "common Christian idea . . . Calvinism goes much farther than Lutheranism or Catholicism."

2. Stanley Elkins and Eric McKitrick, *The Age of Federalism: The Early American Republic, 1788–1800* (New York: Oxford University Press, 1993), passim, but particularly chapter 4.

3. George Lakoff, *Moral Politics* (Chicago: University of Chicago Press, 1996).

This complex culture of individualism was much more functional on the frontier (though it certainly had destructive consequences there as well) than it can be in the complex, interdependent society we have become today. If some readers of *Habits* saw us as nostalgic for an idealized past, we would now like to disabuse them. We still believe that the biblical and republican traditions are in many ways preferable to utilitarian and expressive individualism, but there is no form of them that we can appropriate uncritically or affirm without reservation.

The Crisis of Civic Membership

The consequences of radical individualism are more strikingly evident today than they were even a decade ago, when *Habits of the Heart* was published. In *Habits* we spoke of commitment, of community, and of citizenship as useful terms to contrast to an alienating individualism. Properly understood, these terms are still valuable for our current understanding. But today we think the phrase "civic membership" brings out something not quite captured by those other terms. While we criticized distorted forms of individualism, we never sought to neglect the central significance of the individual person or failed to sympathize with the difficulties faced by the individual self in our society. "Civic membership" points to that critical intersection of personal identity with social identity. If we face a crisis of civic identity, it is not just a social crisis, it is a personal crisis as well.

What we mean by the crisis of civic membership is that there are, at every level of American life and in every significant group, temptations and pressures to disengage from the larger society. Two consequences follow from this: social capital (a term we will define in the next section) is depleted, and personal identity is threatened as well. The confident sense of selfhood that comes from membership in a society in which we believe, where we both trust and feel trusted, and to which we feel we securely belong: this is exactly what is threatened by a crisis of civic membership. It is not simply a matter of disillusionment with politics, though that is bad enough. It involves a more radical disengagement that is even more threatening to social coherence than alienation from politics alone would be.

Because we think that the crisis of civic membership takes different forms in different social classes, a consideration of the widening disparities in our class system is necessary as a step toward clarifying the crisis. Americans often feel uncomfortable talking about class. Isn't ours basically a classless society? Far from it. In *Habits of the Heart* the consideration of class is largely implicit, since the book focuses on cultural ideals of middle-class identity that most Americans share. But in the past decade changes in our class structure have occurred that raise grave moral issues. An explicit treatment of class has now become unavoidable.

The pressures of the global market economy are impinging on all societies in the world. The chief consequence of these pressures is the growing disparity between winners and losers in the global marketplace. The result is not only income polarization, with the rich growing richer and the poor poorer, but also a shrinking middle class increasingly anxious about its future. Let us consider some of the tendencies these global pressures are creating everywhere, but with particular sharpness in the United States. First is the emergence of a deracinated elite composed of those Robert Reich calls "symbolic analysts," that is, people who know how to use the new technologies and information systems that are transforming the global economy.[4] Such people are located less securely in communities than in networks linking them, flexibly and transiently, to others like themselves who are scattered all over the world. Educated in the highly competitive atmosphere of excellent universities and graduate schools, such persons have learned to travel light with regard to family, church, locality, even nation. It is here, though not exclusively here, that we clearly see the cultural profile of individualization that we studied in *Habits of the Heart*.

Among this powerful elite the crisis of civic membership is expressed in the loss of civic consciousness, of a sense of obligation to the rest of society, which leads to a secession from society into guarded, gated residential enclaves and ultra-modern offices, research centers, and universities. Its sense of a social covenant, of the idea that we are all members of the same body, is singularly weak.

What is even more disturbing about this knowledge/power elite than its secession from society is its predatory attitude toward the rest of society, its willingness to pursue its own interests without regard to anyone else. Lester Thurow has spoken of the difference between an establishment and an oligarchy.[5] Japan, he argues, has an establishment, while much of Latin America suffers under an oligarchy. Both are privileged elites; the essential difference is that an establishment seeks its own good by working for the good of the whole society *(noblesse oblige)*, whereas an oligarchy looks out for its own interests by exploiting the rest of society. Another way of putting it would be to say that an establishment has a strong sense of civic membership while an oligarchy lacks one. One of the principal differences has to do with taxation: an oligarchy taxes itself least; an establishment taxes itself most. In American history we have had establishments—most notably in the founding generation and the period after World War II—but we have also had oligarchies. It is not hard to see what we have today.

Thurow has pointed out more recently the growing disparity in incomes when an oligarchy replaces an establishment: "[N]ever before have a majority of American workers suffered real wage reductions while the per capita domestic product was advancing." The real per capita gross domestic product went up 29 percent between 1973 and 1993. That was a lower rate of increase than in the preceding twenty years, but it was still a significant increase. Yet that increase in per capita GDP was not shared equally: 80 percent of workers either lost ground

4. Robert B. Reich, *The Work of Nations: Preparing Ourselves for 21st Century Capitalism* (New York: Knopf, 1991), part 3, "The Rise of the Symbolic Analyst."

5. Lester Thurow, *Head to Head: The Coming Economic Battle Among Japan, Europe, and America* (New York: Warner, 1992), pp. 266–67.

or barely held their own. "Among men, the top 20 percent of the labor force has been winning all of the country's wage increases." This is not a feature of all high-tech economies. Other countries comparable to ours, such as Japan and Germany, shared their increase in GDP across the board.[6] And if we look at the top 20 percent of workers in the United States, we will see inordinate differences. It is the top 5 percent that has gained the most, and particularly the top 1 percent.

. . .

In 1970, after twenty-five years of economic growth in which almost everyone shared, America reached the greatest degree of income equality in its recent history and enjoyed a vigorous civic culture. The challenges of the sixties were deeply unsettling but also stimulating, and a sense of civic membership continued to characterize the society as a whole. In 1995, after twenty-five years in which the profits of economic growth went entirely to the top 20 percent of the population, we have reached the high point of income inequality in our recent history, and our civic life is a shambles. We have seen what Michael Lind calls the revolution of the rich and what Herbert Gans calls the war against the poor.[7] A society in which most of the population is treading water, the bottom is sinking, and the top is rising is a society in which a crisis of civic membership is vividly evident at every level.[8]

Declining Social Capital

One way of characterizing the weakening of the practice of social life and civic engagement that we have called the crisis of civic membership is to speak of declining social capital. Robert Putnam, who has brought the term to public attention recently, defines social capital as follows: "By analogy with notions of physical capital and human capital—tools and training that enhance individual productivity— 'social capital' refers to features of social organization, such as networks, norms, and trust, that facilitate coordination and cooperation for mutual benefits."[9] There are a number of possible indices of social capital; the two that Putnam has used most extensively are associational membership and public trust.

6. Lester Thurow, "Companies Merge; Families Break Up," *New York Times,* September 3, 1995, p. E11.

7. See Herbert J. Gans, *The War Against the Poor: The Underclass and Antipoverty Policy* (New York: Basic Books, 1995), which is particularly good on the stereotyping and stigmatizing of the poor. See also Michael Lind, *The Next American Nation: The New Nationalism and the Fourth American Revolution* (New York; Free Press, 1995), chapter 5, "The Revolution of the Rich."

8. The best current treatment of American inequality is Claude S. Fischer, Michael Hout, Martin Sanchez Jankowski, Samuel R. Lucas, Ann Swidler, and Kim Voss, *Inequality by Design: Cracking the Bell Curve Myth* (Princeton: Princeton University Press, 1996).

9. Robert D. Putnam, "The Prosperous Community: Social Capital and Public Life," *American Prospect,* 13 (Spring 1993): 35. Putnam has derived the notion from James S. Coleman, *Foundations of Social Theory* (Cambridge: Harvard University Press, 1990), pp. 300–321, who in turn credits Glenn Loury with introducing the concept.

Putnam has chosen a stunning image as the title of a recent article: "Bowling Alone: America's Declining Social Capital."[10] He reports that between 1980 and 1993 the total number of bowlers in America increased by 10 percent, while league bowling decreased by 40 percent. Nor, he points out, is this a trivial example: nearly 80 million Americans went bowling at least once in 1993, nearly a third more than voted in the 1994 congressional elections and roughly the same as claim to attend church regularly. But Putnam uses bowling only as a symbol for the decline of American associational life, the vigor of which has been seen as the heart of our civic culture ever since de Tocqueville visited the United States in the 1830s.

In the 1970s dramatic declines in membership began to hit organizations typically associated with women, such as the PTA and the League of Women Voters, in what has often been explained as the result of the massive entry of women into the workforce. In the 1980s falling membership struck traditionally male associations, such as the Lions, Elks, Masons, and Shriners, as well. Union membership has dropped by half since its peak in the middle 1950s. We all know of the continuing decline in the numbers of eligible voters who actually go to the polls, but Putnam reminds us that the number of Americans who answer yes when asked whether they have attended a public meeting on town or school affairs in the last year has fallen by more than a third since 1973.

Almost the only groups that are growing are the support groups, such as twelve-step groups, that Robert Wuthnow has recently studied. These groups make minimal demands on their members and are oriented primarily to the needs of individuals; indeed, Wuthnow has characterized them as involving individuals who "focus on themselves in the presence of others," what we might call being alone together.[11] Putnam argues that paper membership groups, such as the AARP (American Association of Retired Persons), which has grown to gargantuan proportions, have few or no civic consequences, because their members may have common interests but they have no meaningful interactions. Putnam also worries that the Internet, the electronic town meeting, and other much ballyhooed new technological devices are probably civically vacuous, because they do not sustain civic engagement. Talk radio, for instance, mobilizes private opinion, not public opinion, and trades on anxiety, anger, and distrust, all of which are deadly to civic culture. The one sphere that seems to be resisting the general trend is religion. Religious membership and church attendance have remained fairly constant after the decline from the religion boom of the 1950s, although membership in church-related groups has declined by about one-sixth since the 1960s.

What goes together with the decline of associational involvement is the decline of public trust. We are not surprised to hear that the proportion of Americans who reply that they trust the government in Washington only some of

10. In *Journal of Democracy,* January, 1995, pp. 65–78.

11. Robert Wuthnow, *Sharing the Journey: Support Groups and America's New Quest for Community* (New York: Free Press, 1994), p. 3.

the time or almost never has risen steadily, from 30 percent in 1966 to 75 percent in 1992. But are we prepared to hear that the proportion of Americans who say that most people can be trusted fell by more than a third between 1960, when 58 percent chose that alternative, and 1993, when only 37 percent did?

The argument for decline in social capital is not one that we made in *Habits of the Heart*. *Habits* was essentially a cultural analysis, more about language than about behavior. We worried that the language of individualism might undermine civic commitment, but we pointed to the historically high levels of associational membership in America and the relative strength of such memberships here compared with those in other advanced industrial nations. Whether there has really been such a decline is still controversial, but we are inclined to believe that tendencies that were not yet entirely clear in the early 1980s when *Habits* was written are now discernible and disconcerting.[12]

. . .

To summarize the relationship of the decline of social capital to political participation we might consider how this relationship works out in the several social classes. Overall, with the exception of the activities centered in religious institutions, political participation has shifted away from those forms that require civic engagement to those that are essentially private, and above all to that of making monetary contributions.

. . .

Individualism and the American Crisis

Most Americans agree that things are seriously amiss in our society—that we are not, as the poll questions often put it, "headed in the right direction"—but they differ over why this is so and what should be done about it. We have sought for answers in the structural problems that we have described under the rubrics of the crisis in civic membership and the decline of social capital. What are some of the other explanations? Perhaps the most widespread alternative explanation locates the source of our problems in a crisis of the family. The cry that what our society most needs is "family values" is not one to be dismissed lightly. Almost all the tendencies we have been describing threaten family life and are often experienced most acutely within the family. Being unemployed and thus unable to get married or not having enough income to support an existing family due to downsizing or part-timing, along with the tensions caused by these conditions, can certainly be understood as family crises. But why is the crisis expressed as a failure of family values?

12. Seymour Martin Lipset, in a judicious review of Putnam's argument about the decline of Americans' involvement in voluntary organizations along with the relevant data, concludes that it is "not proven but probable." See his "Malaise and Resiliency in America," *Journal of Democracy*, July, 1995, p. 15.

It is unlikely that we will understand what is going on here unless we once again take into account the culture of individualism. If we see unemployment or reduced income because of downsizing as a purely individual problem rather than a structural problem of the economy, then we will seek to understand what is wrong with the unemployed or underemployed individual. If we also discern that such individuals are prone to have children out of wedlock, to divorce, or to fail to make child support payments, we may conclude that the cause is weakened family values. In *Habits of the Heart* we strongly affirmed the value of the family, and in both *Habits* and *The Good Society* we argued for renewed commitment to marriage and family responsibilities. But to imagine that problems arising from failures rooted in the structure of our economy and polity can primarily be traced to the failings of individuals with inadequate family values seems to us sadly mistaken. It not only increases the level of individual guilt, it also distracts attention from larger failures of collective responsibility.

The link between cultural individualism and the emphasis on family values has a further consequence. Families have traditionally been supported by the paid labor of men. Failure to support one's family may be taken as an indication of inadequate manhood. It is easy to draw the conclusion that if American men would only act like men, then family life would be improved and social problems solved. Some such way of thinking undoubtedly lies behind the movement known as Promise Keepers, as well as the Million Man March of 1995. While we share many of the values of these movements, we are skeptical that increased male responsibility will prove to be an adequate solution to our deep structural economic and political problems or even that it will do more than marginally diminish the severe strains on the American family. The notion that if men would only be men then all would be well in our society seems to us a sad cultural delusion.

Another common alternative explanation of our difficulties is to explain them as the failure of community. This is indeed valid, we believe, but only if our understanding of community is broad and deep enough. In many current usages of the term, however, community means face-to-face groups formed by the voluntary efforts of individuals. Used in this way, failure of community as the source of our problems can be interpreted to mean that if only more people would volunteer to help in soup kitchens or Habitat for Humanity or Meals on Wheels, then our social problems would be solved. As in the case of family values, *Habits of the Heart* strongly affirms face-to-face communities and the valuable contributions voluntary groups can make to society. But we do not believe that the deep structural problems that we face as a society can be effectively alleviated by an increase in devotion to community in this narrow sense. We would agree that an increase in the voluntary commitments of individuals can over the long haul increase our social capital and thus add to the resources we can bring to bear on our problems. But to get at the roots of our problems these resources must be used to overcome institutional difficulties that cannot be directly addressed by voluntary action alone.

We see another difficulty in emphasizing a small-scale and voluntaristic understanding of community as the solution to our problems. As we noted in discussing the work of [Sidney] Verba and colleagues,[13] voluntary activity tends to correlate with income, education, and occupation. "Joiners" are more apt to be found in the overclass than in the underclass or the anxious class, again with the significant exception of religious groups. This means that voluntary activities are less often designed to help the most deprived, though we don't want to overlook those that are, than to serve the interests of the affluent. This is particularly true of political voluntarism, as Verba and his associates have shown conclusively. Thus, dismantling structures of public provision for the most deprived in hopes that the voluntary sector will take over is misguided in three important respects. First, the voluntary sector has by no means the resources to take up the slack, as churches, charities, and foundations have been pointing out repeatedly in recent years. The second reason is that our more affluent citizens may feel they have fulfilled their obligation to society by giving time and money to "making a difference" through voluntary activity without taking into account that they have hardly made a dent in the real problems faced by most Americans. The third reason is that, as we noted, the voluntary sector is disproportionately run by our better-off citizens and a good many voluntary activities do more to protect the well-to-do than the needy.

There is another sense of community that also presents difficulties if we think the solution to our problems lies in reviving community, and that is the notion of community as neighborhood or locality. *Habits of the Heart* encourages strong neighborhoods and supports civic engagement in towns and cities. But residential segregation is a fact of life in contemporary America. Even leaving aside the hypersegregation of urban ghettos, segregation by class arising from differential housing costs is becoming increasingly evident in suburban America. Thus it is quite possible that in "getting involved" with one's neighborhood or even with one's suburban town one will never meet someone of a different race or class. One will not be exposed to the realities of life for people in circumstances different from one's own. One may even succumb to the natural human temptation to think that people who are different, particularly those lower in social status, are inferior. The anxious class does not want itself to be confused with the underclass. One of the least pleasant characteristics of the overclass, including its lower echelons in the educated upper middle class, is that they do not want to associate with middle Americans, with "Joe Six-Pack" and others who lack the proper cultural attributes. Even in the underclass, those who are not on welfare look down on those who are, and those who are on the dole briefly look down on those on it for a long time.[14] Under such circumstances an exclusive emphasis on

13. Sidney Verba, Kay Lehman Schlozman, and Henry E. Brady, *Voice and Equality* (Cambridge: Harvard University Press, 1995).
14. Loic J. D. Wacquant in "Inside the 'Zone': The Social Art of the Hustler in the Dark Ghetto,"

neighborhood solidarity could actually contribute to larger social problems rather than solving them.

What the explanations of our social problems that stress the failure of family values or the failure of community have in common is the notion that our problems are individual or in only a narrow sense social (that is, involving family and local community), rather than economic, political, and cultural. A related feature that these common explanations of our troubles share is hostility to the role of government or the state. If we can take care of ourselves, perhaps with a little help from our friends and family, who needs the state? Indeed, the state is often viewed as an interfering father who won't recognize that his children have grown up and don't need him anymore.[15] He can't help solve our problems because it is in large measure he who created them.

In contrast, the market, in this mindset, seems benign, a mostly neutral theater for competition in which achievement is rewarded and incompetence punished. Some awareness exists, however, that markets are not neutral, that some people and organizations have enormous economic power and are capable of making decisions that adversely affect many citizens. From this point of view big business joins big government as the source of problems rather than their solution. Still, in America more than in most comparable societies, people are inclined to think that the market is fairer than the state.

Individualism and Neocapitalism

The culture of individualism, then, has made no small contribution to the rise of the ideology we called neocapitalism in chapter 10 of *Habits*. There we drew a picture of the American political situation that has turned out not to be entirely adequate. We suggested that the impasse between welfare liberalism and its countermovement, neocapitalism, was coming to an end and that two alternatives, the administered society and economic democracy, were looming on the scene. As it turned out, this incipient pair of alternatives did not materialize, or at least they are enduring a long wait. Instead, neocapitalism has grown ever stronger ideologically and politically. Criticism of "big government" and "tax-and-spend liberalism" has mounted even as particular constituencies, which in the aggregate include most citizens, favor those forms of public provision that benefit them in particular, while opposing benefits they do not receive.

We do not believe we were wrong in seeing ten years ago the severe strains that

Russell Sage Foundation, Working Papers, 1994, writes: "'It's people doin' *worser* than me,' often remark ghetto residents, including the most dispossessed of them, as if to comfort themselves, innovating a double superlative that speaks volumes about the finely differentiated microhierarchies elaborated at the very bottom of society."

15. Lakoff, *Moral Politics*.

the neocapitalist formula was creating for the nation. Today those strains are more obvious than ever. But we clearly underestimated the ideological fervor that the neocapitalist position was able to tap—ironically for us, because so much of that fervor derives from the very source we focused on in our book: individualism. The neocapitalist vision is viable only to the degree to which it can be seen as an expression—even a moral expression—of our dominant ideological individualism, with its compulsive stress on independence, its contempt for weakness, and its adulation of success. Its intensity rises in time of economic trial, when individuals who "work hard and play by the rules" fail to find the rewards they feel they deserve.

Thus neocapitalism has been able to turn even its policy failures into ideological successes, at least up to the present. It has persuaded many Americans that the problems it has produced, such as a quadrupling of the national debt since 1980, are really the result of welfare liberalism, even though welfare liberalism has not set the American policy agenda for over twenty years. It manages to interpret problems arising from the drastic reduction of public provision for the poor as caused by the pitifully inadequate welfare system that still manages to survive despite decades of cuts. It holds that it would actually be charitable to the poor to cut them loose from their "dependence" on the state.

. . .

Neocapitalist ideology aims to convince us that all government social programs have been disastrous failures. Millions of beneficiaries of Medicare and Social Security find that position hard to believe, in spite of its ideological appeal. Those programs, then, are attacked not as intrinsically evil but as too expensive, as mortgaging the future of our children and grandchildren for the sake of older Americans. What is not adequately recognized is just how successful those programs actually are.

. . .

During the first decades after World War II, high levels of social spending went hand in hand with high levels of economic growth. In the last twenty years, as the ideology of neocapitalism has taken hold, social spending has decreased dramatically. As spending on material and social infrastructure has declined, economic growth rates have slowed and economic inequality has rapidly increased, as we have seen.

The economic and political changes that have occurred in the United States in recent decades parallel change in Western Europe (although not, interestingly enough, in East Asia), but they are more extreme in America than anywhere else. Structural causes are certainly at work here, some of them not well understood. We are convinced, however, that the extreme position of the United States compared to other countries in matters such as income inequality and the attack on public provision is due in important part to the culture of individualism, with its inability to understand the capacities and responsibilities of government.

Where Do We Go from Here?

We believe that neocapitalism offers a fatally flawed political agenda. It claims to be opposed to the state, yet it uses the state ruthlessly to enforce "market discipline." It creates problems that the market alone only exacerbates and that require for their solution effective government intervention and a strong independent sector. When we wrote *Habits* the term communitarianism had not yet come into vogue, nor had the concern with civil society, sparked as it was by the fall of Communism and the concern for the bases of democracy in post–Communist societies. *Habits* got pulled into the debate in ways beyond our anticipation. As we pointed out in the preface to *The Good Society,* if communitarianism means opposition to the neocapitalist agenda and to a theoretical liberalism for which autonomy is almost the only virtue, then we are communitarians. But if it means a primary emphasis on small-scale and face-to-face relations, with the nineteenth-century small town as its exemplar, we are not communitarians.[16] As we argued in *The Good Society* and reiterate here, only effective institutions — economic, political, and social — make complex modern societies livable.

. . .

Toward the end of *Habits of the Heart,* we used the notion of a social ecology to evoke a vision of a larger community that was formed out of a variety of smaller communities, each with its own agenda and needs but each affecting the whole and depending on the well-being of the whole. The forms of social relations are different at each level; each level should have its own rights and responsibilities, the nature of which should be constantly revised through public debate. In our book on social institutions that was a sequel to *Habits* we did not make community our central term but spoke instead of *The Good Society*. We emphasized that at every level this society must, while respecting the dignity of each of its members, seek the common good. We believe that this approach can provide a helpful framework for both communitarians and civil society theorists.

As long as neocapitalist ideology maintains its hegemony all these matters may seem to be academic. It is one of the danger of the neocapitalist vision that it is determinist. It implies that there are no institutional choices: the market decides. Indeed, one of the conundrums of contemporary individualism is that it can combine an absolute belief in the freedom of individual choice with market determinism. But we believe this determinism is an ideological delusion: neither the global economy, nor the stock market, nor the profit margin can determine our institutional choices unless we as citizens let them. But the capacity to make institutional choices rests on cultural resources that are, along with material and

16. We believe this regressive notion of communitarianism is largely the product of its critics; those who call themselves communitarians are not motivated by nostalgia or by fear of the modern world. See Amitai Etzioni, *The Spirit of Community* (New York: Touchstone, 1993).

social resources, seriously depleted. *Habits of the Heart* was a call to replenish those resources as the basis for moving our society in new directions. It is worth restating that argument in terms of the issues raised in this introduction.

Meaning and a Renewal of Civic Membership

While the idea of community, if limited to neighbors and friends, is an inadequate basis for meeting our current needs, we want to affirm community as a cultural theme that calls us to wider and wider circles of loyalty, ultimately embracing that universal community of all beings of which H. Richard Niebuhr spoke.[17] We should remember that when Jesus was asked, "Who is my neighbor?" he answered with the parable of the Good Samaritan (Luke 10:29–37), in which the true neighbor turns out to be a Samaritan, a member of a group despised in Israel. It is not that Jesus didn't think that a person living next door, or an inhabitant of one's own village, or a member of one's own ethnic group could be a neighbor. But when asked directly, he identified the neighbor as a stranger, an alien, a member of a hated ethnic group. Any community short of the universal community is not the beloved community.

Much of what has been happening in our society has been undermining our sense of community at every level. We are facing trends that threaten our basic sense of solidarity with others: solidarity with those near to us (loyalty to neighbors, colleagues at work, fellow townsfolk), but also solidarity with those who live far from us, those who are economically in situations very different from our own, those of other nations. Yet this solidarity—this sense of connection, shared fate, mutual responsibility, community—is more critical now than ever. It is solidarity, trust, mutual responsibility that allows human communities to deal with threats and take advantage of opportunities. How can we strengthen these endangered capacities, which are first of all cultural capacities to think in certain ways?

When we consider how to renew the cultural capacity for community and solidarity in each of the three classes into which our society is divided, it would be well to remember something we have already mentioned: that in American society religious associations have the strongest hold on their members and almost alone have the capacity to reach individuals in every class. We can formulate the need for a fundamental reorientation toward community and solidarity as a kind of conversion, a turning of consciousness and intention. In the biblical tradition

17. H. Richard Niebuhr, *The Responsible Self* (New York: Harper and Row, 1978 [1963]), p. 88. It is interesting in view of our argument to learn from H. Richard Niebuhr's son, Richard R. Niebuhr, that "[i]n the early years of the 1930s, I sensed though scarcely comprehended my father's increasing apprehension at what he described as the 'class crucifixion' then taking place in our unhappy country." (From the foreword by Richard R. Niebuhr to H. Richard Niebuhr, *Theology, History and Culture: Major Unpublished Writings* [New Haven: Yale University Press, 1996], as reported in *Harvard Divinity Bulletin,* 25, 1 [1995]: 8.) Class crucifixion is the opposite of universal community.

conversion means a turning away from sin and a turning toward God. An idea of turning away from preoccupation with the self and toward some larger identity is characteristic of most of the great religions and philosophies of mankind. Conversion cannot come from willpower alone, but if it is to be enabled we must recover the stories and symbols in whose terms it makes sense.

If we think first of the overclass, the thirty-year critical assault on the dominance of white Euroamerican males in our society has not greatly dented that dominance in practice, but it has been used to justify a decline in civic responsibility on the part of the powerful and a selfish withdrawal into monetary aggrandizement. In an open society we can work to make room for more inclusive leadership without derogating the contributions of older elites. We need at least a portion of the overclass acting as a true establishment if we are to deal with our enormous problems. If the members of the overclass can overcome their own anxieties they may realize that they will gain far more self-respect in belonging to an establishment than to an oligarchy. They may come to see that civic engagement—a concern for the common good, a belief that we are all members of the same body—will not only contribute to the good of the larger society but will contribute to the salvation of their own souls as well. Only some larger engagement can overcome the devastating cultural and psychological narcissism of our current overclass. A return to civic membership, to commitments to community and solidarity, on the part of the overclass would be good not only for society as a whole but also for its individual members.

It would be well to point out that the majority of the people we interviewed in *Habits* belong to the lower echelons of the overclass, to what is commonly called the upper middle class, however much they (and we, who belong to the same class) would be uncomfortable with that terminology. Of course these are not the people who make the big decisions or who profit most from our current economy. They could even be called, in Pierre Bourdieu's pointed phrase, "the dominated fraction of the dominant class."[18] But, as we argued in *Habits,* they are the symbolic center of our society, their style of life is that to which most Americans aspire, and they do indeed prosper more than 80 percent of their fellow citizens. Their resources are far greater than those of other classes: they have the cultural and social capital and the civic skills to influence the direction in which our society goes. The question is, can they recover a coherent view of the world which will allow them to use these resource for the common good rather than for their own aggrandizement?

The anxious class faces equally serious challenges, for its problems are not only cultural and psychological but sharply material. The average income for a white male has slowly drifted down from an all-time high in 1992 dollars of $34,231 in 1973 to $31,012 in 1992.[19] Even worse than that income decline,

---

18. Pierre Bourdieu, *Distinction: A Social Critique of the Judgment of Taste* (Cambridge: Harvard University Press, 1984 [1979]).

19. Thurow, "Companies Merge; Families Break Up," p. E11.

which in considerable degree is offset by increasing female participation in the workplace (though that creates its own problems), is the concomitant rise in economic uncertainty. We are becoming a society of what has been called "advanced insecurity." Downsizing, part-timing, and loss of benefits have become a way of life.

The anger and fear generated by acute economic anxiety are easily displaced onto "welfare queens" and illegal immigrants. These feelings also contribute to the decline of voting and associational membership, even union membership, as well as to the rise of divorce. While economic anxieties are real and must ultimately be dealt with structurally, the resulting decline of civic engagement in the anxious class only deepens its cynicism and despair. Renewed engagement with the larger society—for many, through churches first of all, certainly through labor unions, and then through civic organizations—is the most likely way to meet the very real problems that face society's largest group. And on top of its material problems the anxious class shares more than a little in the psychological and cultural problems of the overclass, for which a renewed sense of meaning giving coherence to ideas of solidarity and community would be the best antidote.

Meeting the problems of the underclass and attempting to reincorporate its members into the larger society is the most challenging task of all. The basic problem stems from economic developments that have simply rendered the twenty or thirty million members of the underclass superfluous (and, we should not forget, have rendered much of the anxious class merely marginally relevant). Only a fundamental change in public policy will begin to alter the situation, and in the present atmosphere such a change is hardly to be expected.

But even indispensable changes in public policy cannot alone meet the situation. Where social trust is limited and morale is blasted, one of the most urgent needs is a recovery of self-respect and a sense of agency that can come only from the participation that enables people to belong and contribute to the larger society. Participatory justice asks each individual to give all that is necessary to the common good of society. In turn it obliges society to order its institutions so that everyone can work to contribute to the commonweal in ways that respect their dignity and renew their freedom.[20] Not by transfer payments alone or the compassion of social workers will the problems of the underclass be solved.

In responding to the problems of the underclass, perhaps we need to turn to the principle of subsidiarity, which is derived from Catholic social teaching. The idea is that groups closest to a problem should deal with it, receiving support from

20. A particularly eloquent statement of this position can be found in *Economic Justice for All: Pastoral Letter on Catholic Social Teaching and the U.S. Economy* (Washington, D.C.: National Conference of Catholic Bishops, 1986). Catholics do not have a monopoly on this position, of course. It is rooted in the covenantal tradition that goes back to the Hebrew Scriptures and is also evidenced in Calvinist corporatism as expressed, for example, in the passage from John Winthrop's sermon "A Model of Christian Charity," quoted below. But the modern tradition of Catholic social teaching has affirmed it with especial vigor.

higher-level groups where necessary but, wherever possible, not being replaced by those higher-level groups. This principle implies respect for the groups closest to the persons in need, but it does not absolutize those groups or exempt them from the moral standards that apply to groups at any level. A process of social reconstruction of the underclass would require massive public resources, but these should be brought to the situation by third-sector agencies, local so far as possible. Today subsidiarity language is, in contradiction to its basic meaning, used to justify cuts in government spending. In truth, subsidiarity is not a substitute for public provision but makes sense only when public provision is adequate.

Ultimately what the underclass needs is not so different from what the overclass or the anxious class needs. Its social capital is more depleted and its morale more thoroughly shattered, but, like everyone else, what its members most require is a clear sense of solidarity and community and of a future shared with the rest of society.

A House Divided

In conclusion it may be helpful to put our present situation into relation to two earlier moments in American history. The first is the crisis of the republic in the 1850s, during the dark years that would lead to the Civil War. David Greenstone has suggested that the American politics of the day were divided between what he calls a reform liberalism represented by Abraham Lincoln and a utilitarian liberalism represented by Stephen Douglas.[21] The Lincoln–Douglas debates, which took place during the Illinois senatorial campaign of 1858, were a defining moment in American history. The issue was whether slavery should be extended to the territories in the West. Douglas took the line of popular sovereignty: if they want slavery, let them have slavery. In other words, freedom to do what you want was, in this case, freedom to do what the white majority wanted. The basis of Douglas's position was a utilitarian liberalism that asked only for the summing of preferences, not about the moral quality of the preferences.

But Lincoln said that slavery was wrong, that it contradicted the nation's most fundamental principles and should not be extended to the territories no matter what the majority there might want. In other words, freedom is the right only to do

21. J. David Greenstone, *The Lincoln Persuasion: Remaking American Liberalism* (Princeton: Princeton University Press, 1993). It should be noted that Greenstone's own terminology is somewhat different. His contrast term to reform liberalism is humanist liberalism, called humanist because it has no transcendent reference. The editor defines humanist liberalism using Greenstone's own words as follows: "*Humanist liberalism* refers to a set of beliefs that place primary emphasis on 'equitably satisfying individual desires and preferences,' and on achieving 'the welfare of each human being as he or she defines it'" (p. 36 n. 1). We believe that is an accurate description of a utilitarian liberalism. Humanist seems a particularly unfortunate way of describing this position in the light of Greenstone's characterization of reform liberalism as "humanitarian."

that which is morally justified. The basis of Lincoln's position was a reform liberalism that had its roots in New England Puritanism. It drew upon biblical and republican sources and was committed not only to the notion of an objective moral order ("the laws of nature and of nature's God") but also to the notion that individuals live in a society that has a common good beyond the sum of individual goods. It was this moral politics that led Lincoln to his great "House Divided" speech in Springfield, Illinois, on June 16, 1858. "'A house divided against itself cannot stand,'"[22] Lincoln said. "I believe this government cannot endure, permanently half *slave* and half *free*."[23]

If we apply Lincoln's words to our situation we can say that the house today is divided not by slavery but by deepening class divisions. Douglas had no problem with a house divided, since he saw society as nothing more than the sum of individual choices and their consequences. Lincoln, however, judged certain conditions to be objectively wrong and held society accountable for changing them. Our situation today is historically linked to what Lincoln was talking about, for though slavery has been abolished, equality for African Americans has not been achieved. But we believe that it is not so much race discrimination that is the problem, though that continues to be serious enough, but, rather, the racialization of the class hierarchy—the Brazilianization of America, as Michael Lind calls it.[24]

Race differences are real in our society, but we should not let them obscure how much we have in common. Jennifer Hochschild in *Facing Up to the American Dream* has recently analyzed the ways in which Americans differ by race.[25] She shows that black and white Americans share most of the ideology of the American dream—by which she means not only material but moral aspirations—though they differ as to how far African Americans have realized it. Focusing exclusively on race differences obscures an important truth about our society: race differences are rooted in class differences. Class differences transcend race and divide all Americans.

We believe the degree of class difference today is wrong in the same sense that Lincoln believed slavery was wrong: it deprives millions of people of the ability to participate fully in society and to realize themselves as individuals. This is the festering secret that Americans would rather not face. Many nations have persisted while divided into a small elite that lives in luxury and a large mass in various

22. "And if a house be divided against itself, that house cannot stand." Mark 3:25, King James Version.

23. Abraham Lincoln, *Speeches and Writings, 1832–1858* (New York: Library of America, 1989), p. 426.

24. "By Brazilianization I mean not the separation of cultures by race, but the separation of races by class. As in Brazil, a common American culture could be indefinitely compatible with a blurry, informal caste system in which most of those at the top of the social hierarchy are white, and most brown and black Americans are on the bottom—*forever*." Lind, *The Next American Nation*, p. 216.

25. Jennifer L. Hochschild, *Facing Up to the American Dream: Race, Class, and the Soul of the Nation* (Princeton: Princeton University Press, 1995).

stages of insecurity and misery, but this nation, with the ideals and hopes of the last 220 years, cannot permanently so endure.

This brings us to our second historical reference: John Winthrop's sermon "A Model of Christian Charity," delivered on board ship in 1630 just before the Massachusetts Bay colonists disembarked. In that sermon Winthrop warned that if we pursue "our pleasures and profits" we will surely perish out of this good land. Rather, what Winthrop, paraphrasing the Apostle Paul, tells us is that we must "entertain each other in brotherly affection, we must be willing to abridge ourselves of our superfluities, for the supply of others' necessities . . . we must delight in each other, make others' conditions our own, rejoice together, mourn together, labour and suffer together, always having before our eyes . . . our Community as members of the same Body."[26]

Under the conditions of today's America, we are tempted to ignore Winthrop's advice, to forget our obligations of solidarity and community, to harden our hearts and look out only for ourselves. In the Hebrew Scriptures God spoke to the children of Israel through the prophet Ezekiel, saying, "I will take out of your flesh the heart of stone and give you a heart of flesh" (Ez. 36:26). Can we pray that God do the same for us in America today?

January 1996

26. John Winthrop, "A Model of Christian Charity," in Conrad Cherry, ed., *God's New Israel: Religious Interpretations of American Destiny* (Englewood Cliffs, N.J.: Prentice-Hall, 1971), p. 42. Spelling has been modernized.

Sources

Chapter 1 Aristotle, *The Politics,* ed. by Steven Everson (Cambridge, U.K.: Cambridge University Press, 1988).

Chapter 2 Immanuel Kant, "Idea for a Universal History with a Cosmopolitan Purpose," in *Political Writings,* ed. Hans S. Reiss, trans. H. B. Nisbet (Cambridge, U.K.: Cambridge University Press, 1991), 44–53.

Chapter 3 Immanuel Kant, "Perpetual Peace," in *Political Writings,* ed. Hans S. Reiss, trans. H. B. Nisbet (Cambridge, U.K.: Cambridge University Press, 1991), 98–109.

Chapter 4 Adam Ferguson, *An Essay on the History of Civil Society,* ed. Fania Oz-Satzberger (Cambridge, U.K.: Cambridge University Press, 1995).

Chapter 5 Thomas Paine, *Rights of Man* (Baltimore: Penguin Books, 1969).

Chapter 6 James Madison, *The Federalist, No. 10* in David C. Hammack, ed., *Making the Nonprofit Sector in the United States: A Reader* (Bloomington: Indiana University Press, 1998).

Chapter 7 G. F. W. Hegel, *Hegel's Philosophy of Right* (Oxford, U.K.: Clarendon Press, 1962).

Chapter 8 Karl Marx, "On the Jewish Question," in Robert C. Tucker, ed., *The Marx-Engels Reader* (New York: W. W. Norton, 1978), 26–46.

Chapter 9 Alexis De Tocqueville, J. P. Mayer, ed., *Democracy in America* (New York: Anchor Books, 1969).

Chapter 10 John Dewey, "The Public and Its Problems" in *John Dewey: The Later Works, 1925–1927,* Vol 2., Jo Ann Boydston, ed., Bridget A. Walsh, textual ed. (Carbondale: Southern Illinois University Press, 1984).

Chapter 11 David B. Truman, *The Governmental Process* (New York: Alfred A. Knopf, 1967).

Chapter 12 Gabriel A. Almond and Sidney Verba, "Organizational Membership and Civic Competence," in *The Civic Culture: Political Attitudes and Democracy in Five Nations* (Boston: Little, Brown, 1963), 244–265.

Chapter 13 Antonio Gramsci, Quintin Hoare, Geoffrey Nowell Smith, eds., *Selections from the Prison Notebooks of Antonio Gramsci* (New York: International Publishers, 1971).

Chapter 14 Adam Michnik, "A New Evolutionism 1976," in *Letters from the Prison and Other Essays* (Berkeley: University of California Press, 1976), pp. 135–154.

Chapter 15 Peter L. Berger and Richard John Neuhaus, *To Empower People: The Role of Mediating Structures in Public Policy* (Washington, D.C.: American Enterprise Institute for Public Policy Research, 1977), 1–13, 15–17, 19–20, 26–32, 34–45.

Chapter 16 Benjamin R. Barber, "Citizenship and Community: Politics as Social Being," in *Strong Democracy: Participatory Politics for a New Age* (Berkeley: University of California Press, 1998), 213–237.

Chapter 17 Sara M. Evans and Harry C. Boyte, *Free Spaces: The Sources of Democratic Change in America* (New York: Harper & Row, 1986), 182–202.

Chapter 18 Jean L. Cohen and Andrew Arato, "Introduction," in *Civil Society and Political Theory* (Cambridge, Mass.: MIT Press, 1992), 1–26 and endnotes.

Chapter 19 Edward Shils, "The Virtue of Civil Society," text of a *Government and Opposition* lecture delivered at the Athenaeum Club on 22 January, 1991.

Chapter 20 Michael Walzer, "A Better Vision: The Idea of Civil Society," in *Dissent*, Spring 1991: 296–304.

Chapter 21 Robert D. Putnam, with Robert Leonardi and Raffaella Y. Nanetti, *Making Democracy Work: Civic Traditions in Modern Italy* (Princeton, N.J.: Princeton University Press, 1993), 86–91.

Chapter 22 Robert N. Bellah, Richard Madsen, William M. Sullivan, Ann Swidler, and Steven M. Tipton, "Introduction to the Updated Edition: The House Divided," in *Habits of the Heart: Individualism and Commitment in American Life* (Berkeley: University of California Press, 1996), vii–xiii, xv–xvii, xxi–xxxv.

Index

Abbé St. Pierre, 22

Activism, *xxiv;* Barber's views on, 246–248, 252–254; civility, 299–302; Cohen's and Arato's views on, 275–276; Putnam's views on, 323–324; vs. passive roles, 182–188, 314–315; Walzer's views on, 307–308, 320–321. *See also* Citizenship; Movements

Agricultural work, 81–82, 91

Allport, Gordon W., 161–162

All That Is Solid Melts into Air (Berman), 257

Almond, Gabriel A., *xix,* 173–189

Ambition: Ferguson's views on, 60–62; role of associations, 120–121

Ancient civilizations: division of labor, 59–60; equality, 43–44; legal codes, 85; war-making manners, 47–49, 52

Antagonism, 19–20, 22

Anti-Politics (Konrad), 317

Aquinas, Thomas, *xiii–xiv*

Arato, Andrew, *x, xxiv,* 270–291

Arendt, Hannah, 246, 308

Aristocracy: Aristotle's views on, 9–10, 13; Kant's views on, 29–31, 29n2; need for associations, 123–124

Aristotelian thought, *xi–xii, xxiii–xxiv;* associations, 158; citizenship, 1, 7–12, 141, 237, 244, 247; friendship, 325; social aspects of human nature, 235

Aristotle, *ix,* 1–18

Armed citizenry, *xii, xii*n5

Associations, *xiii, xiii*n7, *xvii–xix;* and accountability, *xx–xxi;* active *vs.* passive roles, 182–188, 314–315; Almond and Verba's views on, 173–189; Aristotelian thought, 158; civic, 122–126, 128–132; civic competence and, 173–174; class divisions and, 343; creation of comunity in, 145–147; de Tocqueville's views on, 113–132, 252–253, 252n24, 283–286, 325–326, 335; developing countries, 326–327; Dewey's views on, 135–138, 158; in the early United States, *xvi–xvii,* 133–135, 155–156; Evans and Boyte's views on, 255–269; factionalism and, 70–75; forbidding of, 130–131, 130n3; freedom of assembly, 114; Gramsci's views on, 199–200; grass roots level, 271; Hegel's views on, 196; interest groups, *xv, xix,* 154–157, 160–170, 273–274n7, 326; liberalism and, 313–317; Madison's views on, 155–156, 170; Marx's views on, 196; mediating structures, 173–174, 213–218, 227–231, 252, 257–258; membership, *xix,* 334–336, 336n12; and multiple memberships, 186 (table), 188, 200, 252–253; officer roles in, 183 (table), 184 (table), 185 (table); Paine's views on, 65; pluralism and, 284–285, 285n37, 317–321; political, 113–118, 128–132, 154–157, 163–172, 179–182; political competence, 178–187, 262; Putnam's views on, 325–327; radical left views on, 258–259; relationship between civil and political, 128–132; role in political movements, 258–269; role of newspapers and, 126–128; survey data and, 173–189, 326, 338; symbiotic relationship with the state, 317–321; Truman's views on, 164–165; Walzer's views on, 306–307. *See also* Factions; Voluntary associations

Attitudes: association membership, 176–177, 178–179; group development and common, 161–162, 172

Autonomy, *xxiv;* Cohen and Arato's views on, 287–288, 290–291, 290n47; *vs.* communitarianism, 341; Evans and Boyte's views on, 260–261; Marx's views on, 296; Shils's views on, 292–293, 295, 298, 302

Baczko, Bronisław, 204

Bagehot, Walter, 135

Banfield, Edward, 324, 327

Barber, Benjamin, *xxiii–xxiv,* 234–254

Bauer, Bruno, 96–108

Beaumont, Gustave de, 100

Being at Time (Heidegger), 235n4